THE LEGACY OF SÁNDOR FERENCZI

Ferenczi wanted his colleagues and pupils to think and work in their own unique ways and according to their own interests and personality. This is one of the reasons that therapists and analysts of various theoretical origins continue to be drawn to his propositions. Ferenczi was probably the first and perhaps still even the only psychoanalyst who did not speak of *training* in psychoanalysis, but of *learning* it according to one's own rhythms rather than merely following a prescribed course. This important new book illustrates Ferenczi's unique vision of psychoanalysis and summarizes and expands on the gifts psychoanalysts can find in the abundance of his work. It also offers a glimpse into Ferenczi's personal history, and how this affected the ways in which he considered human beings, the world, psychoanalysis, and himself.

—**Judith Dupont, Ph.D. Editor,** *The Clinical Diary of Sándor Ferenczi,* **Literary representative of Sándor Ferenczi, Recipient of the 2013 Sigourney Award**

This fine collection of essays, written by clinicians and scholars of diverse backgrounds, honors the memory of Sándor Ferenczi, Sigmund Freud's closest friend and collaborator, whose groundbreaking contributions to the theory and practice of psychoanalysis were scorned and marginalized by many of his contemporaries. The contributors to this volume have adroitly and sensitively demonstrated the relevance of Ferenczi's ideas to current trends in psychoanalytic thinking and are taking a major step toward restoring his legacy to its rightful place in history.

—**Peter T. Hoffer, Ph.D. Psychoanalytic Center of Philadelphia; Translator,** *The Correspondence of Sigmund Freud and Sándor Ferenczi*

When *The Legacy of Sándor Ferenczi* appeared in 1993, Ferenczi was often ignored or maligned in psychoanalytic circles. That book was a significant part of the Ferenczi Renaissance—a striking example of the psychoanalytic notion that the past keeps changing. The present volume appears in a different climate—Ferenczi, to our great benefit, returned from exile—and testifies to the continued liveliness of contemporary Ferenczi scholarship by eminent authors around the world, illuminating his life and the development of his stimulating revolutionary ideas.

—Emanuel Berman, Ph.D. Israel Psychoanalytic Society

The Legacy of Sándor Ferenczi, first published in 1993 and edited by Lewis Aron and Adrienne Harris, was one of the first books to examine Ferenczi's invaluable contributions to psychoanalysis and his continuing influence on contemporary clinicians and scholars. Building on that pioneering work, *The Legacy of Sándor Ferenczi: From Ghost to Ancestor* brings together leading international Ferenczi scholars to report on previously unavailable data about Ferenczi and his professional descendants.

Many—including Sigmund Freud himself—considered Sándor Ferenczi to be Freud's most gifted patient and protégé. For a large part of his career, Ferenczi was almost as well known, influential, and sought after as a psychoanalyst, teacher, and lecturer as Freud himself. Later, irreconcilable differences between Freud, his followers, and Ferenczi meant that many of his writings were withheld from translation or otherwise stifled, and he was accused of being mentally ill and shunned. In this book, Adrienne Harris and Steven Kuchuck explore how newly discovered historical and theoretical material has returned Ferenczi to a place of theoretical legitimacy and prominence. His work continues to influence both psychoanalytic theory and practice and covers many major contemporary psychoanalytic topics such as process, metapsychology, character structure, trauma, sexuality, and social and progressive aspects of psychoanalytic work.

Among other historical and scholarly contributions, this book demonstrates the direct link between Ferenczi's pioneering work and subsequent psychoanalytic innovations. With rich clinical vignettes, newly unearthed historical data, and contemporary theoretical explorations, it will be of great interest and use to clinicians of all theoretical stripes, as well as scholars and historians.

Adrienne Harris, Ph.D. (co-editor) is faculty and supervisor, NYU Postdoctoral Program in Psychotherapy and Psychoanalysis, Faculty and Training Analyst at the Psychoanalytic Institute of Northern California, serves on the *Editorial Boards of Psychoanalytic Dialogues, Studies in Gender and Sexuality, Psychoanalytic Perspectives* and the *Journal of the American Psychoanalytic Association*. Co-editor, *Routledge's Relational Perspectives Book Series*.

Steven Kuchuck, LCSW (co-editor) is a faculty member, supervisor, Board member, and codirector of curriculum for the adult training program in psychoanalysis at the National Institute for the Psychotherapies and faculty, Stephen Mitchell Center for Relational Studies. Steven is Editor-in-Chief of *Psychoanalytic Perspectives,* and Associate Editor of *Routledge's Relational Perspectives Book Series*.

Relational Perspectives Book Series

Lewis Aron & Adrienne Harris
Series Co-Editors
Steven Kuchuck & Eyal Rozmarin
Associate Editors

The Relational Perspectives Book Series (RPBS) publishes books that grow out of or contribute to the relational tradition in contemporary psychoanalysis. The term *relational psychoanalysis* was first used by Greenberg and Mitchell[1] to bridge the traditions of interpersonal relations, as developed within interpersonal psychoanalysis and object relations, as developed within contemporary British theory. But, under the seminal work of the late Stephen Mitchell, the term *relational psychoanalysis* grew and began to accrue to itself many other influences and developments. Various tributaries—interpersonal psychoanalysis, object relations theory, self psychology, empirical infancy research, and elements of contemporary Freudian and Kleinian thought—flow into this tradition, which understands relational configurations between self and others, both real and fantasied, as the primary subject of psychoanalytic investigation.

We refer to the relational tradition, rather than to a relational school, to highlight that we are identifying a trend, a tendency within contemporary psychoanalysis, not a more formally organized or coherent school or system of beliefs. Our use of the term *relational* signifies a dimension of theory and practice that has become salient across the wide spectrum of contemporary psychoanalysis. Now under the editorial supervision of Lewis Aron and Adrienne Harris with the assistance of Associate Editors Steven Kuchuck and Eyal Rozmarin, the Relational Perspectives Book Series originated in 1990 under the editorial eye of the late Stephen A. Mitchell. Mitchell was the most prolific and influential of the originators of the relational tradition. He was committed to dialogue among psychoanalysts and he abhorred the authoritarianism that dictated adherence to a rigid set of beliefs or technical restrictions. He championed open discussion, comparative and integrative approaches, and he promoted new voices across the generations.

Included in the Relational Perspectives Book Series are authors and works that come from within the relational tradition, extend and develop the tradition, as well as works that critique relational approaches or compare and contrast it with alternative points of view. The series includes our most distinguished senior psychoanalysts, along with younger contributors who bring fresh vision.

1 Greenberg, J. & Mitchell, S. (1983). *Object relations in psychoanalytic theory.* Cambridge, MA: Harvard University Press.

THE LEGACY OF SÁNDOR FERENCZI

From Ghost to Ancestor

Edited by Adrienne Harris and
Steven Kuchuck

Routledge
Taylor & Francis Group

LONDON AND NEW YORK

First published 2015
by Routledge
27 Church Road, Hove, East Sussex BN3 2FA

and by Routledge
711 Third Avenue, New York, NY 10017
Routledge is an imprint of the Taylor & Francis Group, an informa business

British Library Cataloguing in Publication Data
A catalogue record for this book is available from the British Library

Library of Congress Cataloging-in-Publication Data

Legacy of Sándor Ferenczi (2015)The legacy of Sándor Ferenczi: from ghost to ancestor / edited by Adrienne Harris & Steven Kuchuck.
   p. ; cm.
Includes bibliographical references.
   I. Harris, Adrienne, editor. II. Kuchuck, Steven, editor. III. Title. [DNLM: 1. Ferenczi, Sándor,
   1873–1933. 2. Psychoanalysis. 3. Psychoanalytic Theory.
WM 460] RC506
616.89'17—dc23   2014042310

ISBN: 978-1-138-82011-1 hbk
ISBN: 978-1-138-82012-8 pbk
ISBN: 978-1-315-74399-8 ebk

Typeset in Bembo
by codeMantra

Printed and bound in the United States of America by Edwards Brothers Malloy on sustainably sourced paper

In memory of Martin S. Bergmann (1913–2014) and György Hidas (1925–2012)
Keepers of the flame.
Preservers of Ferenczi's work, traditions, and meaning.

We thank them and everyone in this volume who has helped to preserve and enliven the work of Ferenczi. We are all in their debt.

CONTENTS

LIST OF CONTRIBUTORS

Lewis Aron, Ph.D., ABPP is the director of the New York University Postdoctoral Program in Psychotherapy and Psychoanalysis. He is a past president of the Division of Psychoanalysis (39) APA, founding president of the International Association for Relational Psychoanalysis and Psychotherapy (IARPP), and founding president of the Division of Psychologist-Psychoanalysts of NYSPA; the co-founder and co-chair of the Sándor Ferenczi Center at The New School for Social Research; an honorary member of the William Alanson White Psychoanalytic Society, and adjunct professor, School of Psychology, Interdisciplinary Center (IDC) Herzliya, Israel; a co-founder of Psychoanalytic Dialogues and the co-editor of the Relational Perspectives Book Series; author of *A Meeting of Minds* (1996), *A Psychotherapy for the People* (with Karen Starr); editor of *Relational Psychoanalysis: The Emergence of a Tradition* (with Stephen Mitchell); co-editor of the Relational Perspectives Book Series; and author and editor of numerous articles and books. For more information, see www.lewaron.com.

Galit Atlas, Ph.D. is a psychoanalyst, creative arts therapist, and clinical supervisor in private practice in New York City. She is a clinical assistant professor on the faculty of the New York University Postdoctoral Program in Psychotherapy & Psychoanalysis, a faculty member of the Institute for Expressive Analysis (IEA), and a faculty member of the National Training Programs (NTP) and the Four-Year Adult Training Program of the National Institute for the Psychotherapies (NIP) in NYC. Galit serves on the Editorial Board of Psychoanalytic Perspectives, is on the Board of Directors of the Division of Psychoanalysis (39) APA, and is the author of articles and book chapters that focus primarily on gender and sexuality. Galit teaches ongoing private study and supervision groups. Her book *The Enigma of Desire: Sex, Longing and Belonging in Psychoanalysis* will be published by Routledge's Relational Perspectives Book Series next year. More information is available at www.galitatlas.com.

Anthony Bass, Ph.D. is on the faculty of the New York University Postdoctoral Program in Psychotherapy and Psychoanalysis, The Columbia University Center for Psychoanalytic Training and Research, the Stephen Mitchell Center for Relational Studies, The National Institute for the Psychotherapies National Training Program, and the Institute for Relational Psychoanalysis of Philadelphia. He is a joint editor-in-chief of *Psychoanalytic Dialogues: The International Journal of Relational Perspectives* and a founding director of The International Association for Relational Psychoanalysis and Psychotherapy.

Carlo Bonomi, Ph.D. is a faculty member and supervising analyst at the Istituto di psicoanalisi H. S. Sullivan (Florence, Italy), associate editor of the *International Forum of Psychoanalysis*, and co-founding president of the Associazione culturale Sándor Ferenczi. Together with Judit Mészáros, he has promoted the Ferenczi-House project.

Franco Borgogno, Ph.D. is full professor of clinical psychology at the Psychology Department of Turin University (Italy), full member of the International Psycho-analytical Association and of the American Psychoanalytic Association, training and supervising analyst of the Società Psicoanalitica Italiana, and author of *Psychoanalysis as a Journey* (London, Open Gate, 2007) and *The Girl Who Committed Hara-Kiri and Other Clinical and Historical Essays* (London, Karnac Books, 2012).

B. William Brennan, ThM, MA, LMHC is a psychoanalyst and psychoanalytic historian in independent practice in Providence, Rhode Island. He is a graduate of the National Training Program of the National Institute for the Psychotherapies, NYC. He has written on Izette de Forest, as well as the identities of the patients in Ferenczi's *Clinical Diary*, and is currently working on a book about Ferenczi and his American circle.

Christopher Fortune, Ph.D. is a historian of psychoanalysis who focuses on the work of Sándor Ferenczi. He has lectured and published internationally and written papers, chapters, reviews, and interviews for scholarly and popular journals. He is the editor of *Sándor Ferenczi-Georg Groddeck Correspondence: 1921–1933* (Open Gate Press, 2002). He has a doctorate from the University of Toronto and is presently an associate of the Institute for the Humanities at Simon Fraser University, Vancouver, Canada.

Jay Frankel, Ph.D. is adjunct clinical associate professor in the New York University Postdoctoral Program in Psychotherapy and Psychoanalysis, professor in the Master's program in Critical Theory and the Arts at the School of Visual Arts, and a faculty member at the Institute for Psychoanalytic Training and Research, all in New York; associate editor of *Psychoanalytic Dialogues*; author of more than two dozen journal articles and book chapters; and co-author of *Relational Child Psychotherapy* (Other Press, 2002).

Adrienne Harris, Ph.D. (co-editor) is on the faculty and supervises at the NYU Post-doctoral Program in Psychotherapy and Psychoanalysis. She is a faculty member and a training analyst at the Psychoanalytic Institute of Northern California and serves on the Editorial Boards of *Psychoanalytic Dialogues, Studies in Gender and Sexuality, Psychoanalytic Perspectives,* and the *Journal of the American Psychoanalytic Association.* She is the author of *Rocking the Ship of State* and *Gender As Soft Assembly* and co-editor of *Storms in Her Head: The Centennial of Studies on Hysteria; Relational Traditions Vol. 3, 4 and 5; First, Do No Harm: Psychoanalysis, War Making and Resistance;* and forthcoming: *Ghosts in the 21st Century Consulting Room.* Dr. Harris has published widely in the areas of gender studies, developmental theory, analytic vulnerability, and self-care and is particularly interested in the analysts living and working in the shadow of World War I. With Jeremy Safran and Lewis Aron, she formed the Sándor Ferenczi Center at The New School for Social Research.

André E. Haynal, M.D. is a philosopher, physician, psychoanalyst (IPA), and author of more than a dozen books and hundreds of other publications. He was a leading editor of the Freud/Ferenczi Correspondence (1992–2000), and a recipient of the Sigourney Award for his life work. His most recent publication was *Disappearing and Reviving* (London, Karnac Books, 2002).

Véronique D. Haynal, M.A. is a psychoanalytic psychotherapist, life coach, and researcher in nonverbal communication (formerly University Hospital of Geneva, Switzerland).

Haydée Christinne Kahtuni, Ph.D. is a clinical psychologist and psychoanalyst, author of *Dictionary on the Thought of Sándor Ferenczi—A Contribution to the Psycho-analytic Contemporary Clinic* (Elsevier Editora: Rio de Janeiro e FAPESP: São Paulo, 2009) and *Brief Psychoanalytic Psychotherapy: Understanding and Care of the Human Soul* (Editora Escuta, São Paulo, 1996), specialist in Adolescent Psychotherapy (IPUSP), specialist in Hospital Psychology (HCFMUSP), university professor, clinical supervisor, and head of Discipline of Psychology of the Personality (teaching Theory and Practice in Psychoanalysis on Sigmund Freud, Sándor Ferenczi, Melanie Klein, and Donald Woods Winnicott) between 1998 and 2004 (UNIP). She is a member of the Sándor Ferenczi Society and an expert on Trauma Theory of Sándor Ferenczi. She treats adolescents and adults in her office in São Paulo.

Lewis A. Kirshner, M.D. is a clinical professor in Psychiatry, Harvard Medical School; training and supervising analyst, Boston Psychoanalytic Society and Institute; author of *Having a Life: Self Pathology after Lacan* (The Analytic Press, 2004); and editor of *Between Winnicott and Lacan: a Clinical Engagement* (Routledge, 2011).

Steven Kuchuck, LCSW (co-editor) is a faculty member, supervisor, member of the Board of Directors, and co-director of curriculum for the adult training program in psychoanalysis at the National Institute for the Psychotherapies; a faculty member at the Stephen Mitchell Center for Relational Studies, the Institute for Contemporary Psychotherapy, and the Institute for Expressive Analysis; and a Board member of The International Association for Relational Psychoanalysis and Psychotherapy. Steven is editor-in-chief of *Psychoanalytic Perspectives*, associate editor of Routledge's Relational Perspectives Book Series, editor of *Clinical Implications of the Psychoanalyst's Life Experience: When the Personal Becomes Professional* (Routledge, 2014), and author of articles and book chapters that focus primarily on the analyst's subjectivity. He practices psychoanalysis and supervises in Manhattan. More information is available at www.stevenkuchuck.com.

Judit Mészáros, Ph.D. is a founding member and president of the Sándor Ferenczi Society, Budapest, Hungary; a training and supervisory analyst at the Hungarian Psychoanalytical Association; and an honorary associate professor at the ELTE, Budapest, Hungary.

Arnold Wm. Rachman, Ph.D., F.A.G.P.A. is associate professor of Psychiatry at New York University Center; faculty at the Trauma & Disaster Studies Program in the New York University Postdoctoral Program in Psychoanalysis; a member of the Board of Directors for the Sándor Ferenczi Center at The New School for Social Research; a donor to *The Elizabeth Severn Papers*, Library of Congress; and author of *Sándor Ferenczi: The Psychotherapist of Tenderness & Passion, Psychotherapy of Difficult Cases, Analysis of the Incest Trauma.*

Eyal Rozmarin, Ph.D. is co-editor of *Studies in Gender and Sexuality* and associate editor of Routledge's Relational Perspectives Book Series. He has published book chapters and articles in psychoanalytic journals, including *Psychoanalytic Dialogues, Contemporary Psychoanalysis,* and *Studies in Gender and Sexuality.* His writing explores the relations between subjectivity, society, and history.

Peter L. Rudnytsky, Ph.D., LCSW is professor of English at the University of Florida and an analyst in training at the Florida Psychoanalytic Institute. He holds undergraduate degrees from Columbia and Cambridge and a Ph.D. from Yale. Among his many authored and edited books are *Ferenczi's Turn in Psychoanalysis* (NYU, 1996) and *Reading Psychoanalysis: Freud, Rank, Ferenczi, Groddeck* (Cornell, 2002), for which he received the Gradiva Award. He maintains a private practice in Gainesville.

Karen Starr, Psy.D. is an author, with Lewis Aron, of *A Psychotherapy for the People: Toward a Progressive Psychoanalysis*; an editor, with Jill Bresler, of *Relational Psychoanalysis and Psychotherapy Integration*; and the author of *Repair of the Soul: Metaphors of Transformation in Jewish Mysticism and Psychoanalysis.* Dr. Starr is on the Editorial Board of the Psychoanalysis and Jewish Life Book Series, Academic Press. She is a clinical supervisor at The Graduate Center, City University of New York and Long Island University/C.W. Post. Dr. Starr maintains a private practice in New York City and Great Neck, Long Island.

ACKNOWLEDGMENTS

Many people, so deeply knowledgeable about Ferenczi, have helped in the crafting of this book and its many details. In particular, we thank Judit Mészáros for her generosity and guidance.

Adrienne thanks her intellectual, collegial community: Lewis Aron, Anthony Bass, Steven Botticelli, Philip Bromberg, Nancy Chodorow, Susan Coates, Steven Cooper, Ken Corbett, Muriel Dimen, Sam Gerson, Virginia Goldner, David Lichtenstein, Donald Moss, Eyal Rozmarin, Stephen Seligman, Jane Tillman, and Lynne Zeavin, all of whom create the intellectual conversation and climate around me, which is like oxygen.

I thank my family for so much support and care: Lorna, Kate, Justin, Jake, and Philip.

And always I remember my beloved Robert Sklar (1936–2011), who encouraged me to write and put work into the world.

Steven thanks dear friends and colleagues Lewis Aron, Galit Atlas, Sally Bjorklund, Hillary Grill, Sharyn Leff, and Caryn Sherman-Meyer, for enriching my life in so many ways. Thank you, too, to Kim Bernstein, Margaret Black, Pamela Feldman, Ken Frank, Ellen Fries, Linda Hopkins, Steven Knoblauch, Clem Loew, Kristin Long, Pamela Raab, Marc Sholes, and Rachel Sopher for their professional and personal support. I am grateful to my study and reading group-mates, and thank my family and friends, especially Phyllis, Danny and Art Kuchuck, Judith Young, the Peligris, Strausses, Jodd Readick, Herb Stern, and of course Emma, Yali, and Mia Koch. As always, I thank David Flohr for love and devotion that helps to sustain me.

I am very fortunate to have an intellectually stimulating and emotionally nurturing professional home at the National Institute for the Psychotherapies and thank my fellow Board members and members of the larger community for providing that. Thank you friends and colleagues at *Psychoanalytic Perspectives* and fellow Board members at The International Association for Relational Psychoanalysis and Psychotherapy.

Together, we offer our deep appreciation to Routledge Taylor & Francis Group, which has for many years published and championed the Relational Perspectives Book Series. In particular, we thank our publisher Kate Hawes, Senior Editorial Assistant Kirsten Buchanan, and Editorial Assistant Susan Wickenden for their patience, support, and great care in guiding us and ushering our book through production. Thank you, too, to Annelisa Pedersen for her skillful help in preparing the manuscript.

And finally, we offer our gratitude to the authors of these chapters, who have worked through revisions, edits, and many conversations in order to produce work that we are so proud to represent.

INTRODUCTION

The Legacy of Sándor Ferenczi: Lost and Found

In the nineteen years since the release of the Freud–Ferenczi correspondence (1996), twenty-two years since the publication of *The Legacy of Sándor Ferenczi* (Aron and Harris, 1993), and thirty years since the original French publication of *The Clinical Diary* in 1985, much has changed in the conversation about Ferenczi and psychoanalysis. Relational psychoanalysis, then only recently coined as a term and newly emerged on the scene (Greenberg and Mitchell, 1983; Mitchell, 1988), is now a dominant influence for many theoreticians and practitioners. Through a merging of British object relations theory (Klein, 1992; Fairbairn, 1952; Winnicott, 1971; among others) and interpersonal psychoanalysis (Sullivan, 1953; Fromm, 1956; Thompson, 1953; and others), relational psychoanalysis has shifted the focus from the drive theory of sex and aggression to real external, as well as fantasized internal object relationships. In relational psychoanalysis, object seeking and relationships are central to development and motivation more than, or rather than, drives, according to some (Mitchell, 1988; Greenberg and Mitchell, 1983). Contemporary Freudian (Bach, 2001; Richards, 1999; among others) and post-Bionian field theories (Civitarese and Ferro, 2013; Stern, 2013a, 2013b), which each in their way also emphasize the centrality of the therapeutic relationship and many of Ferenczi's ideas, have also become more integral in the psychoanalytic conversation during this period.

These have been scientifically, philosophically, and culturally fertile years. Postmodern, dialectical thinking has now supplanted or at least overshadows Cartesian assumptions in psychoanalysis and other disciplines, and a two-person psychology, in which the analyst's psyche is also mined—mainly for clinical data—and scanned for its impact on the patient and treatment, is now central (Aron, 1996). Previously marginalized voices of women, people of color, the economically challenged, and lesbian, gay, bisexual, and transgendered people—among others previously over-looked or disowned by society and psychoanalysis more specifically—have been invited into this modernized psychoanalytic tent. Ferenczi was perhaps the first to devote significant time and energy to clinical work with the disenfranchised and traumatized, half a century before the postmodern, contemporary Freudian, and relational turns. He was also among the first to routinely treat severely disturbed patients. In this respect especially, he not only changed the course of classical psychoanalysis, but also prefigured all the schools to follow.

This volume of essays attests to the inescapable truth that Ferenczi is now canonical. In the recuperation of his theoretical ideas—the importance of countertransference, the importance of early object relations and mother-child relationships, and the centrality of trauma—we see his formative place in our own history. In his work at an institutional level, we see how crucial he was in the genesis of an international psychoanalytic movement. In understanding his links to culture and to socially and politically progressive ideals, we have a model of psychoanalytic citizenship that offers much to admire and aspire to.

To encounter Ferenczi, his work, his colleagues, and his thinking is to recognize at once the consequences of lost psychoanalytic knowledge and wisdom when history is dismissed or otherwise discarded, and forefathers are pushed to the side. Psychoanalysis, as practice and theory, has paid a high price for Ferenczi's forced exile. Discovering, amplifying, and reclaiming Ferenczi's legacy are ways to restore severed connections to our past without underplaying the importance of more modern innovations. Indeed, a number of contemporary theorists and a majority of the authors in this volume have noted the direct links between Ferenczi and early interpersonal and object relations theorists and therefore the direct connection between Ferenczi and relational psychoanalysis. Freud, of course, is in the psychoanalytic DNA of us all (Brown, 2011; Galit Atlas, in press) and continues to inform our work and ongoing evolution. There is an additional through-line though. Lost from sight for some time but never fully diminished in influence, this line has traveled in particularly direct ways from Ferenczi, perhaps in large part because age, generation, and modern, even prescient sensibilities positioned him as father or grandfather to all incarnations of classical and contemporary perspectives, psychoanalytic schools, and movements. More specifically, as noted above and as many of the authors here have pointed out, Ferenczi's thinking about mutuality, trauma, the analyst's psychology, and the environment not only foretold contemporary psychoanalytic perspectives, but when held in tension with more classical theories also adds to and deepens the dialogue between Freud and those who followed (Aron and Starr, 2013). This pathway from classical thinking to present-day psychoanalytic theory and practice is a central part of Ferenczi's legacy and marks his status as not merely ghost, but also, ancestor (Loewald, 1989).

In 1991, Lewis Aron and Adrienne Harris organized an international Ferenczi conference in New York City, the first of its kind in the United States. A diverse group of European voices including Judit Mészáros, André Haynal, György Hidas, and Judith Dupont joined with Aron, Harris, and other Americans in the throes of discovery or rediscovery, including Therese Ragen, Sue Shapiro, Arnold Rachman, Jay Frankel, Christopher Fortune, Axel Hoffer, and Ben Wolstein. Two years later, inspired by the proceedings and inclusive of many of those presentations as well as additional original contributions, Aron and Harris's *The Legacy of Sándor Ferenczi* (1993) introduced a larger, print audience of psychoanalysts to Sándor Ferenczi. No longer merely the bad boy of early psychoanalytic history, seen as deserving of banishment from Freud's inner circle and status as laughingstock of the larger professional community, Ferenczi emerged in those pages as he did in that earlier conference; a complex, often gifted theoretician and practitioner.

At the conference, American psychoanalysts who were discovering Ferenczi and claiming a long lost ancestor met up with European (primarily Hungarian and English) analysts who had made this possible because of what they salvaged. We have Michael Balint to thank for the ongoing preservation and eventual English translation of Ferenczi's *The Clinical Diary* (1932/1988). Many individuals, some of whom presented at the conference and published in the original and current volume, kept Ferenczi's ideas alive and his manuscripts safe from destruction for decades. Balint, perhaps foremost in this group of preservationists, was determined to keep Ferenczi's technical research and writing present in the postwar period in England, where he became an initiating force in object relations theory. He brought the manuscript of *The Clinical Diary* from Budapest to London but, perhaps correctly, remained fearful of having it translated and published. Publication occurred some years after Balint's death in a different, more evolved psychoanalytic climate from the one in which Balint (and for that matter, Ferenczi) had worked. In his writing about Ferenczi and Freud's disagreement, he sets a graceful, loving tone, feeling and conveying the tragedy of their conflict and its cost to psychoanalysis. Rather than demonizing or idealizing, Balint saw the troubles on each side of that dyad. His manner is measured, mature, and deeply emotionally attuned to both men. Balint's voice remains one of the important ways to tell this story (Balint, 1969). Mészáros, Haynal, Hidas, and Dupont also demonstrated courageous and devoted persistence in keeping Ferenczian work alive and intact, even if not very much in sight until more recent years. The debt owed to these psychoanalysts is incalculable. Both the 1993 book and this current work reflect the importance of the rediscovery of Ferenczi, the enormous evolution of scholarship and theory building in Ferenczian mode, and the valiant efforts of those who saved his legacy and therefore made these strides possible.

Along with the conference, Aron and Harris's book (1993) served as an introduction to and defense of Freud's most famous patient, colleague, inheritor, and opponent. As the editors explained:

> Sándor Ferenczi was dismissed by mainstream psychoanalysts, disregarded because of his radical clinical experiments, because of his revival of interest in

the etiological importance of external trauma, and because he was perceived as encouraging dangerous regressions in his patients and attempting to cure them with love. All these criticisms were reinforced with personal aspersions on his character and accusations that he had mentally deteriorated and even gone mad in the final years of his life at the height of his clinical experimentation and in the midst of disputes with Freud. (p. 2)

Their influential book was an attempt to rescue Ferenczi from these aspersions and resulting professional exile. In Aron and Harris's view, his contributions to early psychoanalysis were second only to Freud's. They note his central role in organizing and representing the psychoanalytic movement and influence as a lecturer, theoretician, and clinician. Indeed, Ferenczi founded the International Psychoanalytical Association and the Budapest Psychoanalytic Association, was the first university-based professor of psychoanalysis, helped found the *International Journal of Psychoanalysis*, and conducted the first formal training analysis (of Ernest Jones). In psychoanalytic historian Edith Kurzweil's introduction to the book, she notes that, "Adler thought Ferenczi was the most brilliant of Freud's disciples" (1993, p. xxii). As analyst to Michael Balint, Ernest Jones, Melanie Klein, and John Rickman in England, as well as to Clara Thompson, Geza Roheim, and Sándor Rado in the United States, he influenced generations of leading psychoanalytic thinkers and writers as well as their patients and subsequent generations of clinicians. Although there were significant missteps, mistakes, boundary violations, and, beyond his control, political forces in play—namely in relation to Freud and Freud's disciples—a rich literature and talented elder statesman and guide were lost for over half a century.

Contributions to the Literature

At the time of Aron and Harris's publication, the Freud–Ferenczi correspondence (1993) was not yet translated into English, and Ferenczi's previously mentioned *The Clinical Diary* (1932/1988)—published in the same year as Stephen Mitchell's first solely relational book (as Bass points out in this volume)—had only been available in English for five years, although a French edition had been released in 1985, the year that many believe ushered in the Ferenczian renaissance. Also in 1985, the Sándor Ferenczi Society was established in Budapest, and international Ferenczi conferences have been held across the world every two to three years since then. Aron and Harris and their contributors were pioneers, aided by the aforementioned crucial acts of courage that preserved Ferenczi's work, and they helped pave the way for future Ferenczi scholars.

A number of important contributions have been made to the literature since 1993, including Rudnytsky, Bokay, and Giampieri-Deutsch (1996), Rachman (1997a), Haynal (2002), Szekacs-Weisz and Keve (2012), and Mészáros (2014). In 2008, Jeremy Safran, Lewis Aron, and Adrienne Harris established the Sándor

Ferenczi Center at The New School for Social Research, exactly one hundred years after Ferenczi's first meeting with Freud, and just over eighty years after Ferenczi spent four months in New York City in 1926, seeing a full roster of patients and giving a series of ten lectures at The New School on topics including psychosis, psychoanalytic theory, and technique. Ferenczi's lectures were well attended, and in fact he notes that three hundred people were present on the first evening. The Sándor Ferenczi Center was established as a tribute to his New School tenure and with the goal of sponsoring conferences and promoting research, scholarship, and publications regarding Ferenczi, promoting new translations and publications of Ferenczi's writings, and in conjunction with similar centers in Europe, contributing to the ongoing vitality of psychoanalysis as a cultural, intellectual, and psychotherapeutic discipline.

In recent years, various journals have devoted special issues to Ferenczi's legacy (*Le-Coq-Héron*, 1999; *International Forum of Psychoanalysis*, 1998 and 2004; *Integrative Therapy*, 2003; *Psychoanalytic Inquiry*, 1997 and 2014). In 2010, under the editorial direction of then co-editors Steven Kuchuck and Deborah Pines, *Psychoanalytic Perspectives* published a special "Ferenczi issue" that included a new, updated introduction to *The Legacy of Sándor Ferenczi* written by Aron and Harris. This new introduction and the currently out-of-print 1993 book are available for download at the Ferenczi Center website. In 2011, after a six-year, extensive fundraising project, the Sándor Ferenczi Society and the International Sándor Ferenczi Foundation (founded in 2006) purchased part of the former Sándor Ferenczi house which had been used as his office in order to house the International Ferenczi Center.

From Ghost to Ancestor

Ferenczi, probably more than any other well-known psychoanalyst, truly exemplifies an integration of classical and contemporary ways of thinking about and practicing his craft. Through our current lens and even during his life, Ferenczi stood with one foot in the classical world and one foot in the modern. His professional vocabulary and emphasis on the intrapsychic still speak to classical and more contemporary Freudian scholars and practitioners, while his experiments in mutuality and emphasis on the here and now and healing potential of the relationship—among numerous other factors—resonate for relational and other contemporary psychotherapists. There are likely additional reasons that he speaks so cogently to so many of us. There may be an identification with Ferenczi as an outsider or "other" that many psychoanalysts also feel in their lives that causes them to experience a corresponding resonance with his work. Also, relational analysts, graduates of non-International Psychoanalytical Association training programs, and those who do not obtain psychoanalytic certificates and therefore are sometimes accused of not being truly psychoanalytic (Aron and Starr, 2013) may experience an understandable identification with his forced exile from the academy and the psychoanalytic mainstream.

The contributions you are about to read come to us from some of the most influential Ferenczi scholars in the world. We are fortunate to be able to include new work by a number of authors from the original volume, and they have been joined by other senior scholars and newer, important voices in international Ferenczian and psychoanalytic scholarship. This is a gathering of geographically and theoretically diverse, at times overlapping, concordant, and complimentary writers; in that sense the collection is perhaps a fitting tribute to a man summarily dismissed for his difference from the dominant psychoanalytic culture and, like many colleagues and citizens of his day, because of the prevailing religious–political ethos.

Part I: The Context

Although we have divided this collection into three sections, some of the chapters cross-reference both each other and historical developments, and therefore as in psychoanalysis—or life—chronology and categories are more nonlinear than the organizational structure of the book might indicate. The chapters in "The Context" could also have been included in "History," and the chapters that we have placed in "History" are certainly interrelated with those folded into "Theory and Technique," as developments in these three areas always are. Regardless of whether or not readers choose to read this work in the order presented here, we do hope this volume will enhance your own experience of "discovery and rediscovery" (Aron and Harris, 1993, 2010) of Sándor Ferenczi.

Few people have done more to further the international Ferenczi renaissance than Hungarian psychoanalyst and Ferenczi scholar Judit Mészáros. In 1993, she provided the contextual framework for the chapters that followed by introducing readers to the social and ideological worlds that gave birth to and supported Ferenczi's educational and professional life and evolution. Building on this foundation two decades later, she asks several key questions and provides answers that help orient readers to Ferenczi's current position of prominence in the psychoanalytic canon. What attracts us to Ferenczi? What does he represent that has been bringing clinicians and academics from various scholarly fields together for decades? What is it in our current era of feuds between psychoanalytic schools of thought that draws people from otherwise opposing theoretical perspectives to connect with Ferenczi and allows for a common way of thinking among professionals who live in a variety of personal and professional cultures and political systems throughout the world? What is it about Ferenczi that leads contemporaries to connect to psychoanalysis and to Ferenczi now, just as they did in the past before his fall from grace?

Carlo Bonomi begins his essay with a very disturbing dream. He suggests that Ferenczi presents this dream in his letter to Freud as a sign of subjugation, though Bonomi reads the complexity of that dream and its transmission as a cover for rebellion as well as a wish to treat—ultimately, perhaps, even to save—Freud and psychoanalysis. Bonomi traces the complexities of Ferenczi's relationship to Freud as compliant and rebellious son, student, patient, friend, colleague, and would-be analyst through a careful consideration of Ferenczi's *The Clinical Diary* (1932/1988), correspondence, publications, and additional well-cited sources. He explores Ferenczi's views about the split found in psychoanalysis between what Ferenczi viewed as Freud's initial passion and caring for his patients and his eventual move toward a colder, more calculating surgical precision. Bonomi considers the toll that carrying these thoughts and feelings of dissent and deep disappointment—mostly in secret—took on Ferenczi and how these dynamics shaped his personal and professional evolution.

In the 1993 volume, psychoanalytic historian André Haynal engaged in a search for the origins of then current psychoanalytic technique in the work of Freud and his pupils, especially Ferenczi. His consideration of correspondence, professional writing, and theoretical evolution shed light on Freud and Ferenczi's complex relationship, including areas of personal and professional similarities and differences. In this earlier contribution, Haynal began to explore what he called Ferenczi's attitude, a topic he and Véronique Haynal now take up in great depth and with remarkable scholarship, insight and zeal. They present Ferenczi in the context and as a product of a rich cultural heritage and describe how the evolution of Ferenczi's personal and psychoanalytic attitude unfolded and became an integral part of his psychoanalytic identity.

The Haynals provide us with a vision of Ferenczi's individuality as a crucial element in his creation of theory and technical experiment. They employ the term "ethics" in showing us how deeply Ferenczi cared to help patients and how deeply his clinical mission went. His character, which the Haynals term "attitude," was one of intensity and passion. He was not proscriptive and moralizing, but rather, was interested in working within relationships, whether institutionally or clinically. He had good critical judgment and cooperated in a highly intellectually elaborate world of ideas and projects. All of these aspects of Ferenczi's character render him a very imaginative and creative innovator in psychoanalysis, yet the Haynals take great pains to show us Ferenczi the team player, the collaborator, and the powerful creator of a movement. This essay goes very far in repairing the construction of Ferenczi as damaged, ill, and marginal to the psychoanalytic movement. It also includes a useful analysis of the difficult-to-unpack book *Thalassa: A Theory of Genitality* (Ferenczi, 1924/1989) and focuses on Ferenczi's seminal contributions to trauma theory, including the reality of externally originating abuse, a modern turn that was long in coming due in large part to the occlusion of Ferenczi's work.

Part II: History

If Freud and others have likened psychoanalytic treatment to detective work (Freud, 1916), with B. William Brennan we are no doubt in the company of an actual psychoanalytic sleuth. Brennan has devoted a large portion of his psychoanalytic research and writing (for example, 2009, 2011) to decoding Ferenczi's *The Clinical Diary* (1932/1988) and to considering related ethical issues and resulting insights into Ferenczi and his patients. This chapter explores Ferenczi's work with Clara Thompson, whose identity as Dm is revealed in *The Clinical Diary* by Dupont (Ferenczi 1932/1988, pp. 2–3) and who became a leading figure in the development of interpersonal psychoanalysis. Brennan offers new insights into Thompson and her controversial analysis based on her candid interview with Kurt Eissler about her treatment with "Papa Ferenczi," which until recently had been sequestered in the Freud archives.

Christopher Fortune, in his earlier contribution (1993), offered a moving narrative of Elizabeth Severn, the patient who appears in *The Clinical Diary* as RN. His chapter shed tremendous light on the strengths and weaknesses of the mutual analysis Ferenczi entered into under pressure from this challenging patient and colleague. Fortune's current work is also about an important figure in Ferenczi's (and Freud's) life, Georg Groddeck, a German physician and psychoanalyst who may have been the first to seriously explore the relationship between physical and mental illness. Fortune discusses Groddeck's influence on Ferenczi as gleaned primarily through a fascinating examination of their twelve-year correspondence.

A prolific contributor to the Ferenczi literature (for example, 1989, 1993, 1997a, 1997b, 1997c, 2000, 2003, 2007, 2010a, 2010b, 2014, among others), Arnold Rachman focused his earlier contribution on Ferenczi's ideas about sexuality, especially as explored in Ferenczi's work with what was then called a transvestite patient (1993) and was prescient of a much later and still burgeoning literature of transgender studies. Rachman's current work, like Fortune's earlier chapter (1993), concerns itself with Elizabeth Severn. Based on newly available data including the discovery of the Elizabeth Severn papers and the Kurt Eissler Interview of Elizabeth Severn (Severn, 1952), Rachman accomplishes a sophisticated deconstruction of Severn's treatment (including the development and impact of what came to be known as mutual analysis) and professional acumen. He provides well-documented support for his claim that Elizabeth Severn should be credited with helping Ferenczi to develop his ideas about the diagnosis, treatment, and theory of trauma.

Adrienne Harris reflects on Ferenczi's "Two Types of War Neuroses" (1926/1994), tying his essay to an interest not only in trauma but also psychotic process and primitive states, and to the work of Ferenczi's colleagues treating and writing in the shadow of the First World War. Ferenczi developed many of his ideas about trauma by observing and working with combat veterans during World War I. The war took its toll on the psychoanalytic community in numerous ways, and in Harris's view, the erasure of Ferenczi within psychoanalysis prevented this war-generation of analysts from having a greater impact on the profession. Her essay is an attempt to at least identify and even begin to amplify their voices.

That we decided to include three chapters devoted primarily to Elizabeth Severn (not counting her appearance in several others) is a testament to her influence on Ferenczi and therefore contemporary psychoanalysis and is indicative of the complexity of their relationship and its resulting historical, theoretical, and clinical implications. It is also reflective of the significant original sources that exist—some only recently available for examination—as well as the varied research interests of these talented Ferenczi–Severn scholars. In his chapter, analyst and historian Peter Rudnytsky notes that *The Discovery of the Self* (1933) contains a thinly disguised case history of Ferenczi, as well as of Severn, which makes the book one of the essential texts in the history of psychoanalysis and of crucial supplemental value to *The Clinical Diary*. For the first time Severn emerges as a subject in her own right with an entire body of work that warrants a thorough reconsideration. Severn's book and Rudnytsky's investigation allow us to more fully appreciate her work as a theoretician and clinician and to gain insight into Ferenczi's struggles as a patient.

In addition to coediting the 1993 volume and other contributions to Ferenczi-related scholarship already mentioned, Lewis Aron wrote a comprehensive introductory chapter with Adrienne Harris that introduced Ferenczi to a new audience by providing a historical and theoretical context and overview (1993, 2010). Also in the earlier volume, with Therese Ragen, he wrote about Ferenczi's daring experiment of mutual analysis, a cutting edge (especially twenty-two years ago) if problematic and flawed paradigm worthy of modification and reconsideration. Writing now with Karen Starr, Aron explores the personal and professional relationship between Freud and Ferenczi, two Jewish Enlightenment men who enacted between them dynamics shaped in large part by internalizations and reactions to an anti-Semitic and homophobic culture.

Part III: Theory and Technique

While babies are hungry for objects and affects they need in order to develop, they have no choice but to take in everything without being able to select and defend themselves from the toxic elements of what they ingest. Franco Borgogno writes that as Ferenczi focused his thinking on the important role of introjections, he asked what it was that the baby puts inside itself and how these things are offered to the infant. Borgogno contends that from Ferenczi's point of view, it is the specific quality of the response of the other that shapes our ensuing identifications and resulting views and perceptions of ourselves and the world.

In her writing about sexuality (2011, 2012a, 2012b, 2013, 2014) and informing her newly coined terms "enigmatic and pragmatic knowing" (in press), Galit Atlas synthesizes primarily Kleinian, object relations, and relational psychoanalytic perspectives of the mind. In her current chapter, she also explores the "confusion of tongues" (1933) that arises in the spaces between the language of tenderness and the language of aggression, especially as this confusion unfolds in two extended case examples. Atlas believes that patients and therapists use playfulness to collude in avoiding aggression in order to protect the fragile sense of tenderness that evolves in the treatment for both parties.

The analyst privileges the patient's inner world and creates the necessary conditions of so-called analytic "neutrality"—at least according to more classical thinkers, and non-intrusiveness (for a more contemporary exploration of this topic, see Robert Grossmark, 2012) in order for internal content to emerge in the consulting room. On the other hand, there is an opposing, more contemporary position that suggests the therapist always participates in the clinical relationship and can therefore never be merely an anonymous "neutral" observer. In the 1993 volume, Jay Frankel explored this paradox and Ferenczi's attempts to address if not reconcile the seeming contradiction. In his most recent work, Frankel continues to focus on the analyst's efforts to both explore the patient's inner world and the analyst–patient relationship, particularly with regard to Ferenczi's perhaps most well-known concept, identification with the aggressor.

Although Freud wrote that psychoanalysis was a "healing through love" (F/JU, 6.12.1906), he attempts to separate the notions of psychoanalytic "transference" love from real world "actual" love. Of the two men, Ferenczi is far more interested in exploring the healing potential of love, and unlike Freud who worried about transference contamination as the result of the analyst's strong countertransference, Ferenczi believed that the analyst must be able to love in order to be of use to his traumatized patients. Steven Kuchuck explores this idea as it applies to the analyst's loving and erotic feelings and their relation to contemporary notions of therapeutic action, gender, and sexual orientation.

Anthony Bass, building on Ragen and Aron's earlier work (1993), Benjamin Wolstein (1993), and others, engages in an in-depth consideration of Ferenczi's "mutual analysis." Bass considers the links between Ferenczi's radical notions of psychoanalysis as a mutual endeavor finally on its way to a two-person psychology, his experiments in mutual analysis, and the direct line from Ferenczi's work in this area to contemporary interpersonal and relational theory and practice. Bass of course acknowledges the problems and limitations of the far lengths to which Ferenczi went to apply his understanding of mutuality. But he also brings in examples from his own personal treatment and practice to illustrate contemporary applications of Ferenczi's theories of mutuality. In the process, Bass shows us how sometimes minor—albeit significant—modifications of Ferenczi's original technique allow for powerful interventions that still adhere to conventional contemporary wisdom about appropriate boundaries and the therapeutic frame.

Although Lacan was familiar with Ferenczi's work, he arrived on the scene too late to have met him. He does mention Ferenczi several times in his seminars and writings, and some features of Ferenczi's work apparently made an impact on Lacan. Nonetheless, the overall tone that he took with regard to Ferenczi's work was dismissive. Lewis Kirshner's chapter summarizes the major references to Ferenczi in Lacan's work and elaborates upon some of the parallels between these two visionaries.

Eyal Rozmarin raises a number of profound questions, as he wonders with us about the nature of development and trauma. Rozmarin brings us two different but related seminal notions: Ferenczi's "confusion of tongues" (1933) and Laplanche's concept of the "enigmatic message" (1995). As he suggests, both notions are concerned with the enigmatic and potentially traumatic differences between adults and children. Although there is some overlap of meaning, the confusions explored by each are very different. Laplanche presents a version of confusion in which the language of the adult is excessive, but for the most part benevolent and implicit, while Ferenczi exposes a form of confusion where the language of the adult is explicitly raw, often toxic, and therefore catastrophic.

The end of Ferenczi's life, like many endings, eventually led to a new beginning—a renaissance, as we and others have referred to the renewed interest in his contributions to the field. As time passed, old professional feuds faded, wounds healed, and psychoanalytic theories, epistemologies, and hegemonies eventually caught up to this visionary thinker. We end this collection with another beginning. Brazilian psychoanalysts Haydée Christinne Kahtuni and Gisela Paraná Sanches have published the first dictionary of Sándor Ferenczi's work. Their goal was to provide both beginning and more advanced psychoanalytic readers with an integrated, extensive but curated collection of his definitions and excerpts of his writings. Entries include his main concepts, original ideas, new expressions, and additional related ideas that are presented in order to guide and facilitate further study of Ferenczi's work. Although the dictionary was published in Portuguese only, funding efforts are underway to translate this ambitious work into English and other languages. Kahtuni arranged for a small portion of the dictionary—the section concerning Ferenczi's trauma theory—to be translated into English for this volume.

Surfaces and Separations

Perhaps in some cases one can actually begin to judge or at least understand a book by its cover. Completed in 1896 when Ferenczi was a young man of 23 and just three years after he moved to Hungary's capital, the (Emperor) Franz Joseph Bridge connects the cities of Buda and Pest, previously separate cities that were united in 1873, the year Ferenczi was born. We chose a photograph of the bridge emerging from shadows into light and clarity. The parts of the city hidden by clouds and darkness include the area where Ferenczi lived in the last years of his life. Destroyed by the German army during their retreat at the end of World War II, the bridge was reconstructed and reopened in 1946 as the Liberty (sometimes called Freedom) Bridge on St. Stephen's day, Hungary's most important holiday and celebration of the nation's founding. This photograph conjures up tragic losses and eclipses of many freedoms, but also symbolizes an opening to the future.

As was the case with Aron and Harris's first volume, our goal is to celebrate Ferenczi's (in this case continuing) return from theoretical exile. These essays shine a new, bright light on Ferenczi's contributions to, influence on, and integration into more contemporary schools of psychoanalysis. Some of them introduce new historical discoveries. Each illuminates Ferenczi's and in some cases his patients' and mentors' personal and professional development and theories.

Final Thoughts

We are in the middle of a fascinating set of conversations; we do not hope for conclusions. Rather than the certitude which sometimes accompanies finality and which we know can lead to intellectual stagnation, our wish is for questions to follow the questions and tentative answers this collection, like its predecessor, presents. We hope for what Mészáros relays to us about Ferenczi, an ability to endure the tension created by uncertainties without rushing into rash or prejudiced conclusions (this volume). And in this spirit we are also buoyed by Michael Balint's words about his former analyst, colleague, and friend, "Even the most common, the most everyday, the most routine experience was never rounded off and finished for him; he never filed anything away as finally dealt with or definitely solved" (Balint, 1948/1957, pp. 245–246 in Mészáros, this volume).

In addition to questions, we also desire more and multiple beginnings. We would like to believe that returned to respectability—indeed, to a position of professional appreciation, admiration, and for some, inspiration—Ferenczi has for some time now been available to learn from and use. As theories develop and evolve, our expectation is that each generation of psychotherapists and psychoanalysts will discover Ferenczi anew and in their own particular ways, just as different generations and individual authors within the same generation have done in this volume and have been doing in offices and clinics for many years.

In the words of Hans Loewald, who passed away in 1993, the same year that Aron and Harris's volume was published:

> Those who know ghosts tell us that they long to be released from their ghost life and led to rest as ancestors. As ancestors they live forth in the present generation, while as ghosts they are compelled to haunt the present generation with their shadow life … In the daylight of analysis the ghosts … are laid and led to rest as ancestors whose power is taken over and transformed into the newer intensity of present life. (1989, p. 249)

So it is for Sándor Ferenczi.

References

Aron, L. (1996). *A Meeting of Minds: Mutuality in Psychoanalysis.* New York: Routledge.

Aron, L. and Harris, A. (1993). Discovery and rediscovery. In L. Aron and A. Harris (eds), *The Legacy of Sándor Ferenczi.* London: The Analytic Press, pp. 1–36.

Aron, L. and Harris, A. (2010). Sándor Ferenczi: Discovery and rediscovery. *Psychoanalytic Perspectives,* 7:5–42.

Aron, L. and Starr, K. (2013). *A Psychotherapy for the People: Towards a Progressive Psychoanalysis.* New York: Routledge.

Atlas, G. (2012a). Sex and the kitchen: Thoughts on culture and forbidden desire. *Psychoanalytic Perspectives,* 9:220–232.

Atlas, G. (2012b). East of Freud. *Division Review,* 1(3).

Atlas, G. (2013). What's love got to do with it? Sexuality, shame, and the use of the other. *Studies in Gender and Sexuality,* 14:51–58.

Atlas, G. (2014). Sex, lies, and videotape. In S. Kuchuck (ed), *Clinical Implications of the Psychoanalyst's Life Experience: When the Personal Becomes Professional.* New York: Routledge, pp. 26–35.

Atlas, G. (In press). *The Enigma of Desire: Sex, Longing, and Belonging in Psychoanalysis.* New York: Routledge.

Atlas-Koch, G. (2011). The bad father, the sinful son, and the wild ghost: A psychoanalytic exploration of the *Dybbuk. Psychoanalytic Perspectives,* 8:238–251.

Bach, S. (2001). On being forgotten and forgetting one's self. *Psychoanalytic Quarterly,* 70: 739–756.

Balint, M. (1957). Sándor Ferenczi, Obit. 1933. In M. Balint (ed), *Problem of Human Pleasure and Behaviour.* New York: Liverright, pp. 243–250. (Originally published 1948).

Balint, M. (1969). The disagreement between Freud and Ferenczi and its repercussions. In *The Basic Fault.* London: Tavistock, pp. 149–158.

Brennan, B. W. (2009). Ferenczi's forgotten messenger: The life and work of Izette de Forest. *American Imago,* 66(4):427–455.

Brennan, B. W. (2011). On Ferenczi, a response—from elasticity to the confusion of tongues and technical dimensions of Ferenczi's approach, *Psychoanalytic Perspectives,* 8(1):1–21.

Brown, L. (2011). *Intersubjective Processes and the Unconscious: An Integration of Freudian, Kleinian and Bionian Perspectives.* New York: Routledge.

Civitarese, G. and Ferro, A. (2013). The meaning and use of metaphor in analytic field theory, *Psychoanalytic Inquiry: A Topical Journal for Mental Health Professionals,* 33(3):190–209.

Fairbairn, W. R. D. (1952). *Psychoanalytic Studies of the Personality* (Intro. D. E. Scharff and E. F. Birtles). London: Tavistock Publications.

Ferenczi, S. (1933). The confusion of tongues between adults and children: The language of tenderness and passion. In M. Balint (ed), *Final Contributions to the Problems and Methods of Psycho-analysis,* Vol. 3. New York: Brunner/Mazel, 1980, pp. 156–167.

Ferenczi, S. (1988). *The Clinical Diary.* (J. Dupont, Ed.). Cambridge, MA: Harvard University Press. (Original work published 1932).

Ferenczi, S. (1989). *Thalassa: A theory of genitality.* London: Karnac Books. (Original work published 1924).

Ferenczi, S. (1994). Two types of war neuroses. *Further Contributions to the Theory and Technique of Psycho-Analysis.* London: Karnac, 1926, pp. 124–141.

Fortune, C. (1993). Sándor Ferenczi's analysis of 'R. N.': A critically important case in the history of psychoanalysis. *British Journal of Psychotherapy,* 9:436–443.

Freud, S. (1906). Letter from Sigmund Freud to C. G. Jung, December 6, 1906. *The Freud/Jung Letters: The Correspondence Between Sigmund Freud and C. J. Jung,* pp. 11–13.

Freud, S. (1916). Introductory lectures on psycho-analysis. *SE,* 15:1915–1916.

Freud, S. and Ferenczi, S. (1996). *The Correspondence of Sigmund Freud and Sándor Ferenczi, Volume 2: 1914–1919.* E. Falzeder and E. Brabant (eds). Cambridge, MA: Harvard University Press.

Fromm, E. (1956). *The Art of Loving.* New York: Harper & Brothers.

Greenberg, J. and Mitchell, S. A. (1983). *Object Relations in Psychoanalytic Theory.* Cambridge, MA: Harvard University Press.

Grossmark, R. (2012). The unobtrusive relational analyst. *Psychoanalytic Dialogues,* 22:629–646.

Haynal, A. (2002). *Disappearing and Reviving. Sándor Ferenczi in the History of Psychoanalysis.* London: Karnac.

Klein, M. (1992). *Love, Guilt and Reparation: And Other Works, 1921–1945.* London: Karnac.

Kurzweil, E. (1993). Introduction. In L. Aron and A. Harris (eds), *The Legacy of Sándor Ferenczi.* London: The Analytic Press.

Laplanche, J. (1995). Seduction, persecution, revelation. *International Journal of Psychoanalysis,* 76:663–682.

Loewald, H. (1989). *Papers on Psychoanalysis.* New Haven: Yale University Press.

Mészáros, J. (2014). *Ferenczi and Beyond: Exile of the Budapest School and Solidarity in the Psychoanalytic Movement in the Nazi Years.* London, UK: Karnac Books.

Mitchell, S. A. (1988). *Relational Concepts in Psychoanalysis: An Integration.* Cambridge, MA: Harvard University Press.

Rachman, A. W. (1989). Confusion of tongues: The Ferenczian metaphor for childhood seduction and emotional trauma. *Journal of the American Academy of Psychoanalysis,* 17:181–205.

Rachman, A. W. (1993). Ferenczi and sexuality. In L. Aron and A. Harris (eds), *The Legacy of Sándor Ferenczi.* Hillsdale, NJ: Analytic Press, pp. 81–100.

Rachman, A. W. (1997a). *Sándor Ferenczi: The Psychotherapy of Tenderness and Passion.* Northvale, NJ: Aronson.

Rachman, A. W. (1997b). The suppression and censorship of Ferenczi's confusion of tongues paper. *Psychoanalytic Inquiry,* 17:459–485.

Rachman, A. W. (1997c). Sándor Ferenczi and the evolution of a self psychology framework in psychoanalysis. *Progress in Self Psychology,* 13:341–365.

Rachman, A. W. (2000). Ferenczi's "confusion of tongues" theory and the analysis of the incest trauma. *Psychoanalytic Social Work,* 7:27–53.

Rachman, A. W. (2003). *Psychotherapy of Difficult Cases: Flexibility and Responsiveness in Contemporary Practice.* Madison, CT: Psychosocial Press.

Rachman, A. W. (2007). Sándor Ferenczi's contributions to the evolution of psychoanalysis. *Psychoanalytic Psychology,* 24:74–96.

Rachman, A. W. (2010a). The origins of a relational perspective in the ideas of Sándor Ferenczi and the Budapest School of Psychoanalysis. *Psychoanalytic Perspectives,* 7:43–60.

Rachman, A. W. (2010b). An "invitro" study of intersubjectivity: Sándor Ferenczi's analysis of Mrs. Elizabeth Severn Presentation. XVII. International Forum for Psychoanalysis. Athens, Greece.

Rachman, A. W. (2014). Sándor Ferenczi as "the bridge": My journey from phenomenology and humanistic psychotherapy to relational analysis. *Psychoanalytic Inquiry,* 34:182–186.

Ragen, T. and Aron, L. (1993). Abandoned workings: Ferenczi's mutual analysis. In L. Aron and A. Harris (eds), *The Legacy of Sándor Ferenczi.* Hillsdale, NJ: Analytic Press, pp. 217–226.

Richards, A. (1999). Ritual and spontaneity in the psychoanalytic process: A dialectical constructive point of view: Irwin Hoffman, Hillsdale, NJ: Analysis Press, 1998. *Psychoanalytic Psychology,* 16:288–302.

Rudnytsky, P. L., Bokay, A., and Giampieri-Deutsch, P. (eds) (1996). *Ferenczi's Turn in Psychoanalysis.* New York: New York University Press.

Severn, E. (1952). Interviews and Recollections, Set B, 1952–1960 with K. R. Eissler/Interviewer. Sigmund Freud Papers, (Box 126). Manuscripts Division, Library of Congress, Washington, D.C.

Stern, D. (2013a). Field theory in psychoanalysis, Part I: Harry Stack Sullivan and Madeleine and Willy Baranger. *Psychoanalytic Dialogues,* 23:487–501.

Stern, D. (2013b). Field theory in psychoanalysis, Part 2: Bionian field theory and contemporary interpersonal/relational psychoanalysis. *Psychoanalytic Dialogues,* 23:630–636.

Sullivan, H. S. (1953). *The interpersonal theory of psychiatry.* New York: Norton.

Szekacs-Weisz, J. and Keve, T. (2012). *Ferenczi and His World: Rekindling the Spirit of the Budapest School.* London: Karnac.

Thompson, C. M. (1953). Towards a psychology of women. *Pastoral Psychology,* 4(34):29–38.

Winnicott, D. W. (1971). *Playing and Reality.* London: Tavistock Publications.

Wolstein, B. (1993). The problem of truth in applied psychoanalysis. *Psychoanalytic Review,* 80:661–664.

PART I
The Context

1

FERENCZI IN OUR CONTEMPORARY WORLD[1]

Judit Mészáros

Why Ferenczi today? This question formed the title of a special issue of the *International Forum of Psychoanalysis* in 2004. This is only one example of the many periodicals, books, and papers published on the legacy of Ferenczi over the last twenty years. By now, Ferenczi's main theoretical and therapeutic initiatives have been discovered/rediscovered and integrated into the mainstream of the contemporary theoretical and therapeutic knowledge of psychoanalysis, from countertransference as an indispensable contribution to the dynamic of the psychotherapeutic process, to the essential importance of the early object relationship between mother and child, and to his paradigm shift in trauma theory.

What attracts us to Ferenczi? What does he represent that has been bringing clinicians and academics from various scholarly fields together for decades? What is that glue/essence that we find for ourselves in the oeuvre of this man who was both an *enfant terrible* and a *wise baby* at the same time, who created the Budapest School, a school with no walls, no director, and no students in a formal sense. He was a man who did not like institutional structures, but nonetheless recognized their inescapable necessity and initiated the establishment of organizations, among them the International Psychoanalytical Association (IPA) more than a hundred years ago, which continues to operate today. What is it in the conflict-burdened world of the twenty-first century that provides us with points of connection to Ferenczi, a common way of thinking among professionals who live in a variety of cultures and political systems throughout the world?

What is it in Ferenczi's personality and way of thinking that smoothes the way for contemporaries to connect to psychoanalysis and to Ferenczi now, just as they did in the past? By now, it is thanks to the tireless work of research, publishing, and education on the part of so many colleagues that a real Ferenczi renaissance has come about. The emergence of this renaissance obviously has numerous components, but some of them can most certainly be linked to Ferenczi's liberalism, the fact that he was not a dogmatic person, his widespread network in Hungarian society at that time, as well as his outstanding presence in the international psychoanalytic movement during his life.

In this chapter, I have collected a number of examples of Ferenczi's way of thinking and his approach, of his relationship to his contemporaries and to the culture around him, and of his theoretical and therapeutic innovations that have enriched psychoanalysis and influenced our professional generation. These point to a liberal-mindedness, a tolerance, and a spirit of cooperation—whether in scholarship or medicine—that developed through respect for the autonomy of others, including the patient!

An Optimal Mix of Liberalism, Respect, and Interactive Communication

It is an unmistakable sign of Ferenczi's liberalism that he respected patients' autonomy and saw psychoanalysis as a joint effort between analyst and analysand both in intellectual and emotional terms; just consider his incorporation of countertransference as part of the unconscious dialogue of transference–countertransference into psychoanalytic treatment in the early 1920s. Psychoanalysis became a system of multidirectional processes of relational elements between the patient and the analyst. Ferenczi's positive thinking on the phenomenon of countertransference represented a fundamental shift in viewpoint (Ferenczi, 1919/1980, 1928/2006; Haynal, 1988; Cabré, 1998; Mészáros, 2004; Aron and Harris, 2010). This paved the way for psychoanalysis to become a system of interactive communication, a "relationship-based" process (Haynal 2002, p. xi) or, as Paul Roazen so aptly put it, "a two-way street" in psychoanalysis (Roazen, 2001).

Psychoanalysis presupposes the simultaneous existence of transference–countertransference *relational dynamics* and *intrapsychic* processes based on *trust between analyst and analysand*. A new psychoanalytic discourse developed. Communication that stressed interpretation and therapy based on teaching was replaced by the need for emotional awareness and a relationship reflective of the unconscious processes of oneself and others, while focusing on the patient's current affective and cognitive capacities. According to Ferenczi, "over-keenness in making interpretations is one of the infantile diseases of the analyst" (Ferenczi 1928/1980, p. 96). He went on to say that:

> [The analyst] has to let the patient's free associations play upon him; simultaneously he lets his own fantasy get to work with the association material; from time to time he compares the new connections that arise with earlier results of the analysis; and not for one moment must he relax the vigilance and criticism made necessary by his own subjective trends.
>
> *(Ferenczi 1928/1980, p. 96)*

As can be seen, the analyst and analysand enter into a mutually reflective relationship. A quality reflective relationship is the price to be paid for therapy. *Authentic communication*, as Axel Hoffer (1996) emphasized, became a fundamental requirement on the part of the psychoanalyst, as false statements result in dissociation and repeat the dynamic of previous pathological relations. In his later writings, Ferenczi often discusses false, insincere communication with the therapist as a repetition of the patient's previous negative relationship experiences. It emerges as a way of speaking that distorts reality, both threatening the trust of the therapeutic relationship and encasing a previous traumatic experience. As we would phrase it today, false reflections result in false self-objects. The technique of using one's countertransference and attitude of authentic communication was incorporated into the psychoanalytic method of the majority of the Budapest analysts. Michael and Alice Balint (1939), Fanny Hann-Kende (1993), and Therese Benedek, who were also close to Ferenczi, were all guided by this conviction from the early 1930s, and it had a strong impact on the development of psychoanalysis after they left Hungary. In fact, Benedek was practically among the first to teach use of the countertransference to students under her supervision at the Chicago Institute from the early 1940s (Gedo, 1993). After Ferenczi's lectures in the United States and through Harry Stack Sullivan and one of his American analysands, some of Ferenczi's ideas became popular among the non-conservative American psychiatrists and psychoanalysts by the late 1920s and were integrated into new theories and approaches.

With every experiment and innovation, Ferenczi endeavored to use psycho-analysis as a two-sided cooperative process between patient and analyst (Rachman, 1997). How many analysts would have signed a letter to a patient undergoing therapy with him—one in which Ferenczi was cancelling a session due to his own mother's death—with a complimentary ending like "Kind regards, *your* doctor, Sándor Ferenczi"?[2] (emphasis mine).

Ferenczi not only considered healing itself important to changing the fates of individuals, but also thought that psychoanalysis could influence society. He thought "that there should be a reasonable individualist, socialist course between anarchism and communism which would be able to weigh precisely how much *repression* was necessary and inevitable to nurture a cultivated man. *Necessary but no more*" (Erős, 2001). When Ferenczi was asked about the destructive conflict gripping Europe in 1914, he said:

> The war had suddenly ripped off the mask and made people keenly aware of their true inner selves, it showed them the child inside, the primitive and the wild … The lesson to be learned here may well be this: in peacetime, let's not be ashamed to recognise the primitive man or even the animal; it's no shame to have such close ties to what is natural. In wartime, let's not deny our finest cultural values, like so many cowards, and let's not compromise them more than absolutely necessary.
>
> *(Ferenczi 1914/2000, p. 71)*

One of Ferenczi's fundamental approaches was to find *optimal* solutions. This was a leitmotif and a compass, of sorts, in both his personal and professional life. For example, for him *optimal* meant the most acceptable treatment for the patient in line with her or his own life situation, even one suffering from boils and thus in need of surgical intervention. He felt the interests of the patient, and not the personal priorities of the physician, should determine decision making. For instance, to remain with the patient with boils, quick surgical exploration and cleaning are certainly more convenient for the physician than a traditional poultice. However, incisions in inflamed tissue leave a permanent scar on the patient's body. As Ferenczi urged, "We must do whatever we can to prevent the formation of scar tissue in women" (Ferenczi 1899/1999, p. 36). And just as he contended that "over-keenness in making interpretations is one of the infantile diseases of the analyst" (Ferenczi 1928/1980, p. 96), so too did he see such overkeenness as the "horrible streptococci" of the young physician (Ferenczi 1899/1999, p. 35). Without thinking, he said, "They hurry ... to free themselves from the fear of the distant danger and simply cut the Gordian Knot in two" (Ferenczi 1899/1999, p. 35). Ferenczi himself was a young physician when he noted this phenomenon and other similarly widespread excesses in child rearing, that is, overly strong prohibitions on the part of adults that hinder children's development.

In 1908, he wrote that moral education based on "unnecessary repression" must be replaced by a learning process based on mutual cooperation (Ferenczi 1908/1980, p. 282). His liberalism was naturally critical of the principle of authority, which not only had an unhealthy effect on human relationships, but also represented a retarding force in terms of scientific progress. Ferenczi often argued that if new experiences cannot be matched to existing theories, then it is not the validity of the experience that must be called into question. One can find this attitude from the very beginning of his work (see Ferenczi's earliest scientific paper on spiritism, 1899) through his clinical experiments with active techniques until the end of his life with mutual analysis. As we all know, experiments and their results are always influenced by the critical attitude of those who represent the current mainstream. It was the fate of Ferenczi, too, who had a creative mind and was not nearly as emotionally independent as he was intellectually autonomous. Ferenczi suffered a lot from Freud's criticism.

The principle of finding the *optimal* also appeared in the thinking of many other authors. Margaret Mahler, who was close to Ferenczi, considers terms such as "optimal symbiosis" (Mahler 1967, p. 746), in which she describes the process of separation and individuation as the psychological birth of the individual, the "ordinary devoted mother" (Mahler 1961, p. 345). Winnicott's brilliant term of the "good enough mother" (Winnicott 1953, p. 94) alludes to optimal motherly behavior.

In the early 1930s, Ferenczi, Michael Balint, and his wife Alice Balint, as well as the young Therese Benedek, all worked with their patients the way we do today. The transference–countertransference dynamic was part of the psychoanalytic process, including the first interview and first anamnesis (Lévy, 1933). They were also aware of the main principles of the early object relationship. Most members of the first two generations of the Budapest psychoanalysts spoke a common language. A shared knowledge base had accumulated by the time they emigrated, one to which everyone enjoyed access. This was carried on with one person at a time taking out one link in the chain of collected knowledge and forging it further, modifying and reshaping the original idea. For example, Lajos Lévy, who was a charismatic internist, a key figure in early psychosomatics, and the physician to both the Ferenczi and Freud families, put it as follows in his report on first patient interviews: "We [must] recognize the patient's physical and mental individuality. Indeed, the task of the physician is not to cure the ailment but the ailing individual" (Lévy 1933, p. 301). He also observed that "the subtle play of the facial expressions that accompany complaints arouses in us an almost unconscious resonance" (Lévy 1933, p. 303). Just like Georg Groddeck, Ferenczi, Balint, and Lévy clearly grasped how the patient communicates her or his illness and how the transference–countertransference dynamic of the doctor–patient relationship can be used in understanding this unconscious communication. However, it was Michael Balint who took this notion the furthest, being the first to discuss this dynamic in a study in 1926 (Balint, 1926; Mészáros, 2009) and then, in 1957, publishing what is still a standard book on the subject, *The Doctor, His Patient and the Illness* (Balint, 1957a). One can recognize in this title the notion expressed by Lévy, "the task of the physician is not to cure the ailment, but the ailing individual" (Lévy 1933, p. 301), which had by then clearly become part of the shared knowledge base of the Budapest psychoanalysts of the day.

"Right down to the Mothers"—The Early Object Relationship

Ferenczi sensed the significance of the mother–infant relationship early on. He was referring to it in *The Clinical Diary* when he wrote: during analysis we must probe deep, "right down to the mothers" (Ferenczi 1932/1988, p. 74).

Ferenczi knew about, and described, the fact that a child left to himself or herself, unwelcome or emotionally rejected, or one brought up without love, can even die (Ferenczi, 1929/1980). This recognition later appeared in work on *hospitalization syndrome*, made famous in the United States by Hungarian-born psychoanalyst René A. Spitz. The notion of the emotional needs of a child was there very early on in the work of Harry Stack Sullivan, when he wrote, for example, of the child's *need for tenderness* (Sullivan, 1953). This phrase was introduced to the psychoanalytic literature by Ferenczi (1933) in his last paper "Confusion of Tongues." Tenderness and love—these are the elements of the optimal primary object relationship between the baby and the mother. According to Ferenczi and Balint, this love is not tied to any erogenous zone. Without this primary love, optimal development is not possible for the baby. The dominant biosocial view of emotional development maintains that the mother and infant form an affective communication system in which the mother has the fundamental role in modulating the baby's affective and mental states. Similarly, Winnicott wrote "A baby can be *fed* without love, but lovelessness or impersonal *management* cannot succeed in producing a new autonomous human child" (Winnicott 1971, p. 108)[3]. Numerous research findings in modern attachment theory verified the previous empirical studies (Bowlby, 1969, 1973, 1980; Fonagy, 2001).

Psychoanalysis and Its Interdisciplinary Connections

Today, when we consider the interdisciplinarity of psychoanalysis, we take for granted the mutual effect between the field and other scholarly areas on the one hand and various modes of artistic expression (film, fine art, and literature) on the other. However, this was considered unique in the early twentieth century. Freud was keen to have this relationship between psychoanalysis and other disciplines, but, according to his bitter note from 1914, "the hostile indifference of the learned and educated … in Vienna" was not receptive to it (Freud 1957, p. 39). That this did not hold true for Budapest was due not only to the possibilities offered by the openness of the city's contemporary avant-garde intelligentsia and its receptiveness to modernism, but also to Ferenczi's widespread network of relationships with outstanding cultural figures, primarily writers, whose work has become among the classics of literature, such as Sándor Márai, Dezső Kosztolányi, and Frigyes Karinthy. All of them came to know Ferenczi through psychoanalysis and incorporated it into their writing.

Ferenczi was a *receptive character* and respected people's interest in psychoanalysis. Many of them came from different disciplines. This made it possible for those in the fields of education, philosophy, literary studies, sociology, and anthropology to connect to psychoanalysis in a relationship that was marked by cross-fertilization. This is how, for example, psychoanalytic anthropology was developed as an independent discipline by Géza Róheim very early on, and this is how psychoanalytic thinking took root among the avant-garde intellectuals of Budapest in the 1920s. With this, Ferenczi not only furthered the multifaceted development of the Budapest School, but he advanced psychoanalysis as well, which could not have prospered without being embedded culturally, or without reflecting questions and problems concerning societies. Today there is no question that a strong connection has developed between psychoanalysis and other disciplines, especially visual art and literature.

Experience as a Mind-Shaping Force

The notion of experience, or generally speaking and in the philosophical sense of *Erlebnis* as Carlo Bonomi discusses it in one of his studies (Bonomi, 2000), stands at the heart of Ferenczi's thinking. Experience represents a mind-shaping force, and the psychodynamic projection of this force emerges, for example, in "Confusion of

Tongues," Ferenczi's most frequently cited paper on his paradigm shift in trauma theory (Ferenczi, 1933/1980; Mészáros, 2010). Ultimately, the intrapsychic formation of interpersonal experiences represents the psychological basis for the traumatic experience. In this approach, the decisive element points to the source that derives trauma from both interpersonal relations and actual experiences. Thus, Ferenczi was rejecting Freud's second trauma theory, according to which the tension created by fantasized experiences can also bring about trauma; that is, it is sufficient to have an intrapsychic process bearing in a pathological direction. Ferenczi's theoretical construction clarifies the interpersonal and intrapsychic processes between victim and persecutor, including the operation of such ego-defence mechanisms as identification with the aggressor, splitting, minimization, denying, or projection. Identification with the aggressor—that became widely known after forty years as Stockholm syndrome—represents a complete forfeiting of the ego, which may lead to destruction in extreme cases. In *The Clinical Diary*, Ferenczi says, "In the absence of alloplastic physical and mental tools of aggression, nothing remains but to perish for lack of love, or to adapt by autoplastic adaptation to the wishes (even the most hidden wishes) of the attacker, in order to calm him down. Identification in place of hatred and defence …" (Ferenczi 1933/1980, p. 175). It is precisely through ego–defence mechanisms that Ferenczi demonstrates how the aftermath of a traumatic event impacts the traumatized individual. Today, we would say that if there is at least one person that provides the traumatized individual with security and enables her or him to share the traumatic experience, and if that individual begins to become aware of the broken fragments and to tie them together in a narrative, then there is a chance for a healing process to be mobilized immediately. In contrast, the shame/anxiety/fear tied to the traumatic experience and attitude of rejection isolates the individual in a social environment that is a pathogenic factor and is itself the source of the process of trans-generational trauma.

To Be Able to Live with Uncertainty

Michael Balint says of Ferenczi, "Even the most common, the most everyday, the most routine experience was never rounded off and finished for him; he never filed anything away as finally dealt with or definitely solved" (Balint 1957b, pp. 245–246).

This is not merely a sign of intellectual openness! The deterministic thinking that integrates the points of a phenomenon that can be incorporated into an existing theoretical construction simultaneously acts to shut out the fragments/phenomena/experiences that cannot be. We might simply say it is a shortcut. This shortcut, in fact, represents an attempt to reduce the factors of uncertainty. A great deal of internal security is required for us to be able to bear the frustration borne of uncertainty for a long period of time. Ferenczi was able to live with the uncertainties borne of theoretical shortcomings and to conduct experiments in order to reduce those shortcomings. Consider, for instance, his experiments with active techniques in psychoanalysis in which he endeavored to increase the effectiveness of psychoanalysis. It should be noted that he also described the negative findings of his experiments. While still in his twenties, he wrote:

> The idea that we learn the most from our mistakes is nothing new. The thing is, generally, we jealously hide the lessons we learn this way because we put a lot of stock in being very clever and, if possible, infallible in the eyes of others. This is how it is in society and particularly in the practice of medicine.
>
> *(Ferenczi 1900/1999, p. 63)*

Isn't the capacity to tolerate uncertainty one of the marks of a good researcher? Indeed, it is not merely the talent, resourcefulness, and endurance that one needs for discoveries and for the recognition of new connections, but also the imperturbability to withstand the cognitive dissonance that arises when one's findings become clear and a familiar phenomenon fails to fit into the system of facts available to us. This conflict often tempts us to take shortcuts in our conclusions because we find the tension of uncertainty burdensome. Ferenczi, who experimented with active technique in an effort to improve the effectiveness of the analyst's work, often experienced enduring tension and even failure. His capacity for tolerating complexity and uncertainty was among his extraordinary strengths, this coupled with his desire to share lessons learnt with his colleagues.

> You know, perhaps, that I was originally inclined to lay down certain rules of behavior, in addition to free associations … Experience later taught me that one should never order or forbid any changes of behavior … If we are patient enough, the patient will himself sooner or later come up with the question whether he should risk making some effort, for example to defy a phobic avoidance. … In other words, it is the patient himself who must decide the timing of activity.
>
> *(Ferenczi 1928/1980, pp. 96–97)*

Ferenczi acknowledged his failures and weaknesses; he developed a reflective and critical relationship with them and incorporated them into his publications (Borgogno, 2004). Ferenczi "introduced an innovative praxis, the index of a future paradigm change" (Borgogno 2007, p. 160).

His thoughts on his own acute anemia, which he considered to be psychosomatic in origin, represent an unsettling example of the struggles of a man who is intellectually independent, but emotionally in need. He writes, similarly, about the contradictions of his relationship with Freud in *The Clinical Diary*:

> In my case the blood-crisis arose when I realized that not only can I not rely on the protection of a "higher power," but *on the contrary* I shall be trampled

underfoot by this indifferent power as soon as I go my own way and not his. ...
And now, just as I must build new red corpuscles, must I (if I can) create a
new basis for my personality? ... I have also been abandoned by colleagues ...
who are all too afraid of Freud to behave objectively or even sympathetically
toward me, in the case of the dispute between Freud and me.

(Ferenczi 1932/1988, p. 212)

Energizing the Psychoanalytic Movement

Ferenczi energized the psychoanalytic movement. He attended every psychoanalytic congress from the very beginning to his death, he proposed the formation of
professional organizations (the IPA and the Hungarian Psychoanalytical Society),
he established Budapest's first university department of psychoanalysis (in 1919) and
its first polyclinic (in 1931), he urged on the founding of the *International Journal of
Psychoanalysis* (in 1920), and he gave lectures that were popular well beyond narrow
professional circles. His writing was published not only in scholarly journals, but
also in newspapers and magazines, thus reaching an even broader educated audience. He took great pride in very few things, but among them were his achievements for the international movement. In an interview in 1928, he said, "Of course,
I still see my most enduring creation as the International Psychoanalytical Association to which I gave life, an organisation that by now has constituent groups in
nearly every cultural hub throughout the world" (Ferenczi 1928/2006, p. 206).

Today, in international psychoanalytical circles, the question of whose idea it
was to establish the International Psychoanalytical Association is surrounded with
uncertainty. As several works and informational materials demonstrate, even today,
it is easier to attribute the idea to Freud than to somebody else, like Ferenczi.
This is the case even though both Freud and Ferenczi, and their Hungarian and
foreign contemporaries—people who were close to him and saw Ferenczi's work
and achievements, including István Hollós, Mihály Bálint, Dezső Kosztolányi, and
Max Eitingon—all knew Ferenczi *initiated* the establishment of the IPA, prepared
its founding statute, and submitted it for debate at the Nuremberg Psychoanalytical
Congress in 1910.

And Ferenczi did so like a wise politician with foresight, being aware that he was
creating a structure which was necessary but could be a source of many conflicts
at the same time. Ferenczi published the following about this topic in *Gyógyászat*
[Therapy] in 1911:[4]

I am familiar with the offshoots in the lives of societies, and I know how
often it occurs in political, social and scientific associations that infantile grandeur, vanity, meaningless formalism, blind obedience, and personal
interests get the upper hand instead of honest work devoted to the public
good ... Associations, both in their essence and in their structure, preserve

the characteristics of a family … Life in an association is a space … where (based on the patterns of family life) hatred and adoration take over, restoring the old order in one superior, a new father in a revered hero or party leader, a new sibling in the colleagues, a mother among those women who trusted him, new toys in the children … this is proved, among others, by the regularity that prevails even among us, wild and unorganized analysts, that the figure of our fathers and that of our spiritual leaders are condensed into one dreamlike figure.

(Hollós citing Ferenczi 2000, pp. 138–139)

Then, expressing a little hope, Ferenczi continued as follows:

Although members that have been schooled psychoanalytically would be the most suitable for establishing an association which would combine every advantage of the family organization with the greatest possible individual freedom … in which the father would not be attributed with dogmatic authority … Where the truth could be told to each other mutually … Thus, the former *autoerotic* phase of association life could be replaced by a more developed phase of *object love*, in which it is no longer the tickling of the emotional erogenous zones (vanity, ambition) that provide satisfaction, but the objects of observation themselves.

(Hollós citing Ferenczi 2000, pp. 138–139)

See how Balint remembers: "He was seldom studied thoroughly, seldom quoted correctly, was often criticized, and more often than not erroneously. More than once his ideas were re-discovered later and then attributed to the second 'discoverer.' He was the founder of the International Psycho-Analytical Association, …" (Balint 1949, p. 216). Max Eitingon notes: "Summarizing former and current trends in the development of psychoanalysis, Ferenczi came to the conclusion that the time was ripe for the establishment of an International Psychoanalytical Association …" (Eitingon 1933, 75).

It is truly fascinating to hear Ferenczi, in the fullness of his creative power, subordinate his intellectual innovations to the institutional framework, which, in spite of all its contradictions, ensures the development of psychoanalysis to the present day. At this point, I wish to mention one motif, which is of invaluable significance in terms of intellectual history, whose effect can be felt to this day and which would not have been possible without the existence of a psychoanalytic community gathered into an organization. This was the Emergency Committee on Relief and Immigration—a tiny organization set up by the American Psychoanalytic Association. This committee, in cooperation with the IPA, made it possible for about 150 European analysts and their families to escape from Europe in the ever-tightening grip of fascism between 1938 and 1941 (Mészáros, 2014). Exceptional solidarity was inspired. Flying in the face of U.S. anti-immigration policy and laying aside personal and professional rivalries, this committee, in cooperation with the psychoanalytic community, helped European colleagues escape to America from a likely death. They not only saved individuals, but also preserved for posterity the spirit of European psychoanalysis.

Ferenczi the Missing Link—Closing Remarks

Why Ferenczi? Fifteen years ago, I asked several of my colleagues, among them Carlo Bonomi, André Haynal, György Hidas, Judith Dupont, Ann-Luise Silver, Rudolf Pfitzner, and Judith Vida how they had happened upon Ferenczi (Mészáros, 2000). They had all been looking for the answers to their unanswerable questions and their reflections within the knowledge and systems of dogma which they had acquired so far. The young André Haynal asked himself: "From where can one learn certain things?" A stereotyped answer echoed in his ears: "… they said … that everything was in the Freud" (Haynal 2000, p. 216). He did not find it. Later, on another occasion, he asked his supervisor where this or that knowledge came from, because *that was not in the Freud*. The renowned analyst did not know it, either, but he promised to call his learned friend in New York City. So he did and received the following answer: *from experience*. To which Haynal responded with another question: "but whose experience?" Then, accidentally, in a library he came across a volume that included, among others, Ferenczi's writings "about who falls asleep during analysis, how symptoms change in parallel with the changes in the patient–analyst relationship, … how we understand … what WE feel, what HE/SHE feels …, there is SOMEBODY" (2000, pp. 219–220). So there is somebody who knows something that has so far been missing from our acquired knowledge, whom we can turn to because "he has experimented with a lot of things, who honestly revealed his errors, who tried to think them over and who even wrote all this down …" (2000, p. 220). In the 70s and 80s, colleagues in Paris, Geneva, New York, Boston, Los Angeles, Budapest, Florence, Turin, London, and Munich raised questions similar to those of Haynal's. These people started to get in touch with each other. Ferenczi was one of the missing links whose ways of thinking and feeling and being can/could take us closer to the multidirectional approach of clinical phenomena, to the technique of psychoanalysis, and to the multifaceted nature of theoretical ideas.

Reading Ferenczi, one easily finds oneself reflecting and seeking out alternatives to interpret a particular phenomenon without feeling the pressure of coming up with an instant answer. In the world in and outside of psychoanalysis, Ferenczi offers a humanist perspective that has absolute priority over success-oriented, egocentric, or, we might even say, *ego diastolic* achievement. In Ferenczi's world, a premium is placed on authenticity, a searching spirit, respect for the patient, and intellectual openness in the broadest sense. Ferenczi's war with authority, his rejection of total systems—be they on the level of relationships or society—and the struggle, the way he attained emotional autonomy to match his intellectual inner freedom, represents a model for so many of us. As colleagues have put it, it is "our professional identification with the world vision of Ferenczi" (Kahtuni and Sanches 2009, p. 5).

Ferenczi's legacy is important not only for psychoanalysis, but also for scholarly thought in a broader sense and for a way of thinking that embraces interdisciplinary complexity. Consider that the spirit of Ferenczi is one that has drawn together professionals from places ranging from New York, through Budapest, Florence, Torino, Paris, London, Tel Aviv, Buenos Aires, and on to São Paulo. It has drawn them together to preserve the legacy. Maybe many of you share some of my sense of who Ferenczi was. He knew how to watch, how to keep quiet, and how to listen. He could endure the tension created by uncertainties without making rapid, prejudiced conclusions, and he was aware of his own mistakes and his own responsibilities.

In our clinical work, research, and even in our everyday life, we are always looking for missing links. The question is: how are we able to live with uncertainties and to find scientific answers or optimal solutions for problems that emerge? How, in the conflict-burdened world of the twenty-first century, can we find links/ psychoanalytic reflections on individual and societal problems? We live on different continents and we have different cultural backgrounds, but all of us respect human sovereignty and focus the tools of psychoanalysis on developing autonomous personalities. This remains the basic element for developing less conflicted societies.

Notes

1 An earlier version of this chapter appeared as "Ferenczi in Our Contemporary World" published in *Psychoanalytic Inquiry*, 34: 1–9, 2014 and appears here with permission of the publisher.
2 Ferenczi's letter to Vilma Kovács on July 21, 1921. Manuscript, Sándor Ferenczi Society, Budapest.
3 This is an expanded version of a paper that was published in *Psychoanalytic Inquiry, 34*: 1–9, 2014.
4 The original Hungarian text is different from the English translation (abridged). The English text was published with the following title: On the organization of the psychoanalytic movement. In S. Ferenczi (ed), *Final Contributions to the Problems and Methods of Psycho-Analysis*. London: Karnac Books, Maresfield Reprints, pp. 299–307. (Original work published 1911).

References

Aron, L. and Harris, A. (2010). Sándor Ferenczi: Discovery and rediscovery. *Psychoanalytic Perspectives*, 7:5–42.
Balint, A. and Balint, M. (1939). On transference and counter-transference. *International Journal of Psychoanalysis*, 20:223–230.
Balint, M. (1926). Psychoanalysis és belgyógyászat [Psychoanalysis and internal medicine]. *Gyógyászat [Therapy]*, 66(19):439–445.
Balint, M. (1949). Sándor Ferenczi, Obit. 1933. *International Journal of Psychoanalysis,* 30:215–219.
Balint, M. (1957a). *The Doctor, His Patient and the Illness*. London: Pitman Medical.
Balint, M. (1957b). Sándor Ferenczi, Obit. 1933. In M. Balint (ed), *Problem of Human Pleasure and Behavior*. New York: Liverright, pp. 243–250. Original published 1948.

Bowlby, J. (1969). *Attachment and Loss. Vol. I. Attachment.* New York: Basic Books.

Bowlby, J. (1973). *Attachment and Loss. Vol. II. Separation.* New York: Basic Books.

Bowlby, J. (1980). *Attachment and Loss. Vol. III. Loss.* New York: Basic Books.

Bonomi, C. (2000). Ferenczi vezetett el Freudhoz [Ferenczi led me to Freud]. In J. Mészáros (ed), *In Memoriam Ferenczi Sándor.* Budapest, Hungary: Jószöveg Kiadó, pp. 228–234.

Borgogno, F. (ed) (2004). Why Ferenczi today? The contribution of Sándor Ferenczi to the understanding and healing of psychic suffering. *International Forum of Psychoanalysis,* 13:5–13.

Borgogno, F. (2007). *Psychoanalysis as a Journey.* London: Open Gate Press.

Cabré, M. L. J. (1998). Ferenczi's contribution to the concept of countertransference. *International Forum of Psychoanalysis,* 7:247–255.

Eitingon, M. (1933). Búcsú Ferenczi Sándortól [Farewell from Sándor Ferenczi]. In J. Mészáros (ed), *In Memoriam Ferenczi Sándor.* Budapest, Hungary: Jószöveg Műhely Kiadó, pp. 129–143.

Erős, F. (2001). In E. Szendi (ed), *Film on Ferenczi.* Hungarian Television.

Ferenczi, S. (1899). Spiritism. *The Psychoanalytic Review,* 50, 139–144.

Ferenczi, S. (1980). Confusion of tongues between adults and the child. In S. Ferenczi (ed), *Final Contributions to the Problems and Methods of Psycho-Analysis.* London: Karnac Books, Maresfield Reprints, pp. 156–167. (Original work published 1933).

Ferenczi, S. (1980). The elasticity of psycho-analytic technique. In S. Ferenczi (ed), *Final Contributions to the Problems and Methods of Psycho-Analysis.* London: Karnac Books, Maresfield Reprints, pp. 87–101. (Original work published 1928).

Ferenczi, S. (1980). On the technique of psycho-analysis. In S. Ferenczi (ed), *Further Contributions to the Theory and Technique of Psycho-Analysis.* London: Karnac Books, Maresfield Reprints, pp. 177–189. (Original work published 1919).

Ferenczi, S. (1980). Psycho-analysis and education. In S. Ferenczi (ed), *Final Contributions to the Problems and Methods of Psycho-Analysis.* London: Karnac Books, Maresfield Reprints, pp. 280–290. (Original work published 1908).

Ferenczi, S. (1980). The unwelcome child and his death instinct. In S. Ferenczi (ed), *Final Contributions to the Problems and Methods of Psycho-Analysis.* London: Karnac Books, Maresfield Reprints, pp. 102–107. (Original work published 1929).

Ferenczi, S. (1988). *The Clinical Diary.* (J. Dupont, ed). Cambridge, MA: Harvard University Press. (Original work published 1932).

Ferenczi, S. (1999). A furunkulus gyógyítása [Treating boils]. In J. Mészáros (ed), *Ferenczi Sándor: A Pszichoanalízis Felé. Fiatalkori Írások, 1897–1908.* Budapest, Hungary: Osiris Könyvkiadó, pp. 35–37. (Original work published 1899).

Ferenczi, S. (1999). Két téves kórisme [Two errors in diagnosis]. In J. Mészáros (ed), *Ferenczi Sándor: A Pszichoanalízis Felé, Fiatalkori írások, 1897–1908, [Towards Psychoanalysis: Early Papers, 1897–1908].* Budapest, Hungary: Osiris, pp. 63–65. (Original work published 1900.

Ferenczi, S. (2000). A veszedelmek jégkorszaka [The ice age of perils]. In F. Erős (ed) *Ferenczi Sándor.* Budapest, Hungary: Thalassa, p. 71. (Original work published 1914).

Ferenczi, S. (2006). A szerelem végső titkai [The ultimate secrets of love]. *Thalassa,* 17(2–3): 203–206. (Original work published 1928).

Fonagy, P. (2001). *Attachment Theory and Psychoanalysis.* New York: Other Press.

Freud, S. (1957). On the history of the psycho-analytic movement. In J. Strachey (ed and Trans.), *The Standard Edition of the Complete Psychological Works of Sigmund Freud,* Vol. XIV, 1914–1916. London: Hogarth Press, 1957, pp. 1–66. (Original work published 1914).

Gedo, J. E. (1993). Empathy, new beginnings, and analytic cure. *Psychoanalytic Review*, 80(4):507–518.

Hann-Kende, F. (1993). Az áttétel és viszontáttétel szerepéhez a pszichoanalízisben. In *Lélekelemzési Tanulmányok*. Budapest, Hungary: Párbeszéd és T-Twins kiadó, pp. 229–239. (Original work published 1933).

Haynal, A. (1988). *The Technique at Issue. Controversies in Psychoanalysis from Freud and Ferenczi to Michael Balint*. London: Karnac Books.

Haynal, A. (2000). FerencziM (My Ferenczi). In J. Mészáros (ed), *In Memoriam Ferenczi Sándor*. Budapest, Hungary: Jószöveg Műhely Kiadó, pp. 216–221.

Haynal, A. (2002). *Disappearing and Reviving. Sándor Ferenczi in the History of Psychoanalysis*. London: Karnac.

Hoffer, A. (1996). Asymmetry and mutuality in the analytic relationship: Contemporary lessons from the Freud-Ferenczi dialogue. In *Ferenczi's Turn in Psychoanalysis*. New York: New York University Press, pp. 107–119.

Hollós, I. (2000). Emlékezés Ferenczi Sándorra. [Remembrance to Sándor Ferenczi] In J. Mészáros (ed), *In Memoriam Ferenczi Sándor*. Budapest, Hungary: Jószöveg Műhely Kiadó, pp. 129–143. (Original work published 1933).

Kahtuni, H. C. and G. P. Sanches. (2009). *Dicionário do pensamento de Sándor Ferenczi. Uma Contribuição á Clínica Psicanalítica Contemporânea*. Saõ Paulo, Brazil: Elsevier, Campus.

Lévy, L. (1993). Mire figyeljünk szívbetegek anamnézisében [What to notice in the medical histories of heart patients]. In L. Tanulmányok (ed), *Párbeszéd és T-Twins kiadó*. Budapest, Hungary: Párbeszéd és T-Twins kiadó, pp. 297–311. (Original work published 1933).

Mahler, M. S. (1961). On sadness and grief in infancy and childhood—Loss and restoration of the symbiotic love object. *Psychoanalytic Study of Child*, 16:332–351.

Mahler, M. S. (1967). On human symbiosis and the vicissitudes of individuation. *Journal of American Psychoanalytic Association*, 15:740–763.

Mészáros, J. (ed). (2000). *In Memoriam Ferenczi Sándor*. Budapest, Hungary: Jószöveg Műhely Kiadó.

Mészáros, J. (2004). Psychoanalysis Is a Two-Way Street. International Forum on Psychoanalysis, 13:105–113.

Mészáros, J. (2009). Contribution of Hungarian psychoanalysts to psychoanalytic psychosomatics. *American Journal of Psychoanalysis*, 69:207–220.

Mészáros, J. (2010). Building blocks toward contemporary trauma theory: Ferenczi's paradigm shift. *American Journal of Psychoanalysis*, 69:328–340.

Mészáros, J. (2014). *Ferenczi and Beyond: Exile of the Budapest School and Solidarity in the Psychoanalytic Movement in the Nazi Years*. London, UK: Karnac Books.

Rachman, A. W. (1997). *Sándor Ferenczi: The Psychotherapist of Tenderness and Passion*. Northvale, NJ: Jason Aronson.

Roazen, P. (2001). In E. Szendi (ed), *Film on Ferenczi*. Hungarian Television.

Sullivan, H. S. (1953). *The Interpersonal Theory of Psychiatry*. New York: Norton.

Winnicott, D. W. (1953). Transitional objects and transitional phenomena—A study of the first not-me possession. *International Journal of Psychoanalysis*, 34:89–97.

Winnicott, D. W. (1971). *Playing and Reality*. Middlesex, England: Penguin.

2

THE PENIS ON THE TRAIL[1]

Re-reading the origins of psychoanalysis with Sándor Ferenczi

Carlo Bonomi

The Split Embedded within the Foundation of Psychoanalysis

During the final years of his life, Sándor Ferenczi arrived to express his dissatisfaction with the direction in which psychoanalysis had been developing and attempted to reorganize its entire field on the basis of a less defensive and more open attitude of analysts toward their patients. His revision of psychoanalysis featured a different approach to regression, a relational understanding of the psychoanalytic situation and the reviving of the theory of real or actual trauma that Freud had abandoned. Ferenczi did not see himself as a dissident and did not wish to break from the psychoanalytic movement *per se*. He well understood, however, that he had little chance of prevailing over Father Freud in an overt and open conflict with him.

Ferenczi crafted *The Clinical Diary* in 1932 as a memorandum on the evolution of his theory and technique as well as a testimony of his conflicts and differences with Freud. Doing so not only provided him the chance to present his own clinical views on treatment but also to pinpoint what he felt were the faulty paths that psychoanalysis had traveled up to then. Ferenczi's diary was published in 1985, more than half a century following his premature death in 1933. Its appearance finally allowed his vision and voice, suppressed for years, to be heard by members of the psychoanalytic community.

Ferenczi was both interested and deeply troubled by the question of why Freud had abandoned his initial views on trauma and symptom formation. Ferenczi's position on this question was structurally related to his thoughts on the faulty development of psychoanalysis: a single problem stood at the heart of both, he felt, the emotional defense of the clinician before his or her traumatized patient— what Ferenczi identified, from the opening pages of his diary, as the *insensitivity* [*Fühlosigkeit*] *of the analyst*. Freud himself introduced this problem and theme into the field of psychoanalysis. Freud's insensitivity toward his patients, as Ferenczi saw it, had been partly rooted in the difficulty and challenges that every psychoanalyst faces by virtue of having to withstand the emotions that surface within the interpersonal setting of the psychoanalytic encounter given the patient's verbalization and recounting of his or her story and personal suffering. Within the medical profession, it was generally held that the physician's insensitivity to his or her patient offered the clinician a necessary protection. According to Freud, a certain degree of coldness and aloofness was required by the analyst if the emotional embroilment between doctor and patient was to be kept in check and the interpersonal dimension of the analytic situation was to be rendered neutral. The analyst, in Freud's view, had necessarily to function as a sort of "surgeon" within the analytic setting. A certain degree of insensitivity was thus required for the doctor to successfully perform the work of analysis, indeed for preserving balance and clarity as a scientist and for responding to the patient's transference with objectivity and neutrality.

Ferenczi viewed the relationship between patient and analyst in terms very different from Freud. On the basis of his clinical experience, he saw the position of the analyst being promulgated as a standard by the analytic community as featuring insensitivity, indeed the abandonment by the doctor of his patient. As Ferenczi wrote in the opening page of his diary, this position only contributed to and favored unconscious re-enactments and repetitions by patients. Ferenczi also wondered how and when Freud came to embrace this position and became insensitive to his patients.

Ferenczi had previously traced the faulty development of psychoanalysis back to Freud's decision to withdraw and take a step back from the intense emotional participation that had characterized his initial work with patients and efforts to cure them through the use of a cathartic method. In *The Principle of Relaxation and Neocatharsis* (1930), for instance, Ferenczi indicated that the highly emotional relation between physician and patient that Freud had initially embraced "gradually cooled down to a kind of unending association experiment" with the analytic process then slowly morphing into an "intellectual" matter and procedure (p. 110). Ferenczi reflected on this theme in his clinical diary and did so precisely in an effort to explain Freud's emotional abandonment and retreat from his patients. Ferenczi had most likely kept his personal views on this theme to himself for years.

According to Ferenczi, Freud originally "followed Breuer with enthusiasm and worked passionately, devotedly on the curing of neurotics." He was, however, "first shaken and then disenchanted" when "the problem of countertransference opened [up] before him like an abyss." Ferenczi's hypothesized that Freud, after his initial shock and disillusionment, simply turned away and abandoned his traumatized patients. Doing so helped him to then safely land in the materialism of nineteenth-century science and to adopt the position of a natural scientist. Freud, Ferenczi argued, remained committed and devoted to analysis "intellectually but not emotionally" (Dupont 1985, p. 93).

Ferenczi's views on the treatment situation clashed with the canonical narration handed down to us regarding the origins of psychoanalysis. Psychoanalysis has traditionally viewed Freud's discovery of the unconscious and its role in the formation of symptoms as a direct product of an intrapsychic achievement by him. Freud's self-analysis has typically been seen in our field as the basis for his discoveries on the significance of infantile sexuality, indeed as the principal determinant of why it was that he came to discover the Oedipus complex. As Ernst Kris (1954) described and phrased the matter: "In the interpretation of his own dreams, Freud had made a fateful step; from self-observation and self-experimentation he had proceeded into a new and definite direction, to systematic self-analysis" (p. 183). As Kris tried to explain, it was in this way that Freud's ego functions emerged "from involvement in intense conflict to full and supreme autonomy" (p. 181).

Kris's explanation and thesis was promulgated by him during the golden age of psychoanalysis, when ego autonomy was valued as the axis upon which psychoanalysis had been constructed and built. Kris's position and the views advanced by Ferenczi in *The Clinical Diary* are radically incompatible. What was presented in the canonical narration of psychoanalysis as the mark of full and supreme ego autonomy, namely, the replacement of "involvement in intense conflict" with "self-analysis," was instead viewed by Ferenczi as a retreat from relatedness, indeed, and as we shall see, as involving the "narcissistic split of the self" into a "suffering brutally destroyed part" and a "self-observing" part which knew "everything" but felt "nothing" (Ferenczi 1931, pp. 135–136).

In what follows, I shall attempt to substantiate and give validity to Ferenczi's views regarding the split found at the heart and origins of psychoanalysis.

Freud's Dream of the Self-Dissection of the Pelvis

The starting point of my reconstruction is a piece of Freud's self-analysis that touches on Ferenczi's notion of a narcissistic split of the self, namely, Freud's dream of self-dissection of the pelvis. In this dream, Freud finds himself split in two and looks from above to see his body lying on a table and his pelvis eviscerated (Freud 1900, p. 453). He then sets out on a long journey that ends in his arriving at a house-coffin. Freud wakes up from his dream in a state of mental fright. In his interpretation, however, Freud (1900) maintained that his dream stood as the fulfillment of a wish and that its dream-work managed to achieve a masterpiece by virtue of giving the coffin the appearance of an Etruscan grave he had visited when traveling near the city of Orvieto (Freud 1900, pp. 454–455). The father of psychoanalysis claimed that the self-dissection of his pelvis featured in his dream was a symbolic statement about the process of self-analysis he had begun four years earlier.

Freud had visited the Etruscan necropolis nearby Orvieto in September 1897, while in the midst of his self-analysis. At that time, Freud also arrived at his decision to drop his theory of seduction, abandoning the role that real or actual trauma played in hysteria. Freud loved to travel to the south but also suffered from a travel phobia. As such, he did not like to vacation alone and for years was accompanied by his brother Alexander, ten years younger than him, when traveling on vacation. Freud was accompanied by Alexander when he visited the Etruscan necropolis. On this occasion, he was likely led to recall his childhood dream of the dead mother with bird-beckets figure (Freud 1900, p. 583), a true anxiety-dream he had experienced when his mother Amalia had been pregnant with Alexander. Freud's childhood dream was rich in archeological imageries associated with the Philipsson Bible he read as a boy. When Freud later dreamt of the Etruscan-grave in his own fertile imagination, he likely imagined that he had managed to take possession of his mother's womb by taking the place of his brother.

It was while visiting the Etruscan necropolis that Freud purchased the first objects of his immense collection of antiquities. A few months later, he experienced a dream in which he and his brother Alexander came under attack from the sea. He and his brother became very frightened at the sight of a ship. Their fears in the dream were dispelled, however, when Freud, in his dream, saw a small ship that had been cut off in the middle. The ship, said Freud, bore a striking resemblance to objects that had attracted his interest when he visited the Etruscan necropolis: "rectangular trays of black pottery, with two handles, on which there stood things like coffee- or tea-cups, not altogether unlike one of our modern breakfast-sets" (Freud 1900, p. 465). Freud reported that these were funerary objects of an Etruscan lady. Since the breakfast-ship was broken off and split in the middle, Freud concluded that his dream must have represented "the return after a shipwreck ['*Schiffbruch*', literally 'ship-break']" (p. 466). Scholars have interpreted Freud's dream of a broken or cut-off ship as symbolic of castration (Anzieu 1986, p. 318; Cotti 2007, p. 172). Freud, however, probably had a more specific situation and event unconsciously in mind, namely, the ritual circumcision of his younger brother Alexander in 1866, an event which Freud undoubtedly attended at the age of ten.

Freud's breakfast-ship dream is his only dream that featured his brother Alexander. Freud felt deep affection for his younger brother. It seems likely that a bit of this affection was later transferred toward another "Alexander" with whom Freud also vacationed and who, like his brother, became his traveling companion: Sándor Ferenczi. The observation helps us to turn our attention toward Ferenczi's own "breakfast" and "penis" dream, which Ferenczi experienced on Christmas of 1912. He reported the dream to Freud in a letter he wrote the very next day on December 26, 1912.

Ferenczi's Dream of the Cut-Off Penis

Ferenczi's dream of the cut-off penis, which left him in a state of mental fright, consisted of the following fragment: A cut-off penis is brought in on a "saucer" [*Tasse*]; Ferenczi's younger brother has just cut off his penis in order to perform coitus. The word "*Tasse*" is probably best translated as "cup"; Ferenczi, however, decided to present Freud in his letter with a drawing in which a penis was standing on a rectangular tray with eating utensils.[2] Ferenczi reported to Freud that the penis which appeared in his dream was strikingly erect. The penis was also flayed, its skin having been pulled off with the corpora cavernosa being laid bare. In yet another segment of his dream, a number of individuals are sitting around the table speaking of family resemblances. Commenting on his dream, Ferenczi remarked: "'My younger brother' (= I, myself)."

Ferenczi wrote to Freud that the dream served to confirm the idea that castration stood as a punishment for his incestuous feelings.[3] Ferenczi, it turns out, had been experiencing somatic disturbance on his male member as well as fantasies of bleeding to death just before he dreamt his troubling and unsettling dream. He was also in the middle of his affair with Elma Palos at the time (Berman, 2004). These facts all help to trace his castration fantasies back to his intrapsychic conflicts.

When I first read Ferenczi's dream, however, I received the distinct impression that it represented a totem meal and that it involved the expression of a powerful identification by him with Freud—in particular, the rectangular tray recalled to me Freud's breakfast-ship dream. It is important for us to note that Freud had not only fainted for a second time before Jung just a month earlier but that Ferenczi had foreseen and actually anticipated the event. Freud immediately set out to analyze his "bit of neurosis."[4] Jung, however, did not place much trust in Freud's self-analysis (see his letter to Freud of December 3, 1912). The Swiss psychiatrist was disturbed by the fact that Freud, when reviving from his faint and while lying on a couch in which the stronger Jung had placed him after picking him up from the floor, was heard muttering: "How sweet it must be to die."

Jung became even more annoyed with Freud when the latter attempted to reverse the situation by detecting a slip in a letter of Jung, and then symbolically placing him on the couch. Jung in turn responded to Freud's "little trick" by accusing him of reducing his students "to the level of sons and daughters who blushingly admit the existence of their faults" (December 18). This caused a final and definitive break between the two men. As we recall, it was on January 3, 1913, that Freud wrote to Jung to propose "that we abandon our personal relations entirely."

Ferenczi was kept informed by Freud of events then and even shared a copy of Jung's letter of December 18 with him. Freud's fainting spell, Jung's distrust of Freud's self-analysis, and the theme of Freud's relations with his followers all combined to form the background of Ferenczi's communication to Freud of December 26, 1912, the letter where he shared with Freud his dreams of the cut-off penis.

Ferenczi's letter starts out with a harsh condemnation of Jung and mutual analysis. Ferenczi admitted that he himself had gone through a period of rebellion and proceeded to add that he had now come to the decision that the idea of mutual analysis was "nonsense." Ferenczi then wrote the following in his letter: "You are probably the only one who can permit himself to do without an analyst; but that is actually no advantage for you." Ferenczi proceeded to add: "Despite all the deficiencies of self-analysis, we have to expect of you the ability to keep your symptoms in check."

Ferenczi appears to have been scared and puzzled by Freud's fainting spell. Since their trip to America in 1909, when he was a silent witness of the interpretation of dreams that Freud and Jung exchanged while on the deck of the ship on which they traveled, Ferenczi had harbored a deep desire to engage Freud in mutual analysis (see his letter to Freud of October 3, 1910). But this desire, obviously fueled by his curiosity and interest in Freud's "secrets," was now condemned and suppressed by him.

Jung and Ferenczi each felt impotent and shocked by the intensity of Freud's fantasies of dying. They were also disappointed by Freud's vulnerability as well as skeptical about self-analysis and its ability to heal and cure symptoms. Instead of challenging and confronting Freud on these topics, however, Ferenczi requested that Freud accept him into analysis. Ferenczi's request is to be found in the very same letter here under consideration, the same letter where he shared his dream of the cut-off penis with Freud. The dream thus serves to announce a change in Ferenczi's desire vis à vis Freud: where there had been an object-relation, an identification now exists.

When I first read Ferenczi's letter, I associated the corpora cavernosa which had been laid bare in his dream with the surgical operation that Wilhelm Fliess had performed on Emma Eckstein's nose seventeen years earlier, in February 1895. Freud himself, we recall, had his nose operated on by Fliess on several occasions. Ferenczi was uniquely acquainted with Freud's traumatic relationship with Fliess. Indeed, Ferenczi was harboring the idea of subjecting himself to a rhinological intervention in Vienna and to visiting Freud during the Christmas holydays in 1912 (letter to Freud of December 7, 1912). Ferenczi decided to change his plans, however, and dropped both his trip and the nose surgery, which was postponed—he would be operated in the spring of 1912 and again on December 25, 1913. Thus, on Christmas 1912, Ferenczi appears to have responded to this change in plan by dreaming his dream of the cut-off penis. Ferenczi, we recall, had argued in his own work that the nose often stood as a representative and symbol for the penis.[5]

Another important element in Ferenczi's dream that drew my attention was the striking resemblance between his dream and Freud's dream of his self-dissection of the pelvis. Though the dream of the cut-off penis was presented by Ferenczi to Freud as a sign of subjugation, it seemed to me that it also carried within it a highly condensed representation of Ferenczi's own doubts and fantasies about Freud's self-analysis. Ferenczi had just recently claimed that speech "suppressed" by a subject often managed to return and reappear as "*Bauchreden*," as discourse of the stomach or "ventriloquism" (Ferenczi 1912, p. 211). In this case, it was not the stomach but Ferenczi's own cut-off penis that spoke.

This same constellation resurfaced when Freud finally agreed to accept Ferenczi into analysis.[6] Just before Ferenczi began his analysis, however, he decided to send Freud a manuscript intended for publication that contained his analysis of the dream of the occlusive pessary (Ferenczi, 1915). In the letter that accompanied the manuscript, dated September 8, 1914, Ferenczi alerted Freud to the fact that the dream featured in it had not been dreamt by one of his patient but rather by Ferenczi himself. In the manuscript, Ferenczi assumed the role of the analyst and presented the pessary dream as one that had been dreamt by a patient of his who had supposedly felt abandoned by his analyst after an analysis had come to an end.

In his dream, Ferenczi had stuffed a foreign body (pessary) into his penis (urethra). This led him to become frightened as a surgical operation might be needed to remove it. In Ferenczi's interpretation, the foreign body stood as a symbol for the penis and for self-analysis as well: it represented, Ferenczi argued, an abandoned child who was being forced to split himself into two in order to replace his analyst. The same theme can be found in Ferenczi's dream of the cut-off penis. The ambiguity remained the same in both dreams. Was Ferenczi speaking of himself or of Freud?

Ferenczi was apparently here presenting himself to Freud, his analyst, as a child who had been abandoned and was being forced to do everything alone and by himself. Yet, as Ernst Falzeder (1996) noted, since Ferenczi's dream of the occlusive pessary had been clearly modeled on Freud's dream of the self-dissection of the pelvis, Ferenczi's dream and his analysis of it stood as "a masterpiece of ambivalence, meta-discourse and hidden messages." At the very moment when Ferenczi was required to entrust himself in Freud's hands, it was the split in his analyst's personality that most frightened him. Ferenczi's dream, however, also seems to anticipate his idea of the "wise baby," namely, his theory of the patient who is forced to become his own analyst's analyst (Ferenczi, 1923, 1933). From this point of view, the occlusive pessary dream can be seen to stage the incorporation of Freud's heritage of emotion that led Ferenczi to experience much anxiety. What exactly was the fate of this incorporation, which, as we have seen, was first announced in Ferenczi's earlier dream of the cut-off penis?

A Cathartic Outlet for the Occlusive Incorporation

In 1993, I presented at the international Sándor Ferenczi conference in Budapest a paper entitled "Freud, Jung, Ferenczi and the Vision of a Cut-Off Penis" (Bonomi, 1994a). I used the term "vision" instead of dream then as it helped me to convey two distinct ideas. The first was that Ferenczi had been struggling with a psychic foreign body. The second was that this foreign body had helped to fertilize Ferenczi's unconscious and became the source of his inspiration. It was following this dream that Ferenczi began to concern himself with genital wounds, undertook research on the traumatic aspects of circumcision, revaluated the theory of real trauma, and proposed that we consider real and actual castration as a "narcissistic wound" (Ferenczi, 1913, 1917a, 1917b, 1921).

The peak of Ferenczi's inspiration then was his work *Thalassa*, the meta-biological theory of the penis which he formulated after his dream of the cut-off penis. Ferenczi had been unable to finish writing and publishing his Thalassa theory for years. Each time he attempted to put pen to paper and to write about the topic, he experienced psychosomatic pains, panic attacks, and a general writing block. Ferenczi finally published his *Thalassa* in German in 1924. However, he also decided to translate his text into Hungarian, his mother tongue, renaming it *Katasz-trofak* (Catastrophe). In his mind, his text represented the biological foundation of Freud's theory of the phallus, which in this essay is described by him as the living monument of a great catastrophe.

I wish to reproduce some of what I wrote in "Mute Correspondence," an article that dealt with the unconscious communications between Freud and Ferenczi (Bonomi, 1997).

Ferenczi's *Thalassa* was itself related to the topic of circumcision. Its central idea was the womb theory of the prepuce, by which circumcision was implicitly assumed as a symbol for a primeval catastrophe. The womb theory of the prepuce allowed a formidable series of bio-symbolic equivalences, especially the equivalence between penis, child, and fish. The enveloping of the gland in the mucous membrane, according to Ferenczi, represented a reproduction of the intra-uterine life of the child, which in turn reproduces the aquatic mode of life of the fish, the philogenetic ancestor of man, before the catastrophic drying-up of the ocean ("Thalassa") occurred.

The penis, as the living monument of past events, thus carries within it the memory of the expulsion of the fish from the mother-sea, which is repeated in the birth of every child and is commemorated through the act of penile erection. The erection itself represents a tendency toward "autotomy" (self-split) or an impulse to self-castration which aims at a complete separation of the genital from the body, only partially achieved by the elimination of fluid and the event of fertilization. Self-castration also represents the prototype of the repression (Ferenczi 1924, pp. 29, 83, 87, 89) by which the original trauma was preserved. When penetrating the womb, the genital functions as the symbol of the child which desires to return to the mother-womb, not unlike the fish which desires and strives to return to the sea; both actions involve a regressive attempt to return and restore a pre-traumatic situation. Finally, the longing for a silent, embracing, and pacifying mother-womb-sea is at bottom nothing but a desire for death, a desire to restore the perfect harmony and rest that existed before the child traumatically enters life and awakes. This is the reason why—as Ferenczi was led to recall in his conclusions—primitive people bury their dead in a squatting or fetal position.

Only after this *Requiem* was Ferenczi able to accomplish his inner separation from Freud. Set free from its biological shell, *Thalassa* surfaces as the poetic transformation of the paralyzing vision of an erect penis which is cut off, offering a cathartic outlet for the occlusive incorporation dramatized in the two dreams previously mentioned. When we connect this fantasy scenario with the dreams and symbols of Freud's self-analysis, we realize that the crucial emotion aroused by the myth presented in *Thalassa* is related to the maternal fantasy of restoring the peace of a mutilated penis, a symbolic equivalent of a dead child.

I have previously attempted to convey this through a simple formula. In my view (Bonomi, 1994a, 1997), Ferenczi's speculation represented an emotional working out of the pathologic mourning encrypted within Freud's phallic cult. It was only after having successfully accomplished his mourning that Ferenczi was finally able to disidentify from Freud and to disconnect and distance himself from his doctrines.

The Creation of a New Language for Trauma

Ferenczi's bio-symbolic analysis of the origins of sexual life was the heir of Freud's *A Phylogenetic Phantasy: Overview of the Transference Neuroses* (1915/1987), a metapsychological essay written by Freud in 1915 but not published by him during his lifetime. The main topic of the essay had been intensively discussed by Freud with Ferenczi. Indeed, in 1916 it gave rise to the plan of writing a book together based on the Lamarckian hypothesis that individually acquired features could be inserted into the genetic code and be inherited. Freud failed to unfold his ideas on this theme, relinquishing the entire thing to Ferenczi. The result was very much valued by Freud who considered *Thalassa* the peak of their "fellowship of life, thoughts, and interests" (Freud to Ferenczi, January 11, 1933). It was soon thereafter that Freud's Hungarian pupil and friend "slowly drifted away" from him, as Freud (1933) wrote in his obituary for Ferenczi (p. 229).

In *Totem and Taboo*, where Freud first presented his founding myth, Freud failed to explicitly indicate whether the father of the primitive horde castrated his sons, an idea that remains essential for Freud's assumption, forged by him during the course of his analysis of the Wolf-Man, that the child "fills in the gaps in individual truth with prehistoric truth" and "replaces occurrences in his own life by occurrences in the life of his ancestors" (Freud 1918, p. 97). The hereditary transmission of unconscious fantasies of castration played an important role in Freud's *Phylogenetic Phantasy*. Thanks to this phylogenetic scenario, the theory of real trauma that he had abandoned was now relocated in a primeval past that became the container of Freud's own fantasies regarding the brutality of origins. Ferenczi, however, expressed some perplexity about this. Despite being convinced that the main weapon employed by fathers against their sons had been the threat of castration. Ferenczi objected to Freud's position, arguing that since castrated individuals were unable to generate, the trauma of castration anxiety could not be transmitted from one generation to the next to become part of the phylogenetic heritage (letter to

Freud on July 24, 1915). It is important to note that when Ferenczi formulated this objection he also associated castration with the "loss of the mother." In the myth forged in *Thalassa*, this would be symbolized by the loss of the first object and source of life: the "ocean."

Ferenczi obviously endorsed Freud's idea that the penis was the organ of pleasure. In his view, however, the significance of the male organ was not primarily narcissistic but consisted in its being "the organic symbol of an infantile fetal union with the mother" (Ferenczi 1930, p. 113). The pleasure-seeking function of the penis was, according to him, inseparable from its semiotic and object-seeking function. Ferenczi thus refused to view the trauma of castration as an ultimate element of the human psyche as Freud did, and forged his *Thalassa* myth as a sort of unconscious explanation.[7]

Dissatisfaction with Freud's hyper-realistic manner of dealing with the theme of castration soon surfaced among his pupils. When Ferenczi and Rank were asked by Freud to collaborate and work on the gap that existed between practice and theory in psychoanalysis, Rank wrote to Freud that they had "decided first to start a scientific campaign against overestimation of the castration complex" and that they were moreover eager to learn of his opinion on the matter (August 22, 1922). Freud discouraged the two men from proceeding in that direction and encouraged them to abandon their plan to rework the theme of castration. The theme was thus effectively removed from their agenda.

Freud viewed castration as the natural language of trauma. He believed, not mistakenly, that the ego reacts to an external trauma by feeling unworthy and by developing a need to be badly treated by the superego, the internal representative of the father. Freud responded to all efforts to move the breakpoint of the psyche in the direction of earlier or pre-oedipal phases with a new formulation that emphasized the primacy of the phallus (Freud, 1923). After Otto Rank wrote *The Trauma of Birth* (1924) in order to help bring trauma back from the phylogenetic scenario to real life, Freud reformulated his theory by postulating castration as the synthetic apriori of trauma: whatever the danger or loss experienced by the ego may be, Freud (1926) argued, the unconscious represented it in the form of the ablation of the penis. Freud was convinced that since "nothing resembling death can ever have been experienced; or if it has, as in fainting, it has left no observable traces behind" (p. 130) the annihilation of life was necessarily represented in the unconscious by castration. This idea can be found throughout the entirety of Freud's work and has a systemic and all-embracing structure impermeable to compromises: one is forced to either accept it or reject it, to remain in or outside the system. Ferenczi, for his part, succeeded in deconstructing the system from within.

As we have seen, in *Thalassa* Ferenczi theorized the erect male organ as a memorial of a great catastrophe that had been repeated through the tendency to "autotomy"—a Greek neologism suggesting the idea of a self-cut or self-dissection. Within biology, the term refers to the behavior of certain animals to cut or eliminate a part of their own body when their life and physical existence is in danger in order to survive. Ferenczi called on the idea to understand and explain how the human psyche reacted to traumatic experiences (Ferenczi, 1921, 1926, 1930–1932). He initially examined the notion of autotomy as paradigmatic of autoplastic adaptation (Ferenczi, 1921, 1926). It served to explain how memory of an external trauma had been inscribed, preserved, and reproduced in the reaction and behavior of an organism.

Later on, he came to conceive of it as the automatic response to an experience of annihilation (1930–1932), prospecting the effect of psychic trauma as a "partial death" and as involving the destruction of certain parts of the psyche that have grown insensitive. An entirely new universe opened up for Ferenczi as a result, one in which the psychotic fragmentation of mental life appeared before him for the first time. It ultimately led him to formulate a new metapsychology and to create an altogether new language to explain the effects of trauma on the human psyche.

The most important symbol of that new language was the notion of a "narcissistic split of the self" (Ferenczi, 1931). In a recent work, I advance the idea that it represented Ferenczi's final interpretation of Freud's dissection of the pelvis dream. Freud, in that key and most revealing of dreams, found himself divided and split in two, left observing himself as a spectator from the outside and without feeling.

This insensitivity to the traumatic element in his dream was identified by Freud (1900) as involving the "suppression of affects." It was also interpreted by him as a neurotic attempt at defense. Freud did this despite his having described it in another part of his dream book as "the peace that has descended upon a battlefield strewn with corpses" with "no trace" being "left of the struggle which raged over it" (p. 467). In his paper *Child Analysis in the Analysis of Adults*, Ferenczi (1931) attempted to provide a new reading of Freud's traumatic insensitivity, tracing the matter back to the splitting of the self into a "suffering brutally destroyed part" and a "self-observing" part which somehow "knows everything but feels nothing" (Ferenczi 1931, pp. 135–136).[8]

The new language for trauma was thus the final product of a very long and articulated process, all made possible by the incorporation, working through, and reformulation of the trauma recorded in Freud's self-analysis. It was also closely connected to Ferenczi's meditation on the split between intellect and emotion, a split that was itself embedded in the very foundation of psychoanalysis. In *The Clinical Diary*, Ferenczi also discussed Freud's fear of allowing himself to be analyzed (p. 185). Freud's insensitivity was associated with his deprecation of abnormalities (p. 93) as well as with his disparaging view of women (p. 187). Ferenczi did not approve of Freud's theory of castration to explain femininity. He felt that it sacrificed the interest of women and neglected the possibility that the masculine fantasy by women to have or acquire a penis might well have set in for traumatic reasons. Finally, Ferenczi traced Freud's aversion to femininity back to his relationship with a "sexually demanding mother" (p. 188), associating Freud's fear of allowing himself to be analyzed to his avoidance of "the traumatic moment of his own castration."

Indirect references to this dream, as we have seen, stretch along throughout the entirety of Ferenczi's work, first marking his identification with Freud before functioning as a compass in forging the myth that he exposed in *Thalassa*. In the end, it enabled Ferenczi to elaborate a new and novel manner of thinking the connection between trauma and the compulsion to repeat.

Freud's Posthumous Dialogue with Ferenczi

How did Freud react to Ferenczi's effort to deconstruct the foundation, indeed the pillar upon which he had built and established psychoanalysis? Freud's initial reaction was positive and even enthusiastic. Ferenczi's "new views about the traumatic fragmentation of mental life," Freud wrote to Ferenczi, had "something of the great characteristic of the Theory of Genitality" (September 16, 1930). Freud, however, also added: "I only think that one can hardly speak of trauma in the extraordinary synthetic activity of the ego without treating the reactive scar-formation along with it. The latter, of course, also produces what we see." According to Freud, traumatic memories were not directly accessible. As Freud wrote in his famous recantation letter to Fliess of September 21, 1897, traumatic memories fail to "break-through" the unconscious and require that they be reconstructed by analyzing psychic reactions and scar-formations.

Ferenczi was disappointed by Freud's reaction "I was pleased to hear that you find my new views 'very ingenious';" he wrote to Freud on September 21, 1930, adding "I would have been much more pleased if you had declared them to be correct, probable, or even only plausible." It was shortly thereafter that the well-known open conflict between the two men arose. It was only after Ferenczi's death that Freud began to assimilate his views. As André Haynal (2005) pointed out:

> The issues and conflicts aroused by this relationship continued to exert an influence in Freud's mind even after Ferenczi's death. After a few years' mourning (from 1933 to 1937), he returned to the theme of trauma in "Analysis terminable and interminable" (1937). He noted—almost as if he had thought through Ferenczi's ideas again—that the effect of the castration threat represented the greatest trauma of all. He was here manifestly seeking to bring his own theory of the Oedipus complex and of the threat of castration, which meant so much to him, into harmony with trauma theory. (p. 464)

Freud's attempt at assimilating the views of Ferenczi informed several of his most important works and is particularly present in a passage found in *Moses and*

Monotheism wherein Freud speaks of the sequestration and fragmentation of the ego (Freud 1939, pp. 76–78). I also think that Freud's last piece of self-analysis was likewise informed by his posthumous dialogue with Ferenczi.

Ferenczi's new views about the traumatic fragmentation of mental life were closely associated with his reformulation of the goal of analysis. Around 1930 the attaining of traumatic memories had become a superseded goal, as psychoanalysis was transforming into an ego-psychology. Ferenczi (1929), however, proposed that "no analysis can be regarded … as complete unless we have succeed in penetrating the traumatic material" (p. 120). He was embracing "an earlier direction" which had been, in his words "undeservedly abandoned" (Ferenczi 1930, p. 108), yet, according to his new perspective, the "traumatic material" was not to be sought in the neurotic reactions and adaptive solutions of the ego but, rather, in more primitive reactions, such as the psychotic turning away from reality, splitting, and fragmentation. Now, this was exactly the material that Freud (1936) chose to review in his last piece of self-analysis, in his famous essay *A Disturbance of Memory on the Acropolis*, a document written and produced by Freud in 1936 in the form of an open letter to Romain Rolland.

Disbelief on the Acropolis

Freud visited the Acropolis in Athens in 1904, seven years after he visited the Etruscan necropolis near Orvieto. He had been accompanied by Alexander on both trips. In my reconstruction, Freud's visit to the necropolis served to stir memories for him that were related to the gestation, birth, and circumcision of his brother Alexander. In his acropolis essay, Freud (1936) noted that he might have said to his brother as they stood together looking over the city:

> "Do you still remember how, when we were young … And now, here we are in Athens, and standing on the Acropolis! We really have gone a long way!" So too, if I may compare such a small event with a greater one, Napoleon, during his coronation as Emperor in Notre Dame, turned to one of his brothers—it must no doubt have been the eldest one, Joseph—and remarked: "What would *Monsieur notre Père* have said to this, if he could have been here to-day?"
> *(Freud 1936, p. 247)*

The pleasure of his crowning achievement was spoiled, however, by a strange *Erinnerungsstorung* [disturbance of memory] which, after it was analyzed, appeared to Freud as a feeling of alienation and incredulity, as though what Freud was seeing in Athens, the Acropolis, was "*not real.*" Such feelings of "derealization," Freud explained, arise "very frequently in certain mental diseases, but they are not unknown among normal people, just as hallucinations occasionally occur in the healthy" (p. 244). Freud's negative hallucination turned out to be so uncanny that he never returned to the Greek capital. The "incident"—as Freud called it—would trouble him for the rest of his life (p. 248).

Freud traced his strange feeling of incredulity before the Acropolis back to the idea that he did not "deserve" and was not "worthy of such happiness." Standing in Athens and looking out toward the Acropolis thus represented an Oedipal achievement, the realization of his desire to supersede his father Jacob. Indeed, it was by siding and adopting a Greek vision of the world, by making the Oedipus myth the key to understanding mankind that Freud, at least in his mind, had superseded his father Jacob. As Richard Armstrong (2001) noted, Freud's reaction appears to be "both a self-accusation and a self-congratulation for being a Hellenizer (in the language of the Maccabees) in the face of Jakob Freud's lineage of Hasidic Judaism" (p. 95).

The initial title that Freud chose for his last piece of self-analysis was "*Unglaube auf der Akropolis*" [Disbelief on the Acropolis], a name suggesting that Freud was broaching the theme of his antireligious feelings. He had expressed his views on this topic in *The Future of an Illusion* (Freud, 1927) and, in 1936, was writing *Moses and Monotheism*, a text wherein he deconstructed the religious beliefs and illusions that his father Jacob and his paternal ancestors held. It was then that Freud decided to pause in order to circle back to Athens and the Acropolis in order to review an "incident" that had occurred years earlier.

In his account and analysis of the incident, Freud (1936) decided to convey his "disbelief" with a provocative simile. As Freud wrote, it was as if, while standing on the Acropolis, he had been "forced to believe in something the reality of which had seemed doubtful, just as if walking beside Loch Ness the sudden sight of the famous [*vielberedeten*, much discussed] Monster stranded upon the shore would force the startled walker to admit: 'So it really does exist—*the sea-serpent* we've never believed in!'" (p. 241).

The elements that arrived to shape Freud's baffling and facetious metaphor are many. Here I will only focus on those aspects that are relevant to our theme, namely, Freud's posthumous dialogue with Ferenczi. The image of the gigantic sea-serpent stranded upon the shore—Freud used the word "*Leib*" (living body) which must have evoked the uncanny idea for him that the dead are not truly dead—appears to be related to Ferenczi's own "ingenious views," more specifically the myth of the exsiccation of the sea that Ferenczi featured in his *Thalassa*. Significantly enough, immediately after his report and interpretation of his Acropolis incident, we find the same "dragon" resurfacing in Freud's discourse. It does so in *Analysis Terminable and Interminable*, a text where Freud cautions his readers against Ferenczi's illusion that it was easy and simple for analysts to gain access to traumatic memories.[9] It was precisely at this juncture that the dragon resurfaced in Freud's text.

Discussing the persistence of libidinal fixations and superstitious beliefs, Freud wrote: "One feels inclined to doubt sometimes whether the dragons of primaeval days are really extinct" (p. 229). It is important for us to mark Freud's precise wording. Freud does not say "extinct dinosaurs" or "non-existent dragons" but instead speaks of extinct dragons, blurring the distinction between the real world of dinosaurs, which is testified to by fossils, and the fantasy world of dragons. This is a dramatic way of asserting that the interplay between external reality and unconscious fantasy, trauma and defenses, life events and predisposition, cannot be disentangled from each other. Freud's words appear to offer a precise response to Ferenczi.

Freud's meditation remained uncompleted and unfinished, however. In a sort of supplement to his Acropolis essay, Freud decided to write *Splitting of the Ego in the Process of Defence*. In it, we find Freud (1938) making the important admission that he had been at fault as a result of his having taken for granted "the synthetic nature of the processes of the ego" (p. 276). Freud now recognized that the ego could be divided and split and, further, that the rift "never heals" but only "increases as time goes on." Freud illustrated his point by returning to a theme that never ceased tormenting him, namely, the reaction of a three-year-old boy to the tremendous fear which the threat of castration had occasioned. Freud's delayed attempt to assimilate Ferenczi's notion of narcissistic split of the self remained unfinished, however. Is it possible for us to take an additional step forward in order to bring Freud and Ferenczi's posthumous dialogue on traumatic memories toward a resolution?

The Abyss of Countertransference Reconsidered

Freud's cosmogonist battle with the biblical creature that lived in the depths—a sea-monster, serpent, or dragon—was more than just a metaphor. When exploring the "background of Freud's 'disturbance' on the Acropolis," Max Schur (1969) felt that Freud's disturbance and feelings of derealization were precipitated by the contents of a letter he had received from Fliess "only a week or so before" he "started his trip" to Athens (p. 130). Since again and again Freud repressed the fact that the idea of a universal bisexual constitution of human beings was originally introduced by Fliess—a symptomatic "memory disturbance" that haunted Freud throughout his relationship with his friend from Berlin—in his letter, Fliess reminded Freud when and how exactly his idea was forged. This occurred in the course of their Nuremberg meeting, on Easter of 1897:

> We talked about it for the first time in Nuremberg and you told me the case history of the woman who had dreams of *gigantic snakes*. At the time you were quite impressed [*sehr betroffen*: very struck] by the idea that undercurrents in a woman might stem from the masculine part of her psyche.
>
> *(Masson 1985, p. 465; emphasis added)*

Who exactly was this woman, likely one of Freud's female patients at the time, who dreamt of *gigantic snakes*? The evidence strongly suggests that it was Emma Eckstein, Freud's most important female patient during the years when he labored to provide psychoanalysis with its foundation. Evidently the baffling case history of Emma stood behind the playful metaphor of the Loch Ness Monster—"*the sea-serpent* we've never believed in!"—that Freud introduced in his 1936 acropolis essay to explain his "disbelief." Just a year later, Freud decided to discuss Emma's case history anonymously in *Analysis Terminable and Interminable*, where the very theory that Fliess had presented to him in Nuremberg was also recalled. As is well known, in his essay of 1937, Freud took steps to identify and comment on the futile attempt by analysts to "persuade a woman" during analysis "to abandon her wish for a penis ..." (p. 252).

Why would phallic fantasies and dreams dreamt by one of Freud's patient in 1897 be related to traumatic material which he came to review in his final piece of self-analysis years later? In a letter to Fliess, written on January 24, 1897, Freud reported that a female patient of his, most likely Emma Eckstein, had presented him a "circumcision scene" during analysis. Beginning with Schur (1966), who was the first to publish the material in Freud's letter where he had reported to Fliess on the "circumcision of a girl," historians of psychoanalysis have responded to Freud's description of the scene by denying the possible truth and reality of the circumcision. Not only is there no rational ground for their position and "disbelief" but the genital mutilation scene reported by Emma itself makes the intensity and quality of her fantasy, including her somatic sensation of having a penis, more understandable. The latter had been evidently rooted on an actual or real traumatic event, to wit, her genital mutilation. As Ferenczi indicated in *The Clinical Diary*, however, Freud failed to consider the possibility that a woman's fantasy of having a penis might have set in for traumatic reasons.

Emma Eckstein is mainly known to analysts today because Wilhelm Fliess operated on her nose during the early phase of her analysis with Freud. Much has been written about Emma's nasal surgery and the debacle that followed. What has escaped the attention of scholars up to now, however, is that her nasal surgery then might have involved an act of re-traumatization which in her case served to activate memories and fantasies related to her childhood trauma, namely, her circumcision. I have presented this hypothesis elsewhere (Bonomi, 2013, 2015). If correct, the narrative that has been handed down to us about the origins of psychoanalysis should and must be reassessed and revised. Emma's circumcision trauma likely also served to reawaken conscious and unconscious memories for Freud which, I wager, not only precipitate his self-analysis but in time also led to his discovery of the Oedipus complex, indeed his experience of castration anxiety as well. Emma Eckstein's circumcision is thus a central element which, during the crucial year when the cornerstone and the foundation of psychoanalysis were being laid down by Freud, served to fertilize Freud's own unconscious. Yet, whereas Freud was deeply affected by Emma's childhood trauma at an unconscious level, and identified himself with her traumatized patient, apparently he didn't categorize her circumcision as a trauma. Likely this is the point where, as intuitively detected by Ferenczi, the problem of countertransference had opened up before Freud "like an abyss."

Notes

1 The author wishes to thank Mario L. Beira for his editorial assistance on this paper.
2 Ferenczi's drawing was not included in the English edition of the letters.
3 These same incestuous feelings were also discussed by Ferenczi in the letter in relation to a second dream that he reported to Freud in it, namely, his dream of the "Little black cat." This second dream was analyzed by Ferenczi in some detail. While his analysis of the black cat dream offers a number of important observations, I wish to place them aside here in order to focus solely on his dream of the cut-off penis.
4 In a letter to Jones, written on December 8, 1912, Freud traced his fainting spell back to a "piece of unruly homosexual feeling" which tied back to his relationship with Fliess. Freud wrote to Ferenczi just one day later to say: "I am again very capable of work, have settled well analytically my dizzy spell in Munich ... All these attacks point to the significance of cases of death experienced early in life (in my case it was a brother who died very young, when I was a little more than a year old)."
5 In the years that followed, a number of nasal symptoms resurfaced for Ferenczi as his analysis with Freud progressed. In March 1916, Freud interpreted Ferenczi's nasal symptom, and his desire to travel to Berlin to consult with a nose specialist, as involving a resistance to analysis, indeed as an expression of Ferenczi's fear of the "father." In his text *The Phenomena of Hysterical Materialization*, Ferenczi (1919) wrote that "in several cases of hysteria in men I was able to prove that congestion of the turbinate represented unconscious libidinal phantasies, the erectile tissue of the genital themselves remaining unexcitable." Ferenczi then added within parenthesis: "Incidentally this connection between the nose and sexuality was discovered by Fliess prior to the inauguration of psychoanalysis" (p. 101).
6 The first period of actual analysis with Freud occurred between September and October 1914 and lasted only few weeks because Ferenczi had to report for military duty. The second period of analysis extends from June 14 to July 5, 1916; the third between September 26 and October 24, 1916.
7 In *The Clinical Diary*, precisely at the juncture where he criticized the "unilaterally androphile orientation" of Freud's theory of sexuality, Ferenczi noted that, despite the fact that Freud's theory of genitality contained many excellent points, its "mode of presentation and its historical reconstruction" nevertheless still clung "too closely to the words of the master; a new edition would mean [a] completely rewriting" (Dupont 1985, p. 187).
8 It is here important to recall that in *The Clinical Diary* Ferenczi not only described Freud as a narcissistic personality but that he also traced back his theory of castration to the disavowal of "the traumatic moment of his own castration" (Dupont 1985, p. 188).
9 This illusion, Freud (1937) remarked, was fostered by the belief that the hypnotic method was a splendid way of achieving this end. While Freud described Ferenczi as a "master of analysis," he also criticized him for having pursued the same end with the same method in his last "therapeutic experiments, which, unhappily, proved to be vain" (p. 230).

References

Anzieu, D. (1986). *Freud's Self-Analysis*. New York: International Universities Press.
Armstrong, R. H. (2001). Unreal city: Freud on the Acropolis. *Psychoanalysis and History*, 3:93–108.
Berman, E. (2004). Sándor, Gizella, Elma: A biographical journey. *International Journal of Psycho-Analysis*, 85:489–520.

Bonomi, C. (1994a). Freud, Jung, Ferenczi et la vision d'un petit pénis coupé. *Le Coq-héron*, 134:69–84.

Bonomi, C. (1994b). Why have we ignored Freud the "Paediatrician"? The relevance of Freud's paediatric training for the origins of psychoanalysis. In A. Haynal, E. Falzeder (eds), *100 Years of Psychoanalysis. Contributions to the History of Psychoanalysis*, Special Issue of *Cahiers Psychiatriques Genevois* distributed by H. Karnac (Books), London, 1994, pp. 55–99.

Bonomi, C. (1994c). "Sexuality and death" in Freud's discovery of sexual aetiology. *International Forum of Psychoanalysis*, 3:63–87.

Bonomi C. (1997). Mute correspondence. In P. Mahony, C. Bonomi, J. Stensson (eds) *Behind the Scenes: Freud in Correspondence*. Oslo: Scandinavian Univ. Press, pp. 155–202.

Bonomi, C. (2007). *Sulla soglia della psicoanalisi. Freud e la follia del bambino* [On the threshold of psychoanalysis: Freud and the insanity of the child]. Torino: Bollati Boringhieri.

Bonomi, C. (2009). The relevance of castration and circumcision to the origins of psychoanalysis. 1. The medical context. *International Journal of Psychoanalysis*, 90:551–580.

Bonomi, C. (2013). Withstanding trauma: The significance of Emma Eckstein's circumcision for Freud's Irma dream. *The Psychoanalytic Quarterly*, 82(3):689–740.

Bonomi, C. (2015). *The Cut and the Building of Psychoanalysis, Vol. I, Sigmund Freud and Emma Eckstein*. New York and London: Routledge.

Brabant, E. and Falzeder, E. (eds) (1993–2000). *The Correspondence of Sigmund Freud and Sándor Ferenczi*, Vol. I, II, and III. Cambridge, MA: Harvard University Press.

Cotti, P. (2007). Hunger and love: Schiller and the origin of drive dualism in Freud's work. *International Journal of Psycho-Analysis*, 88:167–182.

Dupont, J. (1985). *The Clinical Diary of Sándor Ferenczi*. Engl. trans. Cambridge and London: Harvard Universities Press, 1988.

Falzeder, E. (1996). Dreaming of Freud: Ferenczi, Freud, and an analysis without end. *International Forum of Psychoanalysis*, 5(4):265–270.

Ferenczi, S. (1912). Transitory symptom-constructions during the analysis. *First Contributions to Psychoanalysis*. London: Hogarth Press, 1952, pp. 193–212.

Ferenczi, S. (1913). A little Chanticleer. *First Contributions to Psychoanalysis*. London: Hogarth Press, 1952, pp. 240–252.

Ferenczi, S. (1915). The dream of the occlusive pessary. *Further Contributions to the Theory and Technique of Psycho-Analysis*. London: Hogarth Press, 1950, pp. 304–311.

Ferenczi, S. (1917a). Disease or patho-neuroses. *Further Contributions to the Theory and Technique of Psycho-Analysis*. London: Hogarth Press, 1950, pp. 78–87.

Ferenczi, S. (1917b). On the psychical consequences of "castration" in infancy. *Further Contributions to the Theory and Technique of Psycho-Analysis*. London: Hogarth Press, 1950, pp. 244–249.

Ferenczi, S. (1919). The phenomena of hysterical materialization. *Further Contributions to the Theory and Technique of Psycho-Analysis*. London: Hogarth Press, 1950, pp. 89–104.

Ferenczi, S. (1921). Psycho-analytical observations on tic. *Further Contributions to the Theory and Technique of Psycho-Analysis*. London: Hogarth Press, 1950, pp. 142–174.

Ferenczi, S. (1923). The dream of the 'Cleaver Baby'. *Further Contributions to the Theory and Technique of Psycho-Analysis*. London: Hogarth Press, 1950, pp. 349–350.

Ferenczi, S. (1924). *Thalassa: A Theory of Genitality*. London: Karnac Books, 1989.

Ferenczi, S. (1926). The problem of acceptance of unpleasant ideas: Advances in knowledge of the sense of reality. *Further Contributions to the Theory and Technique of Psycho-Analysis*. London: Hogarth Press, 1950, pp. 366–379.

Ferenczi, S. (1930). Masculine and feminine: Psychoanalytic observations on the "genital theory" and on secondary and tertiary sex characteristics. *Psychoanalytic Review*, 17:105–113.

Ferenczi, S. (1930–1932). Notes and fragments. *Final Contributions to the Problems and Methods of Psycho-Analysis*. London: Hogarth Press, 1950, pp. 219–279.

Ferenczi, S. (1931). Child-analysis in the analysis of adults. *Final Contributions to the Problems and Methods of Psycho-Analysis*. London: Hogarth, 1955, pp. 126–142.

Ferenczi, S. (1933). Confusion of tongues between adults and the child. *Final Contributions to the Problems and Methods of Psycho-Analysis*. London: Hogarth Press, 1950.

Freud, S. (1900). The interpretation of dreams. *SE*, 4–5.

Freud, S. (1901b). The psychopathology of everyday life. *SE*, 6.

Freud, S. (1913a). Totem and taboo: Some points of agreement between the mental lives of savages and neurotics. *SE*, 15:1–240.

Freud, S. (1915/1987). *A Phlyogenetic Fantasy: Overview of the Transference Neuroses*. Cambridge, MA: Harvard University Press, 1987.

Freud, S. (1923). The infantile genital organization (An interpolation into the theory of sexuality). *SE*, 19:139–146.

Freud, S. (1926). Inhibitions, symptoms and anxiety. *SE*, 20:77–174.

Freud, S. (1927). The future of an illusion. *SE*, 21:3–56.

Freud, S. (1933). Sándor Ferenczi. *SE*, 22:225–230.

Freud, S. (1936). A disturbance of memory on the Acropolis. *SE*, 22:237–248.

Freud, S. (1937). Analysis terminable and interminable. *SE*, 23:209–254.

Freud, S. (1938). Splitting of the ego in the process of defence. *SE*, 23:271–278.

Freud, S. (1939). Moses and monotheism: Three essays. *SE*, 23:1–138.

Haynal, A. E. (2005). In the shadow of a controversy: Freud and Ferenczi 1925–1933. *International Journal of Psycho-Analysis*, 86:457–466.

Kris, E. (1950). Einleitung zu Freud [Introduction to Freud]. In M. Bonaparte, A. Freud, E. Kris, *Aus den Anfängen der Psychoanalyse. Briefe an Wilhelm Fliess, Abhandlungen und Notizen aus den Jahren 1887–1902* (*The origins of psychoanalysis. Letters to Wilhem Fliess, drafts and notes: 1887–1902*. London: Imago Publishing Company, 1954). Reprinted in S. Freud, *Briefe an Wilhelm Fliess 1887–1904*. Frankfurt am Main: Fisher, 1986, pp. 519–561.

Kris, E. (1954). New contributions to the study of Freud's The Interpretation of Dreams—A Critical Essay. *Journal of the American Psychoanalytic Association*, 2:180–191.

Lieberman, E. J. and Kramer, R. (eds) (2012). *The Letters of Sigmund Freud and Otto Rank: Inside Psychoanalysis*. Baltimore: Johns Hopkins University Press.

Masson, J. M. (ed) (1985). *The Complete Letters of Sigmund Freud to Wilhelm Fliess 1887–1904*. Cambridge, MA: Harvard University Press.

McGuire, W. (ed) (1974). *The Freud/Jung Letters. The Correspondence between Sigmund Freud and C. G. Jung*. London: Routledge and The Hogarth Press, 1994.

Pauskauskas, R. A. (ed) (1993). *The Complete Correspondence of Sigmund Freud and Ernest Jones, 1908–1939*. Cambridge, MA: Harvard University Press, 1993.

Schur, M. (1969). The background of Freud's "disturbance" on the Acropolis. In M. Kanzer and J. Glenn (eds), *Freud and His Self-Analysis*. New York and London: Jason Aronson, 1979, pp. 117–134.

3

FERENCZI'S ATTITUDE

André E. Haynal and Véronique D. Haynal
Translated by Sarah K. Wang

Attitude is "a settled way of thinking or feeling …" (Oxford English Dictionary).

An examination of Sándor Ferenczi's personal attitude is fundamental to under-standing his work and his legacy; one such study is being presented here. Attitude is a regular way of *functioning* sustained by the habitual means of existence, by feeling, understanding, reacting, and avoiding, which all become part of one's personal and professional resources. Attitude is also how we respond, engage, or wrestle with our own usual tendencies to brush aside or dismiss what disturbs us emotionally. All these processes have to take into account one's own sensitivities. This can be summed up with the term "internal *attitude*," the outcome of which can be con-sidered external behavior. We will touch as well on what can be called the "*ethics of the psychoanalyst*" (bearing in mind that "ethos" means, in the first place, attitude, behavior). Take, for example, Ferenczi's quasi-limitless devotion to the suffering of human beings (like in the case of RN), to a level that Freud even denounced as *"furor sanandi"*—a frenzy to heal. In the first volume of *The Legacy of Sándor Ferenczi* (Aron and Harris, 1993), I addressed Ferenczi's contribution to the technique of psychoanalysis along the lines of historical development of related ideas. The pres-ent chapter focuses on this contribution as influenced by contemporary culture and life events on the one hand, and his personality and lifestyle on the other.

Culture

An examination of the historical context of the birth and evolution of psycho-analysis transports us to the heart of the *cultural crisis* at the turn of the twentieth century in the great urban centers of central Europe's Hapsburg monarchy. This entire history is situated on the periphery of the continent in these strange city centers in Eastern Europe and beyond—Vienna, Budapest, Salonika, Cairo, and Alexandria—which were distinguished by their urban, commercial, and intellectual civilizations, and by diverse populations that included many immigrants and few ties to the surrounding agricultural countryside. Nowadays, we may find a similar phenomenon in Western Europe, as in France, for example, where the city of Paris disassociates itself from its more conservative and nationalistic, "provincial" surroundings. Thus, Hungary was split between its major metropolis on the Danube and its sleepy, often nostalgic countryside. These cultural "isolates" no longer play a part in our story, as their heterogeneous populations went to other countries, taking in new immigrations and leaving the *old cities* to new arrivals from the surrounding countryside.

Psychoanalysis would emerge out of these urban centers on the fringe. Freud's work was born out of his neurological studies and his specialist practice in "nervous diseases," a term which indicates a curious mixture of irritability; "nervousness"; digestive, sexual, work- and sleep-related difficulties; and the general "dis-ease" of a difficult life. Certainly, he had always aimed to stay within the sturdy frame of science, with the ambition of becoming a professor and even a Nobel Prize winner.

Freud thus became a great contributor to "modernity" almost *in spite of himself.* In effect, his literary and artistic preferences, most notably his taste in painting, architecture, and music, remained conservative. Although he lived in an extremely stimulating city, he remained isolated from the pioneers and innovators of his *culture* (Freud, 1933a [1932]).

Ferenczi, on the other hand, experienced the cultural crisis intensely, living in circles soaked with literary, psychological, sociological, and anthropological discourse. Either feeling or wanting to be excluded from official enterprises of the universities of the State, he and his friends established their own kind of academy in cafés, where it was not just agitation from caffeine but new ideas that kept them awake into the night. These intellectuals on the fringes, forward thinkers, *philo*-sophers adhering to the Socratic method amid the cultural imbroglio of their Austro-Hungary, considered themselves with pride and defiance as the "Budapest type" (Ferenczi/Jones, 3.16.1914).

Ferenczi contributed not only to the *Huszadik Század* ("Twentieth Century," a cultural monthly), but also to the birth of the century to which the title refers: the twentieth century became *his affair.* He wanted to be an *active contributor,* to determine its character and its future. Perhaps we may consider that he succeeded, but with great delay. Not in his lifetime, certainly.

Interested in those who had difficulties in this society—in the sexopathic, psychotic, alcoholic, and others on the fringe—the curious Ferenczi penetrated their world beyond the conventional limits of traditional medicine through hypnosis, explorations of spiritualism, and alternative ways of thinking. Provocation and challenge to conventional thought were his constant companions. His incessant research into the new led him to accompany his colleague, Fülöp Stein, on a 1908 visit to Zurich's *Burghölzli*, home of Eugen Bleuler and Carl Jung, to learn about new treatment methodologies for mentally ill alcoholics. Meeting with Jung allowed him a trial, if not a game, experimenting with the associations of ideas, which was a major preoccupation of Jung's at the time. In regard to this subject, we cannot speak of a first *analysis* in the contemporary sense of the term, but rather of an initial experience—an aperitif.

The most important aspect of this encounter for Ferenczi's future, however, was that the way was now open for him to pay a visit in the following year to the Master of Vienna, Sigmund Freud.

It was a fundamental turning point in Ferenczi's life: he found himself not only face to face with the promise of therapy, but also with a *new vision* of man, in the line of other intellectual initiatives which one might call *Isms*. These doctrines were meant to shed a new light on the lives of men: for expressionist artists, such as Klimt, Schiele, and Kokoschka, there was the promise of a sensuality more delightful and more free for men as well as for *women (!)*; for Austro-Marxists, an egalitarian man; for proto-communists (in Berlin, Budapest, and St. Petersburg), a future which sang of a utopian society, satisfied in the budding paradise of Soviet communist workers; for the Jews, a new identity in Zionism. These ideas easily aligned with the utopia of the *analyzed man,* mentioned as early as the first chords in Ferenczi's correspondence with Freud—at a time when they hardly knew each other but nevertheless dared to travel together to work in Palermo, Sicily, in 1910.

Thus, Ferenczi thought he had found a vision for the creation of a *new man*, the "ψα" man, which emerged as early as the beginning of his correspondence and would be realized in relationship to other liberated men, by and through psychoanalysis. The "scene at Palermo"[1] brings us into the presence of Freud wanting to impose his own thoughts through writing and Ferenczi wanting to *discuss* with him in a shared creative process. This illustrates Ferenczi's expectation of a perfectly transparent relationship, while Freud had cherished other dreams that centered on advancing his *life's work*.

At that point, Ferenczi already had a fundamentally different attitude from Freud, and it certainly contributed to their eventual drifting apart. Nevertheless, in spite of Ferenczi having asserted a very different mindset, Freud evidently tried forcefully to influence Ferenczi's thinking. The image of Ferenczi as a man on the margins, an experimenter, in sum an *"enfant terrible,"*[2] has since been established.

Ferenczi nonetheless remained faithful and fundamentally admiring of the constructive theoretical force of he who remained his Master. Sigmund Freud, the thinker, continued to be this *developer* of a *new vision* of man and his inner functioning, whereas Ferenczi hoped to be primarily effective in *changing life* through *action*. As a young psychoanalyst, Ferenczi the bohemian lived for a decade in a hotel on a wide, boisterous, gritty boulevard of Pest, and consulted in the same district.

Ferenczi, the writer and sometimes journalist—an artist among other artists, wanted to be one of the builders of the future through his own contributions.

Freud would defend tooth and nail the smallest iota of his grandiose theoretical construction (*metapsychology*), an anthropology that took into account all of the European cultural heritage as well as Darwinian-Lamarckian understandings in biology. For Ferenczi, however, theory was subject first and foremost to the measure by which it emerges in *experience*, in the daily exercise of practice, in life lived.

Ambiance

"I am still taking my patients' affairs too much to heart."
—*Ferenczi, in a letter to Freud, November 22, 1908*

After what we have come to know of Ferenczi's personal background, are we surprised to notice that his work was done with *others*, in *relationships* with partners, and not by writing a book in which he might record his own dreams?

Ferenczi was already a therapist before his introduction to psychoanalysis. He understood several of Freud's ideas, most notably on the subject of dreams, without having been completely convinced right away of these new views. It is only gradually that he moved toward understanding the complex forces that he encountered in practicing hypnosis and in the phenomena of catharsis and trance. It was the Other that interested him, as Ferenczi had always been surrounded by others: by his brotherhood of twelve, later on by fellow students and medical colleagues, and even during his never-ending soirées of debate and discussion.

Until the end, all of his professional activity was based on his ties with people who sought help under him and on those for whom he could make great sacrifices. During his early beginnings, he thought that ridding oneself of disturbing pathological elements seemed to be a less sophisticated approach than developing the finer points of a subject's interior existence. Ferenczi rapidly realized that the boundaries between pathological and normal are not easy to draw but rather they are confluent, as he experienced personally.

Initially, at the beginning of his career as an analyst, a question arose about the analysand's "true request." Was the analyst being asked to address the so-called neurotic defensive structures as described in the DSM's precursors? Or, was he or she really face to face with people who wanted to examine and work on their fundamental attitudes, on the shifts of their existence, and the roots of evil that made them suffer, with the goal of reaching a better life of greater freedom?

Among the analyst's clientele, we often find cases of rigid structure, nearly completely shut down by defense mechanisms which bar the way to expressing emotion and/or internal conflicts. Thus are born the phobic—obsessive neuroses of definitive nosography that call for a proper "curative" work. Nevertheless, the latent demand beneath the symptoms is always fundamental and still persists despite every effort of simplistic medicalization. Those who complain of a general malaise, of failure in life, of suffering due to aggressions from the external world can be referred to by such nomenclature as "anxious" or "depressive" states, whereas we psychoanalysts encounter some of them as borderline personalities, the psychosomatically ill, and as traumatized. The desire of these sufferers to live better, to change and find themselves may represent a challenge for the psychoanalyst in situations where other caregivers no longer have an answer.

Ferenczi, gripped by his own problems and surrounded by analysands with whom he could easily identify, managed to recognize the *complexity* of these questions. It is what motivated him to be at the disposal of his patients two times a day (as was the case at times with RN), to go out of his way to meet them or even to bring them with him on vacation, for example when visiting Groddeck in Baden-Baden. He was aware of the influence of his own unconscious on his life, particularly as it emerged within his friendships or in relation to his health, two realms that were particularly accessible to his curiosity.

In analysis, what is it that the analyst hears? Who speaks? Then, who responds? In transference, the analysand can address his father or his mother, against whom he may justify himself, or rebel, as each one is symbolically present in the analyst. The analyst also sometimes hears his own father or his brother—we call these "part" objects, but their importance is without question. Ferenczi would insist that these observations do not contradict an Oedipal perspective. The analyst may reach an understanding of an analysand through understanding of his own mind.

In this context, Ferenczi's attitude meant asking himself questions about the meaning of the customs of the psychoanalytic field before blindly accepting them without reflection or re-reflection. Thus, he did not allow them to be reduced to rituals, repetitions having lost their original meaning. *Prescription* has no place in Ferenczi's understanding of the analytic situation. What might be called the "analytic Superego"—that is, what it means to be a good analysand, to deliver what the analyst expects and what he does not willingly expect—is beyond the analysand's desire and freedom. What will be said should not be predetermined. There should not be a particular end goal already in mind. There is no point of view which one must say or not say, no intended purpose of the discourse. Even the other's expectations will be raised for discussion, but nothing determines at the outset what the follow-up will be—not even for purposes of presenting oneself as a good analyst or a good analysand. There are certain predictable, traditional bodily positions (for example, on the couch) that favor relaxation, but they are not indispensable. Ferenczi could well tolerate a patient pacing the length of the room. Analysis is not determined by the fact that the analysand is lying down or not.

Only the *frame*, the basis of a mutual understanding, is a limit of the internal time and space in which the work is done, so that the work does not go beyond it to become intangible, elusive, or scattered. The frame provides an *enclosure* not created by the spirit of prohibition.

Let us bear in mind that Ferenczi was a psychoanalyst devoted to listening to sessions for the duration of his life. He revealed a psychoanalytic creativity *nurtured by* "the psychoanalytic situation" (Ferenczi & Rank, 1924b), and *not solely by speculation outside* of this frame. Nonetheless, he remained a precise and keen observer of life for the length of his own. Let us refer to a letter to Freud (Ferenczi/Freud, 10.26.1915) on the subject of the phylogenetic background of phenomena such as: "sleep, laughter, and tears, hypnotic super-performances, the feeling of chastisement, fainting." Experiences such as training horses and his encounter with "The Little Rooster-Man" only added themselves to the long list of phenomena that captivated his curiosity.

In his search to understand himself above all, and with the insights gained from Freud's teaching, Ferenczi's enthusiasm and generosity led him to benefit others with his new theoretical and methodological discoveries. It is theory, however, inspiring and guiding, that always enriched and enlightened his observations in his *encounters* in the field of interpersonal *games* where everything took place.

For Ferenczi, psychoanalysis, as it slowly takes shape, is not a meditation; rather, it is a creative work engaged in during an exchange between *two* persons. Without the compulsion of these libidinal forces, there is no analysis. As Maxwell Gitelson (1962) reminded us later, there is a first moment of deep acceptance of the analysand when the creation of a *libidinal* alliance between analyst and analysand occurs. In the same sense, for Ferenczi, analysis is an *engaging* of *two* persons. The *free association* of one is enhanced by the *free-floating attention* of the other, a mental functioning as free as possible between one another. As was already stated, no prescription and no predetermined conscious goal are the first steps toward creating a certain freedom. It is in this *created freedom* that analysis takes place. Many think that this interaction begins with messages from the analysand, but often it is the analyst who begins with his seducing offer to regularly receive and attentively pursue the other. Even if what follows is simply to remain in silence. In some circumstances, this silence may not suffice or may even be counterproductive. Identification can offer guidance in such cases. In Ferenczi's subsequent work, introjection carries with it an extension of autoerotic interests—the expanding of the ego in an encounter with the Other. This comes about through lifting the repression and thereby taking in the *object*. Since the beginning, Ferenczi conceived of the aspects of transference as the introjection of the analyst in the subjective economy. In this purview, he is an early predecessor to Winnicott and Bion.

The following section presents Ferenczi's chief works as well as some of his correspondences; notes accompany each text as a guide through his personal and professional evolution.

Early Works

Just one year after meeting Freud in person, Ferenczi published a psychoanalytic article, "Introjection and Transference" (1909), about the relationship between the self and others. This theme is at the heart of what Ferenczi experienced with his patients. One year after his plunge into the new world of psychoanalysis, the field was already being shaped by his foundational attitude. Understanding others, identification, or even introjection played a major role. What would become the theory of "object relations" emerged from his attention to this dimension of "you and me."

Along the long path from 1909 to about 1924, he undertook hundreds of remarkable intellectual excursions. The publications from his first decade as an analyst were already full of astonishing, little observations—true clinical gems. Later, we find more ample theoretical works, such as *Stages in the Development of the Sense of Reality* (Ferenczi, 1913), the first evidence of a strong commitment to a developmental line of thinking. This emphasis followed Freud's example and was a feature that would play an important role in his later works, most notably in *Goals for the Development of Psychoanalysis* ([*Entwicklungsziele der Psychoanalyse*], referred to in this chapter as "Goals," Ferenczi and Rank, 1924b).

The 1918 Congress in Budapest marked a turning point in Ferenczi's thinking: Freud had entrusted him with reflecting on the subject of "psychoanalytic practice." This theme would become his primary preoccupation for the rest of his life. It is as if Freud ceded his own position to Ferenczi (and to some extent to Rank), himself retiring from the subject. In fact, in the years that followed, Freud wrote very little on the large themes of practice, as he seemed to be saving his energy for theoretical contributions (*The Future of an Illusion,* 1927, SE 21; *Civilization and its Discontents,* 1930a, SE 21).

Had Freud turned away from people as well? It was often said—by many, including Jones—that he was not a *Menschenkenner* (a good judge of character). A curious remark about someone who socialized with *Menschen* (human beings) only to understand them better! This discrepancy shows him as primarily interested in theories nourished by his self-analysis in a kind of isolation. Several testimonies confirm it, including that of Raymond de Saussure, the famous European psychoanalyst who described his memories of his own personal analysis in an article commemorating the 100th anniversary of his analyst's birth in 1956. Saussure does not hide the fact that to him:

> [Freud] had practiced suggestion too long not to have been materially affected by it. When he was persuaded by the truth of something, he had considerable difficulty in waiting until this became clear to his patient. Freud wanted to convince him immediately. Because of that, he talked so much ... [It was easy to sense the] special theoretical question [uppermost in his mind] for often during the analytic hour he developed at length new points of view he was clarifying in his mind. This was a gain for the intellect but not always for the patient's treatment. (1956, pp. 357–359)

It is as if he describes an experience with a great thinker. By contrast, in reading Ferenczi, we are struck by his efforts in researching understanding, as they are those of a therapist.

Encouraged by Freud, Ferenczi addressed directly the difficult and sometimes controversial questions of practice—of psychoanalytic *action*—that required reflection on his own *attitude*. It is here that we visibly meet the differences in thought of these two figures. Ferenczi, nevertheless, stayed well in line with Freud, that is to say in his research of understanding the unconscious despite differing opinions on the best ways to go about it ... This research brings us to a later period, around 1920, and the publication of several books, one of which would mark his transition.

An "Attempt" ... *Thalassa*

In the intermediary period between the more theoretical publications of one side and those that focused on the practical activities of psychoanalysts on the other, Ferenczi undertook a work that would span the decade from 1914 to 1923: *Thalassa*.

During the war, he was chief physician with a regiment of Hussars in a remote town, called Pápa, in western Hungary. Despite the situation, he remained in frequent contact with Freud in Vienna. Their communication served to crystallize the project. A curious work was born out of it that encompassed science and fantasy, psychoanalysis and Lamarckian biology, which carried the title *Thalassa* in its English translated publication. The Greek word imparts a mythological divinity evoking the sea. The ideas that preoccupied him since 1913, in dialogue with Freud and following *Three Essays on the Theory of Sexuality* (Freud, 1905), slowly took their shape after a development clearly full of hesitation. Freud searched for a scientific foundation for his theoretical construction, which he hoped to find initially in neurology and then in *sexology*.

Freud meanwhile encouraged Ferenczi to seek the foundation for these theories in onto- and phylo-genesis, following the footsteps of Lamarck (Freud/Ferenczi,10.26.1915). As a result, *adaptation* in evolution would play an important role in Ferenczi's thought process, and foreshadows his later idea that it is the analyst who must find access to patients, and who should adapt to his analysand: "I believed rather that therapy was good, but perhaps we were still deficient, and I began to look for our errors" (Ferenczi, 1932/1985). He thus considered adopting a position of *evolution* through successive adaptations, like Lamarck. This position led him to assume, regarding failures of analyses, that is it not that the analysand is "too ill," but rather that the analyst is insufficient or ill prepared for the demands of his profession.

Moreover, we see two themes emerge in this work that continued to underlie his reflections and characterize his concerns. The first theme that arises is the importance of the *mother*. Ferenczi imagines that we harbor a nostalgia to return to her breast, even to the amniotic fluid, to her blissful protection as a reunion with the Sea Goddess—an elusive, evanescent, idealized image, behind which is hidden Ferenczi's ambivalent attitude towards his mother and women in general. These ideas allowed other important perspectives to follow, such as those of letting go or relaxing, thus foreshadowing the idea of relaxation in the analytic situation.

Ferenczi also addresses the theme of "autoplasty" (in the Goethean sense of the term) as opposed to alloplasty, which is the necessity to transform oneself in favor of or in the image of another, as according to a conventional form imposed in an authoritarian manner. The ideal of autoplasty, however, is supported by the courage to accept marginality, that is to say that Ferenczi did not look to be a part of a compact majority, but followed his own evolution and encouraged other psychoanalysts to follow their own.

Thalassa, more of a mythological than a theoretically clear entity, is a "*Versuch*," *an "attempt of a theory of genitality,"* as indicated by the original main title which became a subtitle in several translations (Ferenczi, 1924).[3] Ferenczi's intent, moreover, encompasses nothing more than a "deepening of the explanation of coitus" among other things. His intellectual bravery and his defiant attitude went above and beyond their boundaries. It is this Ferenczi who spoke of his own ejaculation to the heavens "*Ejakulatio usque ad coelum*" (Ferenczi, 1932/1985)!

The formation of *Thalassa* was not completely devoid of ambiguity. Was it recognition of an emerging weakness in the biological foundations that made Freud take his distance little by little over the course of his epistolary exchanges on the subject of *Thalassa* with Ferenczi? How do you explain that, even in his obituary for Ferenczi, Freud considered this text—which would not have great influence, and was focused on a theme from which Freud eventually distanced himself—as "the boldest application" of psychoanalysis to science (1933b, SE 22, p. 228)?

Freud also wrote about him: "I maintain that this is your real field, in which you will be without peer [orig.: *Konkurrenz*]" (Freud/Ferenczi, 4.29.1916). Did he simply want Ferenczi to continue his experiments on the *changes* in psychoanalytic cure? Or, did he want to keep him as "son" in the solid, fortified paternal house of Science, without allowing him either to extend himself or open himself up for dangerous criticism? We will probably never know.

Nevertheless, it is interesting to notice how often Freud showed himself seduced by this theme that he calls "Lamarckian," but despite that did not advance or publish anything on the subject. Rather, despite all his protection, he sent Ferenczi to the front to do so. Freud did not take a public position, nor did he intervene beyond his personal correspondence with Ferenczi, not even in other personal correspondences. Was Ferenczi truly "without competition"[4] in the "overarching themes" of this "great project" (1933b, SE 22, pp. 227–229)? Perhaps the shadow of Jung's high interest in phylogenesis leading to the theory of archetypes had a lively presence in Freud's mind and also became responsible for this avoidance?

The text finally came out at the very end of 1923, at a time when Ferenczi's mind, like that of Freud's, was preoccupied with other problems. In fact, four important books appeared at the same time, within intervals of several months. These texts would inspire a germination of new ideas and perspectives among Freud and his entourage, all the while triggering significant internal dissensions that would lead to the rupture of friendships, and little by little the fading and eventual dissolution of the Secret Committee.

1924 and the Issuing of a Contest: Revolution

> "May I suggest … that you give us some of the scientific ideas of which you are so prolific. We all agree, I am sure, that it would be valuable and interesting …"
>
> —*Jones to Ferenczi in* Circular Letters, *April 19, 1922*

In 1922, Freud issued the challenge to describe exactly the relationship between theory and practice. It was the only time that Freud addressed his entourage with this question, even offering a *prize*[5] to the one who could shed light on the enigma: "It should be examined in what measure the technique influences the theory and to what extent the technique and the theory mutually influence each other" (Freud, 1922). The call for the competition of course piqued the interest of Ferenczi, who, with his friend Otto Rank, quickly announced their intention. They wanted to address this intriguing question with a joint text. So collaborative was their project that, to this day, we do not know which chapter or which section of a chapter belonged to which of the two authors. The translator, Caroline Newton, concludes in her foreword that according to her research, the book "was written in the summer of 1922, somewhat modified and altered by the events of the International Psycho-analytical Congress, held in Berlin in September of that year and completed in 1923." She declares: "The critical part of the work was originally written by Dr. Ferenczi, the didactic chapter 'The Analytical Situation' by Dr. Rank and the work then jointly revised" (Ferenczi & Rank, 1924a, p. iii). Another suggested makeup of authorship is based on the memory of Gizella, Ferenczi's widow; Rank never responded to questioning on the subject. The only other thing we know with more security is that both authors reviewed the final text in a joint meeting.

They vowed, unsurprisingly, that before the proposition of a "prize," even before Freud encouraged a competition to put forth works on this theme, they were already occupied with the problem, which they had observed and dared to approach well before any others, in the summer of 1922.

The atmosphere was tense: disputes, rifts, practically a revolution, broke out (Jeannet-Hasler, 2002; Kramer and Lieberman, 2012; Leitner, 1998). It is not a coincidence that, in his historical account Jones, evoked a scene in which only Freud, at the exclusion of all other members of the Secret Committee, was privy to the preparation of these texts. Jones was thus able to say that the members were taken "by surprise,"—discovering that the two innovative authors broke with the "usual" practice of production. Abraham's and Jones's incisive, acerbic critiques clearly demonstrate the fear of our two authors' ability to circumvent the control of their equals and rivals, and foreshadowed how they would punish the authors with marginalization and exclusion.

Often in cultural history, an era ends with a great synthesis allowing a new departure in an original perspective. What we meet in these four texts is as much a résumé as an innovation, most notable in view of the perspectives of psychoanalysis. Perhaps Freud also felt this need for regeneration in his practice, and that is what urged him to take stock of the situation. If Freud expected a summary of insights, the two young men from Budapest and Vienna went much further in presenting their plans for the future. They summed up their own development, thus ending an era not only by exposing archaic perspectives and their weaknesses, but also by opening the door to new horizons primarily on the subject of the *purposes* of psychoanalytic activity.

Goals for the Development of Psychoanalysis

It is important to note that the title of their work does not pertain to the development of procedures in psychoanalysis, as some translations would suggest (*The Development of Psycho-Analysis*, February 8, 2012), but rather marks a turn toward the "Entwicklungs*ziele*," the *Goals for the Development of Psychoanalysis*.

In the first chapter of *Goals*, we find a presentation of the development that was referred to at the time as "psychoanalytic technique," or in other words, how to proceed (Ferenczi and Rank, 1924b). This metaphor came not from Freud and his entourage, but from the artistic world of Vienna of the time. The expression does not refer to the technology of the second half of the last century. The new "techniques" of Klimt, Schiele, and Kokoschka drew forth the unconscious, particularly the sexual unconscious, of contemporary urban culture (Kandel, 2012). They were thus connected to the great discoveries of Freud and his school. Similarly, the musical compositions of Mahler, Berg, and Schönberg expressed the pulses coming from the depths of the human soul through new tonalities in a civilization surrounding the birth of psychoanalysis. This "technique," the authors of *Goals* declare in the first chapter, does not aim only at *commemorating the past*, but particularly at its *repetition* in the analyst–analysand dyad, or as they would call it, in the "analytic situation." They continue to analyze the conception of this situation in the second chapter, which would eventually hold particularly great importance in the treatment of traumatized patients.

Our authors add that in the experience (*Erlebnisse*) of analysis, new memories are also created in place of the old, meeting with the important idea of introjection (Ferenczi & Rank, 1924b, p. 28). Thus, according to their understanding, memories continue to play a role. The authors also stressed the difficulties met by compulsive neurotics of the time who after a long analysis would have "the complete knowledge of their analyst in their little finger without having *experienced* anything that would have given them this knowledge" (Ferenczi & Rank, p. 24).[6]

The third chapter confronts the reader with a critique of the outdated and *erroneous* ways of proceeding, such as collecting associations. They further add to this list the direct analysis of symptoms, or the "fanaticism of interpretation." All of these techniques work against the spontaneity and liberty of the associative processes.

The rest of the book, on the other hand, recommends constructive postures for achieving desirable results. The distinction between experience and personal knowledge as opposed to theoretical understanding was a new concept, rarely addressed afterwards (much later by Polanyi, 1958).

In the final chapters, the authors emphasize the importance of innovative theoretical reflection, as opposed to a tentative practice stripped of guiding thoughtfulness. The authors denounce the imbalance between different theoretical parties (valuing one aspect at the cost of the other) and the overestimation of theory at the cost of neglecting minute clinical details. Their proposed technical modifications show up in different publications from both Rank and Ferenczi, which soon followed later in 1924.

In the end, in *Goals*, Ferenczi and Rank discussed the approach of helping the individual restore his- or herself in the "fountain of youth" of the psychoanalytic cure, even though the question posed by Freud had been about the *link* between theory and practice, especially about the influence that practice could have on theory. Without this valuable perspective, theory courts the danger of becoming completely detached and untethered, floating through the air. The candidates waived receiving the prize, probably having noticed that they did not supply an answer to the original question of the contest.

Ferenczi maintained that renewal and development of the person should be made in a communication without barriers. The "Palermo Incident" showed him the failure of such an attempt with Freud, and he had been extremely disappointed. Afterwards, and throughout his whole life, Ferenczi strove to surmount the obstacles that might have prevented the coveted, fluid communication that he so desired. His efforts were fueled by his fundamental *attitudes*. His propositions suggested, however, a modification of the "technique."

In *Goals*, Ferenczi and Rank argue that psychoanalysis is not simply a question of development, but rather an arena for the analysand's real transformation of his or her goals toward gaining more freedom. The idealized "genitality" prescribed and imposed by theory was no longer an acceptable goal in the eyes of Ferenczi.

One could say that the books by Rank (*The Trauma of Birth*, 1924) and Ferenczi (*Thalassa*) as well as their collaborative work (Ferenczi & Rank, 1924b) sum up what they considered to be acquired knowledge. But is it really acquired? Did their colleagues share the same idea of a new man liberated by the analytic experience that Ferenczi and Rank defended? The responses of a faction of the Secret Committee would cloud the subject with doubt. Conservative forces prevailed and, in fact, revitalization barely took place. Or, if it did, it did so very discreetly and much later, as written in Ferenczi's practically secret *The Clinical Diary* and in his farewell address, *The Confusion of Tongues* (1932).

Freud was initially satisfied after the publication of *Goals*, but he later wrote, "now I wouldn't know how to say what I don't agree with" (Freud/Ferenczi, 4.2.1924). The confusion was not insignificant and the tone of the debate was sharp. For example, Ferenczi wrote with regard to Abraham, "behind his cautious politeness I always also recognized the signs of boundless ambition and jealousy" and adds he "could slander the joint work and *The Trauma of Birth* as garbage publications" (Ferenczi/Freud, 3.18.1924). We have to add that the English translator apparently misunderstood *Abfallserscheinungen* as "garbage publications" instead of taking Abfall in the sociological–political sense (e.g., *Abfallbewegung*) as dropping out, deviance, heresy.[7] Freud, however, reassured him, "My trust in you and Rank is unqualified (*unbedingt*)" (Freud/Ferenczi, 3.20.1924).

In the meantime, worry (regarding Freud's illness and therefore his succession) persisted among the men of the Secret Committee. Freud tried to ease the concern by writing to Abraham that "after a few years' work it would become evident whether one side had exaggerated a valuable finding or the other had underrated it[8] (Freud/Abraham, 3.4.1924). His concern for institutional unity of the inner circle seemed to prevail. What appeared to be a general renewal became an object of criticism for the influential members of Freud's entourage such as Jones and Abraham.

Ferenczi and Rank suffered the fate of disruptive innovators. Rank was taken up with a lengthy process of alternating breaks and momentary reconciliations with Freud and the committee, followed by new splits, followed by moving to a new city (Paris, "City of Lights") and even a new continent (the New World, the America that Freud feared and mistrusted, as did many central European intellectuals of the time). Rank, not being a medical doctor, faced the perspective of a poorer living than his colleagues in his new surroundings, where the tendency of following the Berlin model and favoring doctors was predominant. He would be compelled to care primarily for social workers while preparing for his desired move to the "*new*, New World," sunny California. But death awaited him just before he realized his dream. As he wrote: "The struggle of youth, the battles of manhood, the fights for success and against stupidity are all over" [omitted sentence in the preface of *Beyond Psychology* (1939)]. His interesting later contributions are difficult to find even today. Rank's ideas on "the trauma of birth" have been recovered only very little in their original form.

Meanwhile, Ferenczi clung to Freud with the desire to restore the same ideal relationship he had expected between the two psychoanalysts. He lived the last decade of his life tormented by the tension held between a fear of distance and feelings of abandonment, and his respect and fidelity to his commitment to Freud. A desire to preserve the originality of his mind became increasingly important to him, but the relationship with Freud continued to preoccupy him. In fact, it was no longer sustained by the same mutual trust. During the final years of his life, Ferenczi found himself in a labor of divorce with Freud, which led neither to a reestablished partnership nor separation. Such are the lingering effects of *Goals* in the progression of the years following.

In fact, peace never returned. But Ferenczi remained steadfast. When he shared with Freud his desire to present "the position of psychoanalysis" (Ferenczi/ Freud, 3.16.1925), practically a résumé of his new ideas, Freud responded immediately and almost fearfully: "I advise you against it. Don't do it ... The only thing new in your lecture would be the personal factor ... With it you are throwing a bomb into the psychoanalytic edifice" (Freud/Ferenczi, 3.20.1925).

Even more of a shock was that Freud also feared isolation. Regarding the spread of psychoanalysis, he wrote, "What personal pleasure is to be derived from analysis I obtained during the time when I was alone, and since others have joined me it has given me more pain than pleasure. The way people accept and distort it has not changed the opinion I formed of them when they non-understandingly rejected it. An incurable breach must have come into existence at that time between me and other men" (Freud & Pfister 1963, p. 79).

Association? Committee? What for?

Behind these problems, we find the watermark of psychoanalytic institutions—or of any institution at all. Regarding the utility of an *organization* of psychoanalysts, Ferenczi promptly responded to Freud's call in 1910. This gesture corresponded to the ideal of establishing a *movement* following the other *Isms* of the time: to reunite people in order to improve their lives, their society, and to create a greater harmony. Ferenczi knew for a long time, like the Greek philosophers, that man is not meant to live alone, but that he is very much a "social creature." Institutions created to bring together people with different subjectivities, qualities, mentalities, and origins are not composed solely of these positive aspects, but as Ferenczi knew well, they become hotbeds of neurotic childishness of all kinds:

> I know the excrescences that grow from organized groups, and I am aware that in most political, social, and scientific organizations childish megalomania, vanity, admiration of empty formalities, blind obedience, or personal egoism prevail instead of quiet, honest work in the general interest.
>
> *(Ferenczi 1911, p. 302)*

Professional organizations often become personal organizations, following the "family" model, going beyond their primary purpose and thus setting the stage for conflict.

Without returning to the problem of the authoritarian, hierarchical structure of these societies, recall that Freud remained for his followers *Herr Professor* and that no one was able to graduate from the distant *Sie* to the more familiar *Du*. Moreover, Freud was used to inhabiting an academic hierarchy and took his titles into account, whereas Ferenczi's egalitarian conception of human relationships was evident everywhere, not only in his life but also in his relationship to analysands, whom he considered his equals.

In the meantime, the background changed as women came on the psychoanalytic scene. In 1920, Melanie Klein spoke at Den Haag on child development and started working in Berlin in 1921; Anna Freud became a member of the Vienna Psychoanalytic Society in 1922; and we find Lou-Andreas Salomé, who held a very high opinion of Ferenczi and saw the future in him, entering Ferenczi's circle. We can say that 1927 marked the end of the male-only domination in the field: Jeanne Lampl-de Groot, Ruth Mack-Brunswick, and Marie Bonaparte were more and more among Freud's closest colleagues. Ferenczi moved geographically as well, beyond Vienna. Against Freud's wishes, he undertook the several months' voyage to the United States in September of 1926.

Clinical Diary

From the first pages of *The Clinical Diary* (Ferenczi, 1932/1985), complete sincerity remains the focus of the psychoanalytic relationship: "*tell everyone the truth*, one's father, teacher, neighbor, and even the king" (Ferenczi/Freud, 2.5.1910). Something he declared as early as the golden years of the Austro-Hungarian monarchy and Old Vienna in 1910 continued to form part of his general *attitude*.

Ferenczi's *The Clinical Diary*, shrouded in mystery, bears witness to his final reflections and his last struggles. The question remains, even today, to whom was Ferenczi writing: was it to the author himself, for further reflection? Was he addressing his colleagues in an instructional text? Did he speak to Freud, confessing the direction that his thoughts always went in the continual quest for relational sincerity? Is the diary simply a question of legacy? Or the preliminary notes for a text to be published later (which would explain why the names of patients were made anonymous)?

A collection of reflections on the analytic experiences of their author logged day by day, the diary is characterized by sincerity without restraint, as if in psychoanalysis. His countertransference clearly shows. Without being tempered, nor eventually censured, the critical remarks regarding Freud could not have been considered to be addressed to a greater audience. It is not by accident that the people who were consulted at the time, Michael Balint, Vilma Kovacs, and Alice Balint, advised his widow against publishing the work "as is" after his death. With the majority of the text (80% according to Balint) typewritten, probably dictated to his secretary, the rest remains handwritten, almost certainly by Ferenczi himself. Although Ferenczi had clearly spoken to his circle about his intention to draft such a journal, he never indicated exactly for what purpose the work should see the light of day. Even the title did not come from Ferenczi but rather from his heirs.[9] According to Michael Balint, Freud could have read the texts preceding *The Clinical Diary* that addressed similar themes and were published posthumously in the fourth volume of the original edition of his complete works (*Bausteine*). Freud is said by Balint to have been admiring of "Ferenczi's ideas until then unknown to him" (Ferenczi 1932/1985, p. 219). But he seems never to have read *The Clinical Diary* in its totality.

The Clinical Diary, which one could also consider as notes for a full text on trauma, covers additional themes encountered in the clinical material of the analysands in question—devoid of any systematics—such as psychosis, masochism, or homosexuality. The recent research of William Brennan (2011) was able to identify the individuals in question, those in analysis with Ferenczi at this exact moment (in New York and in Budapest). Ferenczi scattered his commentaries on quotes from his innovative colleagues, such as Groddeck, Clara Thompson, Rank, Pfister, Balint, Rado, and Brill, showing that he was in contact with them, at the very least through reading. This selection is not due to blind chance. Moreover, he also refers to classic literature by such authors as Schiller, Goethe, and Anatole France.

In this journal, after having addressed the theme of mutual analysis, an unusual framework of his own invention, Ferenczi emphasized the *involvement* of the analyst and what "springs out" of such an interaction and finally from every psychoanalytic encounter. In fact, it becomes a *co-construction*, and through it, a *common work*. Freud's critique of the *uferlose Experimente* (boundless course of experimentation) (1933c, SE 22, p. 153) in the New Introductory Lectures could very well refer to this.

Ferenczi explains his way of working and understanding. To illustrate, let us simply take one passage:

> … complete renunciation of all compulsion and of all authority on both sides: they give the impression of two equally terrified children who compare their experiences, and because of their common fate understand each other completely and instinctively try to comfort each other. Awareness of this shared fate allows the partner to appear as completely harmless, therefore as someone whom one can trust with confidence.
>
> *(Ferenczi 1932/1985, p. 56)*

In this, we find a synopsis of his way of thinking. We could find a thousand other important elements in this text of immense maturity and experience from the one called "the specialist of impossible cases." The characteristics of his *attitude* are reflected in his vision of the other as equal, as of one and the same importance, two frightened children searching together for solutions; it is not from a position of authority that one analyzes; the created atmosphere allows one to confide. The analyst is a partner, unoffending and respectful.

Simultaneously, ego psychology emerges following Freud's *The Ego and the Id* (Freud, 1923, SE, 19, pp. 12–59), triggering the return of a "one-person psychology" (John Rickman) as well as the increasingly growing interest in the study of the defensive work of the ego (which reaches its acme with Anna Freud's *The Ego and the Mechanisms of Defence*, in 1936). A perfectionism of self-regulation influenced by rule (the psychoanalytic, heteronomic superego) is established, contrary to the autonomic freedom desired and facilitated by Ferenczi. For him, ego psychology is set too close to the study of obsessive neuroses and encourages analogous thinking in the analyst.

Like Ferenczi, Freud tried to facilitate the blossoming of these subjects thanks to self-reflection according to the Socratic method, which was revived and expanded by the scientific–biological and cultural views of their time. But this was all taking place in the increasingly hierarchical, authoritarian atmosphere characteristic of central Europe at the time. Freud expected that his students would be submissive. Jung was interested in psychoses, telepathy, and mysticism, themes Freud was wary to treat in public, for fear of endangering the scientific reputation of psychoanalysis. Jung thus found himself immediately under suspicion of potential deviance reinforced by the Spielrein affair in which Freud was asked to take a side against his liking. Freud's choice, in this case, was separation and not discussion. With Rank, however, he tried to maintain dialogue, but he became increasingly ambivalent. Then, even Ferenczi, who had stayed close to Freud at all costs, drifted away as well. For example, when by chance he crossed paths with Rank at Pennsylvania Station in New York City, he would not even greet him. The former great friends!

In the same vein, Klein, as head of her school, also expected submissive colleagues and not autonomous innovators (as illustrated by the well-known case of her taking distance from Paula Heimann). Ferenczi, intellectual and independent, was attracted by and hoping to be surrounded by people of the same fabric who would enrich the group in Budapest with many shades of originality. In fact, he did not want an organized *school* with constraining regulations. Later, his student Balint would want it no more than Ferenczi: he adhered in his research of intellectual freedom to the British Middle Group.

The Confusion of Tongues

Ferenczi's *The Clinical Diary* was a precursor to *The Confusion of Tongues*, a lecture he presented at the Wiesbaden Congress in the fall of 1932 while already suffering from Biermer's disease (a pernicious anemia). The text, a tragic landscape, depicts a struggle in communication where *several* adults—a singular group, as if they were all the same—face *one* solitary child, left to himself, helpless, not understood. The *sole* child tries to understand the adults amid the *confusion*, the cacophony. It is quite the opposite of a speech of comprehension. This was precisely the atmosphere of the influential psychoanalysts surrounding Ferenczi at the time.

Not long before, on September 2, Freud had telegraphed to Eitingon that Ferenczi had read to him his essay, a text he described as "Harmless stupid otherwise inaccessible unfavourable impression" (Freud/Eitingon, 9.2.1932). The next day, he wrote to his daughter Anna more explicitly:

> I listened, shocked … The process of regression in which he is engaged is leading him to maintain one of the etiologies that I believed, but that I have since abandoned 35 years ago: that neuroses are generally caused by sexual traumas suffered during childhood, and he expresses it in terms which were my own.[10] (Freud/Anna Freud, 9.3.1932)

Freud feared a misunderstanding, a devaluation of the importance of the Oedipus complex: "Everything is happening as it did with Rank, but even more sadly" (Freud/Anna Freud, 9.3.1932). Freud was interested very little in exploring the realm of relationships previous to the Oedipus complex. Contrary to what he expressed later in his work on Moses (Freud, 1939, SE, 23, pp. 7–137), here the voice of trauma appears, imperceptible, inaudible.

In *The Confusion of Tongues,* the child, as yet hardly developed, reacts with an anxious identification and then by introjection of the offending person. This identification with the aggressor, attributed to Anna Freud in later psychoanalytic literature, was already fully present in Ferenczi's work in ways that the father of Anna refused to hear. He even cautioned Ferenczi against presenting it at the Congress! Thus, he hoped to save the Oedipus complex and the fantasy of castrating the shadow of pre-Oedipal evolution. Nevertheless, the lecture was well received by its audience, but was not published in English until 1949 because of a censure, in essence due to Jones.

The history of psychoanalytic thought does not always play itself out in harmonious evolution. Rather it is often determined by conflict and matters of preconceived principle, unsupported by clinical experience. Subjectivity and intuition, as well as Ferenczi's *attitude* of immense curiosity, met with the opposition of a protective conservatism and ended in a repetition of a scene in which the one traumatized is not heard.

Children

It is probably not by chance that Ferenczi's swan song would focus on these issues and, more generally, the development and the fate of the child. This interest chased him his whole life—and beyond—by those who continued his work. The importance that Ferenczi and his successors, including Imre Hermann, Margaret Mahler, and René Spitz, attributed to the primary mother–child relationship carries on in theories of attachment (Fonagy, 2001) and intersubjectivity.

Links to Science

A significant feature of the psychoanalytic tradition, namely research, overlaps with other scientific fields. Given that Freud hoped to construct a science, it is understandable that he used methodologies and knowledge of other related sciences, thus the paleo-anthropogy of *Totem and Taboo* (1912–1913, *SE* 13, pp. 1–161), the budding sexology of *Three Essays* (1905, SE 7, pp. 135–243), and the religious science of *Moses and Monotheism* (1939, SE, 23, pp. 7–137).

Ferenczi's attitude, open to the contributions of science, also bears evidence of the convergence of different fields of study. Today we can attempt to make similar advances by taking into account overlaps between neuroscience and psychoanalytic theory. Take, for example, the question of *trauma*: the necessity of repeating the trauma, accompanied by an internal work was one of Ferenczi's ideas later taken up by Balint. It involves not only a recall, but also repetition in the psychoanalytic relationship.

The notion of reconsolidation is presently a focus of memory research in neuroscience. The mechanisms by which the recall of a memory makes its neural pathway temporarily mutable, and therefore subject to change and reassociation or, on the contrary, how recall strengthens the memory, are the processes currently studied in the context of posttraumatic stress disorder (PTSD). In neuroscientific terms, "these memories are not retrieved and therefore not reactivated, perhaps because of a blockade due to repression exerted on the retrieval process per se. Hence, they cannot undergo either reconsolidation or updating" (Alberini, Ansermet, and Magistretti 2013, p. 298). However, the authors elaborate how:

> During psychoanalysis, the subject undertakes the process of becoming aware (or conscious) of the underlying sources of his or her unconscious behavior, both intellectually and emotionally, by re-experiencing them and by redirecting the emotions toward the analyst and then reprocessing them in a new mode. Thus, remembering and elaborating past memories in the new analytic setting is a key component of the psychoanalytic process. (2013, p. 302)

A neurobiological basis of the transmission of emotional states is very similar to what psychoanalysis has grasped in imitation, introjection, identification mechanisms, all thanks to Ferenczi's clinical acumen! Perception of finalized gestures in someone else activates the same neurons—the famous *mirror neurons*—as those that would fire if the subject himself would accomplish the gestures (Rizzolati et al, 1996). Gallese writes correctly, "We share with our conspecifics a multiplicity of states that include actions, sensations and emotions. A new conceptual tool able to capture the richness of the experiences we share with others. ..." (Gallese 2003, p. 171). Is this not the sort of biological basis for which Freud and Ferenczi were searching?

Thus, feelings do not emerge from solipsistic isolation, but in a deep connection with one another. These unconscious, also neural responses, may even explain phenomena such as telepathy and projective identification.

Several years later, after Ferenczi's death in 1933, Freud recognized the importance of trauma and splitting (Freud, 1940), as in his work on Moses (Freud, 1939). In the works of the final years of his life, Ferenczi's influence became increasingly evident, including his reference to the problem of negative transference, its perception in the countertransference and in interpretation (Freud, 1937, SE 23, p. 221).

The legacy is there: undeniable, often hidden, not cited because of its controversial nature, even condemned. However, it is found largely in contemporary psychoanalysis—which *is his legacy.*

Perspective

Ferenczi's fundamental attitude, even before becoming an analyst, inspired him to look into people's *suffering*. In addition to his many clients, Ferenczi was also a traumatized person who had experienced considerable suffering. For him, addressing suffering was not only a sentimental attitude, but it went hand in hand with the campaign for intellectual understanding by a pioneer in the field of *attentive observation* and *introspection*.

The repetition of trauma in analysis and the regressive states that express it pervaded his attitude of devotion and self-sacrifice in the last ten to fifteen years of his life. This repetition/regression, Ferenczi believed, took place in the analytic situation, a co-creation of two protagonists, the product of a two-person work, and the fruit born of their exchanges. This research paved the way for the (post-) modern conception of psychoanalysis and its extensions into interpersonal, intersubjective analysis.

Instead of the expressions employed in our time like mantras, such as countertransference,[11] might we not instead consider notions denoting simple attitudes, such as *sincerity* with respect to oneself and others (as proposed by Ferenczi), and to remember that there are two people involved in treatment? Each of the two has a role to play, and thus the *functioning of both* is *analyzable*, as each party is hoping to be understood. Even Freud concurred, as evidenced by his remark in a letter to Fliess in which he stated, "I analyze myself while analyzing another" (Freud/Fliess, 11.14.1897).

Ferenczi and Rank worked toward a new vision of practice and theory, particularly developmental theory that their work inspired. Ferenczi's earnestness and *attitude* bore fruit in history. These views would not predominate before the end of the Second World War, when innovators (such as Balint, Paula Heiman, Winnicott, and later, Bion) in Great Britain, and little by little elsewhere, as in the United States, would adopt, rediscover, or reinvent them. Psychoanalysis is not a single flower, but a bouquet, generated by group interaction, which is sometimes difficult and contentious, but profits from the contributions of many talented individuals.

It is evident that Ferenczi preceded many innovative authors. A review of certain perspectives on the traditional psychoanalytic historiography is called for to show how many similar ideas emerged earlier and were often fought by the graying hierarchy of writers of psychoanalysis. Critiques such as the allegations and accusations of Jones may have slowed the recognition of the validity of some new ventures that, nevertheless, have reappeared as modern "new perspectives."

Psychoanalysis was dreamed up by a genius and further elaborated by a group of exceptional people. It remains an open question as to how differently and in what direction this practice, method, and theory would have developed if Ferenczi, Freud's most stimulating "correspondent" after 1913, and Otto Rank, his closest collaborator and neighbor in Vienna, had a greater influence on the co-creation of psychoanalysis after the foundational years. This question, which permeates this chapter, may stimulate our thinking today about new perspectives and alternatives for further development.

Translated by Sarah K. Wang
Special thanks to Ernst Falzeder, Ph.D., for his help in establishing the definitive text.

Texts published December 1923 to March 1924

Ferenczi, S.: *Thalassa: An Attempt for a Genital Theory*

Rank, O.: *The Trauma of Birth*

Ferenczi, S., and O. Rank: *Goals for the Development of Psychoanalysis* (Goals)[12]

Freud, S.: *The Dissolution of the Oedipus Complex*[13]

Notes

1　At the time of the "Palermo Incident," ideas about the renewal of the individual and the development of the person were already considered by Ferenczi to be the result of an interaction without restrictions.
2　Literally translated a "terrible child," the phrase often implies someone who is rather turbulent, rebellious, and unorthodox.
3　*Thalassa* is the title in the first English translation. The original title is: *Der Versuch einer Genitaltheorie* [An Attempt of a Theory of Genitality].
4　The German term appears in the letter cited.
5　At the International Psychoanalytic Congress in Berlin (September 1922), Freud proposed an award: for the contributions of the technique of psychoanalysis to the theory and the theory to the technique [*Es soll untersucht werden, inwiefern die Technik die Theorie beeinflusst hat und inwieweit die beiden einander gegenwärtig fördern oder behindern* (Freud 1922, p. 712)].
6　My translation of the original text; italics preserved from the original text.
7　"Heretic: a person holding an opinion at odds with what is generally accepted" (Oxford Dictionary). The little devil of parapraxis.
8　In any case, in the formulation of Freud, it was a *valuable finding*.
9　The German translator (or publisher) thought it best to change the title to "*Ohne Sympathie, keine Heilung*" [Without Sympathy, No Cure], a phrase taken directly from the text.
10　My translation from the original German.
11　A joke: Two analysts meet. One asks, "What are you doing?" The other says, "I am looking after my countertransference."
12　The title used here is a literal translation of the original publication, not taking into account later modifications introduced by the publisher.
13　Importance of this complex as a central phenomenon.
14　The figures in square brackets, here and throughout this paper in the references to Ferenczi's publications, refer to Balint's chronological numericization of Ferenczi's works as proposed in S. Ferenczi, *Schriften zur Psychoanalyse* (2 vols., Frankfurt/Main: Fischer, 1970–1972).

References

Alberini, C. M., Ansermet, F., & Magistretti, P. (2013). Memory Reconsolidation, Trace Reassociation and the Freudian Unconscious. In C. Albarini (Ed.), *Memory reconsolidation*. London: Academic Press, pp. 293–309.

Aron, L. and Harris, A. (eds) (1993). *The Legacy of Sándor Ferenczi.* London: The Analytic Press.

Balint, M. (1969). *Draft Introduction to "The Clinical Diary of Sándor Ferenczi."* Cambridge, MA: Harvard University Press, pp. 219–220.

Brabant, E., Falzeder, E., and Giampieri-Deutsch, P. (eds) (1993). *The Correspondence of Sigmund Freud and Sándor Ferenczi.* Vol. 1, 1908–1914. Cambridge, MA: Harvard University Press.

Falzeder, E. and Brabant, E. (eds) (1996). *The Correspondence of Sigmund Freud and Sándor Ferenczi.* Vol. 2, 1914–1919. Cambridge, MA: Harvard University Press.

Falzeder, E. and Brabant, E. (eds) (2000). *The Correspondence of Sigmund Freud and Sándor Ferenczi.* Vol. 3, 1920–1933. Cambridge, MA: Harvard University Press.

Brennan, W. B. (2011). *Decoding Ferenczi's Clinical Diary: Biographical Notes on Identities Concealed and Revealed.* Private manuscript. Conference at the New School of Social Sciences, NYC.

Ferenczi, S. (1909 [67][14]). Introjection and transference. In Ferenczi, S. 1952, *First Contributions,* pp. 35–93.

Ferenczi, S. (1911 [79]). On the Organization of the Psycho-analytic Movement. In: *Final Contributions of Psycho-Analysis.* pp. 299–307.

Ferenczi, S. (1913). Stages in the development of the sense of reality. In *First Contributions to Psycho-Analysis.* London: Hogarth Press, 1955, pp. 213–239. (Reprinted London: Marresfield Library, 1980).

Ferenczi, S. (1924). *Thalassa. A theory of genitality.* New York: The Psychoanalytic Quarterly, 1938. (orig.: *Versucheiner Genitaltheorie* [Attempt of a Genital Theory]).

Ferenczi, S. (1949). Confusion of the tongues between the adults and the child (The language of tenderness and of passion). *International Journal of Psychoanalysis,* 30:225–230.

Ferenczi, S. (1985). *The Clinical Diary of Sándor Ferenczi.* Cambridge, MA: Harvard University Press. (Original work published 1932).

Ferenczi, S. and Jones, E. (2013 [1911–1933]). *Correspondence.* London: Karnac.

Ferenczi, S. and Rank, O. (1924a). *The Development of Psycho-Analysis.* New York and Washington: Nervous and Mental Diseases Publishing Co.

Ferenczi, S. and Rank, O. (1924b). *Entwicklungsziele der Psychoanalyse. Zur Wechselbeziehung von Theorie und Praxis.* Vienna: Internationaler Psychoanalytischer Verlag.

Fonagy, P. (2001). *Attachment Theory and Psychoanalysis.* London: Karnac.

Freud, A. (1936). *The Ego and the Mechanisms of Defence.* London: Hogarth Press.

Freud, S. (1905). Three essays on the theory of sexuality. *SE* 7:123–243.

Freud, S. (1912–1913). Totem and taboo. *SE* 13:1–161.

Freud, S. (1922). Preisausschreibung. *Gesammelte Werke,* Nachtragsband, 1987.

Freud, S. (1923). The ego and the id. *SE* 19.

Freud, S. (1924). The dissolution of the Oedipus complex. *SE* 19:173.

Freud, S. (1927). The future of an illusion. *SE* 21:1–56.

Freud, S. (1930a [1929]). Civilization and its discontents. *SE* 21:57–145.

Freud, S. (1933a [1932]). In F. B. Davis, Three letters from Sigmund Freud to André Breton. *Journal of American Psychoanalytic Association,* 21:127–134, 1973.

Freud, S. (1933b). Sándor Ferenczi. *SE* 22: 225–229.

Freud, S. (1933c). New introductory lectures on psycho-analysis. *SE* 22:1–182.

Freud, S. (1937). Analysis terminable and interminable. *SE* 23: 209–254.

Freud, S. (1939). Moses and monotheism. *SE* 23:1–137.

Freud, S. (1940). Splitting of the ego in the process of defence. *SE* 23:275–278.

Freud, S. and Abraham, K. (1965a). *A Psycho-Analytic Dialogue. The Letters of Sigmund Freud and Karl Abraham, 1907–1927.* H. Abraham and E. Freud (eds). New York: Basic Books.

Freud, S. and Eitingon, M. (2004). *Briefwechsel 1906–1939 [Freud-Eitingon correspondence, 1906–1939], Vol. 1 and 2.* M. Schröter (ed). Tübingen: edition diskord.

Freud, S. and Fliess, W. (1985 [1887–1904]). *The Complete Letters of Sigmund Freud to Wilhelm Fliess, 1887–1904.* J. M. Masson (ed). Cambridge, MA: Harvard University Press.

Freud, S. and Pfister, O. (1963). *Psychoanalysis and Faith: The Letters of Sigmund Freud and Oskar Pfister.* E. Freud and H. Meng (eds). New York: Basic Books.

Gallese, V. (2003). The roots of empathy: The shared manifold hypothesis and the neural basis of intersubjectivity. *Psychopathology,* 36:171–180.

Gitelson, M. (1962). The curative factors in psycho-analysis. *International Journal of Psycho-analysis,* 43:194–205.

Jeannet-Hasler, M. (2002). *Thérapie contre théorie? Les enjeux d'un concours.* Paris: PUF.

Jones, E. (1957). *The Life and Work of Sigmund Freud,* Vol. 3. New York: Basic Books; London: Hogarth Press.

Kandel, E. (2012). *The Age of Insight.* New York: Random House.

Kramer, R. (1996). *A Psychology of Difference.* Princeton, NJ: Princeton University Press.

Kramer, R. and Lieberman, E. J. (2012). *The letters of Sigmund Freud and Otto Rank.* Baltimore: The Johns Hopkins University Press.

Leitner, M. (1998). *Freud, Rank und die Folgen. Ein Schlüsselkonflikt für die Psychoanalyse.* Wien: Turia+Kant.

Lieberman, E. J. (1985). *Acts of Will.* New York: Free Press.

Newton, C. (1925): Translator's Preface. In: *The Development of Psycho-Analysis* [by S. Ferenczi and O. Rank]. *Nervous & Mental Disease Monograph Series No. 40.*

Paskauskas, A. R. (1993). *The Complete Correspondence of Sigmund Freud and Ernest Jones, 1908–1939.* Cambridge, MA: The Belknap Press of Harvard University Press.

Polanyi, M. (1958). *Personal Knowledge. Towards a Post-Critical Philosophy.* London: Routledge.

Rank, O. (1924). *The Trauma of Birth.* New York: Dover, 1994.

Rizzolati, G., Fadiga, L., Gallese, V., and Fogassi, L. (1996). Premotor cortex and the recognition of motor actions. *Brain Res Cogn Brain Res,* 3:131–141.

Rudnytsky, P. L. (2011). *Rescuing Psychoanalysis from Freud.* London: Karnac.

Saussure, R. de (1956). Sigmund Freud. In H. M. Ruitenbeck (Ed.), *Freud as We Knew Him.* Detroit, MI: Wayne State University Press p. 357.

Wittenberger, G. and Tögel, C. (eds) (1999–2006). *Die Rundbriefe des "Geheimen Komitees"* [The Circular Letters of the "Secret Committee"], Vol. 1–4, [1913–1927]. Tübingen: diskord.

PART II
History

4

OUT OF THE ARCHIVE/UNTO THE COUCH

Clara Thompson's Analysis with Ferenczi

B. William Brennan

"When you are in the middle of a story it isn't a story at all, but only a confusion; a dark roaring, a blindness, a wreckage of shattered glass and splintered wood; like a house in a whirlwind, or else a boat crushed by the icebergs or swept over the rapids, and all aboard powerless to stop it. It's only afterwards that it becomes anything like a story at all. When you are telling it, to yourself or to someone else."

(Margaret Atwood, *Alias Grace)*

"It needs, of course, to be stressed, that they can only ever be accounts and readings; no one, not even the participants themselves, knew in any exact or exacting sense what Really Happened."

(Adam Phillips, 2011)

Introduction: Inside Ferenczi's Consulting Room

As one of the early pioneering women in American psychoanalysis, Clara Thompson staked out the terrain of the interpersonal school of psychoanalysis. A founding mother of the Washington-Baltimore Psychoanalytic Society and the William Alanson White Institute, Thompson was also a close friend of Harry Stack Sullivan and Erich Fromm. Although her family descended from New England puritan stock, Thompson was not without contradictions or controversy. To her family she was Mabel, to everyone else she was Clara (except for those college years when she signed her name Maggie after George Eliot's protagonist in *The Mill on the Floss*). At the age of 15, Thompson fantasized about being a missionary, but in her 1916 college yearbook she noted her future plans were to "murder people in the most refined way possible" (perhaps a fantasy of one day failing as a physician).

Rebelling against being the "good girl," she eschewed authoritarian orthodoxy, at times self-sabotaging her own progress. Thompson's promising career as a young psychiatrist at the Phipps Clinic, and protégé of Adolf Meyer, ended abruptly, shrouded in salacious rumors. Despite her cool detachment, her pupils remarked on her warmth, and her summer house at 599 Commercial Street, in Provincetown, was often the hub of parties and social gatherings.

Previously, Shapiro's (1993) examination of Thompson as the emissary of Ferenczi's ideas found her coming up short, as only "half a messenger," as Thompson did little to develop or carry forward Ferenczi's ideas of trauma and childhood sexual abuse, which were central to his later writings.[1] The annals of psychoanalytic history are most likely to remember Thompson as the patient who boasted that she could kiss Papa Ferenczi whenever she liked. The incident forever tarnished Ferenczi's reputation and intensified the growing tension with Freud. Although this incident is often examined in terms of Thompson's intrapersonal dynamics, or as an example of Ferenczi's failed experiments in technique, the triangular enactment in which Freud is also a key player is often overlooked. In this chapter, as her interview with Eissler is explored in greater detail, we shall see that the geometry of Thompson's analysis and the personal equation of her relationships is one of intersecting and overlapping triangles in which Thompson became entangled quite consistently and ambiguously.

Ferenczi's *The Clinical Diary* (1988) offers a unique glimpse into his consulting room with candid reports of his work with patients in 1932. Clara Thompson appears prominently in the diary as Dm.[2] This chapter will examine Thompson's (1952) account of her analysis as revealed in an interview she gave to Kurt Eissler, for the Freud archives. For many years, this interview, along with many others, languished in the Freud archive, sequestered in the vaults of the Library of Congress, and has only recently been made available. Eissler's interviews, while focused on anyone who met or knew Freud, also contain first person accounts of the early days of psychoanalysis—voices from the other side of the couch.[3] Of all the interviews Eissler conducted, his interview with Thompson contains the most information on Ferenczi, offering another portal into his life and work with patients.

An archive, while serving as a repository for collective memory, is also haunted by ghosts from the past—holding the intergenerational transmission of trauma—the cover-ups, the secrets, the backstories, the unofficial history which through the decades have been repressed, dissociated, or disavowed. Scattered among the relics and the ephemera, one finds records of the personal, the asides, the "off the record," the marginalia. Moreover, an interview, like an analytic hour, can reveal the unconscious at work, as material emerges, is moved away from and is defended against; affective constellations coalesce and dissociations rupture narrative lines. Similar to the analytic hour, process is as important as content. The interviewer's question has the power to evoke the spectre of transference, summoned from the spirit underworld, which continues to haunt memory, recollection, and desire. The reports from the couch cannot escape the ubiquity of transference, embedded in a field where the unconscious is *always* at work, weaving the Penelopian fabric of psychic reality. For Loewald, it was the analysis of the transference which transformed these ghosts into ancestors. As many interviews continue to be haunted by unresolved transferences, perhaps it is the work of the psychoanalytic historian that finally helps to lay them to rest. In regard to Ferenczi, his legacy has been ghosted by transgressive stories of kissing patients and mutual analysis, and lacking precise details, these stories have assumed mythic proportions. Thompson's interview helps to tie up some historical loose ends, laying some spectral speculations to rest, but at best it is only a partial account.

The Interview—On and Off the Record

Although "dead men tell no tales," sometimes if they are interviewed before their passing, they do have stories to tell. The Thompson interview was conducted on June 4, 1952, when Clara Thompson was 58 years old. The date of the interview is important because it is five years before Thompson wrote her account of Ferenczi's last days for Fromm.[4] The details here can be compared with the account Thompson gave Fromm, which had the intention of clearing Ferenczi's name from Jones's accusations that Ferenczi was psychotic during his final years. In this interview, Thompson wasn't under any particular pressure to defend Ferenczi, making her narration of events more forthright and candid.

It would appear that Thompson was much more privy to intimacies about Ferenczi's life than Severn (1952). Thompson related that Ferenczi was quite open with her about the sexual escapades of his youth, congruent with his own disclosures in the diary. Although Thompson envied other analysands who she felt were closer to Ferenczi, and despite Severn's mutual analysis, Ferenczi was more open in sharing his experiences with Thompson and they may have been closer than she felt. She was one of the three people he sent for when he was dying.

Transference and the Transcript

On a personal level, Thompson's interview reveals particular themes that recur within *The Clinical Diary* and can be compared with the case of Dm in that same text: guilt over getting Ferenczi in trouble with Freud, shame and its connection to Thompson's socioeconomic and class background, and her rivalry and envy of other patients. There are also expressed contradictions around what Thompson felt she was able to take away from the analysis. The main transferential paradigm that emerges from the beginning of the interview is the triangle of Thompson, Ferenczi, and Freud, and it is here that Thompson's transference to the parental couple coalesced. Thompson tells Eissler that when she first went to Budapest in 1928 she wanted to visit Freud, either on the way there or returning, but Ferenczi discouraged her—the reasons he gave were Freud's cancer of the jaw and that he did not want visits from women. However, Thompson knew women who had visited Freud and her fantasy was that Ferenczi disapproved of the visit because he was not on friendly terms with Freud. Ferenczi's relationship to Freud had its own unresolved transferences, as Freud took on the mantle of Ferenczi's mother complex,[5] and so multiple internal dramas converged and were being enacted at once during this period of time, in what could be seen as a "mutual enactment."[6]

The Analysis

Thompson first met Ferenczi in 1926 when he was lecturing in the United States and was immediately drawn to his warmth and egalitarianism. Thompson heard Ferenczi lecture once,[7] talked to him of her analysis,[8] and knew immediately that she wanted to work with him:

> he was the first analyst I had ever seen I thought I could talk to. I don't think I could have been analyzed any more in a more authoritarian way at that time anyway. One can stand anything now, I guess. I would find it very difficult. I also have a very great need of love, which I think I couldn't have stood the deprivation in orthodox analysis.[9] (p. 10)

Unfortunately for Thompson, Ferenczi's hours in New York were already filled. He suggested coming to Budapest but Thompson lacked the financial resources. Unlike many of Ferenczi's other patients, Thompson came from a working class family; her father worked for Blanding and Blanding, a drug store in downtown Providence, Rhode Island. Education had offered Thompson the opportunity to transcend her humble origins; she attended Brown University's Pembroke College for women and John Hopkins Medical School (Green, 1964). Thompson had interned at the Phipps Clinic, and in 1922 embarked on her three-year psychiatry residency there. Thompson was a rising star during her years at the clinic, and Adolf Meyer took a particular interest in her. However, in 1925, Thompson resigned from Phipps. This incident will be explored in more detail later in the chapter. Thompson subsequently struggled to establish herself as an analyst in Baltimore.

Unable to begin treatment in New York, Ferenczi asked Thompson how long it would take to save the money, and Thompson guessed about two years. Thompson then reportedly forgot all about it. Two years later, in February, Thompson describes "a bell going off in her head," and she cabled Ferenczi about beginning treatment. Thompson was having difficulty with a patient and didn't know where to turn for help, and she had managed to save $1000, enough to spend two months with

Ferenczi during the summer. Financial constraints caused Thompson to be analyzed in "chunks" at the beginning; for two months in 1928, and again for two months in 1929, and three months in 1930, although this beginning could also be trans-ferentially thought of as an attachment difficulty, titrating closeness and intimacy. Finally in 1931, Thompson was able to move to Budapest for two years, taking eight patients with her in order to sustain her livelihood.[10] She continued to struggle financially; it was the height of the Great Depression, and not all of her patients were able to pay.[11] The diary (June 20, 1932) describes a first encounter different from Thompson's recollection of meeting Ferenczi at his lecture. According to the diary, Ferenczi was at a dance, and a provocative Thompson acted "improperly"— when not immediately accepted as a patient, she went and lost her virginity. If we are to accept Ferenczi's account, this enactment suggests Thompson testing bound-aries, acting seductively, and in response to rejection, resorting to a compensatory sexual acting out. Thompson struggled against a repressive puritan upbringing, and perhaps the "forward edge" of this transference response was her attempt to inte-grate an embodied sexual aliveness.[12]

The analysis was conducted in English. Ferenczi spoke English "adequately but not well," he "had a very large vocabulary," "difficulty with grammar," and "a very bad Hungarian accent," but "you could always manage to find out what he was talking about" (p. 5). Thompson learned a little Hungarian, enough to talk to taxi drivers and negotiate a menu. She recalled about 35 Americans in Budapest during that time, most of whom knew each other.

On Ferenczi's Technique

According to Thompson, Ferenczi had never really believed in the deprivation tech-nique (active therapy)[13] and "he thought that some devil in him had forced him to carry it to such extremes that it would prove it was absurd" (p. 6).[14] Thompson felt his shift to "relaxation therapy"[15] was largely due to Elizabeth Severn. In the interview, Severn's name is misspelled as "La Verne."[16] Thompson thought Severn's demands for additional hours caused Ferenczi to rethink the issue of gratifying patients' needs. At the beginning of the interview, Thompson hints that Ferenczi's relaxation technique was considered "dangerous" by Freud:

> At that time, of course, he was very much in the grips of his theory of the relaxation technique, which Freud felt was very dangerous. He told me that, that Freud felt it was very dangerous, and that he thought it was very danger-ous to give patients love, that it was very dangerous to encourage them to relive so actively as Ferenczi did. (p. 2)

In the interview, when Thompson first talks of her analysis, she is very positive about the experience and the results. For Thompson, the analysis was life changing.

She reports it "changed my personality quite definitely" and it was "almost 100% positive" (p. 11). Thompson states:

> I always think of Budapest as my, as reliving, as really growing up in a happy childhood—which was his [Ferenczi's] fantasy about his method. But I really experienced it as that. Even to the fact that I didn't know what people were talking about around me—just like a child, it was, to live there in a country that was so foreign. ... I think of it as a time in which I came to—I was a very detached person before that, very schizoid, and I came to have relationships with people for the first time. In a comfortable social way. I still have difficulties with intimacy, although not too much.[17] (p. 11)

The transcript of the interview then records a moment of silence. Silences are seldom noted in Eissler's transcripts of interviews, suggesting a deliberate punctuation of the moment. Thompson's next association is to how Freud figured prominently in her analysis as the "bad mother"—given the sequence of associations, Thompson's "bad mother" is probably the reason for her schizoid withdrawal. Thompson discloses she became very partisan in the conflict.[18] The difference between Freud's and Ferenczi's technique and the evolving tension between the two men was perfect for Thompson to relive her family dynamics:

> Well, I had a great difficulty with a rigid mother, who was very religious and very—she was really a very frightened person but she covered it up with this controlling rigidity: "You must do this and you mustn't do that." And there was something in Freud's thinking that fit into this, which I immediately fastened on to. Especially so much of Ferenczi's attitude was like my father's in that, "Oh, that you must understand him" in the early part of my analysis to try to see him in this setting than to be hostile to him, so that we worked out the drama very well, except that it wasn't my family. Then Mrs. LaVerne [Severn] became a much better bad mother than Freud. (p. 20)

One wonders whether Thompson fully worked through these transference constellations in her analysis with Ferenczi, and later with Fromm, as Thompson continued to feel that Ferenczi was "afraid" of Freud. Perhaps her projection of familial dynamics and her investment in Ferenczi's emancipation replicated Thompson's own internal struggle to free herself from internal bad objects. Moreover, the parental couple transference had also been staged earlier, in Thompson's first analysis with Joseph "Snake" Chessman Thompson. When Clara Thompson was at the Phipps Clinic, under the tutelage of Adolf Meyer, a growing rift occurred when she went into analysis with Joseph Thompson (Edmunds, 2012). Clara Thompson had been very close to Meyer, he supported her interest in psychotic patients, she confided in him, and, in 1923, he nursed her through an episode of typhoid fever when she also had been suicidal.[19] The rift with Meyer was enacted on both a personal and a theoretical level. A split developed between Clara's work at Phipps and her analytic private practice. Meyer accused Clara of filtering patients to Joseph Thompson, who Meyer vehemently disdained. On October 23, 1925, Thompson resigned from the Phipps Clinic. Four years later, Thompson reached out to Meyer in an attempt at reconciliation, and on December 7, 1929, she wrote that she felt the difficulty stemmed from her choosing psychoanalysis, as both a theory and practice, which Meyer was against, and his disapproval of her choice of analyst. She should have left the clinic earlier but:

> if it had not been for my attachment to you (transference), growing out of the fact that I had told my problems to you previously and, as in your method of treatment the transference is not analyzed, my attachment had continued to exist for several years. I was therefore confronted by two attachments, and two individuals not friendly to each other and I did not manage that situation very well.
>
> *(Adolf Meyer Collection, I/3805)*

Again we see the reliving of triangles, Thompson experiencing rejection and alienation, and Meyer unable to understand the enactment. Thompson then addresses a piece of gossip that she thinks Meyer is responsible for, which uncannily foreshadows the gossip about Thompson and Ferenczi's "kissing technique"/eroticized acting out:

> It was reported to me thus—that you said that you had asked me to resign because I was my analyst's mistress. I am not holding you accountable for a rumor. Of course, I suppose something was said by some member of your staff which formed the basis for it. But when I heard it I realized that it was a natural inference to have drawn from some of my behavior and that you probably believed it. A more sophisticated woman and one less secure in her innocence would have been more discreet. It happens that I have never been his mistress at any time. I do not know whether you believe that and I do not know that it matters anyway, but since I am telling you facts tonight that is one of them.
>
> *(Adolf Meyer Collection, I/3805)*

It is striking that although Thompson was aware of this scandalmongering in 1929, she herself would perpetuate a similar enactment with Ferenczi. Moreover, just as Meyer had failed to understand the transference, Freud too hadn't considered how he was also being caught up in an enactment and viewed the incident solely from the perspective of Ferenczi's and his patient's dynamics.

Kiss and Tell

The incident between Thompson and Ferenczi has practically become reified as Ferenczi's "kissing technique." It was clearly a mutual enactment, and one in which Thompson replicated the dynamics of childhood boundary crossings and in particular, her own confusion between childhood tenderness and adult passion. Ferenczi was enacting his own desire to be the loving mother he never had, since his own mother was unavailable and lacked warmth. Early in the interview, Thompson talks about her friend Edith Jackson who was a patient of Freud's, and through Jackson, Thompson would relay to Freud everything that was going on. This may in part have been out of Thompson's rivalry with Jackson around who was getting the better treatment, and it is documented that Jackson felt she was special to Freud (Lynn, 2003). The first enactment occurred when Thompson told Jackson about how Ferenczi would disclose when he was at fault. Jackson relayed this to Anna Freud who discussed it with her father, Thompson recalled that Freud thought this was dangerous, and Ferenczi then started receiving letters from Freud expressing concern about his technique.

Commenting on Ferenczi's technique in the interview, Thompson first confuses the analyst admitting to the patient when they are at fault, with the analyst telling the patient their personal flaws. Thompson then clarifies that this is not the same as letting the patient analyze the analyst, introducing the idea of mutual analysis, but rather a matter of the analyst's disclosure of countertransference feelings. For instance, if the patient felt the analyst was angry, it was better for the analyst to admit this to the patient, rather than hide it. Thompson even recalls to Eissler that Ferenczi translated for her parts of a letter from Freud, in which Freud expressed feeling that he was in his "second childhood," but it is only later in the interview that Thompson ventures to reveal more about this:[20]

> I unfortunately am in a way involved in the struggle with Freud because I was talking with Edith Jackson about his new technique, and she said, "You mean that you actually kiss Ferenczi?" And I said, "Sure, I kiss him any time I want to," And she of course at once went back and told this to Freud and Freud became very upset about this and wrote him quite a letter about it. I must say Ferenczi was very decent to me. He was very upset, naturally, and you see I had proceeded on the theory well if this is what we do, why don't we admit it? And he finally admitted that I was right, that if he was going to do such things, he should admit them and not try to hide it from Freud. (p. 4)

The diary records how this incident created a rupture in the treatment, and for a three-month period Thompson became more resistant, feeling that Ferenczi was more reserved, irritable, and contemptuous toward her (*The Clinical Diary*, March 13, 1932). Thompson thought Ferenczi should not take the matter personally and continue to look for the causes of the enactment. There is something about Thompson's matter-of-factness in reporting the incident, without a deeper reflection on the importance of this incidence which hints that it wasn't fully resolved, that it continued to haunt her all these years later. Ferenczi didn't believe there were "naughty children," and so was unlikely to have reprimanded Thompson, and thought that if those in authority were not hypocritical, and instead adopted a sincere approach, it facilitated the child coming forward with their own proposals for good behavior.

Thompson's lack of awareness of the "Confusion of Tongues" paper and its importance as the culmination of Ferenczi's œuvre presents another revealing moment in the interview. Shapiro (1993) astutely argued that Thompson dissociated her knowledge of the paper and its key ideas—in the interview we find further evidence of this hypothesis. Thompson relates that she didn't hear the paper because it was in German and didn't think it had been published. Thompson tells Eissler:

> What I think the theme of this is, as Ferenczi told me, was his favorite theme: that there are no bad patients, there are only bad analysts, and tried to repeat the idea of the bad parent, making the neurotic child, and that the analyst can do the same sort of thing, can make the patient worse. Now, I don't know what else could have been in that paper but Freud was very disturbed about that paper, and that's the one he told him he must not publish, refused to let him publish, and I don't know whether it still exists or not. (p. 13)

This interview took place in 1952 and Eissler affirms that it had been published. In a letter to De Forest two years later (Brennan, 2009), Thompson again enquires about the paper, still unaware that it had been published. Thompson then looks it up and relates to De Forest that she expected "something more revolutionary."[21] In the interview, Thompson's recollection of the paper is interesting as she omits any mention of Ferenczi's ideas that sexual trauma played a role in the etiology of neurosis, and she presents an oversimplification of one aspect of Ferenczi's thought.[22] It's clear that Thompson had not read the paper, since she didn't hear it at Wiesbaden and is operating on the knowledge of her own assumptions. Moreover, the fact that when Thompson did read the paper she didn't comprehend how it was revolutionary for its time indicates that there is something about trauma that always eludes her.

Critique of the Analysis

Toward the end of the interview, Thompson becomes more critical of the analysis and states that she felt Ferenczi didn't address her hostility directly:

> He never actually had any conception of my character structure. Certainly he dealt plenty with my traumatic experiences and with my relationships to

people, but the ways in which my hostility was expressed I don't think he ever saw. The ways in which I manipulated people, I am sure he never saw. (pp. 23–24)

It is interesting that this material emerges after Thompson had been talking about her tattle-tailing. In the diary, Ferenczi describes Thompson's (Dm's) hostility numerous times, including Thompson's smell and lack of personal hygiene as an expression of her hostility. Perhaps it was more the case that Thompson didn't see that Ferenczi saw her hostility and that he was choosing to respond to it in a different way than she thought was indicated. With the harsh and strict discipline Thompson had received from her mother, Ferenczi was choosing to respond in a way where Thompson could find a way out of her vacillation between rage, anxiety, and exaggerated obedience (*The Clinical Diary*, June 3, 1932). Although Thompson had joked in her college yearbook that her future plans were to "murder people in the most refined way possible," there is evidence that Ferenczi did see her hostility, and that like himself,[23] her efforts to help people at the same time concealed darker motives. On December 31, 1931, in the wake of Freud's reprimanding letter, Ferenczi writes of Thompson "she intends to kill by roundabout ways and can only live with this fantasy. In the analysis she sees the analyst understands her—that she is not bad and must kill" (Notes and Fragments).

On Severn

For both Thompson and Ferenczi, Severn evoked a negative maternal transference. When writing to Fromm, Thompson stated that she felt Severn "bullied" Ferenczi.[24] When Thompson first came to Budapest, Ferenczi had suggested that maybe she could room with Severn, but after a conversation Thompson assessed Severn as high maintenance and difficult, with various house rules, and turned down the offer. Thompson felt that Ferenczi was surprised she had the courage to stand up to Severn. Although Thompson didn't know whether to believe it or not, Severn had told her that Ferenczi used to tie his tongue with a string every night to his bed so that he wouldn't swallow it; Thompson thought this sounded "too fantastic." However, on the subject of Severn, Thompson was not tongue tied, describing her as a "paranoid bitch" and revealing that she used to call Severn "Bird of Prey" because she looked like one.[25] While Thompson is aware that everything she says is being recorded, she wants to set the record straight:

This shouldn't be published, should it? But she was one of these very controlling, hypochondriacal women, extreme hypochondriacal (sic) types. You know the kind that would have to have emergency operations and nothing be solved (?) and so forth. And she could never get up. She spent most of her life in bed, where she ruled from her bed.[26] She had her daughter under her thumb, and so forth, and she presently had Ferenczi, and I think the last three, the last two years when I was there, there was quite a change in him, and I think he was quite under her influence and that it was she who demanded the endless hours. You know it started his idea that maybe a, one hour a day isn't enough; if the patient needs more, you should give it to him. And I think that much of this was his attempt to solve the problem of this woman. (p. 6)

Thompson was aware of the mutual analysis Ferenczi was engaged in with Severn, but did not identify herself as being involved in any mutual analysis. Thompson knew some details of the mutual analysis:

I have no idea what went on between those two, but I think he analyzed her one hour and she analyzed him the next—something like that. I think that— I think that he was completely afraid of her. For some reason it was—his wife felt that she bled him to death; his wife said this. (p. 15)

In the Eissler interview, Thompson portrays a very dramatic ending to Severn's analysis. It is difficult to know how much is hearsay, and how much of it is true, but Severn in her interview did experience the ending of the analysis as very difficult:

She left Ferenczi about three months before he died. He finally got the strength to dismiss her, the day he did, he went into a kind of elation. Her parting words to him were that he would die, that she would see that he died, and that he would be a little man and completely forgotten by the world. This was her parting curse. (p. 7)

Severn makes no mention of this in her interview, but it would replicate how Severn's own abusive father put a curse on her as his parting gesture. From the interview, it is also clear that Thompson had little empathy for Severn and is somewhat dismissive of her trauma and memories of abuse:

Yes, he did tell me quite a bit about her. It's uncanny. I had an uncanny experience in that I've had three analysts and they've all been involved with women who had a great deal of hypochondriasis. I had an analyst before Ferenczi, a totally unknown American—a man named Joe Thompson. He's dead now. He married a patient who also had the same kind of weird childhood memories. Mrs. La Verne [Severn] and this other woman also reconstructed the most sadistic sexual accomplishments having been perpetrated on them as children. Now they were almost identical, those stories, so that this must be something that goes on in that type of person. (p. 21)

Thompson had a lot of experience working with very sick patients, including many psychotics, so her reaction to the depth of Severn's suffering is striking, and the tone sounds like one of skepticism.

On Ferenczi's Illness

In the interview, Thompson is more critical of Ferenczi during the time he was ill and exhibiting symptoms of pernicious anemia than she was prior to this period. Thompson states:

> He apparently felt very strongly the need of more analysis all his life, and I think that towards the end that he did really use his patients in order to try to solve his own problems. I mean that he would do more than just say, "Yes, I felt this way." He would tell—I know towards the, his last illness he told me a great deal about his early life and about his unhappiness, about his sexual escapades and things like that. I think by that time he was already mentally quite disturbed. That was in the last winter, 1932, or 33, 1932 or 33 (sic). (p. 3)

Thompson recalls that he had a red count of about a million and a half when he fell at the railway station (in Biarritz) and notes:

> his mind was definitely affected, I can tell you that. He had combined sclerosis symptoms, I mean he staggered and he was not sure of his walking. Now, Ferenczi always had a great awkwardness of his hands. ... So that how much of that was sort of constitutional, I don't know, but he certainly got to the point where he was not sure of his walking. (p. 3)

Thompson realized that Ferenczi was "mentally disturbed" the morning he uncharacteristically showed up to her hour thirty minutes late. Although Thompson thought Ferenczi was "disturbed," she does not state that he was delusional or paranoid. Gizella, his wife, had also told Thompson that during his last illness he was often reading the newspaper upside down. Compared to the account that Thompson gave Fromm, many of the same details are included but as much as one can infer tone from a text, the tone in the interview with Eissler is more critical.

Termination—Never Can Say Goodbye

In the interview, Thompson recalls her last analytic hour, which depicts a very poignant scene between Ferenczi and Thompson:

> He suddenly took me into the next room and played a Victrola record of—I don't remember what it was, but it was about somebody longing for love—and

he wept over this record. And, this, he just played it as something which—well, it was something I was talking about. He was completely in it, too. (p. 8)

In her account to Fromm, Thompson (November 5, 1957) mentions this incident but states that they were not doing psychoanalysis at the time, although here she clearly views the Victrola incident as a response to her material and feels that Ferenczi was affectively engaged in the moment. The interview poses the question as to whether Ferenczi's illness complicated the termination process. During 1932 in numerous letters to De Forest, Thompson is thinking about terminating, but is aware that she fooled herself into thinking the analysis was ending twice before. On June 19, 1932, Thompson wrote "I'm determined to hang on to the end here this time." Ferenczi had stopped working with patients at the beginning of May 1933, Severn had left in February, and Lowell in March. Thompson lingered. She tells Eissler "I don't think we quite faced the fact that he was dying. I don't know why we didn't, except I don't seem to face that fact about people" (p. 8). Note the confusion in Thompson's statement between "I" and "we." Even the last time they saw each other Ferenczi is saying goodbye, and Thompson is insisting that she will see him again. In Thompson's account to Fromm, she is clearer that she had difficulty accepting that Ferenczi was dying. Undoubtedly, Ferenczi's illness hastened the termination process. Thompson's belief that Ferenczi did not see her hostility may be an indicator that she had not worked through her hostility adequately enough in the analysis and his failing health undoubtedly complicated her ability to do so. I would posit that Thompson hadn't fully worked through her childhood trauma differentiating between innocence and culpability and continued to feel guilty about mistaking her identification with the aggressor for her own hostility.[27]

On Shame

When Eissler enquires about Thompson's thoughts on Ferenczi's need for love, her associations go in the direction of her own need for love and the shame she felt over her socioeconomic background. Thompson doesn't directly answer his question until later in the interview, but here she states:

> And I think he was rather ashamed of me. Now this may be a patient's projection, but I was a person whom he almost never invited to his house. Although his wife told me after he died that he had often told her I would be his best pupil, that he felt I would be his best pupil. Now, I, well I believe he must have said that, but somehow he was not—I didn't have enough polish to, to make him comfortable. (p. 9)

Thompson felt Ferenczi was also ashamed of another patient, Teddy Miller, a Lower East Side Polish Jew, and was impressed by Alice Lowell[28] with her cultured

"American aristocratic background." Thompson doesn't disclose her romantic involvement with Miller, which formed another triangle, and her closeness to Miller may have contributed to her feelings of shame. In the diary, Miller (patient U) is a philanderer, and Ferenczi is aware of the patient's criminality.

There may be some truth to Thompson's observation that Ferenczi didn't find her polished enough. In the diary, Ferenczi describes how he had to work through his own feelings of disgust when in response to initially not taking her on as a patient she went out and lost her virginity. He also struggled with the fact that she was odiferous, at times found her appearance and gestures detestable, and often found her crude, although he felt her smell was connected to her mother's puritanical repudiation of her daughter's body. The diary also records how Alice Lowell harbored antipathy towards Thompson for her "lack of education," "her New England narrow-mindedness," and the lack of "artistic élan" (*The Clinical Diary*, April 24, 1932). Thompson's shame may also be linked to her own lack of financial means and her initial struggle to enter into analysis with Ferenczi. She states "I had no money except what I earned. I had no background of money at all" (p. 10).

An Odd Conclusion

The interview ends on a bittersweet note and one which raises more questions about what Thompson gained from her experience with Ferenczi. Although Thompson related how helpful the analysis had been, including reliving a positive childhood, and making her less schizoid, her "concluding arguments" in the interview were that the neurotic character structure was a closed system. Thompson believed that despite being offered analytic love, neurotic defenses made it impossible to take the love in, and this was an inherent problem of character structure. Consequently, the question arises, had the analysis prematurely terminated before Thompson could fully metabolize its effects? Thompson finally addresses Ferenczi's need to be loved, and answers:

> Well I don't think he saw his own need of love as a neurosis. I think that's where he missed out. I think that's where his whole relaxation therapy missed out, in that he really thought that you could give an adult the love he never had, which you can't because it's shut off. ... and no matter how much you feed them, it's just like diabetes; the sugar isn't digested. (p. 24)

A contemporary relational approach would not frame "the need for love" as a neurosis, and if it is a neurosis then it is one we all suffer from and is part of the human condition (hence Ferenczi's argument in his paper (1929) *The Unwelcome Child and His Death-Instinct*). Interestingly, Ferenczi had written a paper about love in 1901, before he encountered Freud and psychoanalysis, and so love was a preoccupation of his from the beginning to the end of his career. Ferenczi wisely stated "Love itself functions as a kind of 'borderland' between health and sickness for the human soul" (1901, 14). Despite psychoanalysis being a "cure by love," Freud, in the wake of his break with Fleiss, had turned his homosexual libido towards his own narcissistic ends and could not offer Ferenczi the love he longed for in their relationship.[29]

Thompson's view of the psyche as a closed system also indicates that she had failed to introject Ferenczi as a new object. While Thompson believed that the analyst's love couldn't be metabolized, De Forest (1954) took a diametrically opposite position in describing the effects of Ferenczi's treatment as "the leaven of love," where the effects of the analysis continued working years afterwards. Thompson's interview sheds light on the intersecting triangles in which her analysis became entwined, which could easily be construed as traditional Oedipal dynamics. However, Ferenczi was sensitive to the fact that Thompson was "longing for a triangle without envy or jealousy" *(The Clinical Diary*, June 20, 1932), where she could enjoy the love of both parents and even have her rejecting mother accept her tomboy-love and love for her father (*The Clinical Diary*, June 14, 1932). Perhaps there was something about the relational failure between Freud and Ferenczi that ultimately reinforced her family romance/drama rather than resolved it, and this split continued to haunt Thompson. Balint would go so far to say that it was a trauma that affected the whole world of psychoanalysis (Balint, 1968).

In Thompson's early paper *Evaluation of Ferenczi's Relaxation Therapy* (1933), it is clear that Thompson is wrestling with the problem of how to separate childlike tenderness and adult passion in the regressed adult patient, as the analyst may think he is dealing with childlike tenderness when it is a cover for adult passion and a manipulation to potentially destroy the analysis or the analyst. In the context of a child and an adult, these two affective tributaries, tenderness and passion, can be more easily discerned, but perhaps between adults, or between the regressed patient and the analyst, these threads are not so easily teased apart.[30] Like many cases within psychoanalysis, Thompson's story will undoubtedly be discussed and debated for years to come, and in loosening her tongue and gossiping to Jackson, and in her interview with Eissler, she has left us with an important part of our ancestral history.

Notes

1 For an alternative reading of Thompson's trauma, see Leys (2000).
2 For a detailed account of the identities of the patients in *The Clinical Diary*, see Brennan, 2015 (in press), Decoding Ferenczi's Clinical Diary: Biographical Notes. *American Journal of Psychoanalysis.*
3 Thanks to Harold P. Blum, M.D., executive director of the Sigmund Freud Archive, for granting me access to previously restricted material, to Emanuel Garcia, executor of Kurt Eissler's estate; to Rainer Funk, executor of the Erich Fromm Archive; to Henry Taves, executor of the De Forest-Taves Family Papers; to the William Alanson White Institute for access to the Clara Thompson Papers; to the Alan Mason Chesney Medical Archives of The Johns Hopkins Medical Institutions for access to the Adolf Meyer

Papers; to John Balint, M.D., executor of Michael Balint's estate; and to the Special
Collections, Albert Sloman Library, University of Essex.

4 Thompson to Fromm, November 5, 1957, Erich Fromm Papers.

5 Ferenczi's analysis with Freud ended with the emergence of the negative maternal
transference (see letter November 13, 1916, Freud/Ferenczi Correspondence, Vol. 2)
and Ferenczi's mother complex was also responsible for the impasse in his treatment of
Severn. This was worked through in the mutual analysis.

6 By "mutual enactment" I am referring to an enactment where something from the
unconscious of all participants is being enacted and not just that of the patient.

7 Thompson related another story to Helen Swink Perry "I would not have gone to
Ferenczi [for my personal analysis] if Sullivan hadn't insisted that this was the only
analyst in Europe he had any confidence in; and therefore, if I was going to go to
Europe and get analyzed, I had just better go there. So I went" (Perry 1982, p. 202).

8 Thompson's first analysis was with Joseph C. "Snake" Thompson (no relation).

9 As the transcript is an exact verbatim of the recording of the interview, there are times
when the syntax, etc., can appear clumsy or stilted.

10 Two of these patients were analysts: Lewis B. Hill, M.D. and Bernard Robbins, M.D.

11 In a letter to Izette De Forest dated June 9, 1932, Thompson notes that of nine patients
with her only three were able to pay (De Forest-Taves Papers).

12 For instance, De Forest had remarked that "She was enjoying life with great gaiety,
having rescued herself with Ferenczi's help from a life of dried-up intellectual and
puritanical spinsterhood" (1959, 2).

13 Ferenczi's ideas about "active technique" can be traced back to a letter he wrote to
Freud on April 27, 1916, and articulated in his papers *Technical Difficulties in the Analysis
of a Case of Hysteria* (1919) and *The Further Development of an Active Therapy in Psycho-
Analysis* (1920), where the analyst intervenes to increase the libidinal tension and gain
access to the unconscious fantasies by prohibiting the patient from certain habits and
behaviors. As a technique, it privileged abstinence, frustration, privation, and avoiding
pleasurable activities. Also see Stanton (1991) and Grunberger (1980).

14 See Ferenczi's letter to Freud September 15, 1931, Freud/Ferenczi Correspondence,
Vol 3. For a discussion of Ferenczi's technique, see Hoffer (2010) and Brennan (2011).

15 Ferenczi moved away from his active therapy to relaxation therapy in 1925, where
relaxation of the musculature aided free association, and Ferenczi later expanded it to
a "principle of indulgence" which privileged meeting the patients' needs rather than
frustrating them, facilitating a regression to the original trauma and a "neocatharsis."
See Ferenczi's *Contra-Indications to the "Active" Psycho-Analytical Technique* (1926) and
The Principle of Relaxation and Neocatharsis (1930).

16 The misspelling of Severn as "La Verne" confirms the preferred pronunciation
(Se-vern) and that it was not pronounced Sev-ern, like the river in England.

17 It is interesting that Thompson identifies herself as a detached schizoid personality, as
one of her first papers (1938) was *Development of Awareness of Transference in a Markedly
Detached Personality*. In Adolf Meyer's notes on Thompson, he wrote that "she had a
rather detached existence not making very close relations with the other women at the
Clinic" (Notes, November 1, 1925).

18 Thompson's views on the Freud/Ferenczi relationship was deemed so emotional that
Balint, having solicited feedback from Jones, wanted her to revise her preface in the
second volume of the Collected Works (letter 1955, Balint Papers). Balint to Jones
4 May, 1955, Balint Papers, University of Essex.

19 In a letter to Elsa Sprague Field on March 27, 1953, Thompson reflected on her time
at Phipps "it's curious how a building holds a memory. I think I can say the years of my
greatest despair were spent in those walls" (Thompson Papers, WAWI).

20 Thompson's memory of the letter describing a "second childhood" may refer to a
letter that Freud sent Ferenczi on September 18, 1931, where Freud describes a "third

puberty." It would not be until four months later in December that Ferenczi would receive the harsher scolding from Freud.

21 Thompson to De Forest, May 9, 1954.

22 In his obituary of Ferenczi, Balint summarized Ferenczi's idea as "The central idea, to which Ferenczi returned time and again, is the essential disproportion between the child's limited capacity for dealing with excitation and the adults' unconscious and consequently uncontrolled, passionate and simultaneously guilt-laden, over- or under-stimulating of the child" (1949, pp. 218–219). In the unpublished section of Thompson's *Evaluation of Ferenczi's Relaxation Therapy* which was written in 1933, Thompson gives a much closer account of Ferenczi's ideas "It is possible that the trauma is not necessarily of a gross sexual nature, but of the more subtle nature of the reaction of the child to parental erotic tensions and guilt … the child does not suffer from his own Oedipal complex but from that of the parents" (Thompson Papers, 1933, pp. 17–18).

23 In *The Clinical Diary*, Ferenczi describes his own early trauma and his unconscious desire to kill (March 17; May 5, 1932).

24 Thompson suggested that Fromm not reach out to Severn, when he was writing his article on Ferenczi's illness, but Severn heard that Fromm was writing the article and wrote him a very favorable account of her analysis with Ferenczi (Thompson to Fromm, November 5, 1957. Erich Fromm Papers).

25 It should also be noted that in Severn's interview she does not speak disparagingly of Thompson. In fact, she seems to have had empathy toward Thompson's financial struggles.

26 In the Severn interview, Elizabeth Severn discloses that when she was too ill Ferenczi would come to her abode for the analytic session and most of the mutual analysis took place at her villa.

27 Clara Thompson (unpublished version), *Evaluation of Ferenczi's Relaxation Therapy*. Although a version of this paper appeared in her Selected Papers, it was edited. On page 20 of the unpublished version, Thompson writes "It is unsafe for the analyst to permit free expression of tenderness until the analysis is far advanced and the patient's destructive impulses are fairly well understood. … there are certain patients with a compulsive need to get other people in trouble by fair means or foul" (Thompson Papers, WAWI).

28 Alice Lowell, M.D. (1906–1982), grew up in Concord, Massachusetts. The Lowells were one of the Boston Brahmin families. Lowell worked with Ferenczi from 1930–1933 and is patient "B." in *The Clinical Diary*. Lowell completed medical school at Tufts University, and although originally intending to train as a psychoanalyst, she specialized in internal medicine. Lowell was medical director and chief of medicine at New England Hospital, Boston, Massachusetts. Lowell was involved in a relationship with Izette De Forest (Brennan, 2009).

29 In a letter dated October 6, 1910, Freud writes to Ferenczi: "A piece of homosexual investment has been withdrawn and utilized for the enlargement of my own ego" (Freud/Ferenczi Correspondence, Vol. 1). It is also interesting in the Thompson interview that she said of Ferenczi "I don't know whether he ever was homosexual as a young man or not. There were certain qualities in him that makes me think he might have had some strong tendencies that way" (p. 4).

30 This is Mitchell's (1988) "developmental tilt" critique of psychoanalytic theory.

References

Balint, M. (1896–1970). Enid and Michael Balint Papers. Special Collections. Albert Sloman Library, University of Essex.

Balint, M. (1949). Sándor Ferenczi, Obit 1933. *International Journal of Psychoanalysis*, 30:215–219.

Balint, M. (1968). *The Basic Fault*. London: Tavistock.

Brennan, B. W. (2009). Ferenczi's forgotten messenger: The life and work of Izette De Forest. *American Imago*, 66(4):427–455.

Brennan, B. W. (2011). On Ferenczi: A response—From elasticity to the confusion of tongues and the technical dimensions of Ferenczi's approach. *Psychoanalytic Perspectives*, 8(1):1–21.

Brennan, B. W. (2015—in press). Decoding Ferenczi's clinical diary: Biographical notes. *American Journal of Psychoanalysis*.

De Forest, I. (1925–1957). De Forest Family Papers. Private collection in possession of Henry Taves.

De Forest, I. (1954). *The Leaven of Love: A Development of the Psychoanalytic Theory and Technique of Sándor Ferenczi*. New York: Harper Brothers.

De Forest, I. (1959). Letter. *William Alanson White Institute Newsletter*, 7(1):2.

Edmunds, L. and Small, L. (2012). The 90-year divide. *Johns Hopkins Magazine*, 64(Fall):50–56.

Falzeder, E. and Brabrant, E. (eds) With the collaboration of P. Giampieri-Deutsch. (1992). *The Correspondence of Sigmund Freud and Sándor Ferenczi*, Vol. I, 1908–1914 (P. Hoffer, Trans., A. Haynal, Intro). Cambridge, MA: Harvard University Press.

Falzeder, E. and Brabrant, E. (eds) With the collaboration of P. Giampieri-Deutsch. (1996). *The Correspondence of Sigmund Freud and Sándor Ferenczi*, Vol. II, 1914–1919 (P. Hoffer, Trans., A. Hoffer, Intro). Cambridge, MA: Harvard University Press.

Falzeder, E. and Brabrant, E. (eds) With the collaboration of P. Giampieri-Deutsch. (2000). *The Correspondence of Sigmund Freud and Sándor Ferenczi*, Vol. III, 1920–1933 (P. Hoffer, Trans., J. Dupont, Intro). Cambridge, MA: Harvard University Press.

Ferenczi, S. (1901). Love within science. *Selected Writings*, Julia Borossa (ed). London: Penguin, 1991.

Ferenczi, S. (1919). Technical difficulties in the analysis of a case of hysteria. In J. Rickman (ed), J. I. Suttie (Trans.), et al, *Further Contributions to the Theory and Technique of Psychoanalysis*. New York: Basic Books, 1960.

Ferenczi, S. (1920). The further development of an active therapy in psycho-analysis. In J. Rickman (ed), J. I. Suttie (Trans.), et al, *Further Contributions to the Theory and Technique of Psychoanalysis*. New York: Basic Books, 1960.

Ferenczi, S. (1926). Contra-indications to the "active" psycho-analytical technique. In J. Rickman (ed), J. I. Suttie (Trans.), et al, *Further Contributions to the Theory and Technique of Psychoanalysis*. New York: Basic Books, 1960.

Ferenczi, S. (1929). The unwelcome child and his death-instinct. *International Journal of Psychoanalysis*, 10:125–129.

Ferenczi, S. (1930). The principle of relaxation and neocatharsis. *International Journal of Psychoanalysis*, 11:428–443.

Ferenczi, S. (1931). Notes and fragments (1920 and 1930–1932). In M. Balint (ed), E. Mosbacher (Trans.), et al, *Final Contributions to the Problems and Methods of Psycho-Analysis*. New York: Basic Books, 1960.

Fromm, E. (1900–1980). Erich Fromm Papers. Erich Fromm Literary Estate. Tuebingen, Germany.

Green, M. (ed) (1964). *Interpersonal Psychoanalysis: The Selected Papers of Clara M. Thompson*. New York: Basic Books.

Grunberger, B. (1980). From the "active technique" to the "confusion of tongues": On Ferenczi's deviation. In S. Lebovici and D. Widlöcher, *Psychoanalysis in France*. New York: International Universities Press, pp. 127–152.

Hoffer, P. (2010). From elasticity to the confusion of tongues: A historical commentary on the technical dimension of the Freud/Ferenczi controversy. *Psychoanalytic Perspectives*, 7(1):90–103.

Leys, R. (2000). *Trauma: A Genealogy*. Chicago: University of Chicago Press.

Lynn, D. J. (2003). Freud's psychoanalysis of Edith Banfield Jackson, 1930–1936. *Journal of the American Academy of Psychoanalysis*, 31(4):609–625.

Meyer, A. Notes. Adolf Meyer Collection. Alan Chesney Medical Archive. John Hopkins Medical Institutions.

Mitchell, S. (1988). *Relational Concepts in Psychoanalysis*. Cambridge, MA: Harvard University Press.

Perry, H. S. (1982). *Psychiatrist of America: The Life of Harry Stack Sullivan*. Cambridge, MA: Harvard University Press.

Phillips, A. (2011). A reply to Slochower. *Psychoanalytic Dialogues*, 21:22–27.

Severn, E. (1952). *Interviews and Recollections, Set B, 1952–1960 with K. R. Eissler/Interviewer*. Sigmund Freud Papers, (Box 126). Manuscripts Division, Library of Congress, Washington, DC.

Shapiro, S. (1993). Clara Thompson: Ferenczi's messenger with half a message. In L. Aron and A. Harris (eds), *The Legacy of Sándor Ferenczi*. Hillsdale, NJ: The Analytic Press, pp. 159–174.

Stanton, M. (1991). *Sándor Ferenczi—Reconsidering Active Intervention*. Northvale, NJ: The Analytic Press.

Thompson, C. (1933). *Evaluation of Ferenczi's Relaxation Therapy*. Unpublished manuscript. Thompson Papers. William Alanson White Institute.

Thompson, C. (1938). Development of awareness of transference in a markedly detached personality. *International Journal of Psychoanalysis*, 19:299–309.

Thompson, C. (1952). *Interviews and Recollections, Set A, 1914–1998 with K. R. Eissler/Interviewer*. Sigmund Freud Papers, (Box 115). Manuscripts Division, Library of Congress, Washington, DC.

5

GEORG GRODDECK'S INFLUENCE ON SÁNDOR FERENCZI

Christopher Fortune

The Ferenczi–Groddeck correspondence began on April 26, 1921, and spanned twelve years. In the first letter, Ferenczi, age 48, wrote to Groddeck, age 55, to refer a young patient for treatment. That summer, Ferenczi and his wife, Gizella, visited Groddeck's sanitorium for ten days, marking the beginning of a close friendship between the two men and their wives. The relationship between Groddeck and Ferenczi lasted until Ferenczi's death in May 1933. Groddeck died just one year later in June 1934. This chapter argues, and details the reasons, that without Georg Groddeck's influence on Sándor Ferenczi, there may have been no later Ferenczi challenging Freud and expanding the frontiers of psychoanalysis.

Of the early psychoanalysts, Sándor Ferenczi (1873–1933) was considered the most brilliant therapist—acknowledged by Freud to be a "master of analysis." Ferenczi, as this volume attests, is a well-known figure in psychoanalytic history. However, Georg Groddeck (1866–1934), a German physician drawn to Freud and psychoanalysis in 1917, is less known to an English-speaking audience. Groddeck produced a prolific body of writing, much of which remains untranslated into English. An early explorer of the relationship between organic and mental illness, Groddeck established a sana-torium in Baden-Baden in 1900 and has been championed by some as the "father of psychosomatic medicine." In the years before coming to Freud, Groddeck at first rejected the "Freudian school," later admitting he was jealous of Freud. He is then said to have taught himself psychoanalysis. While most of the psychoanalytic world was suspicious of Groddeck, Freud told him that he had to "claim" Groddeck because "the discovery that transference and resistance are the most important aspects of treat-ment turns a person irretrievably into a member of the wild army [of psychoanaly-sis]" (Freud and Ferenczi 1996, N. 1, p. 220). A few years later, in 1923, Freud assured Groddeck's renown when he acknowledged in his book, *The Ego and the Id* (1923), that he had borrowed the term "Id" (Das Es) from Groddeck.

Groddeck's best known work, *The Book of the It* (Das Buch vom Es) (1923/1961), is a psychoanalytic classic in which he spiritedly presents his idea that illness is a symbolic psychic expression and, as the body and mind are inseparable, the treatment must be both psychic and physical. Groddeck, who also wrote literature, is noted for being the author of the first psychoanalytical novel, *The Soul-Seekers* (Der Seelensucher), published in 1921 (unpublished in English). *The Meaning of Illness* (1977) is a collection of Groddeck's essays, autobiographical notes and letters, and in particular his correspondence with Freud from 1917 to 1934.

In 1920, at the Sixth International Psychoanalytic Association Congress in the Hague, Ferenczi delivered his paper "The Further Development of an Active Therapy in Psycho-Analysis" (1921a). At the same meeting, Groddeck presented his paper "On Psychoanalyzing the Organic in Human Beings" (1921a). Groddeck, who was still little known to psychoanalysis at the time, caused a stir at the congress by defiantly introducing himself to Freud and the assembled analysts as a "wild analyst." Thus, Ferenczi was introduced to his future physician, friend, and correspondent. A few years earlier, Ferenczi had positively reviewed Groddeck's brief paper, "Psychic Conditioning and the Psychoanalytic Treatment of Organic Disorders" (1917).

Overview of the Ferenczi-Groddeck Correspondence, 1921–1933

The correspondence, which consists primarily of Ferenczi's letters to Groddeck, provides important new insights into Ferenczi's professional and personal life. For example:

- Ferenczi's letters, particularly the critical Christmas 1921 letter, illuminate the personal roots of his professional drive, suggesting the origins of his radical clinical and theoretical experiments, and his reconsideration of the importance of early trauma. Ferenczi's determination to understand his personal history and heal himself led him to critique fundamental aspects of classical psychoanalysis. This letter reveals the effects of Ferenczi's own childhood traumas—specifically the perception of his mother as critical and unloving. Using Groddeck as a sounding-board and a kind of analyst, Ferenczi attempted to work through his early traumas and integrate them into his evolving ideas on theory and practice. He writes: "I can declare myself totally vanquished by your unpretentious manner, your natural kindness and friendliness. I have never been so open with another man, not even with 'Siegmund'" (Ferenczi and Groddeck 2002, p. 8). Different than his letters to Freud, whom he clearly saw as a father figure, Ferenczi pursued a more open friendship with Groddeck, as though he were a favorite older brother.
- He struggled to find answers to this childhood "terrorism of suffering," describing his painful and repressed childhood, one in which there was too little love and too much discipline. There was no physical affection, and keeping

up appearances was paramount. This search led to many of his innovations in psychoanalysis, as Ferenczi not only sought answers to his own suffering, but also attempted to find methods, structures, and approaches to better help his patients. In directly using himself in his work, he embodied the traditional idea of the wounded healer (Whan, 1987).

The letters also provide insights into:

- Ferenczi's challenge to the traditional limits of the doctor–patient and analyst–analysand relationship. For example, he pursued a much more open professional friendship with his own physician, Groddeck. During Ferenczi's yearly therapeutic holidays to Groddeck's sanatorium in Baden-Baden, the two men engaged in an open dialogue—frequently a vigorous debate of shared interests. For example, they wrestled with the question of whether psychoanalysis could be a science, as well as issues such as self-analysis, mutual analysis—which they tried for a brief time—and an exploration of the body–mind relationship. The letters resonate with critical theoretical and clinical issues today. At times, Groddeck could not follow Ferenczi's irrepressible spirit of scientific investigation and saw in Ferenczi's passionate thirst for psychological knowledge a dangerous desire to "atomise the soul," which he believed could only lead to Ferenczi's self-destruction. In a last letter to Gizella, after Ferenczi's death, Groddeck (Ferenczi and Groddeck, 2002) wrote:

> All these years I could only think about Sándor's life with a heavy heart. He became a victim of his own spirit of inquiry, a fate I escaped only because of my insufficient thirst for knowledge. I must first speak about myself. Even before going over to psychoanalysis one of the underlying principles of my medical thinking was the conviction that in human individuals there are—apart from the psyche which is the subject of scientific investigation—thousands and millions of more or less independently existing souls which continuously unite and separate, group and re-group, working sometimes for and sometimes against each other, and probably exist quite independently at times. Having embraced this view, I was content to leave it at that. I never tried to study this cosmos; it simply isn't in my nature to go into matters which I consider unfathomable. (pp. 112–113)

The above is a reflection of Groddeck's strong identification with his "It." He then continues in the letter explaining how he came to view the demise of Ferenczi's "soul:"

> Being such a close friend of Sándor's, I soon realised that he viewed these matters similarly. I was thus horrified to see him proceed to investigate

this human cosmos scientifically, even attempt to describe it, so that others could participate in this undoubtedly overwhelming spectacle. He became completely consumed by this endeavour. He expressed it thus to me: I atomise the soul. Such atomisation, though, if pursued seriously, can only end in the dissolution of the self, for another human being is, and always will remain hidden to us. We can only atomise our own soul, and that will destroy us. (p. 113)

- The complex emotional triangle involving his wife and stepdaughter. For example, in his critical Christmas 1921 letter, he writes:

> Your letter spurred me on to greater efforts; it helped me remove my mask in front of my wife, too—albeit partially. I spoke to her again about my sexual frustration, about my suppressed love for her daughter (who should have been my wife; indeed who in effect was my bride until a somewhat disparaging remark of Freud's prompted me to fight this love tooth and nail—literally to push the girl away from me).
>
> *(Ferenczi and Groddeck 2002, p. 9)*

Prefiguring the surprising positive analytical outcomes of his negative counter-transference confessions with his patient, Elizabeth Severn, ten years later, and recorded in *The Clinical Diary*, Ferenczi continues in the letter: "Oddly enough, with us these confessions usually end with me drawing closer to her [Gizella] again—overwhelmed by her goodness and forgiving nature" (Ferenczi and Groddeck 2002, pp. 9–10).

- Ferenczi openly reveals himself as a chronic medical patient and likely hypochondriac, plagued by a myriad of physical ailments, including breathing problems, sensitivity to cold, and insomnia.

Groddeck's Letters

> Make up your mind once and for all, not to search in my letters for the things your conscious "I" will value, but to read them as though they were travel books or detective stories. Life is already serious enough without making it worse by taking too seriously one's studies, or lectures, or work, or anything else at all.
>
> *(Groddeck, Introduction by Ashley Montagu, 1961, p. x)*

Groddeck produced rich psychoanalytic ideas. However, by 1925, Freud perceived what he saw as Groddeck's limitation—a fatal flaw. Freud wrote to Ferenczi: "[Groddeck is] not the man to complete an idea" (Freud/Ferenczi, 12.1.1925).

Freud was probably right; Groddeck was not particularly interested in completion and would rather leave his playful, chastising sparks of ideas for others to develop. Groddeck's intelligence, freshness, and rebelliousness in the letters we do have are tantalizing. His few letters tend to be better written and, in some ways, more interesting than Ferenczi's. His letters pique our interest in Groddeck and call for a reexamination of his role in originating creative ideas within the psychoanalytic domain, including the body–mind relationship, the mother transference, and the transitional object.

Groddeck's Importance and His Influence on Ferenczi

To what extent did Groddeck influence Ferenczi and his ideas? Ferenczi wrote to Groddeck on October 13, 1926, "I have learned a lot from the carefree courage with which you 'come to grips' with the psychomorphology of the organic, but flatter myself that I have had some influence on your development too" (Ferenczi and Groddeck 2002, p.78). Ferenczi probably admired Groddeck's free thinking spirit as much as his specific ideas.

Ferenczi and Groddeck shared a passionate interest in the relationship between body and mind. In fact, Ferenczi wrote about the body–mind relationship before he knew of Groddeck (Dupont, personal communication, March 1995). In his first letter to Groddeck on June 5, 1917, Freud attempted to connect the two men by mentioning Ferenczi's recent paper, "Disease-or Patho-Neuroses" (1916/1917) (Groddeck 1977, p. 36). Initially, however, Ferenczi told Freud he was suspicious of Groddeck's "mysticism." In turn, Freud reproached Ferenczi for the "long-standing characteristic trait in you, the tendency to leave a stranger standing outside" (Freud and Ferenczi 1996, p. 220). If Ferenczi was in fact pushing Groddeck away, it was quite probably because he was jealous of Freud's enthusiasm for Groddeck. Also, given their parallel interest in the body–mind relationship, and the fact that Ferenczi had been unable to finish his own book, *Thalassa* (Ferenczi, 1924/1984), he may have felt competitive with Groddeck.

However, their relationship developed and is reflected in this correspondence. Almost ten years later, in his October 13, 1926, letter on Groddeck's sixtieth birthday, Ferenczi comments on the history of their friendship and Groddeck's contributions to psychoanalysis:

> There are decided differences between us with regard to the scientific method we employ; yet we always managed to bridge these outward differences with a bit of goodwill on both our parts and essentially to harmonise our views. ... Psychoanalysis has undoubtedly received significant impulses from you; the best in our profession know this only too well, even if they somewhat begrudge you your rights to priority in current psychoanalytic writing.
>
> *(Ferenczi and Groddeck 2002, p. 78)*

Significance of the Mother

Groddeck's recognition of the significance of the mother parallels the development of Ferenczi's own influential views. In his June 9, 1923, letter, Ferenczi acknowledged: "… I consider to be the particular merit of your approach: namely that you have never ceased emphasizing, along with the role of the father, the exorbitant importance of the *mother*" (Ferenczi and Groddeck 2002, p. 49).

Ferenczi, and the Hungarian school generally, is now recognized as a primary source for today's object relations theories (Bowlby, 1988; Eagle, 1987). As well, Michael Balint (1950), who was one of Ferenczi's analysands, most important followers, and founder of the influential British "Middle School" of object relations, acknowledged Ferenczi's critical shift in psychoanalytic theory "from an exclusively one-person model toward conceiving of mind, development, pathology, and treatment in terms of a two-person, relational, psychology" (Aron and Harris 1993, p. 31). Also, since early object relations emerged from acknowledging the central relationship with the mother, Ferenczi may be attributing Groddeck with a significant role in the development of his own thought. This view opposed Freud's writings which gave central importance to the father and the Oedipus complex. Much of today's analytic literature focuses on the mother and pre-Oedipal phases of development. In 1988, Bowlby wrote that Ferenczi "saw the infant as striving from the first to relate to his mother, and his future mental health as turning on the success or failure of this first relationship. Thus was the object relations version of psychoanalysis born" (p. xvi).

Groddeck had an unusually strong identification with women, particularly the mother, and went so far as to declare that "[I] envy that I am not myself a woman and cannot be a mother" (1923, p. 21). In his November 12, 1922, letter to Ferenczi, he wrote:

> In the final analysis, I actually produce nothing myself, I am much too maternal, inclined towards receiving and letting things develop naturally. The games I played with my sister, who by the way was older than me, were called Mother and Child, and I was almost always the mother. Alternatively one could say that I am a digesting machine which consumes other people's ideas, releasing them again as a sausage after due assimilation, so that it requires a lot of work and insight to recognise the various elements in their former guise.
>
> *(Ferenczi and Groddeck 2002, p. 36)*

Francois Roustang (1982) cast Groddeck's charge to confront the mother as a profound challenge to the foundations of psychoanalysis. He writes:

> What proves that the insistence on the paternal transference and on the need for filiation in psychoanalysis is not a way to avoid facing up in the analysis

to the more dangerous and more archaic relation with the mother and her language, which is in fact a mockery of language? If Groddeck believed neither in words nor in science, it was because he placed himself in the mother's position. (p. 129)

Later, Ferenczi took Groddeck's challenge to heart by addressing the mother transference in his mutual analysis with Elizabeth Severn (Fortune, 1993, 1994, 1996). In mutual analysis, Ferenczi experienced a therapeutic shift, in part due to Severn's empathy. Through Severn, Ferenczi approached his ideal of being "remothered." He may have felt he had the chance to work out his negative transference, which he had long criticized Freud for failing to analyze. In his diary, Ferenczi wrote:

> In R.N. I find my mother again, namely the real one, who was hard and energetic and of whom I am afraid. R.N. knows this, and treats me with particular gentleness; the analysis even allows her to transform her own hardness into friendly softness, and here the question arises: should one not have, in spite of all, the courage to expose oneself to the danger of analytic transference and win out in the end. (1932, p. 45)

Later, Ferenczi told Freud that Severn "analyzed him and thereby saved him" (Freud and Jones 1993, p. 721).

The idea of "mother" informs the relationships of both figures in the Ferenczi–Groddeck correspondence. It could be argued that Ferenczi, and probably Groddeck, wanted Freud to be their mother. But Freud ultimately refused them both. So Ferenczi, according to Grosskurth (1991), looked to Groddeck to replace Freud as the mother Ferenczi always wanted" (opp. p. 200). And later, as mentioned earlier, Severn was cast in the mother role in mutual analysis, while Groddeck found his "mother" in a more traditional arrangement—with his wife (Emmy) (Freud and Groddeck, 1977).

Groddeck's Inspiration and His Influence on Ferenczi's Writings

Groddeck likely helped free Ferenczi to produce new work beyond the approved canon of classical psychoanalysis, braving to go beyond Freud, the master. Groddeck may have helped to light a spark under Ferenczi—a "furor sanandi" (rage to cure), as Freud called it—that propelled him into his radical technical experiments and writings of the 1920s. In his Christmas 1921 letter, Ferenczi wrote: "I never plucked up my courage … I always allowed myself to be sidetracked into writing small improvisations instead of the main one." Instead of continuing to produce the many small and imaginative papers of the previous decade, with quaint titles such as "Flatus as an Adult Prerogative" (1913) and "Disgust for Breakfast" (1919),

Ferenczi finally found his writer's backbone, overcame his block, and completed his biological magnum opus, *Thalassa: A Theory of Genitality* (1924)—a bold leap of imagination linking sexuality, gender, psychology, biology, and evolution. 1923 was a breakthrough year for Ferenczi to complete the writing projects on which he had procrastinated—besides *Thalassa* (1924), there was also the collaboration with Rank: *The Development of Psycho-Analysis* (1924). Both were original pieces of writing. Subsequently, after 1923, Ferenczi's work mood improved—he had gained strength and independence through overcoming his writing block.

In *Thalassa*, Ferenczi expounds an almost cosmic theory, that "the whole of life is determined by a tendency to return to the womb, equating the process of birth with the phylogenetic transition of animal life from water to land, and linking coitus to the idea of 'thalassal regression: the longing for the sea-life from which man emerged in primeval times'" (Ferenczi, 1924).

Possibly, Ferenczi was inspired to finish *Thalassa* thanks to Groddeck's own highly original, even daring, writings of the period—such as his psychoanalytical novel, *The Soul-Seekers* (1921a) and *The Book of the It* (1923). Both were radical departures from the form and style of analytic writings at that time.

In his semi-autobiographical *The Soul-Seekers*, also known as *The Seeker of Souls*, Groddeck uses the medium of the novel to present his ideas about illness, life, and institutions. It's an unusual book written as a conscious imitation of Cervantes's *Don Quixote*, combining analysis with coarse situation comedy in a satirical critique of the times. The main character is a fool who has analytical adventures while wandering through pre-war Germany applying "wild" interpretations to everyone and everything that meets his eye. Like a modern Don Quixote, the protagonist battles against repression—mainly sexual repression—and, of course, encounters disapprobation. Groddeck struggled to get the book published, as it was seen as an outrageous piece of literature in many psychoanalytic circles. However, Freud supported the book, and it was finally published in Vienna by the established psychoanalytic press, Internationaler Psychoanalytischer Verlag (Bos 1997, p. 152). Ferenczi wrote a review of *The Soul-Seekers* for the psychoanalytic journal, *Imago* (Ferenczi, 1921b). Before reviewing the book itself, Ferenczi went to great lengths to promote his understanding of Groddeck and his work. Compared to his previous review of Groddeck's paper (Ferenczi, 1917), in this piece, Ferenczi was even more laudatory about Groddeck's creativity and potential in understanding and treating psychosomatic disease.

The Book of the It (Das Buch vom Es), which appeared two years later in 1923, also published by the Psychoanalytischer Verlag, became a popular psychoanalytic work—accessible and openly personal. It is a unique collection of thirty-three "Letters to a Woman Friend," all variations on a central theme—Groddeck's concept of the "wondrous force" which directs man—"both what he himself does, and what happens to him." To this force, Groddeck, probably adapting Nietzsche's terminology, gave the name "Das Es." At the outset of the book, Groddeck attempts to disarm all critics by asserting that he has no intention to be scientific or to follow any particular creed but wishes to discourse and speculate freely upon whatever presents itself for consideration. The book's theme is how the whole body, be it sick or healthy, is an instrument of the soul. Groddeck posits that "Das Es," translated as the "It," is the unconscious force that drives human behavior and underpins its poles of attraction and revulsion, standing as the root source of physical disease. As mentioned, it was Groddeck's notion of "Das Es" that Freud borrowed and adapted into his own somewhat different concept, alternatively translated as the "Id" in his *Ego and the Id* (1923).

Ferenczi knew that Groddeck had long been a writer of literature and wrote in his Christmas 1921 letter:

> I notice that I'm imitating *your* "Letters to a Woman Friend" [working title of *The Book of the It*] in peppering this letter with these entertaining morsels. Are you by any chance this female friend for me, or am I using your friendship in a homosexual way to replace her?
>
> *(Ferenczi and Groddeck 2002, p. 11)*

Was Ferenczi looking to Groddeck, as an experienced writer and his physician, to inspire and help him overcome his writer's block? His Christmas 1921 letter is full of references to his writing struggles, frequently linked to somatic symptoms. In it, he describes his "fear of work," his difficulty in completing *Thalassa*: "Am I trying to become a fish, or do I wish to activate my piscean genital theory [*Thalassa*], which I won't write down?" Ferenczi linked this fear of work to criticisms in childhood. He writes to Groddeck:

> If I was as talented a writer as you I would continue in this vein and discharge my physical and mental pain on paper. (N.B: I wasn't being quite honest then! I do think I am a talented writer; I remember how hurt I was when someone made derogatory comments about something I had written, and, when I was younger, about a poem).
>
> *(Ferenczi and Groddeck 2002, p. 9)*

Or, was it also possibly a fear of Freud's reaction? Even though Freud apparently liked the earlier tentative drafts of *Thalassa,* he may not have been able to inspire Ferenczi, as Groddeck might since his work was based in a body approach, to make the leaps of imagination necessary, and to complete the book.

Ferenczi's discourse on work with Groddeck was embedded with somatic references:

> But I'm far from feeling well yet. I will list the symptoms for you. The first thing that comes to mind is my inhibition about work. (Association of ideas: You mustn't outshine the father.) In 1915/16 when I was garrisoned (for

eighteen months) in a small Hungarian town, and had time on my hands I devised a great, indeed a "grand" theory that genital development evolved as a reaction on the part of animals to the threat of dehydration whilst adapting to life on land [*Thalassa*]. *Not once* could I get myself to write down this valuable theory—my best to date. The relevant data lie dozing in my writing-desk, scattered about all over the place. I'm happy enough to "talk" about the theory; once—actually twice—I explained it all to Freud, Rank, Jones, Abraham, etc., ... but write about it, and I get a backache, due of course, to my aorta, which, according to the X-ray, is enlarged. A few weeks ago I developed arthritic swellings in my right wrist, which, of course, again, kept me from writing. The wrist now feels free again.

(Ferenczi and Groddeck 2002, p. 10)

A key to the embodied Ferenczi may be found in *Thalassa*. The symptoms that he describes above could be seen as metaphors for the evolutionary movement from sea to land, and they specifically relate to not writing his genital theory book (*Thalassa*); the complications and attention paid to his difficulty in breathing, his acute sensitivity to heat and cold, his sleep disturbances, and his blood problems (Ferenczi and Groddeck, 2002).

Metaphorically, Ferenczi may not have made a successful adaptation from the womb to the world, from childhood to adulthood. Hence the fantasy expressed in *Thalassa*, the desire throughout life to return—particularly to "return to the mother," and to the womb. This notion, and his championing of the child, suggests that Ferenczi was pulled back to the innocence of childhood. Groddeck not only supported Ferenczi's childlike qualities, but shared and celebrated it as a rebellion. He wrote to Ferenczi: "... the pompous aura surrounding the grown-ups god-forsaken head, to ensure that nothing goes in or goes out, is in the eyes of us children no more than a game, thank God, only play" (Ferenczi and Groddeck 2002, p. 36).

Actually, Ferenczi's desire probably wasn't so much to return to childhood—did he ever really leave it?—as a deep respect for, and sensitivity to, the child's perspective, which resonates with the idealization of the child and notions of innocence. The 1990s New Age notion of the "Inner Child," made popular by self-help guru, John Bradshaw (1990) and former psychoanalyst, Alice Miller (1981), linked this childhood innocence with the growing recognition of child abuse. It also allowed Ferenczi to identify such a profound, yet subtle, concept in early trauma as the "Wise Baby" (Ferenczi, 1923). Perhaps it's not too extreme to suggest that in his strong identification with the honesty and innocence of the child, Ferenczi seemed to idealize the child as a kind of mini-god.

In the later 1920s to early 1930s, Ferenczi had to reconsider the views he expressed in *Thalassa* in light of his work on trauma. That *Thalassa* continued as a significant reference point is confirmed by his note at the end of his "Confusion of Tongues" paper, when he writes: "The 'Theory of Genitality' that tries to found the 'struggle of the sexes' on phylogenesis, will have to make clear [the] difference between the infantile-erotic gratifications and the hate-impregnated love of adult mating" (p. 167). It is interesting to note Ferenczi's scathing view of adult sexuality. It fits with his idealization of the child.

The Body Between Ferenczi and Groddeck

Ferenczi's dialogue with Groddeck about the relationship of body and mind was a discourse not found in psychoanalysis until that time. Perhaps Groddeck's positive view of the body—his instinctual "It"—drew Ferenczi to him. Ferenczi recognized that the actual body had been neglected and needed to be considered in psychoanalysis. For Groddeck, the "It" was a positive natural force—wise beyond all—as compared to Freud's "Id" which was sexual, mistrusted, threatening, and needed to be controlled.

Groddeck's approach resonates with today's body-oriented therapies that espouse rhetoric such as "the body doesn't lie." He treated the body through water therapy, diet, exercise, and massage. To what degree it is true or not, and there is new research suggesting this aspersion needs to be re-contextualized (Brennan, this volume), Ferenczi is known for kissing and hugging his patients (Freud to Ferenczi, December 13, 1931, Jones, 1957, pp. 174–176). Groddeck's language of the body spoke to Ferenczi, particularly his own psycho-pathological body symptoms. This emphasis on the body augmented, and even opposed, Freud's privileging of language in analysis. And, ironically, for all the importance given to sexuality, the body was absent from classical analysis.

For Ferenczi, the body was the new frontier in psychoanalysis, and, on a personal level, it was a return to his deeper nature, a return to himself. In retrospect, given the developments of object relations perspectives in psychoanalytic theory over the decades, it was also a return to the idea of mother—if not the maternal body. In the later 1920s in his clinical work, Ferenczi investigated the embodiment of early trauma. His attention to the body in analysis was a critical component in his return to a theory of trauma.

In summing up Ferenczi after his death, Groddeck wrote in his letter of February 19, 1934 (Ferenczi and Groddeck 2002, p. 112), to Ferenczi's wife, Gizella, that Ferenczi had been on an "ascent to the stars." While that may be true, it is obvious from the letters that Ferenczi had also been on a descent into the body—his own body. In this descent, Ferenczi at times sank into sleepless, sickly, melancholic, and even depressed states; he was besieged by physical complaints. In his last letter to Gizella, Groddeck implied that Ferenczi went too far, even abandoning Groddeck's advice, and refused to acknowledge his limitations—physically, mentally, and emotionally. Groddeck wrote that in his desire to "atomise the soul," Ferenczi "became completely consumed by this endeavour" and this ambition got the better of him and he fell victim to his drive for discovery. Groddeck seems to suggest that Ferenczi had betrayed his own body by allowing it to be destroyed. By giving his passions and neurosis free rein, and not acknowledging his limitations, Ferenczi transgressed nature (the "It"?) and his own being. Groddeck, who may have felt betrayed by Ferenczi and later by his loss of him, almost accuses Ferenczi of his own demise. Ferenczi failed by not surviving. This echoes Dupont's (1988) question in her introduction to *The Clinical Diary* regarding Ferenczi: "Hasn't it been said that the first task of the guerrilla fighter is to stay alive?" (p. xii).

Ferenczi: Chaos and Expanding Psychoanalytic Horizons

Ferenczi seems to have sought chaotic forces, at times possibly destructive, uncontained by the body. Overwhelmed with a sense of needing to indulge the child, he never learned to cope, to overcome, and so he suffered as if a child still. Like another eternal child, Peter Pan, Ferenczi equated children with good and adults, including parents, with bad. And, like Peter Pan, Ferenczi may have been caught in the child imago, unable to mature, and in this sense to endure, to survive, even to stand up to Freud and become an adult. In the end, commenting on Ferenczi's clinical directions, Freud himself simply dismissed him as being stuck in childhood complexes: "[Ferenczi's] technical innovations were connected with ... regressions to his childhood complexes" (Freud and Jones, May 29, 1933, p. 721). However, Ferenczi's last papers, which very much took a view from the child's perspective, and challenge Freud's and Jones's rejection, made great contributions to psychoanalytic theory and practice.

As well, it could be argued, to some degree, that Ferenczi's experiment in mutual analysis was a fantasy of merging. Through mutual analysis "[Ferenczi] was determined to engage his patients, to descend with them into his own psyche to see what emerged in the analytic encounter. What he discovered has enriched all of psychoanalysis" (Fortune, 1996, p. 184). Ferenczi refused to acknowledge his limits, and at the expense of his own well-being, he yet again opened new horizons for psychoanalysis (Fortune, 1993, 1994, 1996). "However, [it must be said] it was both a hero's and a fool's journey. Sándor Ferenczi caught therapeutic fire, and tragically it ultimately consumed him" (Fortune, 1996, p. 184). After his death, Groddeck wrote: "External events only acquired meaning in the life of this rare human being as he belonged to the givers, to those who give again and again" (Ferenczi and Groddeck February 19, 1934, p. 114).

Freud saw Groddeck as a Rabelaisian figure—earthy, joyously coarse, and gross. Ferenczi was also hearty in his tastes. For example, he acted out his psycho-physical pathologies early on when he sought out prostitutes. He wanted to marry the life of the mind with the body. Groddeck provided the bodily side of the equation for Ferenczi after his long association with Freud.

Ferenczi was probably by nature a poet, artist, and scientist as well as a psychoanalyst. In the last decade of his life—parallel to his friendship with Groddeck, and emboldened by that friendship—Ferenczi's spirit embodied these realms. He was no longer comfortable as a flag-bearer in the Freudian army. It may have been that by learning to trust this side of his nature, and bridling at the constraints of the psychoanalytic movement, he finally challenged his friend, analyst, and mentor, Sigmund Freud.

As mentioned earlier, Freud judged Groddeck as "not the man to complete an idea" (Freud and Ferenczi, December 1, 1921). While Freud's opinion is debatable, and even if true, not necessarily a failing, we do know that Groddeck made a great contribution to the development of psychoanalysis by "remothering" Ferenczi and inspiring Ferenczi to follow his creative instincts. Based on the perspectives outlined in this chapter, I would conclude that without Groddeck there may have been no later Ferenczi challenging Freud, and pushing to extend the frontiers of psychoanalysis.

References

Aron, L. and Harris, A. (1993). Sándor Ferenczi: Discovery and rediscovery. In L. Aron and A. Harris (eds), *The Legacy of Sándor Ferenczi*. Hillsdale, NJ: The Analytic Press, pp. 1–35.

Balint, M. (1950). Changing therapeutic aims and techniques in psychoanalysis. *International Journal of Psychoanalysis,* 31:117–124.

Bos, J. (1997). *Authorized Knowledge*. Holland: University of Utrecht.

Bradshaw, J. (1990). *Homecoming: Reclaiming and Championing Your Inner Child*. New York: Bantam Books.

Bowlby, J. (1988). Foreword. *The Origins of Love and Hate,* by Ian Suttie. London: Free Association Books, pp. xv–xviii.

Dupont, J. (1988). Introduction. *The Clinical Diary of Sándor Ferenczi*. J. Dupont (ed) and M. Balint and N.Z. Jackson (trans.). Cambridge, MA: Harvard University Press. (Originally published as *Journal clinique*. Paris: Payot, 1985).

Eagle, M. (1987). *Recent Developments in Psychoanalysis: A Critical Evaluation*. Cambridge, MA: Harvard University Press.

Falzeder, E., & Brabant, E. (2000). *The Correspondence of Sigmund Freud and Sándor Ferenczi. Volume 3, 1920–1933*. Cambridge, MA: Harvard University Press.

Ferenczi Collected Works. *Further Contributions to Psychoanalysis*. Compiled by J. Rickman. Trans. J. Suttie, et al [London: Hogarth Press, 1926 (2nd ed., 1950)]. *Final Contributions to the Problems and Methods of Psycho-Analysis*. M. Balint (ed) and E. Mosbacher et al (Trans.). London: Hogarth Press/New York: Basic Books, 1955. London: Karnac, 1980.

Ferenczi, S. (1913). Flatus as an adult prerogative. *Further Contributions to Psychoanalysis,* p. 325.

Ferenczi, S. (1916/17). Disease- or patho-neuroses. *Further Contributions to Psychoanalysis,* pp. 78–89.

Ferenczi, S. (1917). Review of psychic conditioning and the psychoanalytic treatment of organic disorders. *Final Contributions to the Problems and Methods of Psycho-Analysis,* pp. 342–343.

Ferenczi, S. (1919). Disgust for breakfast. *Further Contributions to Psychoanalysis,* p. 326.

Ferenczi, S. (1921a). The further development of an active therapy in psycho-analysis. *Further Contributions to Psychoanalysis,* pp. 198–217.

Ferenczi, S. (1921b). Review of Groddeck's, The soul-seekers: A psychoanalytic novel. *Imago,* 1921, 7:356. *Final Contributions to the Problems and Methods of Psycho-Analysis,* pp. 344–348.

Ferenczi, S. (1923).The dream of the clever [wise] baby. *Further Contributions to Psychoanalysis*, pp. 349–350.

Ferenczi, S. (1924). *Thalassa: A Theory of Genitality*. London: Karnac, 1984. *Versuch Einer Genital Theorie*. Vienna: International Psychoanlytischer, 1924 and New York: *Psychoanalytic Quarterly*, 1938.

Ferenczi, S. (1930–1932). Notes and fragments (& 1920). *Final Contributions to the Problems and Methods of Psycho-Analysis*, pp. 216–279.

Ferenczi, S. (1932). *The Clinical Diary of Sándor Ferenczi*, J. Dupont (ed) and M. Balint and N. Z. Jackson (trans.). Cambridge, MA: Harvard University Press, 1988. (Originally published as *Journal Clinique*. Paris: Payot, 1985).

Ferenczi, S. (1933). Confusion of tongues between adults and the child. *Final Contributions to the Problems and Methods of Psycho-Analysis*, pp. 156–167.

Ferenczi, S. and Groddeck, G. (2002). *Sándor Ferenczi Georg Groddeck Correspondence: 1921–1933*. C. Fortune (ed). London: Open Gate Press/New York: The Other Press.

Ferenczi, S. and Rank, O. (1924). *The Development of Psycho-Analysis*. New York/Washington: Nervous and Mental Disease Pub. Co., 1925.

Fortune, C. (1993).The case of RN: Sándor Ferenczi's radical experiment in psychoanalysis. In L. Aron and A. Harris (eds) *The legacy of Sándor Ferenczi*. Hillsdale, NJ: The Analytic Press, pp. 101–120.

Fortune, C. (1994). A difficult ending: Ferenczi, "R.N.", and the experiment in mutual analysis. In A. Haynal and E. Falzeder (eds), *100 Years of psychoanalysis* (Cahiers Psychiatriques Genevois, special issue), Geneva: Universitaires de Psychiatrie de Geneve, pp. 217–223.

Fortune, C. (1996). Mutual analysis: A logical outcome of Sándor Ferenczi's experiments in psychoanalysis. In P. Rudnytsky, A. Bokay, and P. Giampieri-Deutsch (eds) *Ferenczi's Turn in Psychoanalysis*. New York: New York University Press, pp. 170–186.

Freud, S. and Ferenczi, S. (1993). *The Correspondence of Sigmund Freud and Sándor Ferenczi, Vol. I, 1908–1914*. E. Brabent, E. Falzeder, and P. Giampieri-Deutsch (eds) and P. Hoffer (Trans.). Cambridge, MA: Harvard University Press/Belknap.

Freud, S. and Ferenczi, S. (1996). *The Correspondence of Sigmund Freud and Sándor Ferenczi, Vol. II, 1915–1919*. E. Brabent, E. Falzeder, and P. Giampieri-Deutsch (eds) and P. Hoffer (Trans.). Cambridge, MA: Harvard University Press/Belknap.

Freud, S. and Ferenczi, S. (2000). *The Correspondence of Sigmund Freud and Sándor Ferenczi, Vol. III, 1920–1933*. E. Brabent, E. Falzeder, and P. Giampieri-Deutsch (eds) and P. Hoffer (Trans.). Cambridge, MA: Harvard University Press/Belknap.

Freud, S. and Groddeck, G. For Freud/Groddeck correspondence, see Groddeck, 1977.

Freud, S. and Jones, E. (1993). *The Complete Correspondence of Sigmund Freud and Ernest Jones, 1908–1939*, R.A. Paskauskas (ed). Cambridge, MA: Harvard University Press/Belknap.

Groddeck, G. (1921a). *Der Seelensucher: Ein Psychoanalytischer Roman (The Soulseeker: A Psychoanalytic Novel)*. Vienna/Leipzig: Internationaler Psychoanalytischer Verlag.

Groddeck, G. (1921b). On psychoanalyzing the organic in human beings. *Internationale Zeitschrift fur Psychoanalyse*, 7.

Groddeck, G. (1923). *The Book of the It (Das Buch Vom Es)*. London: Vision Press, 1950/New York: Vintage, 1961. Originally published Vienna/Leipzig: Internationaler Psychoanalytischer Verlag, 1923.

Groddeck, G. (1961). *The Book of the It*. Introduction by Ashley Montagu. New York: Mentor: The New American Library.

Groddeck, G. (1977). *The Meaning of Illness: Selected Psychoanalytic Writings* (Including his correspondence with Sigmund Freud), Selected with introduction by L. Schacht. London: Hogarth Press.

Grosskurth, P. (1991). *The Secret Ring: Freud's Inner Circle and the Politics of Psycho-Analysis.* Reading, MA: Addison-Wesley.

Jones, E. (1957). *Sigmund Freud: Life and Work, Vol. 3.* London: Hogarth Press.

Miller, A. (1981). *The Drama of the Gifted Child.* New York: Basic Books.

Quinn, S. (1988). *A Mind of Her Own: The Life of Karen Horney.* New York: Addison-Wesley.

Roustang, F. (1982). *Dire Mastery: Discipleship from Freud to Lacan.* Baltimore, MD: Johns Hopkins University.

Whan, M. (1987). Chiron's wound: Some reflections on the wounded-healer. *Chiron: A Review of Jungian Analysis,* pp. 197–208.

6

ELIZABETH SEVERN

Sándor Ferenczi's Analysand and Collaborator in the Study and Treatment of Trauma

Arnold Wm. Rachman

Elizabeth Severn as the "Evil Genius" of Psychoanalysis

In an obscure passage, toward the end of the third volume of Jones's biography of Freud, Jones communicated to the analytic world Freud's negative view of Severn:

> ... an expatient—*a woman Freud called Ferenczi's evil genius.*
>
> *(Jones 1957, p. 407, italics added)*

Freud believed Severn had an "evil" influence because he blamed her for the following:

1. Encouraging Ferenczi to leave traditional psychoanalysis by involving him in boundary violations in clinical functioning and unusual theoretical concepts which were not in keeping with Freudian thinking.
2. Sapping Ferenczi's physical, emotional, and interpersonal functioning by her constant demands for attention and satisfaction of her unresolved needs.
3. He had no time or energy to maintain contact with Freud or to be part of the political structure of psychoanalysis.
4. Emotionally seducing Ferenczi into believing her pathological lies about her childhood traumas. Freud called her a "pseudo-logical phantastica" (a pathological liar) (Paskaukas 1993, p. 722).
5. Ferenczi's inability to resist her deep-seated needs for love and attention due to his unresolved need for his mother's love (Paskauskas 1993, pp. 721–722).
6. Ferenczi becoming a mother to Severn: "So he [Ferenczi] became a better mother even found the children he needed. Among these a suspect American woman ... (Mrs. Severn?)" (Paskauskas 1993, pp. 721–722).

The antipathy that Freud and the analytic community displayed toward Severn was based on rumors and prejudice. At this time in analytic history, we need to reexamine and reevaluate Severn's reputation and clinical experience with Ferenczi. New data has been discovered previously unknown to the analytic community. This has been the discovery of "The Elizabeth Severn Papers" (Rachman, 2009) and the "Interview with Dr. Elizabeth Severn" (Eissler, 1952).

Elizabeth Severn: The Person and Trauma Survivor

It was Masson (1984) who identified R. N. in Ferenczi's *The Clinical Diary* (Ferenczi 1988) as Severn. She was born Leota Loretta Brown on November 17, 1879, in Milwaukee, Wisconsin, and died on February 11, 1959, in New York City, at the age of 79 (Rachman, 2009). Severn's married name was Mrs. Heywood, which she changed to Elizabeth Severn around 1910 when she divorced Kenneth Heywood. Margaret, her daughter, "… never said why she chose Severn, or what significance the River Severn in England had" (Lipskis 1980, p. 5 in Rachman, 2009). Severn's childhood was marked by a series of severe traumas perpetrated by her father. They were recovered in the analysis with Ferenczi, which took place for eight years, from 1925 to 1933 (Eissler, 1952). The traumas were described in three stages in *The Clinical Diary*:

> Stage I. … at the age of one and a half years (a promise by [her father] to give her "something good"; instead of which drugged and sexually abused) … total disillusionment and helplessness … state of half-stupor … a wish not to be alive … complete repression of her own inclinations and feelings.
>
> *(Ferenczi 1988, p. 8)*
>
> Stage II. The second wave of shocks occurred:
> At the age of five, renewed brutal attacks; genitals artificially dilated, insisted suggestion to be compliant with men; stimulating intoxicants administered … suicide impulses … the sensation of dying (agony) … helplessness and despair of any outside help, propel her toward death.
>
> *(Ferenczi 1988, p. 9)*
>
> Stage III. The last great shock struck this person, who was already split into three parts, at the age of eleven and a half.
>
> *(Ferenczi 1988, p. 9)*

Ferenczi and Severn discussed her personality fragmentation as being divided into three parts: (1) the-suffering-child-in-the-adult. The conscious adult is not aware of the damaged child in the unconscious of the adult. The adult is unaware of the "buried child"; (2) the "Orpha" fragment, which Severn and Ferenczi named for the positive part of her personality remained, intact during her childhood traumas (Ferenczi, 1988; Rachman, 2014a, 2014b; Severn, 1933); (3) "... Soulless part of the personality ... or body progressively divested of its soul, whose disintegration is not perceived at all or is regarded as an event happening to another person, being watched from the outside" (Ferenczi 1988, p. 9).

As a result of her childhood traumas, Severn developed severe psychopathology as an adult (e.g., severe and debilitating headaches, severe depression with suicidal ideation, and periodic hospitalizations). She was able to marry and have a child, Margaret. Severn also enjoyed a successful career, first as a "therapeutic healer" and then as a lay analyst.

Severn as a "Therapeutic Healer"

Elizabeth Severn developed a career as a "therapeutic healer" before she entered psychoanalysis with Ferenczi (Rachman, 2009). She was also a lecturer and author, before and after her analysis with Ferenczi. She developed an interest in therapy through her work as a door-to-door encyclopedia salesperson, where her customers sought advice in personal matters (Fortune, 1993). Her customers responded to Severn's positive personality qualities, which included empathy, assertiveness, intelligence, and an engaging interpersonal style, qualities she brought to her analysis with Ferenczi.

Severn was one of the rare individuals in pre-analytic times who, when formal training for psychotherapy was not available, developed a therapeutic understanding of how to treat psychological issues. She combined the personal qualities of assertiveness, likeability, capacity for empathy, and interpersonal skill with a study of spirituality (Rachman, 2014). At first, she used therapeutic massages to help her customers at a woman's salon. Her therapeutic massage work was so popular that she was able to open up a private practice for nervous women (M. Severn, 1988 in Rachman, 2009).

Beginning in about 1908, Severn practiced her brand of therapy in the states of Colorado, New York, and Texas. One of her first clinical announcements said:

> Elizabeth Severn Metaphysician ... desires to announce ... Hours 10 to 12 p.m. 4 to 6 p.m. ... San Antonio, Texas ... In her exhaustive study of the mind, she retains the scientific attitude that aims always to make practical the truths promulgated. ...
>
> *(Rachman, 2014b)*

In the years to come, Severn called herself "Dr. Elizabeth Severn Metaphysician and Healer," as she noted in an April 9, 1911, announcement for a lecture before the Oriental Esoteric Society in Chicago and in a series of lectures in Washington, D.C. in the winter of 1912. By 1916, Severn sent out a notice about her clinical practice at 50 West 45th Street, in New York City, listing herself as "Dr. Elizabeth Seven, Psychotherapist" (Rachman, 2014b).

In the period 1925–1933, the years Severn was in analysis with Ferenczi, she had a practice in Budapest with a small group of patients she brought from the United States.

Severn practiced in London for a time after she left Budapest. The final phase of her clinical practice occurred when she returned to the United States. She had a series of offices in New York City, the last one being at 115 East 87th Street, where she practiced until her death in 1959 (Rachman, 2014b).

Severn's Self-Taught Therapeutic Knowledge

Severn was, originally, a self-taught therapist. She was influenced by the founder of Christian Science, Mary Baker Eddy, and Emile Couré, a French psychologist who introduced a method of self-improvement (Dupont 1988b, f2, 3, pp. 33–34). Eddy's ideas under the title of Christian Science (Eddy 1875) emphasized self-healing, free from drugs, medicine, and physicians. Healing for illnesses came from the individual and a belief in his/her own mental capacity for cure. One's illness was a result of one's faulty belief system. Mary Baker Eddy's philosophy was compatible with Severn's sense of spirituality, self-reliance, and self-assertiveness and provided the untrained Severn with a method of healing she could teach herself.

Another influence, called "Applied Psychology," was founded by Emile Coué (Abraham, 1926; Coué, 1920). He believed in "auto-suggestions" (self-hypnosis), that each person had the solution to his or her own problem: "You have in yourself the instrument of your cure." His "Law of Concentrated Attention" involved concentration on an idea over and over again, so you spontaneously tended to realize it. This philosophy produced his famous quotation: "Every day, in every way, I am getting better and better."

Severn as an Author and Lecturer

Severn published three books: (1) *Psychotherapy: Its Doctrine and Practice*. London: Rider (1913); (2) *The Psychology of Behavior*. New York: Dodd, Mead & Co. (1920); and (3) *The Discovery of the Self*. London: Rider (1933). An enthusiastic letter from London suggesting that Severn's establishment of a practice in London after she left Ferenczi was a result of her developing a following there through her books and lectures:

> Since I read your book on Psycho-therapy, I have become interested in the subject. Would you kindly let me know if there is any chance of your coming to England soon, as I would like to see you if possible.
>
> *(Rachman, 2014b, Letter to Dr. Severn from L. Chirnside.*
> *March 31, 1919, London, England)*

Elizabeth Severn, The Analysand

In autumn of 1925, Severn began an eight-year odyssey that became one of the most controversial psychoanalysis cases. Freud and his followers believed Ferenczi was emotionally seduced by Severn, a seriously disturbed individual. She also became his analyst because she triggered his fundamental unresolved childhood neurosis of an unfulfilled need for maternal love. Severn, it can be said, acted out her childhood traumas with an abusive father, urging Ferenczi to become the "all loving, all giving father."

Severn was clearly Ferenczi's "most difficult analysand," and he characterized her as having "schizophrenia progressia" (Ferenczi, 1988). The analysis began in a traditional way, but Severn's emotional issues did not respond to the traditional method of interpretation, analysis of resistance, and transference.

Severn developed her own ideas about how to conduct psychotherapy (Severn, 1920). She also had ideas about her own emotional problems, which developed from trauma stemming from the actual childhood abuse perpetuated by her father (Eissler, 1952; Ferenczi, 1988; Severn, 1933). Her clinical acumen and assertive personality allowed her to express her own ideas to Ferenczi about how she wanted and needed to be treated. She was determined to use her sessions to retrieve, confront, and work through her childhood trauma. Severn's idea is now considered standard procedure for the analysis of trauma (Rachman, 2003).

Severn also used her extensive experience as a psychiatric patient and her clinical functioning as a therapist as a resource to understand her own emotional issues as well as the functioning of the psychiatrists and analysts who had tried to help her:

> ... Dr. Ash ... A very nice fellow ... his own analysis was incomplete. And his analysis of me was limited ... he stopped it on his own ... it was not progressing as it should ... Otto Rank ... I found him completely wrapped up in this one idea of the birth trauma, and incapable of thinking of anything else ...
> ... Dr. Jelliffe ... A very sadistic man ... I was extremely disappointed with my work with him. Got absolutely nowhere.
> *(Eissler 1952, p. 4)*

After her experience with Rank in 1924, she said:

> I was in a desperate state ... because I didn't feel I could live unless I got rid of this thing that was still was troubling my unconscious, causing me violent headaches and deep depressions ... And if I could get rid of it, I certainly didn't want to live. ...
> *(Eissler 1952, p. 5)*

Even after failures in several analyses, she did not give up hope. Severn's Orpha function of her personality, one of her splits, helped her to survive her horrendous traumas and "bad analysis."

The Ferenczi/Severn analysis was a clinical interaction between an insightful, talented, and emotionally courageous analysand and a talented, empathic, and emotionally courageous analyst. Severn found in Ferenczi an analyst who was gentle and kind, especially empathic and responsive to her needs, in a way that no one other analyst had ever been. He "did not blame or criticize" Severn for any difficulties they had in their relationship. In fact, Ferenczi struggled to understand himself and accept her interpretations of his clinical behavior. With Severn, he developed a new kind of analytic relationship, where a democratic and mutual interaction prevailed. For the first time in analytic history, both the analyst and the analysand became participants in co-creating the analytic encounter, which included the "analysis of the analyst" (Ferenczi, 1980e, 1988) and attuning to the subjectivity of analysand and analyst (Rachman, 2010a).

Another unique part of the Ferenczi/Severn analysis was that Severn interpreted Ferenczi's clinical behavior and convinced Ferenczi to analyze his emotional reactions to her. Ferenczi struggled with Severn's suggestions for about a year, which she believed was interfering with the progress of their analysis. This also created a new way of being in the relationship. Freud's discovery of the countertransference reaction was transformed by Ferenczi into "countertransference analysis" (De Forest, 1954). Ferenczi could have said no to Severn's request for self-analysis and terminated the analysis, as Dr. Ash had done to her. Freud, Jones, and others urged Ferenczi to end the analysis with Severn because they felt she was causing him personal and professional harm. Was Ferenczi hopelessly caught in the countertransference reaction of needing Severn to fulfill his yearning for his mother's love, as Freud believed (Freud, 1933)? Ferenczi's willingness to see the analysis to a successful ending cannot be explained solely as psychopathology. Ferenczi's identity was built upon being a "healer," and Severn had a special need to be healed. She was convinced Ferenczi was meant to be "her healer." Ferenczi expanded the boundaries of empathy and activity as no analyst had done:

> When the case [Severn] did not show any progress I re-doubled my efforts, in fact I made up my mind not to be frightened off by any difficulty; gradually I gave in to more and more of the patient's wishes doubled the number of sessions, going to her house instead of forcing her to come to me. I took her with me on vacation trips [Madrid] and provided sessions even on Sunday. With the help of such extreme exertions and the help, as it were, of the contrasting effects of relaxation, we arrived at the point where the evidently traumatic infantile history could emerge, in the form of state of trance, or attacks.
>
> *(Ferenczi 1988, p. 97, Clinical Entry, May 5, 1932)*

Difficulties in the Analysis

"Semi-Trance Session"

When Ferenczi used traditional techniques to interact with Severn, she rebelled and made it clear to him that interpretation was a form of a detached intellectual response that was not helpful (Ferenczi, 1988). A particular dramatic example of this occurred in the later part of the analysis. Severn began a session lying in the traditional analytic position on the couch and remained silent. Ferenczi began speaking to her and she remained silent. Ferenczi thought the silence was protracted. Her eyes remained shut. He became anxious and started to offer a series of interpretations to break the silence, believing he was fulfilling his function to maintain a verbal interaction. Severn, however, was extremely dissatisfied with his interpretations and the breaking of the silence. He was interfering with her capacity to go into a "semi-trance" to re-experience her trauma. Ferenczi's "frantic interpretations" were interfering so she finally told him to "shut up" (Ferenczi 1988, pp. 29–31). Finally, Ferenczi realized that Severn was correct, appreciating that the "therapeutic trance" was more relevant to her treatment than interpreting her behavior as "resistant." Balint (1992), Ferenczi's closest colleague in the Hungarian Psychoanalyst Society, regularly discussed the analysis with Severn with his mentor. These discussions led to Balint elaborating on Ferenczi's new methodology of trauma-analysis in his concept of therapeutic regression.

Ferenczi's Empathic Failure Toward Severn

In 1928, Ferenczi introduced "clinical empathy" into psychoanalysis (Ferenczi, 1980a). This event changed the face of the analytic encounter forever (Rachman, 1989). The analysand was no longer blamed for the difficulties that arose in the analytic encounter. A time-honored tradition in psychoanalysis, the analysis of resistance, was reconfigured. Ferenczi attuned to the subjective experience of the analysand as well as his own, in order to work through the difficulty. It was the beginning of a two-person psychology in the analytic encounter (Aron, 1996; Rachman, 2007).

As had happened before in all her other therapies, Severn also reached a stalemate in the analysis with Ferenczi. She was "desperate" to get help because she was haunted by severe and crippling symptoms that were driving her toward suicide. When Severn and Ferenczi reached their impasse, Severn was convinced that she knew how to overcome the difficulty. She told Ferenczi that he had a negative countertransference reaction because he "hated women." His "antipathy" toward her was causing the therapeutic impasse. Ferenczi needed to analyze his negative feelings toward her in order to work through the impasse and liberate empathy. In the next session, Severn helped to create another historic moment in psychoanalysis. She told Ferenczi that he needed her to help him work through the relational crisis. Was her suggestion arrogance or genius? Did she understand countertransference better than Ferenczi? He spent most of 1932 agonizing over whether or not a mutual analysis was meaningful. An analyst had never allowed the analyst to be analyzed by the analysand. Of course, there also has never been an analysand like Severn. Her insistence on analyzing his antipathy toward her and Ferenczi's anxiety about losing control to a very difficult analysand were the makings of a monumental power struggle. But, in this moment in analytic history, something new was created in the analytic encounter, because he could relinquish his need for power, control, and status (Rachman, 2000). Ferenczi was willing to experiment with the nature of an analytic encounter, conceding to Severn that she had insight into their impasse and his subjectivity. He agreed to analyze his negative countertransference and allow Severn to help him.

Severn Analyzed Ferenczi

As a result of Severn convincing Ferenczi that he needed to analyze his negative countertransference reaction to her, they entered into a mutual analytic interaction. Neither of them realized that their work together would lead to Ferenczi's deepest therapeutic experience (Rachman and Prince, 2014). In the following sequence, Ferenczi uncovered his childhood sexual trauma (Rachman, 2010a, 2010b, 2012, 2014):

> Stage I. … [In] RN I find my mother again, namely the real one, who was hard and energetic and of whom I am afraid. RN knows this. …
>
> *(Ferenczi 1988, p. 45, Clinical Entry, February 24, 1932, italics added)*

When Severn encouraged Ferenczi to go deeper into his counter-transference reaction, a remarkable event occurred:

> Stage II. I submerged myself deeply in the reproduction of the infantile experience; the most evocative image was the vague appearance of female figures, probably servant girls form earliest childhood.
>
> *(Ferenczi 1988, pp. 60–61, Clinical Entry, March 17, 1932)*

Ferenczi was determined to go to "rock bottom" in analyzing his difficulties with Severn. What emerged was a recovered memory of child abuse:

> Stage III. … [a] mad fantasy of being pressed into this wound in the corpse.

> Stage IV. … a house maid probably allowed me to play with her breasts but then pressed my head between her legs … I became frightened and felt I was suffocating.
>
> *(Ferenczi 1988, p. 61, Clinical Entry, March 17, 1932)*

As the countertransference encounter continued, Ferenczi developed insight into his negative reaction toward women:

> Stage V. This is the source of my hatred of females. I want to dissect them for it, that is, to kill them.
>
> *(Ferenczi 1988, p. 61, Clinical Entry, March 17, 1932)*

This led to the insight about the emotional connection between his mother and Severn:

> Stage VI. The patient's demands to be loved corresponded to the analogous demands on me by my mother. I did hate the patient, in spite of all the friendliness I displayed. ...
>
> *(Ferenczi 1988, p. 99, Clinical Entry, May 5, 1932)*

Ferenczi also developed the awareness that Seven's negative reaction to him and their impasse was a transferential re-enactment of the original trauma that she suffered in her childhood with her father:

> Stage VII. ... This was what she was aware of to which she reacted with the same in accessibility that had finally forced her criminal father to renounce her.
>
> *(Ferenczi 1988, p. 99, Clinical Entry, May 5, 1932)*

Ferenczi reported that the mutual analytic encounter produced a diminution in the previously intractable erotic transference so that a more traditional analytic interaction could be reinstated. The transference changed because he was able to self-disclose to Severn his negative feelings toward her and became emotionally vulnerable through mutual analysis to reveal his own childhood sexual trauma (Rachman, 2014). Ferenczi did not recommend mutual analysis as a regular method, rather, only to be used as a last resort. Ferenczi credited Severn with a significant contribution to overcoming the therapeutic impasse. In essence, the most helpful clinical behavior was Ferenczi's attunement to Severn's subjectivity (Rachman, 2010a).

> ... [Severn said] her analysis would never make any progress until I allowed her to analyze those hidden feelings in me. I resisted for approximately a year but then I decided to make this sacrifice.
>
> *(Ferenczi 1988, p. 99, Clinical Entry, May 5, 1932)*

The Trauma of a Unilateral Premature Termination

Ferenczi reluctantly ended the analysis in February 1933 because he was too physically weak to continue, suffering from the advance stages of pernicious anemia. The analysis was in a "malignant regression" stage, uncovering the deepest level of childhood trauma. She and Ferenczi were exhausted from their eight-year struggle:

> ... I saw that he wouldn't be able to stand the analysis for long and I didn't feel I could either. It would mean giving up some more years of my life, and my money and everything else and so I finally managed to get away from Budapest by sheer will force, a complete "wreck."
>
> *(Eissler 1952, p. 7)*

Severn believed that Ferenczi's willingness to enter into a mutual analysis helped her separate from him:

> ... it was the last year I was there that I did his analysis, and that was really what helped me to get on my feet, You see to disconnect from him.
>
> *(Eissler 1952, p. 13, italics added)*

What seemed to be missing from the clinical experience of termination was the analysis of "the crisis of unilateral premature termination." What needed to be accomplished was analyzing the psychodynamics of the traumatic effect that premature termination had on Severn, which became a reenactment of her father's childhood abandonment and abuse. Severn felt Ferenczi leaving her was akin to her father throwing her out of his house and using her for his own purposes and neglecting her needs. There seemed to be a lack of analytical awareness that Severn's needs were not being met. What is more, Severn needed help from Ferenczi to separate from him. Perhaps a combination of his physical weakness and his emotional sense of failure with the analysis (Balint, 1992) produced a depressive reaction that interfered with his usual, brilliant analytic skills.

Ferenczi needed to unilaterally terminate the analysis before the malignant regressive phase could be worked through. Severn needed to continue her analysis to its conclusion. Why didn't Ferenczi refer Severn to another analyst when he knew he was becoming incapacitated, perhaps Michael Balint in Budapest or Izette De Forest in the United States? Did Ferenczi consider using any medications to help Severn with her severe symptoms? The use of psychotropic drugs was in its infancy in the 1930s. Severn would likely have turned down medication because she believed the tenets of Mary Baker Eddy. But, why did Ferenczi treat Severn for such a severe psychological illness without using the Groddeck sanatorium at Baden-Baden to hospitalize Severn, from time to time, when her trauma overwhelmed her? Did Severn convince Ferenczi that only he could treat her, and, only, by psychoanalysis? Did Severn's belief in Ferenczi as "her savior" influence him beyond his capabilities? Was he harboring a megalomaniacal fantasy of curing a severe disorder by virtue of his own personality and clinical skills as a psychoanalyst?

Severn's "Recovery"

Severn left Budapest in early 1933, in a state of near collapse and despair. She told Eissler:

> [I felt] ... a complete wreck. ...
>
> *(Eissler 1952, p. 7)*

Severn was not angry with Ferenczi or psychoanalysis for being in an emotional upheaval at the termination.

> ... it [the analysis] didn't lessen in any way my belief in analysis or its usefulness.
>
> *(Eissler 1952, p. 7)*

When Severn paid three consultation visits to Freud to assess her analysis, Freud did not voice any criticism of Ferenczi. But Severn's daughter, Margaret, was not so generous in her evaluation of the analysis with Ferenczi. According to Fortune (1993), Margaret Severn wrote a letter of protest to Ferenczi complaining about his treatment of her mother (p. 112). After Budapest, Severn went to stay with her daughter to recuperate. Margaret was a pioneer of modern dance working in Paris (Rachman, 2009). The relationship between mother and daughter was very close. Elizabeth Severn, as Freud had done with Anna (Rachman, 2003b), analyzed her daughter Margaret (Rachman, 2009). Whatever difficulties that analysis may have caused Margaret, it did not interfere with her helping her mother to recover.

If it is seen as a daring clinical experiment with limitations (Balint, 1992; Rachman, 2014a, 2014b), not a defect in analytic skill or a sign of psychopathology, Ferenczi provided a sense of empathy, safety, and trust, which helped Severn to retrieve, explore, and recover from her severe childhood traumas (Rachman, 2010a, 2010b, 2012, 2014a, 2014b).

"To Work, To Love"—(Freud): Severn's Functioning After the Termination of Her Analysis

To Work

Freud's standard of "To Work, To Love" (Erikson, 1950) has been used as an indication of analytic success. In Severn's functioning from 1933 until 1959, the twenty-six-year period from the ending of her analysis with Ferenczi until her death, there is evidence to support some success in the Ferenczi/Severn analysis. In the first year of her recovery, Severn wrote the last of her three books entitled *The Discovery of the Self* (Severn, 1933), as she was recovering from her traumas. The book can be seen as a psychoanalytic treatise on trauma disorder, the book Ferenczi and Severn intended to write together (Haynal, 2014; Smith, 1998). It reported the need for empathic understanding, the need for the analyst's responsiveness and flexibility and capacity for tenderness and affection.

Severn was able to resume her clinical practice but as a lay analyst not a meta-physician or psychic. Severn considered herself to have had a training analysis with Ferenczi (Eissler, 1952) as did Ferenczi (Ferenczi, 1988). In her interview with Eissler in 1952, she interacted as an analytic equal (Eissler, 1952).

After her recuperations in Paris, she moved to London where, as previously mentioned, she had developed a following from her earlier practice and the positive reception of her books. In the 1940s, she and her daughter moved to New York City. Her daughter had retired as a modern dancer to run a dance program. Severn practiced at 87th Street and Park Avenue until her death in 1959, apparently with success, as letters of testimony by her analysands indicate (Rachman, 2009).

When I inspected the interview that Kurt Eissler conducted with Severn on December 20, 1952, in New York City, when Severn was 73, the negative view of Severn's functioning rumored in the analytic community pointed to her as a dysfunctional and negative human being was erased. Severn came across as a very intelligent, thoughtful, assertive, and analytically informed individual. She was open and nondefensive in her responses to Eissler, who, at times, pressed her for specific answers. What is more, Severn offered many insightful statements about psycho-analysis, Freud, Ferenczi, Rank, and her own functioning. This interview showed Severn to be a person who seemed to recover from her illness and was functioning at a high level. In print, Severn sounded like a psychoanalyst who could handle Kurt Eissler, "the keeper of the keys" to the Freudian tradition.

To Love

Severn also showed meaningful functioning in her capacity to love after her analysis with Ferenczi. All through her adult life, Elizabeth Severn maintained a close, loving relationship with her daughter, Margaret. Perhaps their relationship was pathologi-cally close. Margaret Severn adored her mother, writing letters to her, sometimes on a daily basis, for about twenty years, while she toured the United State and Europe as a dancer (Rachman, 2009). When, the two moved to New York City, they had regular social contacts with friends and colleagues. On Sunday afternoons, they would invite people to afternoon tea. An eyewitness to these social gatherings reported that Elizabeth Severn was a friendly and responsive host (Rachman, 2009).

Severn's assessment of her analysis with Ferenczi is enlightening:

> As to my own analysis, some of the worst of my symptoms were allayed or disposed of, including the suicidal compulsion and the devastating head-aches, though I was emotionally exhausted and still subject to the devitalizing nightmarish dreams—and from these I have never fully recovered.
>
> *(Eissler 1952, p. 24)*

Michael Balint's assessment of the Ferenczi/Severn analysis is similar:

> The patient, a talented but profoundly disturbed woman, improved considerably ... but could not be considered as cured ... when we discussed his experiments—the case ... was the grandest,—Ferenczi accepted that, in a way, he failed, but added that he himself learned an immense amount, and perhaps even others might benefit from his failure if they realized that this task, in the way he tried to solve it, was insoluble.
>
> *(Balint 1992, p. 113)*

Severn's Contribution to the Evolution of Psychoanalysis

The Ferenczi/Severn analysis was a crucible for the diagnosis of a trauma disorder. Severn and Ferenczi shared sexual trauma backgrounds (Ferenczi, 1988), a sense of independence and rebellion (Rachman, 1997a), and negative parental experiences (Ferenczi, 1988). Was there ever an analysand and analyst matched with more similar psychodynamics than these two? On the basis of Ferenczi's own statements in his papers, *The Clinical Diary*, and the new data uncovered about Severn (Eissler, 1952; Rachman, 2009, 2014a), we can say that Severn was not only his analysand but also his partner or collaborator in the area of trauma studies. Their partnership actually produced a significant evolutionary step for psychoanalysis. Because of the suppression and condemnation of Ferenczi (Rachman, 1997b) and Severn (Rachman, 2014a), it was not previously possible to appreciate these contributions. Severn was a co-participant in many theoretical and technical innovations:

1. The introduction of clinical empathy (Ferenczi, 1980a)
2. The introduction of non-interpretative measures into the analytic encounter (Ferenczi, 1980a, 1980e, 1988)
3. Democratization of the analytic encounter (Ferenczi, 1980a, 1980b, 1980c, 1980d, 1980e; Severn, 1933)
4. Development of the Confusion of Tongues Theory (Ferenczi, 1980e)
5. Establishment of "Trauma-Analysis" (Ferenczi, 1980a, 1980b, 1980c, 1980d, 1980e; Severn, 1933)
6. Conceptualizations of the positive functioning of the self (Ferenczi, 1988)
7. Counter-transference analysis and "Analysis of the analyst" (Ferenczi, 1988)
8. The Orpha function of the individual as a life force for growth, repair, and recovery (Goldstein, 1995)

These innovations began an evolution in theory and technique that had far-reaching effects. First, Ferenczi and his analysand, Balint, formed the Budapest School of Psychoanalysis, which integrated greater flexibility, responsiveness, activity, and empathy into clinical interaction (Balint, 1992). Balint became one of the conduits for the

Object Relations perspective. During the same period, another Ferenczi analysand, Clara Thompson, as well as Henry Stack Sullivan and Eric Fromm were finding his ideas compatible with the Interpersonal Psychoanalysis perspective (Fromm, 1959; Thompson, 1950; Wolstein, 1993). The Ferenczi/Severn approach also influenced American Humanistic psychotherapy via the work of Izette De Forest (1954) and Carl Rogers (1951; Kahn and Rachman, 2000). Although Heinz Kohut did not credit Ferenczi as a forerunner, Michael Basch (1988) and John Gedo (1986) acknowledged Ferenczi as an influence on Kohut. After Kohut's death, the psychology of the Self perspective openly acknowledged Ferenczi's importance as a precursor of Self Psychology (Rachman, 1989, 1997c, 2014b). Through contemporary efforts (Aron and Harris, 1993; Harris and Kuchuck, 2015; Rachman, 2007, 2010b), Ferenczi has been established as one of the intellectual and clinical forerunners of the Relational Perspective. If one pauses to examine the influence of the Ferenczi/Severn relationship, one can conclude that their collaboration has been influential in providing the fertile soil for the evolution of the major psychoanalytic alternatives to the Freudian approach to psychoanalysis.

There have been a series of great cases in psychoanalysis, a special experience between analyst and analysand that contributed to its evolution. Berta Pappenheim is credited with helping Freud discover psychoanalysis as "the talking cure"; Sabina Sprielrein with helping Jung develop the theory and treatment of severe psychological disorder; Miss F. with helping Kohut develop Self Psychology; and Ellen West with helping Ludwig Binswager develop Existential Analysis. Elizabeth Severn should be credited with helping Ferenczi develop the diagnosis, treatment, and theory of trauma.

References

Abraham, K. (1926). Psychoanalytical notes on Coué's method of self-mastery. *International Journal of Psychoanalysis,* VII.

Aron, L. and Harris, A. (1993). *The Legacy of Sándor Ferenczi.* Hillsdale, NJ: The Analytic Press.

Aron, S. (1996). *A Meeting of Minds: Mutuality in Psychoanalysis.* Hillsdale, NJ: The Analytic Press.

Balint, M. (1992). *The Basic Fault: Therapeutic Aspects of Regression.* London: Tavistock; Evanston, IL: Northwestern University Press (Paperback edition) (Original edition 1968).

Basch, M. F. (1988). Reflections on self psychology and infancy, empathy and theory. *Progress in Self Psychology,* 3:55–59.

Coué, E. (1920). *Self-Mastery through Conscious Auto-Suggestion.* New York: Malkan Publishing Co.

De Forest, I. (1954). *The Leaven of Love: A Development of the Psychoanalytic Theory and Technique of Sándor Ferenczi.* New York: Harper & Row.

Dupont, J. (1988a). *Introduction. The Clinical Diary of Sándor Ferenczi.* J. Dupont (ed). Cambridge, MA: Harvard University Press.

Dupont, J. (Ed.) (1988b). *The Clinical Diary of Sándor Ferenczi.* J. Dupont (ed). Cambridge, MA: Harvard University Press, footnote 2, p. 33 and footnote 3, p. 34.

Eddy, M. B. (1875). *Science and Health.* Boston: Christian Science Publishing Company.

Eissler, K. (1952). Interview with Dr. Elizabeth Severn, December 20, 1952. Container 121. Sigmund Freud Papers, Sigmund Freud Collection, Manuscript Division, Library of Congress, Washington, DC.

Erikson, E. H. (1950). *Childhood and Society.* New York: W.W. Norton & Company, Inc.

Ferenczi, S. (1980a). The elasticity of psych-analytic technique. In M. Balint (ed) *Final Contributions to the Problems and Methods of Psycho-Analysis,* Vol. 3. New York: Bruner/Mazel, pp. 87–102 (Original was published 1928).

Ferenczi, S. (1980b). The principle of relaxation and neocatharsis. In M. Balint (ed) *Final Contribution to the Problems and Methods of Psycho-Analysis,* Vol. 3. New York: Bruner/Mazel, pp. 108–125 (Original was published 1929).

Ferenczi, S. (1980c). The principle of relaxation and neocatharsis. In M. Balint (ed) *Final Contribution to the Problems and Methods of Psycho-Analysis,* Vol. 3. New York: Bruner/Mazel, pp. 108–125 (Original was published 1930).

Ferenczi, S. (1980d). Child analysis in the analysis of adults. In M. Balint (ed) *Final Contribution to the Problems and Methods of Psycho-Analysis,* Vol. 3. New York: Bruner/Mazel, pp. 126–142 (Original was published 1931).

Ferenczi, S. (1980e). The confusion of tongues between adults and children: The language of tenderness and passion. In M. Balint (ed) *Final Contribution to the Problems and Methods of Psycho-Analysis,* Vol. 3. New York: Bruner/Mazel, pp. 156–167 (Original was published 1933).

Ferenczi, S. (1988). *The Clinical Diary of Sándor Ferenczi* (ed) J. Dupont [trans. M. Balint and N. Z. Jackson]. Cambridge, MA: Harvard University Press.

Fortune, C. (1993). The Case of R.N.; Sándor Ferenczi's Radical Experiment in Psychoanalysis. In L. Aron and A. Harris (eds). *The Legacy of Sándor Ferenczi.* Hillsdale, NJ: The Analytic Press, pp. 101–120.

Freud, S. (1933). Sándor Ferenczi: Obit. *International Journal of Psychoanalysis,* 14(3):297–299.

Fromm, E. (1959). *Sigmund Freud's Mission; an Analysis of His Personality and Influence.* New York: Harper.

Gedo, J. E. (1986). *Conceptual Issues in Psychoanalysis: Essays in History and Method.* Hillsdale, NJ: The Analytic Press.

Goldstein, K. (1939/1995). *The Organism: A Holistic Approach to Biology Derived from Pathological Data in Man* (Zone Books).

Gottschalk, S. (2006). *Rolling Away the Stone: Mary Baker Eddy's Challenge to Materialism.* Bloomington, IN: Indiana University Press.

Harris, A. and Kuchuck, S. (2015). *The Legacy of Sándor Ferenczi: From ghost to ancestor.* New York: Routledge.

Haynal, A. (1989). *Controversies in Psychoanalytic Method: From Freud and Ferenczi to Michael Balint.* New York: New York University Press.

Haynal, A. (2014). Orpha and trauma. In A. W. Rachman (ed) *Sándor Ferenczi and the Evolution of Psychoanalysis: Psychoanalytic Inquiry,* March.

Jones, E. (1957). *The Life and Work of Sigmund Freud, Vol. III: The Last Phase: 1919–1939.* New York, Basic Books.

Kahn, E. and Rachman, A. W. (2000). Carl Rogers and Heinz Kohut: a historical perspective, *Psychoanalytic Psychology,* 17:294–312.

Masson, J. M. (1984). *The Assault on Truth: Freud's Suppression of the Seduction Theory.* New York: Farrar. Straus & Giroux.

Mitchell, S. A. (1988). *Relational Concepts in Psychoanalysis: An Integration.* Cambridge, MA: Harvard University Press.

Paskauskas, R. A. (1993). *The Complete Correspondence of Sigmund Freud and Ernest Jones 1908–1939.* Introd. by R. Steiner. Cambridge, MA: Harvard University Press.

Rachman, A. W. (1989). Confusion of tongues: The Ferenczian metaphor for childhood seduction and emotional trauma. *Journal American Academy of Psychoanalysis,* 17:181–205.

Rachman, A. W. (1997a). *Sándor Ferenczi: The Psycho-Therapist of Tenderness and Passion.* Northvale, NJ: Jason Aronson.

Rachman, A. W. (1997b). The suppression and censorship of Ferenczi's confusion of tongues paper. *Psychoanalytic Inquiry,* 17(4):459–485.

Rachman, A. W. (1997c). (ed) Psychoanalysis favorite son: The legacy of Sándor Ferenczi. *Psychoanalytic Inquiry,* 17(4), November.

Rachman, A. W. (2000). Issues of power, control and status: From Ferenczi to Foucault. *Group: Journal of Eastern Group Psychotherapy* 7(1):121–144.

Rachman, A. W. (2003). *Psychotherapy of Difficult Cases: Flexibility and Responsiveness in Contemporary Practice.* Madison, CT: Psychosocial Press.

Rachman, A. W. (2007). Sándor Ferenczi's contributions to the evolution of psychoanalysis. *Psychoanalytic Psychology,* 24(1):74–96.

Rachman, A. W. (2009). *The Papers of Elizabeth Severn Letters, Papers, Books, Photographs, Personal Items, Personal Recollections A Lost Legacy of Psychoanalysis* (Unpublished).

Rachman, A. W. (2010a). An "invitro" study of intersubjectivity: Sándor Ferenczi's analysis of Mrs. Elizabeth Severn Presentation. XVII. International Forum for Psychoanalysis. Athens, Greece.

Rachman, A. W. (2010b). The origins of a relational perspective in the ideas of Sándor Ferenczi and the Budapest School of psychoanalysis. *Psychoanalytic Perspective,* 7(1):43–60.

Rachman, A. W. (2012). The Confusion of Tongues between Sándor Ferenczi and Elizabeth Severn. *Plenary Presentation.* The International Sándor Ferenczi Conference. "Faces of Trauma" Budapest, Hungary, Saturday, June 3.

Rachman, A. W. (2014a). Sándor Ferenczi's analysis of Elizabeth Severn: "Wild Analysis" or pioneering attempt to analyze the incest trauma. In A. W. Rachman (ed) Sándor Ferenczi and the evolution of psychoanalysis: Innovations in theory and technique. *Psychoanalytic Inquiry,* March.

Rachman, A. W. (2014b). The "evil genius" of psychoanalysis, Mrs. Elizabeth Severn: Dr. Sándor Ferenczi's partner in the pioneering study and treatment of trauma. *Presentation.* The Library of Congress, Washington, D.C., June 20.

Rachman, A. W. and Prince, R. (2014). *The Three Analyses of Dr. F.* (In preparation).

Roazen, P. (1975). *Freud and His Followers.* New York: Alfred A. Knopf.

Rogers, C. R. (1951). *Client-Centered Therapy: Its Current Practice Implications and Theory.* Boston: Houghton Mifflin.

Severn, E. (1913). *Psychotherapy: Its Doctrine and Practice.* London: Rider.

Severn, E. (1920). *The Psychology of Behavior.* New York: Dodd, Mead and Company.

Severn, E. (1933). *The Discovery of the Self: A Study in Psychological Cure.* London: Rider & Co.

Smith, N. A. (1998). Orpha reviving: Toward an honorable recognition of Elizabeth Severn International *Forum of Psychoanalysis,* 7(4):241–246.

Thompson, C. (1950). *Psychoanalysis: Evolution and Development. A Review of Theory and Therapy.* New York: Hermitage House.

Wolstein, B. (1993). Sándor Ferenczi and American interpersonal relations: Historical and personal reflections. In L. Aron and A. Harris (eds). *The Legacy of Sándor Ferenczi.* Hillsdale, NJ: The Analytic Press.

7

FERENCZI'S WORK ON
WAR NEUROSES[1]

Adrienne Harris

Ferenczi's paper "Two Types of War Neuroses" appeared in the *Zeitschrift* in 1916–1917 (Bd IV. 131) and is reprinted in the second book of his collected papers, *Further Contributions to the Theory and Technique of Psychoanalysis* (Ferenczi, 1928/1980). In the footnotes to that collection, we learn that the paper was presented at a "Scientific Congress of Hospital Physicians" (Ferenczi 1928/1980, p.124).

Ferenczi starts by describing his work in an army hospital he had been transferred to in early February 1916, during the First World War. He begins, modestly, by saying how preliminary his understanding is, based as it is, on work over a two-month period, when, nonetheless, he had "two hundred cases under observation." I find it telling that even if only at the beginning of his understanding, he felt the need to write and publish his thoughts on the damage to soldiers in the context of that war. The scale of damage, the unprecedented experience of trench warfare, the long exposures to inaction and powerlessness, and the effects of the machine gun led to breakdowns in unexpected ways and to unexpected degrees in many soldiers (Shepherd, 2000). The term *shellshock* illustrates the early ideas that these mental and physical collapses were organically driven.

The war was still ongoing when this paper appeared first as a talk and then as a publication. Not very much later, in 1919, when the Symposium on War Trauma appears at the International Congress, Ferenczi is mindful that this "new" preliminary knowledge is already disappearing.

In a collection of edited papers on war trauma, Steve Botticelli and I (Harris and Botticelli, 2010) note the overwhelming pattern of work on war trauma over this century. There is concern and rehabilitative and caretaking activity during the war and then the startling arrival of almost immediate "forgetting" in the postwar period, followed by the long slow leaking of traumatic residues over the next decades (Davoine, 2010). Now, no repetition of forgetting should be too surprising. We are in the presence of the uncanny, the erasure of anguish; really, its repeated disavowal. This repeated forgetting haunted the Second World War and many combats since, although there is some sign of the lifting of that amnesia. This paradox of forgetting and not forgetting seems to have a resonance in Ferenczi's own deeply held beliefs about dissociated states and the long sequaelae to trauma.

Ferenczi begins the 1917 essay by taking the reader along on a walk through the wards. He moves through rooms in which hundreds of men sit, stand, freeze, or shudder, caught in unimaginable anguish. Ferenczi also describes his thoughts about these men, taking us from the exotic ideas of "shellshock" to the sober realities of war neurosis, the psychic collapses and fragmentation that affect the mind as acutely as the newly fragmenting weapon of the machine gun.

In his rendering of the work done in the hospital, Ferenczi details a long rumination and period of discovery in order to get to the point of deciding that war trauma was psychogenic. He starts with the intense and startling bodily symptoms: chills, twitching, tremors, and paralyzed limbs with no organic basis for the paralysis. Soldiers with no observable injuries manifested inabilities in walking, standing, and moving. Many have atypical and odd gaits. He listens to the histories as they are remembered by the men: being buried, dumped into water or earth, dramatic temperature changes, knockdowns from up close, exploding shells, and watching the death or dismemberment of companions.

Ferenczi begins to see that many of the mono-symptomatic men carry as their symptom, their stance or movements just at the moment before a catastrophe occurs—stop time. He comes to think of these as a form of conversion hysteria. Ferenczi notes the intense repetitive dreams that relive the traumatic events, accompanied upon waking by amnesia, but with physical and motor manifestations of injury and damage. He sees in the incomprehensible actions an arm raised to shoot just before a devastating attack, a body turning away from a shell, or a body buried in earth or mud. He reads the bodies of these soldiers, guided by his psychoanalytic compass; sometimes with obsessive loyalty to Freud's focus on the sexual etiology of symptoms.

Ferenczi continues to think about the tenacity of these symptoms, the odd mismatch of gallant and often powerfully courageous soldiers and the manifestations of overwhelming fear. He begins to see regression in the pattern of symptoms, as though time and development have reversed. He sees hypervigilence and amnesia in the same soldier and makes the subtle point that phobia masks deeper levels of anxiety. He sees the flooding of war-specific induced trauma into sexual functioning, developmental level, and the fragmenting of mind and affect states. Ferenczi outlines a second kind of war neurosis that is driven by anxiety. In both types, he sees the powerful functioning of unconscious phenomena, regression, and fragmentation.

I read this essay and its report on Ferenczi's unique experiences in a wartime psychiatric hospital as creating experience and theoretical reflection that operated for the rest of Ferenczi's life. He goes back to an earlier interest in sexual abuse and trauma in the *Confusion of Tongues* (Ferenczi, 1933) and to fragmentation and dissociation that he wrote about in many clinical and theoretical papers (Ferenczi, 1928). The work reported in the paper on war neuroses contains the signature Ferenczian preoccupations with somatic representation and the interdependence of body and mind (see Chapter 5 by Fortune in this text), his personal evolution of Freud's idea that the ego is first a body ego.

I read this essay with a mixture of wonder and sadness. Ferenczi's observations seem so fresh, so modern, and so compassionate. He understands that these soldiers' bodies hold trauma, speaking it and denying it often in the same act. His observations are so humane, without the judgment or cynicism that dominated so many psychiatric and military encounters with shellshock and war trauma. Jones and Wessely (2005) have done an extensive historical review of the medical debates prior to 1914. It is important to know that there were precursors to the analyst/ psychiatrist who recognized the link between symptoms and psychic functioning, but it is also clear that certain conditions of this war (e.g., the industrialized character of trench warfare) required the leaps of diagnosis and care that Ferenczi and his colleagues promoted.

The sadness, for me, comes in what I know to be the long history of forgetting. Ferenczi's work and influence were occluded for reasons not especially associated with his work during and about the war. Because his reputation was so attacked in the 1930s after his death, much that he had to say about dissociation and trauma remains shadowed. But this forgetting of war trauma goes beyond Ferenczi and psychoanalysis per se. Many trauma theorists [(Gaudilliere, 2010), (van der Kolk et al, 1984), and (van der Kolk, 1994)] report the erasure of concerns for PTSD or other manifestations of war in every move towards peacetime life after warfare.

Returning to the context of Ferenczi's original essay, I want to first take up the way literary theorists have considered the impact of the 1914–1918 war. Paul Fussel (1975) wrote a fascinating and important book about the impact of that war on poetry and memory. He believed that fragmentation—the huge impact of powerlessness, mass death, and extermination—changed the whole context and shape of poetry and literature, indeed of memoir and memory itself. Fussell's text is devoted to literary sources and has been critiqued for its narrowness, but the sharp impact of his point remains important. The nature and conduct of that war left alterations in consciousness. Fussel saw that voice, syntax, structure, and form were all shattered by the war experiences of a generation of poets. There was a shattering of language (an echo of the shattering of bodies due to the introduction of mass trench warfare and the machine gun) that resulted in the collapse of many illusions, empires, and institutions. The very concept of shattered, fragmented selves is both locatable in Ferenczi's work and broadly found in the mass experiences of the First World War.

The literary arts were not the only art form that reflects the horrors of this war. In a 2007 show on surrealism at the Museum of Modern Art in New York City, the viewer is confronted in the anteroom to the show with a series of documentary films, yielding images that are both predictable and unimaginable. Trench warfare, strafing airplanes, cannons, dismemberment—all iconic forms of that war's imagery—flash by. But, shockingly, there is actual footage made in a military hospital, in which wounded men—faces smashed or battered—are outfitted with prosthetic faces. After viewing this show, you will never look at the canvases of the 1920s and 1930s, littered with damaged veterans, or the split faces and bodies in the works of Picasso and Braque, in the same light again.

Ferenczi's deep sensitivity to the impact of war shaped, I believe, his understanding of primitive mental states, regression, fragmentation, and trauma. But his work needs to be situated in the context of other prominent psychoanalytic figures of that period: Tausk, Groddeck, Grosz, Bion, and Simmel. These figures expanded their ideas and theories to encompass extreme trauma and fragmentation far in excess of Freud's own contribution to these matters in *Beyond the Pleasure Principle* (1920).

One feels that in his writing and clinical work, Ferenczi had a capacity to face and metabolize extreme trauma, in many different kinds of patients. These abilities were no doubt developed from many sources. But his experience as a psychiatrist/ psychoanalyst in the First World War was formative. The psychiatry and medical approach to shellshock in this period was just beginning to develop and in fact even the term *shellshock* was initially treated in a literal way—something mechanical and organic must have happened (Shepherd, 2000). In the space of the essay, we see Ferenczi working his way to a psychogenic theory of trauma. This theory leads toward a different model of mind, a perspective on dissociation and levels of functioning, a theory of trauma as a disrupter of time in the micro and macro sense of temporality.

Thinking about Ferenczi's work on war trauma and now knowing more about his work in the United States in New York from fall 1926 to spring 1927, I have found myself increasingly interested in the group of psychoanalysts/psychiatrists who lived through and were (I believe) deeply affected by the First World War. Men like Bion, Groddeck, Tausk, Simmel, and Feigenbaum (whom Ferenczi met in New York) wrote from a direct and immediate experience of trauma. Bion famously wrote, "I died on August 7th (1917) on the Amiens-Roye Road" (1982). Grotstein (1998, p. 612), in a review of Bion's memoir, interprets this sentence as a sign of Bion's enduring guilt and shame about the death in that battle of a brave and beloved friend. Many of these early analysts knew trauma firsthand.

Freud, in *Beyond the Pleasure Principle*, surely writes exquisite theory in regard to trauma and the repetition compulsion. But there is, for me, a chilly distance to that essay, most acutely in the footnote in the fort/da section, clearly a lynchpin to his whole argument. In that footnote, he notes briefly that the child repeated the fort/da process when a sibling was born and felt that rupture more keenly than the actual death of his mother. Commenting on the fort/da text, Freud says in this foot-note: "When this child was five and three-quarters, his mother died. Now that she was really 'gone' ('o-o-o'), the little boy showed no signs of grief. It is true that in the interval a second child had been born and had roused him to violent jealousy" (Freud 1920, p.16).

Now we know that the death referred to is of Sophie, Freud's beloved oldest daughter and that in more private communications he could express his under-standing that this was not a death to recover from. Yet, in print, this family trauma is read out of the child's play and story. It seems shocking under any circumstances. But I think that the distancing (certainly one would say traumatized) forms Freud's writing took (two years after Sophie's death in the 1919 influenza epidemic when his wife was pregnant with another child) compared to the more intense and haunted work of Ferenczi and others who saw war firsthand is striking. This very emotionally distanced perspective on loss and mourning has been noted by histo-rians and cultural theorists (von Unwerth, 2005; Breger, 2000), and for many, this stance is linked to accounts of Freud's difficulties with mourning and register-ing loss, difficulties in regard both to the death of his mother and of his beloved daughter.

Reading the Freud–Ferenczi correspondence in this early wartime period is quite odd (Falzeder and Brabant, 1996). In these letters, Ferenczi tracks the progress of his military work following his move to the Marie Valerie Hospital in Budapest for war-traumatized veterans (Feb. 1916, #598). He begins by calling these patients "brain crippled" (#556) but, eight months later, is describing conditions of "war psychoses and war neuroses'" (#561). It strikes me that Ferenczi is really using his wartime letters to Freud for continuing analysis. Almost every letter reads like an analytic session. Inner wars are referred to. Sexual life is relayed, in deep detail, with analytic commentary by Ferenczi. Related, it is worth pondering the link between his preoccupations with the vitality of sexual and relational life in the context of death and terror; Eros and Thanatos.

There is another way to read the odd bifurcation of Ferenczi's letters to Freud and his work on war trauma. The tensions within the psychoanalytic community in regard to the role of trauma and the role of drives, fantasy, and sexuality were particularly acute after 1913 (Makari, 2008). The question of character and trauma is no doubt complex, but it is also true that the key figures in the wartime era were constantly adjusting their ideas about trauma and sexual drives and their impact on neuroses. That tension remains in Ferenczi's conception of war trauma as conver-sion hysteria and/or phobia.

Despite Ferenczi's intense outpouring of personal detail and self-analysis in these letters—really streams of free association—Freud keeps his eye on psychoanalytic institutions and pragmatic matters. As Ferenczi gets ready to publish the paper on war neuroses, Freud is complimentary but says in #598, "keep your nice theoretical points of view there to yourself" and resolutely denies that he would ever have had the thought that traumatic neurosis could be a somatic representation of having died. This is a chilly and defensive reaction to Ferenczi, one might say. Freud is always interested in having some field of inquiry recruited to psychoanalysis. He is pleased, for example, to see Simmel's (1921) book on war neurosis, but mostly for its conveyed meaning that German psychiatry now absorbed a psychogenic view of war trauma. In other words, Freud's concerns are more institutional and pragmatic than clinically or empathically driven.

In the 1919 Symposium on War, presented at the International Congress in Budapest and published in 1921, the basic psychoanalytic point of view on war trauma and war neurosis is laid out with an introduction by Freud and papers by, among others, Ferenczi and Ernst Simmel, whose views are remarkably in tune with Ferenczi's. Simmel, by virtue of greater independence from Freud, is more able to focus on trauma, per se. He speaks definitively against the use of restrictive therapies to treat war neurosis, calling them a kind of "torture." He is cautious about the use of hypnosis and psychotherapy to treat war neuroses, because of the need for more thorough analytic treatment to effect deep personality change. Simmel's thinking about the interface of traumatic events of war and personality is fascinating. Sexuality, he explains, must clearly be implicated in traumatic experiences, particularly where such acutely primitive body states are involved. But he is also interested in how one's relation to authority may interface with war trauma. In one of his most harrowing examples, he traces an almost complete paralysis to an experience of being buried. He links the power of being dominated by comrades or officers with the resulting collapse of identity. Again, we might note the tension between a focus on contemporary trauma and the force of drive upon character, a tension similar to the one under which Ferenczi labored. Like Ferenczi, Simmel approaches war trauma with great compassion for suffering. One sees that his clinical work during the war taught him about the damaging horror of particular conditions: noise, mud, changes in temperature, and, above all, the impossible, unbearable experience of powerlessness.

I have gone back to this work of Ferenczi's on war neuroses for several reasons. First, I think it sheds light on his subsequent development and perhaps on ways he deviates from Freud, and not solely on the matter of sexual trauma. But I also want to tie this essay and Ferenczi's interest in psychotic process and primitive states to the work of his colleagues who worked and wrote in the shadow of the First World War. The war took different kinds of tolls on the psychoanalytic community. In my view, the erasure of Ferenczi within psychoanalysis limited not just his impact but also the powerful impact of many other war-generation analysts. They deserve a deeper hearing, and this chapter is a project in that direction.

Note

1 An earlier version of this text appeared in *Psychoanalytic Perspectives*, Volume 7, Issue 1, 2010 and appears here with permission of the publishers.

References

Bion, W. R. (1982). *The Long Week-End 1897–1919: Part of a Life*. Abingdon, England: Fleetwood.

Breger, L. (2000). *Freud: Darkness in the Midst of Vision*. New York: John Wiley.

Davoine, F. (2010). Casus Belli. In A. Harris and S. Botticelli (eds), *First Do No Harm: The paradoxical encounters of Psychoanalysis, Warmaking, and Resistance*. New York: Taylor and Francis.

Falzeder, E. and Brabant, E. (1996). *The Correspondence of SIgmund Freud and Sándor Ferenczi*, Volume 2, 1914–1919. Cambridge, MA: The Belknap Press of Harvard University Press.

Ferenczi, S. (1928, 1980). Two Types of War Neurosis. In *Further Contributions to the Theory and Practice of Psychoanalysis*. New York: Brunner Mazell.

Ferenczi, S. (1933). The confusion of tongues between adults and children: The language of tenderness and passion. In M. Balint (ed), *Final Contributions to the Problems and Methods of Psycho-Analysis, Vol. 3* (New York: Brunner/Mazel, 1980, pp. 156–167).

Freud, S. (1920). *Beyond the Pleasure Principle. The Standard Edition of the Complete Psychological Works of Sigmund Freud*, Volume XVIII (1920–1922): *Beyond the Pleasure Principle, Group Psychology and Other Works*, 1–64.

———— (1921). *Introduction to Symposium on War*.

Fussell, P. (1975). *The Great War and Modern Memory*. Oxford University Press.

Gaudilliere, J. M. (2010). Men learn from history that mean learn nothing from history. In A. Harris & S. Botticelli (Eds.), *First Do No Harm: The paradoxical encounters of Psychoanalysis, Warmaking, and Resistance*. New York: Taylor & Francis, pp. 15–28.

Grotstein, J. (1998). Bion, W. R. *War Memoirs 1917–1919* Francesca Bion (ed). London: Karnac Books, 1997, pp. vii and 312. *J. Anal. Psychol.*, 43:610–614.

Harris, A. and Botticelli, S. (2010). *First Do No Harm: The paradoxical encounters of Psychoanalysis, Warmaking, and Resistance* (Taylor and Francis, Relational Book Series, Volume 40).

Jones, E. and Wessely, S. (2005). *Shell Shock to PTSD*. Maudsley Monographs, Hove and New York: The Psychology Press.

Makari, G. (2008). *Revolution in Mind: The Creation of Psychoanalysis*. New York: Harper Collins.

Shepherd, B. (2000). *A War of Nerves*. Cambridge, MA: Harvard University Press.

Simmel, E. (1921). *Symposium on Psychoanalysis and the War Neurosis* Held at the Fifth International Psycho-Analytical Congress Budapest, September 1918. *Int. Psycho-Anal. Lib.*, 2:30–43.

van der Kolk, B. A. (1994). The body keeps the score: Memory and the evolving psychobiology of posttraumatic stress, *Harvard Review of Psychiatry*, 1:253–265.

van der Kolk, B. A., Blitz, R., Burr, W. A., and Hartmann, E. (1984). Nightmares and trauma: Life-long and traumatic nightmares in veterans, *Am. J. Psychiatry*, 141:187–190.

von Unwerth, M. (2005). *Freud's Requiem: Mourning, Memory and the Invisible History of a Summer Walk*. New York: Riverhead Books.

8

THE OTHER SIDE OF THE STORY

Severn on Ferenczi and Mutual Analysis

Peter L. Rudnytsky

> "Is the purpose of mutual analysis perhaps the finding of that common feature which repeats itself in every case of infantile trauma?"
>
> —Ferenczi, *The Clinical Diary*

A Ferenczian Experience

In scholarship, too, we have our Orphas. Thus it was that on December 16, 2013, as I was struggling to come up with a topic for my contribution to this volume, I received an e-mail with the subject line, "Ferenczi student visiting Gainesville." Its author, Katy Meigs, a writer and editor living in Ojai, California, reminded me that we had spoken at the 2012 conference of the Ferenczi Society in Budapest and asked if we could meet during her visit to Gainesville to see her daughter. One week later, Ms. Meigs appeared in my office, where she produced a photocopy of Elizabeth Severn's *The Discovery of the Self* and directed my attention to a case history beginning on page 134. Scanning the work, which I had to confess I had not read, I swiftly confirmed her surmise, "It has to be Ferenczi ..."

Discovering Severn

Severn's importance as the patient with whom Ferenczi engaged in his experiment of mutual analysis has been widely acknowledged since the publication of *The Clinical Diary*. What has hitherto been known about her life is indebted to Fortune (1993), and Severn has also found champions in Masson (1984), Stanton (1991), Wolstein (1992), Rachman (1997), and Smith (1998). But these authors have relied either on Ferenczi's portrait of her as "R.N." in *The Clinical Diary* or on impressionistic readings not simply of Severn's first two books (1913; 1917) but of *The Discovery of the Self* (1933), the distillation of her relationship with Ferenczi, which began with her arrival in 1925 and did not end until February 1933. Even Smith (1998), who discerns the muffled echoes of Severn's sexual and physical abuse in the "anesthetizingly comforting" (p. 242) rhetoric of her earlier books, in contrast to the "depth of healing" (p. 241) evidenced by *The Discovery of the Self*, concentrates on Severn's concept of "Orpha" as a protective shield against trauma and does not convey the landmark quality of her crowning achievement.

The realization that *The Discovery of the Self* contains a thinly disguised case history of Ferenczi, as well as of Severn herself, immediately transforms the book into one of the essential texts in the history of psychoanalysis and an indispensable companion volume to *The Clinical Diary*. For the first time, Severn truly emerges as a subject in her own right whose entire body of work warrants thoroughgoing reappraisal. *The Discovery of the Self*, by the same token, takes its place in the venerable tradition—extending from Freud and Ferenczi through Horney and Kohut—of covertly auto-biographical psychoanalytic writing, while also tacitly employing material from the analysis of a colleague, though Severn, unlike many others who have engaged in the latter practice, did so in an ethically responsible fashion by securing her analysand's informed consent and allowing him to see how she had rendered his case.

Competing Legacies

In a superlative feat of research, Brennan (2014) has established the identities of the eight principal patients referred to by code names in the diary. In addition to Severn, these include Clara Thompson ("DM.") and Izette de Forest ("Ett."). The renewed attention that should now go to Severn makes clear the extent to which these three formidable American women, while all marginal from the perspective of the hegemonic school of ego psychology, espoused competing versions of Ferenczi, the roots of which lie not only in their individual characters but also in the group dynamics of their time together during his final years in Budapest.

Of the three, Thompson is the most critical in her attitude toward Ferenczi. When de Forest (1942), in the first article on Ferenczi to appear in the *International Journal of Psychoanalysis*, argued that the analyst should help the patient "to face dramatically the trauma or traumatic series by re-living it emotionally, not in its original setting but as an actual part of the analytic situation" (p. 121), Thompson published a rejoinder (1943) in which she took aim at the premise that the analyst should facilitate the patient's reliving of traumatic experience by insisting on the analyst's obligation "to keep the patient in touch with reality," and that he ought therefore on no account to "make the patient believe the analyst is really involved" (p. 66) in any kind of joint enactment.

Although Thompson disputes de Forest's endorsement of Ferenczi's radical views, she does so respectfully and with an absence of rancor. Matters stand quite otherwise with Severn, whom Thompson evidently loathed. When Fromm was gathering testimonials for his rebuttal (1958) of Jones's (1957) impugning of the sanity of Rank and Ferenczi, Thompson wrote to him that Severn was "one of the most destructive people I know" and that Ferenczi "had the courage to dismiss" her after she "had bullied him for years" (Fortune 1993, p. 115), and she urged Fromm not to contact Severn. What is more, in the interview Thompson gave to Kurt Eissler on June 4, 1952, she maligned Severn as "a much better bad mother than Freud" and called her a "paranoid bitch" as well as a "Bird of Prey" (Brennan, this volume).

In the first entry of *The Clinical Diary*, Ferenczi (1932a) discloses that Thompson "had been grossly abused sexually by her father" (p. 3) in childhood. As Shapiro (1993) points out, however, Thompson failed "to spread the word when she returned to America about the reality of abuse and its impact on children's lives" (p. 162). Shapiro likewise notes that in his final diary entry Ferenczi (1932a) posed the question, "must every case be mutual?," and he commented that Thompson "feels hurt because of the absence of mutuality on my part" (p. 213).

Ferenczi's reference to Thompson's history of sexual abuse furnishes a context for his statements that she had "allowed herself to take more and more liberties" with his relaxation technique by kissing him, and then boasted to patients "who were undergoing analysis elsewhere: 'I am allowed to kiss Papa Ferenczi, as often as I like'" (p. 2). As Brennan (this volume) has shown, one of those to whom Thompson spoke was Edith Jackson, who was in analysis with Freud, and it was by this route that Freud heard about Ferenczi's supposed "kissing technique," which evoked Freud's condemnation and has led orthodox analysts, such as Arlow (1958) in his rejoinder to Fromm, to dismiss Ferenczi's technical innovations as "not psycho-*analysis*" (p. 14). At least indirectly, therefore, Thompson is responsible not only for exacerbating the conflict between Ferenczi and Freud but also for much of the damage to Ferenczi's posthumous reputation.

Compelling evidence that Ferenczi's indulgence of Thompson's behavior did not stem from any erotic desire on his part may be found in Thompson's posthumously (and only partially) published manuscript, "Ferenczi's Relaxation Method" (1933). There, Thompson writes of a woman "who had grown up in an intolerant small-town community" where she had been ostracized for her "childhood sexual activities with boys," for whom it became important in her analysis not only "to talk of whether her body was repulsive to the analyst, but to test it" (p. 67). Accordingly, she was encouraged by the analyst "to try a natural expression of her feelings," which made it seem "necessary for her to kiss the analyst not only once but many times and to receive from her not simply passivity but an evidence of warm friendliness and a caress in return before she could be conscious of the degree of degradation she had felt" (pp. 67–68).

In her case report, Thompson makes it seem that the patient and analyst are both women, and she professes to wonder whether the procedure would have been different had the analyst been a man. But it is obvious from what is known of Thompson's life, as well of her behavior during her analysis, that she is here giving an account of her own experience with Ferenczi, which she proceeds to justify by arguing that "the technique of not touching the patient except in the most formal way might easily act as a permanent reliving of the childhood experience so that an abreaction of the experience and change of attitude might remain permanently impossible" (p. 68).

Despite this veiled confession, however, Thompson incontrovertibly did not get what she needed from her treatment with Ferenczi. The bitterness of this disappointment must have heightened Thompson's antipathy to Severn, who took up so much of Ferenczi's time and emotional energy, and who cast the spell that led him to embark on the experiment in mutual analysis that Thompson herself so ardently desired.

Mutuality, Marginality, Magnanimity

Like Thompson, Severn preoccupies Ferenczi (1932a) throughout *The Clinical Diary*. But where he failed with Thompson, he succeeded with Severn. In his opening entry, Ferenczi reports that in what can only be her case "the communication of the content of my own psyche developed into a form of mutual analysis, from which I, the analyst, derived much profit" (p. 3), while in his closing entry he records not only Severn's hope that "what will *remain*" of their joint work "is a *reciprocal* 'honorable' recognition of mutual achievement," but also his own sense of accomplishment: "I released R.N. from her torments by repeating the sins of her father, which then I confessed and for which I received forgiveness" (p. 214).

Ferenczi's conviction that he "released R.N. from her torments" gains credence from Severn's interview with Eissler on December 20, 1952. Although Severn (1952) could not have known what Thompson had said to him, she calls into question the allegation that Ferenczi "dismissed" her from her analysis when she declares that, after a year of mutual analysis, neither she nor Ferenczi could stand it any longer, "and I was at the end of my strength and my money and everything else, and so I finally managed to get away from Budapest by sheer will force, a complete wreck" (p. 7). She reiterates, "it was the last year I was there that I did his analysis, and that was what helped me get on my feet, you see—to disconnect from him" (p. 13).

Beyond providing an alternative account of the end of her analysis, Severn exhibits a magnanimity toward Thompson that stands in stark contrast to Thompson's vituperativeness toward her. Concerning the fee arrangements for the mutual analysis, Severn explains that Ferenczi did not pay her anything but also stopped accepting money from her. In addition to disregarding a debt she had accumulated, Ferenczi had in analysis a wealthy American woman married to a Hungarian count. Ferenczi persuaded this woman, who had previously been Severn's patient, to lend or give her several hundred dollars, which Severn found "very humiliating" (p. 16), and he later told Severn that he was not charging this woman anything. "At the same time," Severn informs Eissler, "he was charging a young woman who was an analyst and earning her own living. I felt it was quite unfair. That the countess could pay, and it was hard for the other lady to pay. And he thought so, too, but he didn't do anything about it."

Thanks to Brennan (2014), we know that the wealthy woman married to a Hungarian count is Harriot Sigray ("S.I."), and the financially struggling analyst is Thompson, although Severn tactfully refrains from identifying Thompson in this connection. Thompson must have been aware not only that Ferenczi was coming to Severn for analysis but also that he was not charging either her or Sigray, while she herself was expected to pay for her sessions. These inequities added insult to the injury of being excluded from mutual analysis, and they undoubtedly fueled Thompson's grudge against Ferenczi and hatred of Severn.

After Ferenczi's death, his wife assured Thompson that "he had often told her that I would be his best pupil" (Brennan, this volume). But this did not outweigh her sense of not being close to Ferenczi's heart. Paradoxically, therefore, whereas to all outward appearances Thompson was Ferenczi's "best pupil" in the United States, with Severn on the remotest margin, the truth as seen from inside is rather the reverse, with Severn being, as Ferenczi wrote to Groddeck on December 21, 1930, his "main patient, the 'Queen,'" to whom he devoted as much as "four, sometimes five hours daily" (Fortune 2002, p. 96), and Thompson nursing an inferiority complex. Given Severn's unmatched closeness with Ferenczi, the notion "that Thompson was much more privy to intimacies about Ferenczi's life than Severn" (Brennan, this volume) appears to be an unwarranted inference arising from Severn's reticence, compounded by an unfamiliarity with her case history of Ferenczi in *The Discovery of the Self*. Despite being, as her daughter Margaret recalled, "a one-woman show," with "no friends or colleagues, only patients" (Fortune 1993, p. 105), and lacking an institutional base of any kind, Severn (1933) understood Ferenczi more profoundly than anyone. Certainly, in her espousal of "*Psycho-Gnosis*" (p. 222), she was more attuned than either Thompson or de Forest to his mystical tendencies, or what Groddeck, in a letter to Gizella Ferenczi after Sándor's death, termed his "ascent to the stars" (Fortune 2002, p. 114).

Severn on Psychoanalysis

By the time Severn began her eight-year odyssey with Ferenczi in 1925, she had published two books that engaged with Freud and his ideas, and long regarded herself as a practitioner of psychoanalysis. She had, moreover, as she informed Eissler, previously attempted analysis with Smith Ely Jelliffe, Joseph Asch, and

Otto Rank. *The Discovery of the Self* (1933) is, therefore, the distillation not simply of her experience with Ferenczi but of her sustained immersion in psychoanalytic culture. The depth of her understanding, her anticipation of later trends, and the cogency of her criticisms can all be gleaned from a handful of quotations. She pays tribute at the outset to Freud: "The truth is that there is a very large part of the mind, actively functioning, which is completely unknown to the conscious self. ... The lifting of the invisible into visibility was a prodigious work and has entitled Freud to a distinguished place among the scientists and benefactors of mankind" (pp. 12–13).

Although she acknowledges Freud as the indispensable starting point, Severn's emphasis on the permeability of the child's mind to environmental influences articulates a fundamental principle of relational thinking: "It is little realized how sensitive the child's mind is, and especially how even in its 'unconscious' years— that is generally until the third year—it is the constant recipient of the words, actions, and behavior (and I believe also the thoughts) of those in his environment" (p. 19). Her comments on a boy who stole money and craved sweets cannot fail to remind contemporary readers of Winnicott on the antisocial tendency: "These too told that he did not receive enough love from his mother, and the angry outbursts were a positive symptom expressing his unconscious rage at the deprivation" (p. 143). Both Winnicott and Kohut would concur with Severn that the analyst ought "to provide the patient with just that psychic atmosphere which must have been absent in his early life, or he would not be compelled to seek the kind of help he is seeking now" (p. 87), while Kohut especially would applaud her recognition that the patient requires "endless understanding and 'Einfühlung,' as the Germans say it, a kind of 'feeling in' or identification with him and his problem, whatever it may be" (p. 61).

Beyond these prescient theoretical insights, Severn judiciously assesses "the *limitations* of Psycho-Analysis" (p. 58). Just as Ferenczi in *The Clinical Diary* (1932a) faults Freud because he "introduced the 'educational' stage too soon" (p. 62) into analysis, so Severn (1933) stresses that the analytic "relationship should be anything but a pedagogical one" (p. 61). In her interview with Eissler, Severn (1952) states that during the second of her three meetings with Freud, in 1929, she expressed her conviction that his early students "had not been thoroughly analyzed" because "they had been analyzed in an intellectual manner," but "this limitation did not appear to Freud to be a limitation" (p. 3). Entirely in Ferenczi's spirit is Severn's espousal (1933) of the virtues of elasticity, tact, and humility: "The greatest objection to be made against Psycho-Analysis as such is, in my opinion, its *rigidity*. Being devised as a systematic and observational method, it lacks in flexibility and humanness in its personal application to sick people" (p. 59). "The analyst has to be very tactful in this process," Severn adds, while the patient should have the right "to say when he thinks the analyst is wrong, since the person of the analyst represents an authority to him" (p. 60).

The Battle Lines

In a letter to Jones on May 29, 1933, one week after Ferenczi's death, Freud alleged that Ferenczi had fallen victim to "mental degeneration" that was manifested in his "technical innovations," and pointed his finger squarely at a "suspect American woman" with the most bizarre ideas:

> After she left, he believed that she influenced him through vibrations across the ocean, and said that she analyzed him and thereby saved him. (He thus played both roles, was mother and child.) She seems to have produced a *pseudologia phantastica*; he credited her with the oddest childhood traumas, which he then defended against us. In this confusion his once so brilliant intelligence was extinguished.
>
> *(Paskauskas 1993, p. 721)*

Pseudologia phantastica. To Freud, Severn was a compulsive liar, while Ferenczi's willingness to credit her reports of the "oddest childhood traumas" was a symptom of the loss of his mind. Hence Freud's notorious condemnation of Severn as Ferenczi's "evil genius" (Jones 1957, p. 407)—an epithet he had previously used (1914, p. 45) to denounce the German psychiatrist Alfred Hoche, who had attacked the nascent psychoanalytic movement as a sect, and which derives from Descartes' fear that a malicious deceiver was trying to seduce him in his dreams (Freud, 1929).

Ferenczi's rehabilitation of Freud's "seduction theory" is eloquently defended by Severn in *The Discovery of the Self* (1933):

> The importance of *trauma* as a specific and almost universal cause of Neurosis, was first impressed upon me by Ferenczi, who, probing deeply, had found it present in nearly all his cases. He thus resurrected and gave new value to an idea which had once, much earlier, been entertained by Freud, but which was discarded by him in favor of "phantasy." ... Experience has convinced me, however, that the patient does not "invent," but *always tells the truth*, even though in a distorted form: and further, that what he tells is mostly of a severe and specific injury, inflicted on him when he was young and helpless. (pp. 125–126)

From this premise of the reality of traumatic experience, it follows that "emotional recollection and reproduction" is "the *sine qua non* of successful analysis" (p. 93). Severn continues:

> It is an important measure which was worked out between Ferenczi and myself in the course of my own long analysis with him—a development which enables the patient to re-live, as though it were *now*, the traumatic events of the past, aided by the dramatic participation of the analyst.

It is usually considered enough to recollect these events mentally, but the thing that made them harmful in the first place was, in every case, the *shock*, the psychic reaction to them. ... The emotion created was of a nature or degree that made it incapable of assimilation by the person suffering it, and it is this feeling–quality which has to be recovered and experienced again, in order to bring, first, conviction and, secondly, release through reconstruction. (pp. 93–94)

Or, in Severn's epigrammatic formulation: "'Hallucination,' they say—*Memory*, I say, a memory which had been kept alive in the Unconscious, and which was now, perhaps for the first time, projected outward into the objective world where we could see it" (p. 97).

The Case of Ferenczi

According to Fortune (1994), Severn "does not mention mutual analysis, and there are few references to Ferenczi" (p. 221) in *The Discovery of the Self*. Severn, however, told her daughter that Ferenczi had asked her not to divulge that they had engaged in mutual analysis (Fortune 1994, p. 221), while in an addendum to her interview with Eissler she attested (1952) that *The Discovery of the Self* "replaced to some extent the plans Ferenczi and I had had for a more scientific mutual publication," and that "he saw the MSS. before I left and approved it" (p. 24). Thus, while respecting Ferenczi's wishes, Severn's book is not only about the experience of mutual analysis but also a "mutual publication" insofar as it received his blessing before his death, and Ferenczi's spirit permeates every page.

The case history of Ferenczi appears in Chapter 5, "Nightmares Are Real," which forms the clinical heart of Severn's book. Severn (1933) introduces her patient as "a man of especially high moral and intellectual standing, with a very balanced outlook on life and marked serenity of manner. He suffered from various physical symptoms, which he ascribed mostly to bodily causes," and was "in a state of constant depression in regard to his health" (pp. 134–135). Contending that the analysis disclosed not only a "definite psychological clinical picture quite sufficient to account for his state of physical deterioration" but also "a clearly outlined psychosis," Severn affirms, "The patient was not the balanced, well-adjusted person that he, and others, had imagined" (p. 135).

Ferenczi had been worried for decades about his health, and by 1932 he was in a "state of physical deterioration," which he attributed in *The Clinical Diary* (1932a) to the prospect of being "trampled under foot" by Freud's "indifferent power" (p. 212), a "definite psychological clinical picture." Severn's initial perception of her "patient" as "very balanced" and possessing a "marked serenity of manner" comports with Ferenczi's account of how he had been taught by Freud to exhibit a "calm, unemotional reserve" and "unruffled assurance that one knew better" (p. 185). In describing the "antipathy" and "apprehension" aroused in him by Severn, Ferenczi acknowledges, "I appear to have assumed, perhaps uncon-sciously, the attitude of superiority of my intrepid masculinity, which the patient took to be genuine, whereas this was a conscious professional pose, partly adopted as a defensive measure against anxiety" (p. 97). Although Severn's imputing of a "psychosis" to Ferenczi might seem extreme, it is corroborated by his avowal, "Psychoanalytical insight into my own emotional emptiness, which was shrouded by overcompensation (repressed—unconscious—psychosis) led to a self-diagnosis of *schizophrenia*" (p. 160).

Ferenczi's façade of "intrepid masculinity" crumbled during his analysis when, as Severn (1933) recounts, his "psychosis" was "involuntarily enacted": "He spoke to me suddenly one day about Strindberg's play *The Father*, and became himself almost immediately the insane son. He broke down and asked with tears in his eyes, if I would sometimes think of him kindly after he had been put away in the asylum" (p. 135). Severn says that her patient "evidently expected to be thus sent away at that moment," and that he added "with terrible pathos, 'And we like, when the straitjacket must be put on us, that it shall be done by our mother.'" She elaborates, "I immediately saw by this that the patient was re-experiencing a severe trauma in which he expected his mother to send him away as insane."

In recounting Ferenczi's "emotional recollection and reproduction" of his "severe trauma" at the hands of his mother, "aided by the dramatic participation of the analyst," Severn fills in the contours of Ferenczi's description in *The Clinical Diary* (1932a) of how "to use R.N.'s mode of expression: in R.N. I find my mother again, namely the real one, who was hard and energetic and of whom I am afraid" (p. 45). From Severn's (1933) perspective: "We already knew something of this story, of his mother as an angry, hysterical woman, often scolding and threaten-ing her child, and especially for a certain event which she had treated with such harshness and vituperation to make him feel completely crazy and branded as a felon" (pp. 135–136). The "event" is probably when Ferenczi was "threatened with a kitchen knife" by his mother "at the age of about three" for "mutual touch-ing" with his sister Gisela, confessed in a letter to Freud on December 26, 1912 (Brabant, Falzeder, and Giampieri-Deutsch 1993, p. 452). But whereas Freud did not encourage Ferenczi to go beyond intellectual remembering to an emotional catharsis, with Severn (1933) "the unexpected reproduction in the analysis of a part of this painful scene" enabled him "to acknowledge this traumatically-caused insanity for the first time as a living fact in himself, which was the beginning of its dissolution" (p. 136).

After setting forth the primal trauma inflicted on Ferenczi, Severn proceeds to narrate "still another serious trauma, allied to that caused by the mother," namely, "an unscrupulous attack by an adult person on the child's sensibilities, which was ruinous to his mental integrity and subsequent health" (p. 136). In this instance, "he was a boy of six, his nurse the offender. She was a comely young woman of voluptuous type who, for the satisfaction of her own urgencies, seduced the child, i.e. used him forcibly as best she could in lieu of an adult partner" (pp. 137–138). Ferenczi, in the *Diary* (1932a), augments Severn's account by recalling his "reproduction of infantile experiences" in mutual analysis, specifically "passionate scenes" with a housemaid who "probably allowed me to play with her breasts, but then pressed my head between her legs, so that I became frightened and felt as if I was suffocating" (p. 61). This trauma, Ferenczi proposes, is the source of his "hatred of females," leading him to feel not only murderous rage but also "exaggerated reactions of guilt at the slightest lapse."

Severn (1933) rounds out her case history by observing that the child was "horrified, frightened, and emotionally shocked by coming in contact with such emotional violence," but simultaneously "he was in a real sense 'seduced' in that he was made suddenly and unduly precocious, a *desire* was aroused in him which was beyond his years and his capacity but which remained, nevertheless, to act as a constant excitation, with an inclination to a repetition of the experience" (p. 138). Ferenczi, that is, became a "wise baby," exhibiting the "*precocious maturity*" that, as he expounded theoretically in "Confusion of Tongues" (1932b, p. 165), regularly results from trauma, but also undergoing the "*introjection of the guilt feelings of the adult*" (p. 162) that is a further price to be paid for being subjected to such an ordeal. Or, as Severn (1933) puts it, the child is usually "too shocked to recognize the enormity of the sin *against him*," and consequently finds it easier "to feel himself the guilty one" (pp. 138–139). Her patient, Severn concludes, "preserved his sanity" and reestablished "a seemingly normal relation to life after the trauma" by "what Ferenczi would call fragmentation" (p. 139). In other words, "he eliminated the entire affair ... and his own fury" from his "psyche as a whole," although "the exploded bits continued to exist, spatially speaking, outside of him: where we had to 'catch' it, so to speak, before it could be restored" (pp. 139–140).

By such a "remarkable compensatory mechanism," the child who became Severn's patient "grew to be a person of unusual intelligence, balance, and helpfulness," though "at what cost," Severn ruefully notes, "the reader can well imagine. He was deprived of both happiness and health for most of a life-time, for it was fifty years after its occurrence, that this trauma came under observation and treatment" (p. 140).

The Father as Son

The title of Strindberg's *The Father* (1887) is ironic, since the Captain, a military officer and freethinker who initially seems to dominate his household full of women with "intrepid masculinity," becomes obsessed with doubts that he is the father of his daughter, Bertha. The conflicts with his wife, Laura, lead to a regression in which she takes on a maternal role: "Weep then, my child, and you will have your mother with you again. Do you remember that it was as your mother I first came into your life? ... You were a giant of a child and had either come into the world ahead of your time—or perhaps you were unwanted" (p. 39). The Captain confirms, "My father and mother did not want a child; and so I was born without a will of my own."

Strindberg here encapsulates the syndrome delineated by Ferenczi in "The Unwelcome Child and His Death Instinct" (1929), as well as the "precocious maturity" that is a concomitant of trauma. Laura's plan to have her husband declared insane and committed to an asylum is termed by her brother, the Pastor, "an innocent murder that cannot be reached by the law" (Strindberg 1887, p. 45). As the straitjacket is placed on the unsuspecting Captain by his erstwhile nursemaid, Margaret, she reminds him, "Do you remember when you were my darling little child and I used to tuck you in at night and read 'God loves the little children dearly' to you?" (p. 51). Once pinioned, the Captain rages against every woman he has ever known as his "deadly enemy" (p. 53), but soon collapses on Margaret's breast:

> Let me put my head in your lap. There! It's so nice and warm! Lean over me so that I can feel your breast!—Oh, how wonderful to fall asleep at a mother's breast—whether mother or mistress ... but most wonderful at a mother's! (p. 55; ellipses in original)

As the play ends, the Captain wails, "A man has no children, it is only women who bear children" (p. 55), before falling victim to a stroke. Feeling his pulse, the Doctor pronounces, "he may still come back to life ... but to what kind of awakening— that we cannot tell" (p. 56; ellipses in original).

In disclosing Ferenczi's identification with the character of Strindberg's Captain, Severn affords a window into his psyche. It is striking that she should write, "He spoke to me suddenly one day about Strindberg's play *The Father*, and became himself almost immediately the insane son," since the crux of the play is that the father *is* "the insane son," and psychically not a father at all. Ferenczi, of course, had only stepchildren, thus literalizing the Captain's plight. It is equally striking that Ferenczi should have said to Severn, "And we like, when the straitjacket must be put on us, that it shall be done by our mother," since in the play the straitjacket is put on the Captain not by his mother but by his nursemaid. But just as Margaret is conflated by the Captain with his mother, so, too, the childhood traumas relived by Ferenczi in his analysis with Severn were perpetrated by both his mother and his nurse. As we read in *The Clinical Diary*, when Ferenczi (1932a) contemplated holding out against mutual analysis, he imagined Severn responding with a ferocity worthy of the Swedish dramatist:

> And is it not one of your own peculiar analytic weaknesses of character that you are unable to keep any secrets to yourself, ... that you have an uneasy conscience, as if you had done something wrong, and that you have to run to your mother or wife, like a small boy or submissive husband, to confess everything and obtain forgiveness! (p. 35)

Severn on Severn

A case history no less transparent than that of Ferenczi concludes "Nightmares Are Real." Introduced by Severn (1933) as "one on which I worked for a long time," it concerns "a highly intelligent, mentally active, woman of middle-age" who concealed her "internal disintegration" but was nonetheless "a very sick woman, carrying on the necessary activities of her life by means of a superhuman will" (p. 153).

This is, of course, Severn herself, presenting her analysis with Ferenczi as though she were one of her own patients. "The analysis revealed an astonishing story of almost complete amnesia prior to her twelfth year," during which the patient was subjected to "incredible abuse" by "a diabolically clever and secretly criminal father," compounded by "a stupid enslaved mother who completely closed her eyes to all that took place" (p. 153). The father, it transpires, "had left the family after a final and violent crisis in connection with his daughter, evidently being satisfied that the culminating shock to which he subjected her had deprived her of all memory" (pp. 153–154).

All these details are amplified in *The Clinical Diary*. Ferenczi (1932a) tells how R.N., "who was already split into three parts," was struck by "the last great shock … at the age of eleven and a half" (p. 9). He specifies that "the most abominable cruelty" was that "she was forced to swallow the severed genitals of a repugnant black man who had just been killed" (p. 140), which led to her "extraordinary, incessant protestations that she is no murderer, though she admits to having fired the shots" (p. 17). Severn's analysis of the relationship between her "criminal" father and willfully blind mother is echoed when Ferenczi writes, "the most frightful of frights is when the threat from the father is coupled with simultaneous desertion by the mother" (p. 18). Severn (1933) highlights that "as part of the abuse heaped upon the child we found to have been the constant use of narcotic drugs" (p. 154), just as Ferenczi (1932a) comments that R.N. "considers the effect of anesthetics a monstrous act of violence. … To be anesthetized is thus to be temporarily split off one's own body: the operation is not carried out on me, but on a body to which I used to belong" (p. 17).

Although Severn (1933) does not disclose that she had committed a murder, the theme is conspicuous in her dream life. She reports that her "patient" had "a dream entitled 'This is how it feels to be murdered'" (p. 154), in which the scene of abuse by the father was repeatedly reenacted. "We went through the phase of considering it as a phantasy only," she observes, "but the amount and terrific intensity of the emotions which accompanied each and every manifestation, finally convinced both of us beyond any question that it was a historical reality" (p. 155). Her account of what unfolded in her analysis with Ferenczi is complemented by his admonition (1932a) that "patients cannot believe that an event really took place, or cannot fully believe it, if the analyst, as the sole witness of the events, persists in his … purely intellectual attitude," and one should therefore choose "actually to transport oneself with the patient into that period of the past (a practice Freud reproached me for, as being not permissible), with the result that we ourselves and the patient believe in its reality" (p. 24).

Severn (1933) lets it be known that the patient who is really herself "had originally withstood the shock of repeated misuse" by means of "fragmentation," as a consequence of which "there gradually appeared at least three persons with distinctness and clarity" (p. 155). As we have seen, Ferenczi found that R.N. "was already split into three parts" when she received "the last great shock" in her twelfth year. Severn's fragmentation is depicted in a dream in which she dances to music "played by another girl, her double," on the piano, and though "both girls were thus active, they were also both *dead*, and the patient felt dead while dreaming it." In the course of the analysis, "the patient finally came to recognize herself as both these girls *at the same time*." Ferenczi (1932a) writes of R.N. in the diary: "frequently recurring form of dream: two, three, or even several persons represent, according to the completed dream-analysis, an equal number of component parts of her personality" (p. 157).

In addition to her piano dream, Severn (1933) had another "double" dream, "'I attend my own funeral'" (p. 156). Against Freud's claim that "no one ever dreams of his own death," Severn counters that it is "perfectly possible for a person to be psychically 'killed,' or some part of him killed, while he still continues to live in the flesh." Indeed, in her own case, "the patient was not so much looking back upon an earlier psychic catastrophe as she was expressing, exactly as it was registered in her mind, what had actually occurred at the time." In an experiential account of the origins of Ferenczian trauma theory, what Severn relived in her dream "was nothing less than a recognition of the destruction or loss of an integral part of her being, while another part was sufficiently removed from the immediate psychic environment to look at what was occurring and suffer accordingly."

Severn concludes by drawing attention to "another illuminating type of dream" that showed "the remarkable resources of her psyche for preserving itself when thus attacked" (p. 157). She cites as an illustration a dream, "The child's life is insured by magic." Here, the part of her she termed her "Intelligence," which, as in Ferenczi's case, "had developed to unusual proportions as compensation for the damages done, came to her rescue like a ministering angel and took over the care of the child while she was physically and psychically exposed to the evils of her father." "The Intelligence," Severn goes on, was "'magical,' had appeared very early in the child's life and continued to watch over her like a mother, giving her a kind of psychic sustenance by means of which she managed to withstand the cruelties both moral and physical which fate had placed upon her."

To learn the name of Severn's "Intelligence," we must turn to *The Clinical Diary*:

> Patient R.N. even imagines that at the time of the principal trauma, with the aid of an omnipotent Intelligence (Orpha), she so to speak scoured the universe in search of help. ... Thus her Orpha is supposed to have tracked me

down, even at that time, as the only person in the world who owing to his special personal fate could and would make amends for the injury that had been done to her.

(Ferenczi 1932a, p. 121)

Recognizing that to many "it may seem as fantastic to believe in this kind of 'Insurance' as in my proposal that all dreams are 'true' and but the ghosts of our past," Severn (1933) argues that this is "the same process which physiologists know so well in the bodily realm, of compensation and adaptation," and, on a higher plane, "a manifestation of the intelligence of the Unconscious, the trend toward 'good,' toward health, the healing tendency which is apparent throughout Nature" (pp. 157–158).

Soul Mates

In The *Clinical Diary*, Ferenczi (1932a) reports a "dream fragment" of Severn's in which a "withered breast" is forced into her mouth, adding that she saw the dream as "a combination of the unconscious contents of the psyches of the analysand and the analyst" (p. 13). If Ferenczi initially appeared to Severn as a "balanced, well-adjusted person," she struck him as aloof and intimidating, but inside both shells were severely traumatized souls seeking healing and redemption. As children, both had experienced murder in a literal or symbolic form, as a result of which they were "psychically 'killed,'" though also endowed with preternatural gifts. Ferenczi quotes Severn's summary of "the combined result of the two analyses": "'Your greatest trauma was the destruction of genitality. Mine was worse: I saw my life destroyed by an insane criminal'" (p. 14).

Ferenczi recapitulates how he and Severn found their way to mutual analysis. Initially, "the woman 'patient' was unable to put any trust in this man; it was not known why" (p. 110). But when the man discovered that "his hatred of his mother in his childhood had almost led to matricide," the "woman analyst" then took the process further by helping him to see that "in order to save his mother the 'patient' has castrated himself." Only through being reenacted in his transference to Severn could Ferenczi unearth the roots of his "destruction of genitality":

> The entire libido of this man appears to have been transformed into hatred, the eradication of which, in actual fact, means self-annihilation. In his relationship to his friend the woman "analyst," the origin of guilt feelings and self-destructiveness could be recognized *in statu nascendi*. (p. 110)

In Ferenczi's conceptualization of the therapeutic process, which applies to his analysis by Severn as much as to his work with his own patients, although the analyst "may take kindness and relaxation as far as he possibly can, the time will come when he will have to repeat with his own hands the act of murder previously perpetrated against the patient" (p. 52).

Progress in Severn's analysis became possible only when Ferenczi allowed himself to be analyzed by her: "The first real advances toward the patient's gaining conviction occurred in conjunction with some genuinely emotionally colored fragments of the rather systematically conducted analysis of the analyst" (p. 26). Ferenczi responded to Severn's dream of the "withered breast" by associating to "an episode in his infancy" involving his nurse, even as she accessed "scenes of horrifying events at the ages of one and a half, three, five, and eleven and a half" (p. 13). Because of what each gave to the other, Ferenczi was "able, for the first time, to link *emotions* with the above primal event and thus endow that event with the feeling of a real experience," while Severn succeeded "in gaining insight, far more penetrating than before, into the reality of these events that have been repeated so often on an intellectual level" (pp. 13–14). Where both had once been sundered, "it is as though two halves had combined to form a whole soul" (p. 14).

The Last Word

"[He] said that she analyzed him and thereby saved him. (He thus played both roles, was mother and child.)"

Note

A revised and expanded version of this chapter—including a sketch of Severn's life and an examination of her first two books—appears as the introduction to my edition of *The Discovery of the Self*, forthcoming in Routledge's Relational Perspectives Book Series. My discussion of the relationship between Severn and Thompson is likewise reworked in light of my reading of the complete text of Thompson's interview with Eissler, to which I did not have access at the time of writing this essay. Finally, my research has shown that Severn's chapter, "Nightmares Are Real," also contains a disguised case history of her daughter Margaret, whom she herself analyzed, which places Severn's experience of childhood sexual abuse in an intergenerational context and permits us to study the vicissitudes of mutual analysis from yet another standpoint.

References

Arlow, J. A. (1958). Freud, friends, and feuds. 2. Truth or motivations? Toward a definition of psychoanalysis. *The Saturday Review*, June 14, pp. 14, 54.

Brabant, E., Falzeder, E., and Giampieri-Deutsch, P., (eds) (1993). *The Correspondence of Sigmund Freud and Sándor Ferenczi, Vol. 1, 1908–1914* (trans. P. T. Hoffer). Cambridge, MA: Harvard University Press.

Brennan, B. W. (2014). Decoding Ferenczi's *Clinical Diary*: Biographical notes on identities concealed and revealed. *American Journal of Psychoanalysis*, in press.

Brennan, B. W. (2015). Out of the archive/Unto the couch: Clara Thompson's analysis with Ferenczi. This volume.

De Forest, I. (1942). The therapeutic technique of Sándor Ferenczi. *International Journal of Psychoanalysis*, 33:120–139.

Ferenczi, S. (1929). The unwelcome child and his death instinct. In M. Balint (ed) and E Mosbacher et al (trans.), *Final Contributions to the Problems and Methods of Psycho-Analysis*. New York: Brunner/Mazel, 1980, pp. 102–107.

Ferenczi, S. (1932a). *The Clinical Diary of Sándor Ferenczi*, J. Dupont (ed) and M. Balint and N. Z. Jackson (trans.). Cambridge, MA: Harvard University Press, 1988.

Ferenczi, S. (1932b). Confusion of tongues between adults and the child: The language of tenderness and passion. In M. Balint (ed) and E. Mosbacher et al (trans.), *Final Contributions to the Problems and Methods of Psycho-Analysis*. New York: Brunner/Mazel, 1980, pp. 156–167.

Fortune, C. (1993). The case of "RN": Sándor Ferenczi's radical experiment in psychoanalysis. In L. Aron and A. Harris (eds), *The Legacy of Sándor Ferenczi*. Hillsdale, NJ: Analytic Press, pp. 101–120.

Fortune, C. (1994). A difficult ending: Ferenczi, "R.N.," and the experiment in mutual analysis. In A. Haynal and E Falzeder (eds), *100 Years of Psychoanalysis: Contributions to the History of Psychoanalysis, Cahiers Psychiatriques Genevois*, special issue, pp. 217–223.

Fortune, C. (ed) (2002). *The Sándor Ferenczi—Georg Groddeck Correspondence, 1921–1933* (trans. J. Cohen, E. Petersdorff, and N. Ruebsaat). New York: Other Press.

Freud, S. (1914). On the history of the psychoanalytic movement. *SE*, 14:7–66. London: Hogarth Press, 1957.

Freud, S. (1929). Some dreams of Descartes': A letter to Maxime Leroy. *SE*, 21:203–204. London: Hogarth Press, 1961.

Fromm, E. (1958). Freud, friends, and feuds. 1. Scientism or fanaticism? *The Saturday Review*, June 14, pp. 11–13, 55.

Jones, E. (1957). *The Life and Work of Sigmund Freud: Vol. 3, The Last Phase, 1919–1939*. New York: Basic Books.

Masson, J. M. (1984). *The Assault on Truth: Freud's Suppression of the Seduction Theory*. New York: Farrar, Straus & Giroux.

Paskauskas, R. A. (ed) (1993). *The Complete Correspondence of Sigmund Freud and Ernest Jones, 1908–1939*. Cambridge, MA: Harvard University Press.

Rachman, A. W. (1997). *Sándor Ferenczi: The Psychotherapist of Tenderness and Passion*. Northvale, NJ: Aronson.

Severn, E. (1913). *Psycho-Therapy: Its Doctrine and Practice*. London: Rider.

Severn, E. (1917). *The Psychology of Behavior: A Practical Study of Human Personality and Conduct with Special Reference to Methods of Development*. New York: Dodd, Mead.

Severn, E. (1933). *The Discovery of the Self: A Study in Psychological Cure*. Philadelphia: McKay.

Severn, E. (1952). Interview with Kurt R. Eissler. Sigmund Freud Archives, Container X 17. Manuscripts Division, Library of Congress, Washington, D.C., 24 pp.

Shapiro, S. A. (1993). Clara Thompson: Ferenczi's messenger with half a message. In L. Aron and A. Harris (eds), *The Legacy of Sándor Ferenczi*. Hillsdale, NJ: Analytic Press, pp. 159–173.

Smith, N. A. (1998). "Orpha reviving": Toward an honorable recognition of Elizabeth Severn. *International Forum of Psychoanalysis*, 7:241–246.

Stanton, M. (1991). *Sándor Ferenczi: Reconsidering Active Intervention*. Northvale, NJ: Aronson.

Strindberg, A. (1887). *The Father*. In *Seven Plays by August Strindberg* (trans. A. Paulson). New York: Bantam Books, 1972, pp. 6–56.

Thompson, C. M. (1933). Ferenczi's relaxation method. In M. R. Green (ed), *Interpersonal Psychoanalysis: Selected Papers of Clara M. Thompson*. New York: Basic Books, 1964, pp. 67–71.

Thompson, C. M. (1943). "The therapeutic technique of Sándor Ferenczi": A comment. *International Journal of Psychoanalysis*, 24:64–66.

Wolstein, B. (1992). Resistance interlocked with countertransference—R.N. and Ferenczi, and American interpersonal relations. *Contemporary Psychoanalysis*, 28:172–189.

9

FREUD AND FERENCZI

Wandering Jews in Palermo[1]

Lewis Aron and Karen Starr

Sigmund Freud and Sándor Ferenczi were close friends and fellow travelers, wandering Jews who traveled and vacationed together regularly for many years. In our recent book (Aron and Starr, 2013), we examine the problematic place of binaries in the history of psychoanalysis, focusing in particular on Freud's "optimally marginal" position at the crossroads of his Jewish racial and German cultural identities. Freud's friend and colleague, Sándor Ferenczi, shared this divided Jewish Enlightenment identity. Freud and Ferenczi, like most of the early analysts, were part of a tradition of migration, acculturation, and assimilation (Erös, 2004). Both were from Jewish immigrant families who migrated from Eastern to Western Europe, from the shtetl to the large cosmopolitan city. Medicine, particularly private practice, was one of the free professions that allowed upward mobility independent from institutions that would not accept Jews.

Before and during World War I, the Jews of Austria-Hungary were intensely loyal to the state. In Austria, westernized Jews occupied multiple subject positions, thinking of themselves as German by language and culture or bildung, Austrian by political loyalty, and Jewish by race, ethnicity, or religion. In Hungary, Jews were more fully assimilated, or "Magyarized," into the Magyar nation. Identifying as Hungarian, they spoke Hungarian and German along with Yiddish (Rozenblit, 2001). The Freud–Ferenczi correspondence is filled with Yiddish idioms, such as Ferenczi's (1915) describing his own theory that "all libido is based on 'nachas'" (pleasure) (p. 80). We will explore the personal and professional relationship between Freud and Ferenczi, two Jewish Enlightenment men—friends, colleagues, and analytic couple—who enacted between them dynamics shaped to a great extent by their characteristic reactions to their anti-Semitic and homophobic cultural surround.

Sándor Ferenczi: Progressive Enlightenment Jew

Sándor Ferenczi was born on July 7, 1873, the eighth of eleven children who survived childhood. His father, Baruch Frankel, emigrated from Poland as part of a large migration of Jews from the East seeking to escape anti-Semitism. Born in Cracow in 1830, Baruch came from the same sociocultural environment as Freud's father. Over the course of a changing political atmosphere, Baruch Frankel gradually became Bernat Ferenczi. At age 18, he participated in the Hungarian insurrection against Austrian domination. Hungary's Jews had been handicapped by discrimination, particularly by the German guilds in Buda and Pest; thus, almost all Jews identified with the Magyar national cause in 1848 and thereafter. At this time, Magyar liberals welcomed Jewish assimilation, as many more people were needed to populate large portions of the Hungarian Kingdom (Lukacs, 1988). The rebellion was suppressed until 1867–1868, when it led to the constitution of an independent Hungary and emancipation of the Jews. Bernat Frankel was then offered the name Ferenczy with a "y", a sign of nobility in the new Hungary. Being a liberal democrat, he refused this status symbol, and in 1879, took the name Ferenci, a commoner's name. Gradually, usage added the letter "z" (Fortune, 2002).

By 1900, Budapest was a thriving metropolis in which Jews comprised more than 20 percent of the population and about 40 percent of its voters. Their influence in finance, commerce, and culture was even greater than indicated by these numbers. With their rise in population and prominence, the alliance between Jewish and non-Jewish Hungarians broke down and a new form of modern liberal anti-Semitism took hold, one that was populist and democratic, not religious but racial, and was aimed at assimilated as well as religious Jews, who had acquired power, prosperity, and influence (Lukacs, 1988). This was the Budapest in which Ferenczi lived and worked as an adult. As we will soon see, the years 1918–1920 brought the disintegration of the Austro-Hungarian monarchy and the collapse of the sociopolitical premises of the prewar era. This is an important historical distinction in comparing Freud's and Ferenczi's experiences with anti-Semitism. In Vienna, the liberal political philosophy promising Jews full emancipation and participation in German culture broke down far earlier than in Hungary. Freud had early in his life become disillusioned, increasingly so with the appointment of Karl Lueger in 1897, and especially after World War I. In contrast, the Hungarian political atmosphere was liberal until 1919–1920, in spite of growing popular resentment toward Jews. At the time Lueger and the Christian Socialists came to power in Vienna, there was a Jewish mayor in Budapest. Lueger referred to Budapest with the derogatory epithet, "Judapest" (Lukacs 1988, p. 95). Hungarian Jews continued, long after those in Vienna, to seek emancipation and integration into Hungarian society (Sziklai, 2009). By the time Ferenczi faced the loss of his illusion of being a "Hungarian of Jewish faith" (Ferenczi 1919, p. 365), Freud had already lost his own similar illusions.

Baruch/Bernat became the manager of a bookshop in the center of Miskolc that he purchased in 1856 from Michael Heilprin, a Chasidic scholar who returned to his native America. It became a family business, with the family living in the flat above the store. Bernat added a printing press and then a concert agency, as the Ferenczis were a musical family. By 1880, he was elected president of the Miskolc chamber of commerce. The Ferenczi house became a gathering place for artists, musicians, and intellectuals, and Sándor was raised in a lively, intellectually stimulating, and politically and culturally liberal environment. Sándor was his father's favorite child, accompanying him on excursions to his vineyard on the hills near Miskolc (Kapusi, 2010). Bernat was an upwardly mobile reform Jew who, along with Sándor, attended the synagogue on Kazinczy Street in Miskolc, the only synagogue that remains standing in Miskolc today.

Sándor's mother, Rosa Eibenschütz, was born in 1840 in Cracow, but her family soon moved to Vienna. Baruch and Rosa married in 1858. Busy raising eleven children, Rosa had to resign from her prestigious town role as president of the Union of Jewish Women, which she had founded, but whose work required long periods away from home. When Sándor was 15, his father died, and Rosa took over and expanded the business. Very few members of the Ferenczi family survived the deportations of the Second World War.

Sándor graduated from the Miskolc Calvinist Gymnasium, which would have been the only choice of school for a liberal, enlightened Jewish family. He attended medical school in Vienna, living with his relatives and graduating in 1894, and then left for military service in the Austro-Hungarian army. He then settled in Budapest, where he began working at the hospice for the poor and the marginal, with prostitutes and society's outcasts. By 1900, he established himself in private practice, as a neurologist at the Elizabeth Hospice, and as a court-appointed forensic neurologist.

Ferenczi maintained a social orientation throughout his medical career, and from the beginning of his involvement with Freud, considered the progressive implications of psychoanalysis. This liberal socialist political leaning was common among the members of Ferenczi's Jewish circle, as they sat and discussed art, science, culture, and politics in the coffee houses of Budapest. After giving a lecture on Freud's *The Psychopathology of Everyday Life* to members of the Galileo Circle on October 30, 1909, Ferenczi wrote to Freud:

> I was happy that I could speak before approximately three hundred young and enthusiastic medical students, who listened to my (or, that is to say, your) words with bated breath. ... The medical students surrounded me and wanted me to promise them, at any price, to tell them more about these things. ... Budapest seems, after all, not to be such an absolutely bad place. The audience was naturally composed of nine tenth Jews!
>
> *(Ferenczi 1909b, pp. 91–92)*

As early as 1910, Ferenczi (1910a) emphasized to Freud the "*sociological* significance" of psychoanalysis, "in the sense that in our analyses we investigate the *real* conditions in the various levels of society, cleansed of all hypocrisy and conventionalism, just as they are mirrored in the individual" (p. 153). Ferenczi illustrated this sociological significance with several of his analytic cases, including his analysis of a typesetter described as suffering the "terrorism" of oppressed labor conditions; the analysis of the owner of a print shop who was circumventing union rules to swindle his workers; the "inner hollowness" that analysis uncovered in a young countess and members of her social class; and the sexual masochism that kept a young maid working at lower than necessary wages. As early as 1911, Ferenczi spoke of alcoholism as a symptom of a social neurosis that could only be cured by analyzing its social causation (Nyíri Kristóf, cited in Sziklai, 2009). Ferenczi advocated for the rights of homosexuals and transvestites and wrote about his work with prostitutes and criminals, calling for healthier social conditions and better treatment of the disadvantaged (Gaztambide, 2011). Ferenczi was the Budapest representative of the sexologist Magnus Hirschfeld's International Humanitarian Committee for the Defense of Homosexuals founded in 1905 (Stanton, 1991).

Freud, Ferenczi, and Schreber: Homoerotic Longings, Homophobia, and Paranoia

Jewish and German cultural identities carried serious implications with regard to race, gender, sexuality, bigotry, anti-Semitism, and homophobia. We will focus on one incident that occurred in 1910 during Freud's and Ferenczi's joint vacation in Palermo as they collaborated on writing the Schreber case. Freud's *Schreber, Psychoanalytic Notes on an Autobiographical Account of a Case of Paranoia*, was published in 1911. Although developed in collaboration with Ferenczi, it became derailed over a mutual enactment of dynamics related to racism, anti-Semitism, homophobia, and misogyny. The tense interpersonal incident between Freud and Ferenczi both foreshadowed and shaped Ferenczi's personal analysis with Freud as well as their later theoretical and technical divergence.

In the summer of 1910, Freud traveled to Italy via Paris with Ferenczi, who was then 37 years old and single, although involved since 1900 with the married Frau G., Gisella Pallos. Ferenczi's brief and interrupted analysis with Freud would not begin for four more years. Freud and Ferenczi sailed to Palermo. The trip was marred by unpleasant Sirocco winds, but the personal storm was far worse. On Christmas Day 1921, Ferenczi wrote to Georg Groddeck a revealing self-analytic letter recalling the incident in Palermo:

> I could never be completely free and open with him; I felt that he expected too much of this "deferential respect" from me; he was too big for me, there

was too much of the father. As a result, on our very first working evening together in Palermo, when he wanted to work with me on the famous paranoia text (Schreber), and started to dictate something, I jumped up in a sudden rebellious outburst, exclaiming that this was no working together, dictating to me. "So this is what you are like?" he said, taken aback. "You obviously want to do the whole thing yourself." That said, he now spent every evening working on his own, I was left out in the cold—bitter feelings constricted my throat. (Of course I now know what this "working alone in the evenings" and this "constriction of the throat" signifies: I wanted, of course, to be loved by Freud.)

(Ferenczi 1921, pp. 8–9)

Comparing Ferenczi's recollections with Freud's contemporaneous description, we can see that both Freud and Ferenczi understood Ferenczi's desires as homoerotic, derivatives of a negative Oedipus complex. From Rome, Freud wrote to Jung, triangulating him with Ferenczi:

My travelling companion is a dear fellow, but dreamy in a disturbing kind of way, and his attitude towards me is infantile. He never stops admiring me, which I don't like, and is probably sharply critical of me in his unconscious when I am taking it easy. He has been passive and receptive, letting everything be done for him like a woman, and I really haven't got enough homosexuality in me to accept him as one. These trips arouse a great longing for a real woman. A number of scientific notions I brought with me have combined to form a paper on paranoia, which still lacks an end, but takes quite a step forward in explaining the mechanism of the choice of neurosis.

(Freud 1910a, p. 353, emphasis added)

Although Freud (1910a) accused Ferenczi of being "infantile," inhibited," and "dreamy," (p. 215) and of not asserting his equality, according to Ferenczi's account, Ferenczi had stood up for himself as being not a secretary but a collaborator. Ferenczi wanted a shared collaboration, but Freud accused him of wanting the whole thing. Freud seems to have been unable to collaborate as an equal, interpreting a demand to participate in partnership as a demand to take over the whole. Ferenczi wrote back to Freud, agreeing that he was infantile and inhibited, adding, "On this occasion I have also rather ruthlessly brought to light the resistance against my own homosexual drive components (and the uncommon sexual overestimation of women which goes along with it)" (Ferenczi 1910b, p. 217). Ferenczi here explicitly understood his own desires for intimacy with Freud to be homosexual, which he homophobically devalued as infantile, even while recognizing that his own heterosexual excess might be a defense against underlying homoerotic desire. Ferenczi (1910b) wrote that he was looking for something more from Freud:

I did, perhaps, have an exaggerated idea of companionship between two men who tell each other the truth unrelentingly, sacrificing all consideration. Just as in my relationship with Frau G. I strive for absolute mutual openness, in the same manner—and with even more justification—I believed that this, apparently cruel, but in the end only useful, clear-as-day openness, which conceals nothing, could be possible in the relations between two Ψa.-minded people who can really understand everything and, instead of making value judgments, can seek the determinants of their Ψa. impulses. That was the ideal I was looking for: I wanted to enjoy the man, not the scholar, in close friendship. (p. 218)

In his ongoing idealization of telling the truth at all cost, Ferenczi seemed oblivious to the aggression that could be expressed in this way. He was trapped in these dynamics: while seeing himself as longing for genuine equality and mutuality, he was unable to find a third to either competitive aggression (the positive Oedipal—paranoia) or passive submission (the negative Oedipal—hysteria).

Ferenczi (1910b) went on to mention a dream he had in which he saw Freud standing naked before him. Ferenczi analyzed this dream, deriving two motives. The first was unconscious homosexual tendencies. The second was the "longing for absolute mutual openness" (p. 218). Could Ferenczi's longing for openness from Freud simply be explained on the basis of infantile sexual wishes? While recognizing this motive in himself, Ferenczi also believed that the adult wish for personal contact and relatedness should not be reduced to its genetic origins in infantile longings. He longed for Freud to feel comfortable enough with him to expose himself personally, to speak the truth even if it was unpleasant. Ferenczi (1910b) wrote:

Don't forget that for years I have been occupied with nothing but the products of your intellect, and I have also always felt the man behind every sentence of your works and made him my confidant. Whether you want to be or not, you are one of the great master teachers of mankind, and you must allow your readers to approach you, at least intellectually, in a personal relationship as well. My ideal of truth that strikes down all consideration is certainly nothing less than the most self-evident consequence of your teachings. ... The final consequences of such insight—when it is present in two people—is that they are not ashamed in front of each other, keep nothing secret, tell each other the truth without risk of insult or in the certain hope that within the truth there can be no lasting insult ... according to my Ψa. ideal, there are no halfway standards, all consideration for people and conditions disappear beside my ideal of truth. Please don't misunderstand me. I really don't want to "reform" society, I am not a paranoiac. I would only like to see thoughts and speech liberated from the compulsion of unnecessary inhibitions in the relations of Ψα.-minded men.—Unfortunately—I can't begin, you have to! After all, you are Ψα. in person! (pp. 219–220, emphasis added)

Freud told Ferenczi that his dreams while they were away together were entirely concerned with Fliess, with which he understood it would be difficult for Ferenczi to sympathize. And here Freud's letter quickly turns to his thinking about Schreber. While there is much that could be said about this letter, we want to highlight Freud's denial of his superhero status as well as its impact on those around him, the intricate connections between themes of homosexuality and paranoia in Freud's personal relationships and collaborative work, and Freud's study of Schreber.

> I am also not that Ψα superman whom we have constructed, and I also haven't overcome the countertransference … Not only have you noticed that I no longer have any need for that full opening of my personality, but you have also understood it and correctly returned to its traumatic cause. Why did you thus make a point of it? This need has been extinguished in me since Fliess's case, with the overcoming of which you just saw me occupied. A piece of homosexual investment has been withdrawn and utilized for the enlargement of my own ego. I have succeeded where the paranoiac fails.
> *(Freud 1910b p. 221, emphasis added)*

In this exchange, we can see the clash of contrasting visions as they emerge from complementary personalities. In what follows, we will explicate these dynamics. Ferenczi's uncritical idealism about the psychoanalytic value of mutual and reciprocal openness became more central as his own work evolved, and Ferenczi continued to long for Freud's openness and personal closeness. He wrote to Freud that he had not given up hope that Freud would:

> let a part of your withdrawn homosexual libido be refloated and bring more sympathy to bear toward "my ideal of honesty." You know, I am an unimpeachable therapist. I don't want to even give up on the paranoiac as a total loss. So how can I warm up to the fact that you extend your—in part, justified—distrust to the entire male sex! There is certainly much that is infantile in my yearning for honesty—but it certainly also has a healthy core. Not everything that is infantile should be abhorred.
> *(Ferenczi 1910c p. 224, emphasis added)*

What Ferenczi expected from Freud, the master psychoanalyst, was precisely what some two decades later he attempted to offer his own patients: mutual openness and honesty. Ferenczi did not realize that this was his own innovation, but believed it to be the logical and transparent aim of Freud's teachings! Note also the relation of homosexuality and paranoia hovering in the background of these personal exchanges. As we will elaborate, there was an ongoing tension being played out between Freud and Ferenczi, enacting between them the paired binaries: hetero-sexual/homosexual, active/passive, positive/negative Oedipus, paranoia/hysteria, male/female. Hence, it is understandable that these forces would become explosive in their attempt to collaborate on these very themes, elicited by the Schreber case.

The Eternal, Wandering, "Unmanned" Jew

Freud began his theorizing of the relationship between paranoia and repressed homosexuality in 1908, in collaboration with Ferenczi, to whom he was introduced by Jung. In 1910, Jung gave Freud a copy of Schreber's *Memoirs of My Nervous Illness* (Lothane, 1997). The schism between Freud and Jung that climaxed in 1912 revolved around their differing interpretations of the case of Schreber. Freud used Schreber to highlight the role in paranoia of repressed sexuality, which was central to his theory, and had never been fully accepted by Jung.

In contrast, Ferenczi, who was always ready to understand himself in terms of spiri-tualized or sublimated homosexuality, argued that what led to paranoia was not homo-sexuality, but its repudiation. In today's terms, one might read Ferenczi as suggesting that paranoia results from homophobia. Keep in mind that both Freud's and Ferenczi's understandings were prior to any formulation of gender identity as distinct from sexu-ality, and so a man's possession of any culturally designated "feminine" trait was equated with homosexuality. Freud's and Ferenczi's works have been misused for much of the past century to argue that homosexuality was a pathological and regressed outcome of failed heterosexuality (Phillips, 2003). However, neither Ferenczi nor Freud was moralistic or particularly pathologizing of homosexuality, viewing it as a variation in resolving the Oedipus complex. The pathologizing of homosexuality came later.

Let's return to September 1910 in Palermo, the scene of the primal fight between Freud and Ferenczi. Many of these themes—homoeroticism, homosexuality, homophobia, and paranoia—were brewing in Freud's and Ferenczi's minds, leading to this perfect storm. Freud's closeness to and conflict with Ferenczi, his anticipa-tion of Adler's "heresy," his anxious hopes for Jung to become his Aryan successor, reactions stirred by the Wolfman's analysis, and his preoccupation with Schreber, all stimulated in Freud a recurrence of thoughts about his old close friend, Wilhelm Fliess. Freud announced to Jung in December 1910, "My Schreber is finished," but went on to say that he himself could not judge its objective worth "because in working on it I have had to fight off complexes within myself (Fliess)" (Freud 1910a, p. 380). Freud anticipated an upcoming schism with Adler, which indeed came to full bloom before Schreber was published. Freud (1910a) wrote to Jung:

> I am very glad that you see Adler as I do. The only reason the affair upsets me so much is that it has opened the wounds of the Fliess affair. It was the same feeling that disturbed the peace I otherwise enjoyed during my work on paranoia. (p. 382, emphasis added)

Freud later called Adler paranoid, just as he accused Fliess of becoming paranoid following their break. Freud was preoccupied with mastering his homosexual tendencies, writing to Ferenczi, "I … approve of the overcoming of my homosexuality, with the result being greater independence" (Freud 1910c, p. 227). Ferenczi's appeal for Freud's love conjured the Fliess dybbuk, as did Freud's deepening homoerotic ties to Jung. Indeed, Jung's paranoid collapse may have been triggered by his break with Freud (Lothane, 1997).

Adler's "heretical" theories matched these dynamics in a way that can only be described as uncanny. Breger (2000) argues that Adler's "concept of the masculine protest—that one exaggerates certain culturally defined masculine traits to repudiate threatening feelings of weakness and helplessness that are seen as feminine—fit Freud all too closely" (p. 204). Neither Breger (2000) nor Rudnytsky (2002), however, both of whom have astutely clarified the Freud–Ferenczi relationship, take into consideration that this formulation not only fits Freud and Adler in terms of their idiosyncratic psychodynamics, but also captures precisely the Jewish male cultural response to the prevailing anti-Semitic stereotypes in which they were helplessly trapped—regarded as feminine, circumcised, and thus castrated. While Freud's (1937) notion of "the repudiation of femininity" (p. 252) may seem identical to Adler's "masculine protest," Freud argued from a genitally derived, biological basis that the masculine protest results from castration anxiety, whereas Adler examined social and cultural forces. All of these currents were in the background, as these two wandering Jews, Freud and Ferenczi, traveled intimately together, writing about homosexuality, paranoia, and Schreber's identification with the Eternal Jew. In writing Schreber, Freud had to prove Adler wrong: psychosis was not about social issues but about biology, specifically sexuality, and he had to convince Jung that psychosis was rooted in sexual, not spiritual conflict. If in writing Schreber, Freud was overcoming his homoerotic love of Fliess, then he was also simultaneously enacting the relationship with Ferenczi. Recall James Strachey's comment to Ernest Jones about the redacted Freud–Fliess letters, "It is really a complete instance of folie à deux, with Freud in the unexpected role of hysterical partner to a paranoiac" (cited in Boyarin 1997, p. 194). In Freud's collaboration with Ferenczi, Freud and Ferenczi reenacted the complementary roles of hysteric and paranoiac, but in reverse, with Ferenczi acting as hysterical partner to Freud's paranoiac. The thesis we are putting forward is that Freud and Ferenczi, in a relationship of split complementarity (Benjamin, 1988), divided up between them the two polarized poles of reaction to the anti-Semitism and associated homophobia surrounding them, with Freud reacting along paranoid lines and Ferenczi in his more characteristically hysteric manner. Whereas Freud emphasized his positive Oedipal wishes to repress the negative, Ferenczi highlighted his negative Oedipal wishes, attempting to sublimate them. Whereas Freud tried to emulate the Greek–German ideal of the conqueror–hero, Ferenczi tended toward "ironic obedience," a strategy he would only identify much later (Ferenczi 1932, p. 19).

In Freud's championing of the positive Oedipus and in his "overcoming" of his homosexuality, Freud was also rejecting what his society viewed, and what he internalized, as the stereotypically Jewish, passive, feminine, masochistic, castrated position. This was precisely the role Ferenczi played in exaggerated caricature. The "repudiation of femininity" became "bedrock," and Freud identified with warriors and conquerors, including Moses, whom he transformed from a self-effacing, reluctant leader into a ruthless man of action. While the rabbis emphasized Moses's humility and caretaking, Freud's (1939) Moses possessed "decisiveness of thought," "strength of will," and "energy of action," exhibiting "autonomy and independence" and "divine unconcern which may grow into ruthlessness" (pp. 109–110). While Freud's notion of the heroic culminated in autonomous ruthlessness, Ferenczi's vision idealized mutual openness, surrender, and forgiveness.

Boyarin (1997) interprets Freud's formulation of Schreber as an autobiographical commentary on Freud's own unconscious dynamics. While Boyarin emphasizes Freud's defensive reaction against his own homosexuality and away from the negative Oedipus, we are expanding Boyarin's analysis by comparing Freud's reactions to those of Ferenczi, who ultimately criticized Freud's "androphile orientation" (p. 187), viewing masculinity itself as a "hysterical symptom" (p. 188). To his patients, Ferenczi directly expressed his pain that as a man, he was taught to suppress his capacities for caretaking and kindness, as these were considered feminine and childish; he held the analyst guilty for his inability to provide maternal care (p. 53). Freud and Ferenczi differed markedly in their stance toward gender and sexuality. Freud and Ferenczi shared the experience of being upwardly mobile, liberal, professional Jews surrounded by a culture of intense anti-Semitism that feminized them, circumcised/castrated them, and rejected them as truly Hungarian, Austrian, or German men. Nevertheless, their individual reactions to these circumstances were dramatically different, because they each had quite distinct childhood experiences with their own mothers and fathers. In other words, their reaction to anti-Semitism is one—but certainly not the only—element involved in shaping Freud's and Ferenczi's responses to gender and sexuality and broader aspects of misogyny. To be clear: we are not reducing patriarchy and misogyny to anti-Semitism, but rather are exploring the intersection of misogyny, racism, anti-Semitism, and homophobia. Feminism has exposed the inherent relationship between patriarchy and misogyny, and postcolonial studies have investigated the interrelations between racism, misogyny, and homophobia. A psychoanalytic study of the intersection of anti-Semitism, homophobia, and misogyny enriches the findings of feminism; it does not detract from them. Freud and Ferenczi reacted in opposing ways to their society's anti-Semitism and expectations of normative masculinity; they were both drawn to and made anxious by the other's polar opposite style. This clash of polarities was reflected in their theories and clinical approaches and in the versions of psychoanalysis that emerged following their work.

The Familiar Stranger

Ferenczi, while loved by Freud, remained enigmatic and exotic (Erös, 2004). Freud emphasized Ferenczi's Hungarian national character. "Hungary, so near geographically to Austria, and so far from it scientifically, has produced only one collaborator, S. Ferenczi, but one that indeed outweighs a whole society" (Freud 1914, p. 33). Later, others, too, highlighted Ferenczi's Hungarian national character and gypsy nature (Thompson, 1988). But as the Hungarian historiographer of psychoanalysis Erös (2004) argues, "Instead of searching for nonexistent Hungarian roots, we should emphasize the ethnocultural and linguistic pluralism in Ferenczi's background" (p. 125). This pluralism was typical of assimilationist, middle-class, upwardly mobile Jewish families, such as Freud's and Ferenczi's. Ferenczi was Freud's "familiar stranger" (Erös 2004, p. 125), both heimlich and unheimlich. It was not Ferenczi's nationality, language, or culture that evoked this familiar strangeness, but rather his split complementarity with Freud in relation to gender, hysteria, and paranoia. Freud and Ferenczi inhabited the flip sides of positive and negative Oedipal wishes and defenses. Freud's paranoia—his castration anxiety and paternal fear that his sons would band together to kill him—met Ferenczi's hysteria—his excessive "feminine" need to be loved and engaged in direct emotional exchange—even as each unconsciously and ambivalently identified with the other, his uncanny double. Before, during, and after his formal analysis of Ferenczi, Freud repeatedly interpreted to Ferenczi that Ferenczi was trying to obtain the love he missed in childhood from his patients, and via homosexual submission, from Freud. As Ernst Falzeder (2010) puts it:

> Freud did not even dream of giving Ferenczi some of this love himself. No, Ferenczi should get a grip on himself, stop acting like an obnoxious child, and should, as Freud admonished him ... "leave the island of dreams which you inhabit with your fantasy children and mix in with the struggle of men." (p. 401)

Note the equation of femininity and childishness, accepted by both Freud and Ferenczi until Ferenczi began to challenge this assumption in his final years.

In his analysis of Schreber, Freud focused exclusively on Schreber's dynamic conflicts about his longings for his father's love, the negative Oedipus complex—with not a single mention of Schreber's relation to his mother. The neglect of the maternal is characteristic of Freud's work, reflecting, among other things, his own lack of insight into his conflicts concerning his own mother. Not only is the mother neglected, only present as the object of the child's desire, but so too are the loving relations of the boy to his father. Only the competitive and murderous side of the ambivalence is present within the positive Oedipus. Significantly, also neglected in Freud's work was the theme of anti-Semitism, including his society's assumption of the passive, effeminate, perverse, homosexual, and castrated nature of Jewish men. Freud made no mention of Schreber's incorporation of the rhetoric of anti-Semitism into his delusional system. Schreber constructed a complex theology involving a divided God with dark and light incarnations, whose "rays" and "nerves" would sexually violate him. Schreber believed that he was being literally "unmanned," an Eternal or Wandering Jew who was being transformed into a woman, so that God could sexually violate him and conceive a new human race. As part of his transformation, he felt his stomach being replaced with an inferior "Jew's stomach." Unmanning and Jewification are equivalent. Examining the margin comments on Freud's copy of Schreber's book, Gilman (1993) demonstrates that Freud was well aware of this rhetoric. But if Freud commented on Schreber's identification with the Wandering Jew, he would draw attention to the most obvious marker of his own Jewishness and undercut his credibility as a neutral (non-Jewish) scientist. It was therefore important for Freud to present his data as uncontaminated by anything that might inscribe them as Jewish. The image of the Eternal Jew converged with "the eternal feminine"[2] to mark or circumcise the Jew as racially/sexually different (Pellegrini, 1997).

Paranoia and anti-Semitism were closely related. In fin de siècle Germany and Austria, paranoia was often centered on the perceived danger of a Jewish conspiracy. Gilman (1993) contends that Freud displaced the perceived danger from Jews to homosexuals. Similar to his rejection of the hereditary etiology Charcot had championed, Freud rejected Kraft-Ebbing's theory that homosexuality, like Jewishness, was an innate biological flaw. Instead, Freud viewed it as a developmental arrest, not as degenerate, but as primitive. When Freud and Ferenczi stayed together in Palermo to collaborate on the case of Schreber, the deck was stacked for an enactment of the very content they were immersed in writing about—homosexuality, paranoia, and homophobia. Here were two Jewish men, viewed by their society as castrated, homosexual, and feminine, collaborating together in partnership, writing about the themes that were intensely preoccupying them. Freud was determined not to relive his love of Fliess, while Ferenczi, longing for love and intimacy, dreamt of seeing Freud naked.

Freud's (1911) formulation of Schreber was inextricably linked with his own internalized homophobia, stemming from his identity as a feminized Jew living in the larger context of an anti-Semitic and homophobic milieu, just at a time when homosexuality was being transformed into a distinct identity. Freud's recognition of Schreber's desire to be transformed into a woman meant facing his own unresolved feminine desires, which in their society was equated with homosexuality. Anxious to overcome the pathology of feminization and homosexuality that fin de siècle Europe attributed to Jews, Freud proceeded to pathologize them, or at the very least to characterize them as developmentally primitive.

Whereas Freud began his career focusing on hysteria in men (including in himself), now a new pathology became central—paranoia—and hence a new binary emerged. With paranoia as the new prototype of male psychopathology, hysteria returned to its pre-Freudian position as quintessentially female. Vulnerability was displaced from circumcised Jewish men onto hysterical women and paranoid men—men who were unconsciously homosexual. Hysteria and paranoia, caricatures of femininity and masculinity, were explained by positing universal anxieties: penis envy, castration anxiety, and the repudiation of femininity became psychological bedrock. The negative Oedipus was pathologized and men's wish for penetration was repressed. All differences, including race and religion, became minor differences, except for the one big universal difference—the phallic difference—the difference between the sexes (Pellegrini, 1997). This formulation is not meant to imply that misogyny is secondary to racism or religious hatred; rather, we believe that each of these displaces and disguises the others.

Let's examine how the inventor of the term "introjection" (Ferenczi, 1909a) and the first analyst to examine the dynamic of "identification with the aggressor" (Ferenczi, 1933b/1949) dealt with the anti-Semitism that surrounded him. This is a striking illustration of how a colonized people introject the views of the colonizer—how they identify with the aggressor, albeit with disguised ambivalence, or with what Ferenczi (1913) described as "mockery and scorn concealed behind the blind belief" (p. 443). Let's return to Ferenczi's 1921 Christmas Day letter to Groddeck, in which he recalled the incident in Palermo.

Georg Groddeck, a pioneer in psychosomatic medicine, practiced at Baden-Baden. After Freud introduced Ferenczi to Groddeck in 1917, Ferenczi became enamored of him and, as was his wont, opened himself up to obtain Groddeck's love. In fact, for the rest of his life, Ferenczi spent summers at Groddeck's sanatorium and the two engaged in something of a mutual analysis (see Fortune, this volume, for an exploration of Groddeck's influence on Ferenczi). Ferenczi was resentful of Freud because he allowed himself to be pressured by Freud to marry Gizella, a woman older than he who was no longer able to bear children.[3] Ferenczi never felt sexually satisfied in his marriage, writing to Groddeck, "I, my 'It', isn't interested in analytic interpretations, but wants something real, a young wife, a child!" (Fortune 2002, p. 11). Immediately, Ferenczi shifted to his feelings about Groddeck. "Are you by any chance this female friend for me, or am I using your friendship in a homosexual way to replace her?" (Fortune 2002, p. 11). Note the flow of associations and emerging themes of heterosexuality and homosexuality, positive and negative Oedipus complex, and Jewishness and anti-Semitism. Ferenczi next told a dream, which he called an "entirely 'Hungarian' dream," illuminating his Hungarian experience and identity. In the dream, Ferenczi was happily singing a Hungarian folksong, the words of which he recalled:

> This is what the old Jew tells me.
> Here!—it's from my market stall.
> I want nothing from your stall,
> I don't want you, old Jew, either.
> This is what Fay Gyula tells me (name of a dashing man)
> I'll buy you, dearest, dresses, ribbons,
> Don't need your dresses, ribbons, Fay,
> All I want is you.

Ferenczi does not hesitate to provide his associations to the dream. On Christmas Eve, he had a small dinner with his family and there were two "servant-girls," sisters, singing and laughing with their friends. The younger one is 16 and has "remarkably red lips." The older is 19 or 20 and Ferenczi writes, "She has, as I was able to establish during the course of a medical examination, remarkably firm, ripe breasts, with enormous nipples which become erect during the examination. Interpretation: these pretty girls didn't want an old Jew like me!" (Fortune 2002, p. 13). Ferenczi notices that he is growing grey while a friend of his still has black hair and his wife is a "fresh young blonde."

Ferenczi says that he picked up that folksong as a child when he visited the vineyard with his father and heard the peasant women singing it. Strikingly, Ferenczi recalls that he also heard his own parents sing the song. He remembers yearning for the "earthly charms of those peasant girls in that vineyard." Ferenczi then adds that the song was somehow "bisexual" and that the "dashing man" Fay Gyula was simultaneously also a beautiful lady.

In our view, the dream reflects Ferenczi's internalization of the anti-Semitism surrounding him, magnified by his identification with his parents' introjections of these same attitudes. That he could happily sing and laugh about these blatantly anti-Semitic images is an illustration of his and his family's identification with the aggressor. It also speaks to their Hungarian nationalism, longing for acceptance by the culture, and belief that they would be absorbed as Hungarians of Jewish faith, a hope that would soon be crushed. Perhaps Ferenczi and his parents happily singing this anti-Semitic folksong reveals the workings of dissociation, illustrating Homi Bhabha's (1984) formulation of the ambivalence of colonial mimicry, including the wavering between mimicry and mockery, resemblance and menace. Anticipating Bhabha's insight, Ferenczi contended that identification with the aggressor is never complete (Frankel, 2002). The split-off ego is dissociatively contemptuous and sarcastic and displays what Ferenczi importantly designated "ironic obedience." As he elaborated: "The mentally ill person has a keen eye for the insanity of mankind" (Ferenczi 1932, p. 19).

In March 1919, Ferenczi was appointed as the first university professor of psychoanalysis, but by that time, the independence of the university had been suspended under the Hungarian Republic of Councils (Erös, 2004). With the victory of the counterrevolutionary Horthy regime, there were numerous mass executions and arbitrary arrests. Jews were accused of collaborating with the communists. By August, Ferenczi's professorship was annulled and soon he was also excluded from the Budapest Medical Association (Giamppieri and Erös, 1987). Ferenczi (1919) wrote to Freud:

> The ruthless clerical anti-Semitic spirit seems to have eked out a victory. If everything does not deceive, we Hungarian Jews are now facing a period of brutal persecution of Jews. They will, I think, have cured us in a very short time of the illusion with which we were brought up, namely that we are "Hungarians of Jewish faith." (p. 365)

Ferenczi then added a line that, from our perspective, is bitterly ironic. "I picture Hungarian anti-Semitism—commensurate with the national character—to be more brutal than the petty-hatred of the Austrians." He continued, "Personally, one will have to take this trauma as an occasion to abandon certain prejudices brought along from the nursery and to come to terms with the bitter truth of being, as a Jew, really without a country." An eternally wandering Jew. "The blackest reaction prevails at the university. All Jewish assistants were fired, the Jewish students were thrown out and beaten" (pp. 365–366). Freud (1919) responded with "burning disappointment for you, one which has robbed you of a fatherland" (p. 367). Ferenczi found himself unheimlich, uncanny, and without a home—a familiar situation for a wandering Jew.

Never giving up his love for Freud, in one of his last letters, March 29, 1933, Ferenczi wrote to Freud, "Short and sweet: I advise you to make use of the time of the not yet impending dangerously threatening situation and, with a few patients and your daughter Anna, to go to a more secure country, perhaps England" (Ferenczi 1933a, p. 448). Freud responded that it was not certain that Hitler will overpower Austria, and if he does it will not reach the level of brutality as in Germany, and in any event his own life is secure, and besides being an immigrant is not easy, and even if they kill you, one kind of death is as good as another!

On May 4, 1933, as he was dying, Ferenczi wrote to wish Freud a happy birthday. Sándor Ferenczi died in Budapest on May 22, 1933. Ferenczi's younger brother, Karoly, and his wife Vilma Klar died in Auschwitz in 1944. His younger sister Zsofia had an inscription carved in a gravestone in the cemetery of Miskolc. After their names, it reads, "I will keep hold of your memories for ever. Your mourning sister."[4]

We are all deeply embedded in social and cultural assumptions and biases that are beyond our capacity to observe. These include prejudices that influence both our self-understandings and our clinical practices. The mutual enactment in Palermo and the history of the Freud–Ferenczi relationship illustrates how these pre-reflective beliefs and related unconscious dynamics are inevitably enacted in our relationships, particularly as we actualize the very content we are formulating in words. Our hope is that this study of the context beyond the psychoanalytic text will serve as an example of the critical importance of studying the development of psychoanalytic ideas, including our fundamental clinical concepts, within the larger framework of the social, cultural, political, economic, and religious surround.

Notes

1   This chapter is adapted from Chapter 15 in Aron and Starr's (2013) *A Psychotherapy for the People: Toward a Progressive Psychoanalysis*. New York: Routledge. An earlier version was presented by Lewis Aron as the Keynote Address to the Spring Meeting, Division of Psychoanalysis (39), American Psychological Association, New York City, April 15, 2011.
2   "The eternal feminine" is a cultural archetype invoked by Symbolist artists and writers of the late nineteenth century, whereby a woman was an instinctual or spiritual being, whether a wicked temptress or a saintly virgin.

3 A review of the Freud–Ferenczi correspondence makes it abundantly clear that even while claiming to remain neutral, Freud admitted to Gizella that he was doing all he could, both in and out of the analysis, to persuade Ferenczi to marry her. For a thorough account of the quadrangle between Freud and Ferenczi, Ferenczi's wife Gizella, and her daughter Elma, see Berman (2004).
4 For the tragic story of the anti-Semitic and communist persecutions of Hungarian analysts throughout the twentieth century, see Mészáros (2010).

References

Aron, L. and Starr, K. (2013). *A Psychotherapy for the People: Toward a Progressive Psychoanalysis*. New York: Routledge.

Benjamin, J. (1988). *The Bonds of Love*. New York: Pantheon.

Berman, E. (2004). Sándor, Gizella, Elma. *International Journal of Psychoanalysis*, 85:489–520.

Bhabha, H. (1984). Of mimicry and man: The ambivalence of colonial discourse. *Discipleship: A Special Issue on Psychoanalysis*, 28:125–133.

Boyarin, D. (1997). *Unheroic conduct*. Berkeley: University of California Press.

Breger, L. (2000). *Freud: Darkness in the Midst of Vision*. New York: John Wiley.

Erös, F. (2004). The Ferenczi cult: Its historical and political roots. *International Forum of Psychoanalysis*, 13:121–128.

Falzeder, E. (2010). Sándor Ferenczi between orthodoxy and heterodoxy. *American Imago*, 66(4):395.

Ferenczi, S. (1909a). Introjection and transference. In J. Rickman (ed) and J. I. Suttie (Trans.), *First Contributions to Psycho-Analysis* (Ch. 2). London: Hogarth Press, 1952.

Ferenczi, S. (1909b). Letter from Sándor Ferenczi to Sigmund Freud, October 30, 1909. In E. Brabant, E. Falzeder, and P. Giampieri-Deutsch (eds & Trans.), *The Correspondence of Sigmund Freud and Sándor Ferenczi, 1908–1914*, Vol. 1. Cambridge, MA: Belknap Press of Harvard University Press, 1993, pp. 118–119.

Ferenczi, S. (1910a). Letter from Sándor Ferenczi to Sigmund Freud, March 22, 1910. In E. Brabant, E. Falzeder, and P. Giampieri-Deutsch (eds & Trans.), *The Correspondence of Sigmund Freud and Sándor Ferenczi, 1908–1914*, Vol. 1. Cambridge, MA: Belknap Press of Harvard University Press, 1993, p. 153.

Ferenczi, S. (1910b). Letter from Sándor Ferenczi to Sigmund Freud, October 3, 1910. In E. Brabant, E. Falzeder, and P. Giampieri-Deutsch (eds & Trans.), *The Correspondence of Sigmund Freud and Sándor Ferenczi, 1908–1914*, Vol. 1. Cambridge, MA: Belknap Press of Harvard University Press, 1993, pp. 217–221.

Ferenczi, S. (1910c). Letter from Sándor Ferenczi to Sigmund Freud, October 10, 1910. In E. Brabant, E. Falzeder, and P. Giampieri-Deutsch (eds & Trans.), *The Correspondence of Sigmund Freud and Sándor Ferenczi, 1908–1914*, Vol. 1. Cambridge, MA: Belknap Press of Harvard University Press, 1993, p. 224.

Ferenczi, S. (1913). Belief, disbelief, and conviction. In J. Rickman (ed) and J. I. Suttie (Trans.), *Further Contributions to Psycho-Analysis*. London: Hogarth Press, 1950, pp. 437–450.

Ferenczi, S. (1915). Letter from Sándor Ferenczi to Sigmund Freud. In E. Brabant, E. Falzeder, and P. Giampieri-Deutsch (eds. & Trans.), *The Correspondence of Sigmund Freud and Sándor Ferenczi*, Vol. 2. Cambridge, MA: Belknap Press of Harvard University Press, 1996, p. 80.

Ferenczi, S. (1919). Letter from Sándor Ferenczi to Sigmund Freud, August 28, 1919. In E. Brabant, E. Falzeder, and P. Giampieri-Deutsch (eds & Trans.), *The Correspondence of*

Sigmund Freud and Sándor Ferenczi, Vol. 2. Cambridge, MA: Belknap Press of Harvard University Press, 1996, p. 365.

Ferenczi, S. (1921). Letter from Sándor Ferenczi to Georg Groddeck, December 25, 1921. In C. Fortune (ed & Trans.), *The Sándor Ferenczi-Georg Groddeck Correspondence*. London: Open Gate Press, 2002, pp. 8–9.

Ferenczi, S. (1932). *The Clinical diary of Sándor Ferenczi*. J. Dupont (ed) and M. Balint and N. Z. Jackson (Trans.). Cambridge, MA: Harvard University Press, 1988.

Ferenczi, S. (1933a). Letter from Sándor Ferenczi to Sigmund Freud, March 29, 1933. In E. Brabant, E. Falzeder, and P. Giampieri-Deutsch (eds & Trans.), *The Correspondence of Sigmund Freud and Sándor Ferenczi*, Vol. 3. Cambridge, MA: Belknap Press of Harvard University Press, 1996, p. 448.

Ferenczi, S. (1933b). The confusion of tongues between adults and children: The language of tenderness and of passion (M. Balint, ed). *International Journal of Psychoanalysis*, 30(4), 1949.

Fortune, C. (ed). (2002). *The Sándor Ferenczi—Georg Groddeck Correspondence, 1921–1933*. J. Cohen, E. Petersdorff, and N. Ruebsaat (Trans.). New York: The Other Press.

Frankel, J. (2002). Identification and "traumatic aloneness". *Psychoanalytic Dialogues*, 12:159–170.

Freud, S. (1910a). Letter from Sigmund Freud to Carl Jung. In W. McGuire (ed), *The Freud/Jung Letters: The Correspondence between Sigmund Freud and C. G. Jung*. Princeton, NJ: Princeton University Press, 1974, pp. 1–592.

Freud, S. (1910b). Letter from Sigmund Freud to Sándor Ferenczi, October 6, 1910. In E. Brabant, E. Falzeder, and P. Giampieri-Deutsch (eds and Trans.), *The Correspondence of Sigmund Freud and Sándor Ferenczi, 1908–1914*, Vol. 1. Cambridge, MA: Belknap Press of Harvard University Press, 1993, pp. 221–222.

Freud, S. (1910c). Letter from Sigmund Freud to Sándor Ferenczi, October 17, 1910. In E. Brabant, E. Falzeder, and P. Giampieri-Deutsch (eds and Trans.), *The Correspondence of Sigmund Freud and Sándor Ferenczi, 1908–1914*, Vol. 1. Cambridge, MA: Belknap Press of Harvard University Press, 1993, p. 227.

Freud, S. (1911). Psycho-analytic notes on an autobiographical account of a case of paranoia (dementia paranoides). In J. Strachey (Ed. & Trans.) *The standard edition of the complete works of Sigmund Freud*, Vol. 12. London: Hogarth Press, 1961, pp. 1–82.

Freud, S. (1914). On the history of the psycho-analytic movement. In J. Strachey (ed & Trans.), *The Standard Edition of the Complete Psychological Works of Sigmund Freud*, Vol. 14. London: Hogarth Press, 1957, pp. 1–66.

Freud, S. (1919). Letter from Sigmund Freud to Sándor Ferenczi, September 5, 1919. In E. L. Freud (ed), *Letters of Sigmund Freud, 1873–1929*. London: Hogarth Press, 1961, p. 367.

Freud, S. (1937). Analysis terminable and interminable. In J. Strachey (ed & Trans.), *The Standard Edition of the Complete Psychological Works of Sigmund Freud*, Vol. 23. London: Hogarth Press, 1964, pp. 216–253.

Freud, S. (1939). Moses and monotheism. In J. Strachey (ed & Trans.), *The Standard Edition of the Complete Psychological Works of Sigmund Freud*, Vol. 23. London: Hogarth Press, 1964, pp. 1–138.

Gaztambide, D. (2011, April 28). *"A Psychotherapy for the People": Freud, Ferenczi, and Psychoanalytic Work with the Underprivileged*. Paper presented at the Ferenczi Center at the New School for Social Research, New York, NY.

Giamppieri, P. and Erös, F. (1987). The beginnings of the reception of psychoanalysis in Hungary 1900–1920. *Sigmund Freud House Bulletin*, 11(2):13–28.

Gilman, S. L. (1993). *Freud, Race, and Gender*. Princeton, NJ: Princeton University Press.

Kapusi, K. (2010). Toward a biography of Sándor Ferenczi: Footnotes from Miskolc. *American Imago, 66*:405–410.

Lothane, Z. (1997). The schism between Freud and Jung over Schreber. *International Forum of Psychoanalysis,* 6:103–115.

Lukacs, J. (1988). *Budapest 1900: A Historical Portrait of a City and Its Culture.* New York, NY: Grove Press.

Mészáros, J. (2010). Progress and persecution in the psychoanalytic heartland: Anti-Semitism, communism, and the fate of Hungarian psychoanalysis. *Psychoanalytic Dialogues, 20,* 600-622.

Pellegrini, A. (1997). *Performance Anxieties.* New York: Routledge.

Phillips, S. H. (2003). Homosexuality: Coming out of the confusion. *International Journal of Psychoanalysis,* 84:1431–1450.

Rozenblit, M. L. (2001). *Reconstructing a National Identity: The Jews of Habsburg Austria during World War I.* Oxford and New York: Oxford University.

Rudnytsky, P. L. (2002). *Reading Psychoanalysis.* Ithaca, NY: Cornell.

Stanton, M. (1991). *Sándor Ferenczi: Reconsidering Active Intervention.* London: Free Association Books.

Sziklai, A. (2009). *The Jewish Theme in the Relationship of Sigmund Freud and Sándor Ferenczi: Between the State and the Public Sphere* (Vol. 84 of Working paper). Jerusalem: The European Forum at the Hebrew University.

Thompson, C. M. (1988). Sándor Ferenczi, 1873–1933. *Contemporary Psychoanalysis,* 24:182–195.

PART III

Theory and Technique

10
FERENCZI, THE "INTROJECTIVE ANALYST"[1]

Franco Borgogno

Aims

In this chapter, my aim is to highlight why Ferenczi is the "introjective psycho-analyst" *par excellence* in the history of psychoanalysis. Employing the approach to classic psychoanalytic texts adopted in my book *Psychoanalysis as a Journey* (Borgogno, 1999), I will explore and discuss a number of crucial theoretical and clinical issues that, throughout Ferenczi's life and works, shaped his development in this direction. In doing so, I also maintain that this specific characteristic of his analytic commitment is the main reason why today we still look at Ferenczi as a source of inspiration and a contemporary teacher. In my argument, I will focus particularly on Ferenczi's early and late writings in order to illustrate more clearly the development of his "introjective" analytic style, leaving for another paper the equally interesting subject of the evolution of Ferenczi's ideas on the phenomena of imitation, incorporation, and identification that follow the process of introjection.

Ouverture: A "Calling Card"

My starting point will be Ferenczi's very first psychoanalytic writing, his paper "The Effect on Women of Premature Ejaculation in Men" (1908a). The reason for my choice is that, as I will show, this paper represents a sort of "calling card" through which Ferenczi (albeit without realizing it) heralded the *distinctively introjective approach* of his future research. This is a line of investigation that, from Ferenczi's early steps into psychoanalysis at a stage when psychoanalysis itself was still, as it were, "in the making," was aimed at chastising what he called "the sins of psychoanalysts" (Ferenczi, 1932b), which of course included *his own sins* as a novice analyst at that time: first and foremost, insufficient contact with the affective needs of patients and, consequently, a lack of introjection and emotional sharing of their communications on the part of the person who ought to feel concern for and should take care of them (Ferenczi 1932b, pp. 1–3, pp. 199–202, pp. 209–211).

At one level, to those who are familiar with the events of his personal life, Ferenczi himself is quite possibly the premature ejaculator described in the (therefore "self-analytic") remarks of these pages. However, my preferred approach to an author's writings involves a more comprehensive overview that spans his whole corpus of works. From this standpoint, even at this embryonic stage of Ferenczi's thinking, the premature ejaculator appears in fact to be the analyst who, despite his sincere commitment to help the patient, does not adequately fulfill the mental coupling indispensable to the analytic encounter by failing to acknowledge (and sometimes disregarding) the patient's uniqueness and his psychic need for relatedness and recognition.

Thus, if in our reading of Ferenczi's first paper we set aside the physical nature of the symptom (explored through an original focus on how it affects the female partner) and take instead a more metaphoric interpretative stance, we become able to share Ferenczi's keen insight—an insight, it is worth remarking, that stands out as very unusual within the cultural context in which it was formulated. Essentially, Ferenczi asks: can the feelings experienced by the woman when her partner ejaculates prematurely—feelings such as "anxiety," "depression," "restless-ness," and even partial or complete "anesthesia" and "orgasm failure," combined with a large "amount of libidinal excitation"—almost be understood in terms of the effect of the analyst's relational and interpretative haste towards the patient (1908a, p. 291)? By the term "haste," I mean to suggest a psychoanalytic atti-tude whereby the analyst does not sufficiently hold within himself the needs and requests of the patients, or *sympathize with their disadvantaged position* (of course, disadvantaged compared to that of the analyst), and does not respect the rhythms and synchrony necessary to perform a *penetrative–interpretative act* that fulfils both members of the couple, not just one. (According to Paula Heimann, 1949, Roger Money-Kyrle, 1956, and Irma Brenman Pick, 1985, interpretation is to be con-sidered a "projective act," as it is for Racker, 1949–1958, and for the textbook on psychoanalytic technique by Etchegoyen, 1991; I shall return to this point briefly in the last part of this paper.)

To be sure, Ferenczi's later works corroborate such a metaphorical interpre-tation, which might at first sight seem far-fetched (only "at first sight", because Ferenczi himself authorizes such an interpretative shift from body to mind by com-paring "sexual coitus" to "mental coitus" in his 1924 *Thalassa*), by showing very clearly how the premature ejaculator may well be the analyst. This is the case, for instance, when the analyst gets impatient and does not wait long enough in order to achieve a genuine contact with the other, either because of his "fanaticism for interpretation" (Ferenczi with Rank 1924b, p. 25) and "over-keenness" in making interpretation (1928, p. 96),[2] or because, conversely, his response to the messages of the patients is characterized by "exaggerated reserve" and "schizoid abstinence," as Ferenczi will point out at the outset of *The Clinical Diary* (Ferenczi 1932b, pp. 1–4). This attitude will be repeatedly criticized in *The Clinical Diary*, where Ferenczi explicitly claims that it also represents a "masculine" refusal (though observable in men and women alike) to make available the inner space necessary to contain an experience that involves tension, as well as unfamiliar and unexpected feelings that one does not want to experience insofar as they require a temporary modification of one's mindset and identity (pp. 40–42).

Interludio capriccioso: Instructions for Employing the Psychoanalytic Method

Before moving on to address in detail Ferenczi's introduction of the notion of introjection into psychoanalysis, I shall briefly examine what one may appropriately call his "instructions for use" of the psychoanalytic method. As Ferenczi himself observed at the beginning of his own journey, this method always requires that the patient becomes somewhat educated into it. Moreover, if successful mental coupling and effective cooperation from the patient are to be achieved (Ferenczi 1909b, p. 124), the education process should be carried out with "much tact and psychological understanding [...] learned by long practice" (1908c, p. 39). Nevertheless, regrettably but not infrequently, *an excess or a deficit in the expression of the analyst's drives* within this process delays or interferes with its positive outcome.

Several examples of such a "deficit" or "excess" already emerge at this very early stage in Ferenczi's career (at which point he was, nonetheless, fully launched as a psychoanalyst), and they are both extremely relevant to my argument and significant *per se* in terms of the psychoanalytic approach he would develop later on in his clinical thought. For instance, turning his attention to the role of the parents, he briefly discusses the case of a mother who cannot accept her son's maturation and gradual acquisition of mental and existential independence, and that of a father who (like that mother) is an incestuous parent, and when hugging his daughter "puts his tongue into her mouth every time he kisses her" (Ferenczi 1908c, p. 45; this detail has been omitted from the English translation). More generally, he also refers to caregivers who, for "lack of concern and neglect" (1908b, p. 285; this detail, again, has been omitted from the English translation), have the "custom of leaving children alone [...] during the most violent crises," or are too anxious, lie to them, and act hypocritically: on the one hand, underestimating the "understanding and faculty of observation" of children (1909b, p. 116), and on the other being too strict when confronted by their hunger for truth and help with their sexual development. These are all parental attitudes that, as Ferenczi notes, either excite or inhibit growth by eliciting in the child "uncritical obedience" (1909a, p. 93), "unjustified respect," and a sort of "*introspective blindness*" through a "post-hypnotic suggestion of a negative hallucination" (1908b, p. 288), thus triggering not only "unnecessary repressions" (1908b, p. 283) but also "dissociation" and (using a term I have coined) "extraction" (Borgogno, 1999, 2011) of vital parts and resources of the self.

It is for this set of reasons, Ferenczi goes on to suggest as early as 1908, that *homo psychoanalyticus* should be chiefly sober and nondogmatic (1908b, p. 290). In other words, he should first and foremost constantly monitor the characteristics of his own affects, preventing them from degenerating into passions and provoking "unnecessary pain" (1908b, p. 290; 1911b, p. 304). Furthermore, he should "limit the amount of [...] external stimuli" in communicating his own impressions (1908b, p. 284), resorting to "good humour and charity" and, as he recommends, a "pinch of irony" when "pondering on" what the patients say and do (1911a). Finally, in listening to patients he should not forget his own childhood and adolescence, and stick consistently to a principle of "*equal distribution*" of rights and obligations between man and woman, parent and child, and analyst and patient. This is a recurrent leitmotiv throughout Ferenczi's late works, and most notably in "The Adaptation of the Family to the Child" (1927). In this paper, he maintains that, in order to get in touch with the most archaic and nonverbal levels of the patient's psyche, analysts should overcome their *forgetfulness of their own childhood* and take the initiative by getting closer and adapting to the patient and his particular mindset (Borgogno, 2013).

In the concrete practice of an analysis, Ferenczi points out, the analyst should never discount this set of ideal principles—those which he invokes right from the very beginning—nor presume that they are easy to stick to and master. So much so that, in "On the Technique of Psychoanalysis" (1919c), he will underscore how these principles are seriously hindered by the narcissistic parts in the analyst's countertransference as well as by the analyst's own resistances to the self-analytic and working-through process required of him; both these aspects, in turn, often prompt the resistances and negative therapeutic reactions of the patients, becoming in some cases the cause for "retarding and making impossible the appearance of the transference" (1919c, p. 188). Thus, summing up Ferenczi's views on this matter, the analyst's narcissism and his resistance to the analytic task are the factors most likely to actively produce the resistances and negative therapeutic reactions of the patient: a perspective that he will continue to develop in the chapters he contributed to the book co-authored (with Otto Rank), *The Development of Psychoanalysis* (1924b), in his "Child Analysis in the Analysis of Adults (1931) and, of course, his *Notes and Fragments* (1920–1932) and *The Clinical Diary* (Ferenczi, 1932b).

Incidentally, I would like here to remark that in the same year when Ferenczi wrote "On the Technique of Psychoanalysis" Abraham (1919) too addressed the problem of patients who reject or obstruct the use of the analytic method. However, Abraham's conclusions are opposite to Ferenczi's. While Ferenczi claims that the cause of these patients' attitude is a narcissistic deficit in the analyst's ability to listen and respond, Abraham in contrast contends that the cause is the robust narcissism of the patient, who out of envy and greed cannot accept that the analyst has "something good" to offer him. Ferenczi's and Abraham's difference in this respect, by the way, is connected to their diverging views on the issue of introjection. Ferenczi in fact, in *Thalassa* (1924a) and *The Clinical Diary* (Ferenczi, 1932b), like Winnicott, will conceive of the early introjection of the baby as a process that is indeed ruthless but essentially life-oriented (quite literally, the baby eats the mother with pleasure, and the mother feels pleasure in letting her baby eat her); whereas Abraham, like Klein, maintains that introjection is always partially destructive, and that, if unmitigated and not worked-through, its inherent destructiveness is bound to "seal the fate" of a person.

Allegro ma non troppo: Contact, Psychic Contagion, Transference, and Introjection

It is through a series of short, albeit progressively elaborate, remarks on the nature of *psychic contact*, and how it may turn into a sort of *psychic contagion* when the quality and intensity of contact are not adequately handled, that Ferenczi developed the thoughts that eventually led him to formulate the notion of "introjection." Throughout his career, Ferenczi was increasingly to stress the importance of this notion, going as far as to claim that its significance as a psychic process was no less crucial than that of projection—which, at that time, was deemed by Freud and his disciples the *primum movens* of psychic life.

While it is true to say that Ferenczi's ideas on introjection were not yet fully formed when he first introduced the concept (Ferenczi, 1909a), he did nevertheless point out clearly from the outset that, as Laplanche and Pontalis correctly note in *The Language of Psychoanalysis* (1967, p. 230), it is connected with the "passion for transference" typical of neurotic patients. In this respect, it is worth highlighting that not only does this "passion" mark the infantile soul that underlies neurosis, but it also characterizes Ferenczi's own approach as an apprentice Freudian psychoanalyst. It is precisely in exploring thoughts and ideas linked with this *(infantile) passion for transference* that Ferenczi, focusing progressively on children's *yearning for love and objects* and on the *vulnerability* and *permeability* resulting from their intense attachment to and bonds with them (even at this early stage of his thinking he understands libido as object-seeking rather than drive-fulfillment-seeking!), starts to hint in several remarks not solely at the crucial role of introjection as a structuring psychic process, but also at the fact that it can be a source of death, as well as of life. The story of Peter the Great and his son Alexis, based on Merežkovskij's account, that Ferenczi quotes in this paper, speaks volumes on this regard (1909a, p. 78).

To put it somewhat more bluntly, in "Introjection and Transference" Ferenczi does seem to suggest between the lines that even from the earliest stages of life it is possible to "eat shit" and *be poisoned* (rather than nurtured) *by parents* who, in contrast with the dominant sociocultural (and psychoanalytic) paradigms of his age, were by no means "good by definition." In fact, as Ferenczi goes on to write in the same essay, while babies are certainly *hungry for objects and affects* indispensable for their development, because of their very young age and their consequent helplessness they have no choice but take in everything without being able to select and defend themselves from what they take.

"But, then again, what is it that the baby puts inside itself?" Ferenczi seems to wonder as he further focuses his thinking on the important role of introjections. Certainly not only material things—food, attention, affects, and words—but also the actual way they are offered. It is above all the *specific quality of the response of the other* that, from Ferenczi's point of view, shapes our ensuing identifications, together with our views and perceptions of ourselves and the world, including those of a potentially pathogenic nature.

As far as *pathogenic forms of introjection* are concerned, it is worth mentioning at least two relevant examples significantly addressed by Ferenczi. The first is a form of identification—*identification with the aggressor*—that a few years later, in "A Little Chanticleer" (1913c), he will identify and describe as a key process in the formation of personality and in the analysis, a key process of which in the last period of his life he will systematically study the complex phenomenology (1930; 1931; 1932a; 1932b; 1920–1932). The second is a type of *infantile inclination*, which he deemed physiological, *to assimilate into our own character the distinctive traits of our parents*, and most notably the way they react (sometimes completely unconsciously) to our coming into the world. This particular inclination is wonderfully described in the late paper, "The Unwelcome Child and His Death-Instinct" (1929), where Ferenczi illustrates how the "aversion or impatience on the part of the mother" (the fact of non-being, by reflex, "desired and welcome") instills in children a consequent sense of being "*unwelcome guests of the family*" and a "feeling that life was hardly any longer worth living" together with a "streak of pessimism and of aversion to life" (1929, pp. 103–105).

As these examples help to make clear, Ferenczi ultimately appears to place a new and unusual attention on the aspects of inter-psychic transmission; and actually, by introducing the notion of introjection, he promptly pointed out to his colleagues that it is absolutely crucial to take into account a certain kind of *pragmatics of human communication.*[3] Although such a pragmatics of communication always plays a significant role in the process of psychic transmission, its importance is paramount *when the minds involved in the process are not yet completely formed*, as these are much more likely than adult minds to be affected and shaped by the "hypnotic orders" of their caregivers: "maternal" hypnotic orders if they are based on fascination, insinuation, and seductiveness, and "paternal" if they are grounded on intimidation (1909a, pp. 69–70) and "compelling" and "authoritative [...] commands" (1913a, p. 339). Both types of orders, Ferenczi adds, are inevitably received and introjected by newborn babies, and become operative in their minds (and mindsets) without them being aware of hosting such messages in the most intimate part of their selves—until they meet someone who, visualizing and putting them into words, eventually "loosens" their grip (1932a, p. 166).[4] However, as Ferenczi emphasises at the end of "Introjection and Transference," the problem with unconscious hypnotic orders is that very often not even the person who imparts them is aware of doing so, nor of what he actually orders, as he in turn has introjected the same injunctions from his own caregivers by identifying both with the orders and with those who convey them.

This predicament also draws attention to the fact that, in contrast to what Ferenczi believed at the beginning of his reflection on introjection, transference is not solely a form of projection triggered by unconscious fantasy. In effect, it is produced (alas, no less unconsciously!) by the analyst too, who therefore should no longer be considered as merely a "catalytic ferment" (1909a, p. 39) of other people's states of mind or, in other words, a magnet that simply attracts the idiosyncratic affects of the patient and the significant characters in his life, without influencing the process in any way through his own subjectivity.[5]

Especially if one considers when it was formulated, this truly stands out as an extraordinary opinion, one that after a few years would lead Ferenczi to affirm that "the transitory symptoms during analysis" should be understood in the context of the session by starting from focusing on what the analyst did (or did not) say or do before their occurrence. Put another way, from this perspective symptoms are to be understood by investigating the analyst-patient interrelation within which they emerge, as only careful scrutiny of the "here and now" context can help us to learn *en miniature* (1912b, p. 212) how the patient's suffering originated in the first place, illuminating the interpsychic environment where he grew up, the pleasant or unpleasant feelings by which he began to be stimulated at that early age, and the resulting defence reactions and intrapsychic conflicts. A working style that Ferenczi will also extend to the patients' comparisons, as well as of his own dreams and even (in the wake of Pfister) his own scribbling (see "The Analysis of Comparisons," 1915a, and "Dreams of the Unsuspecting," 1917).

Rondò finale: Trauma, Identificatory Play, and Role-Reversal

In coming to the last part of my chapter, in which I shall explore the final developments of the brilliant intuitions Ferenczi had as a "young psychoanalyst," and as a preamble to my conclusions on Ferenczi as an eminently "introjective analyst," I should like to state first that, in his exploration and endeavors in psychoanalytic theory and practice in the later years, Ferenczi clearly resumes the set of themes he had already identified and focused on at the beginning of his career. It should be noted, nevertheless, that these central topics are now addressed from a different angle, i.e., from the standpoint of a *new theory of trauma* and a corresponding *new therapeutic technique to reawaken and transform it*.

As well as marking the first step into contemporary psychoanalysis, these new perspectives (developed by Ferenczi shortly before his untimely death in 1933) continue to stimulate our psychoanalytic inquiry today through the central questions they pose.

Indeed, Ferenczi's late works reflect a stage in which he has set himself free from the massive burden of Freud's authority, managing finally to "be himself" as a clinician and fully elaborate his practice of what he called "child analyses with adults" (1931), that is, analyses aimed at avoiding the significant number of improper attitudes displayed by analysts themselves in the course of treatment.

Yet, in order to move on consistently from Ferenczi's early writings to his late ones, it is important to mention briefly at least two major strands that characterized his research during the "middle stage" and which are also relevant to the subject of my inquiry. The first is an increasingly closer examination of "primary identification" as "a stage preceding object relations" (Ferenczi 1932b, p. 147): a survey that includes the numerous archaic and autoplastic survival strategies that arise in response to extreme and non-representable pain.[6] The second line of investigation leads to Ferenczi's repeated assertions that, in order to revitalize the "dead points" in the treatment (1919a, p. 196),[7] it is vital to make use of a more intense "libidinal mobility" and a more unsparing, ductile, and "untiring sensitivity" (1933, p. 153). Bearing this in mind, according to different needs and situations, in Ferenczi's opinion psychoanalysts at any rate must be the first to *take on*, temporarily, *the various roles that the unconscious of the patients "prescribes"* them to personify, so as to be able to grasp not only intellectually but also intimately the circumstances that initially produced their pathogenic suffering and their psychic "malaise" and "unwell-being" (Ferenczi with Rank 1924b, p. 43).

If Ferenczi's research from 1927 to 1932 is considered from this twofold perspective—i.e., a standpoint that combines a focus on primary identification and connected archaic defense strategies with the advocacy of a more intense imaginative identification with the patient—it becomes clear that it actually revolves around one core question: are psychoanalysts (and, most notably, is he himself) sufficiently permeable and open in the analytic encounter so as to let themselves momentarily *become the patient* and *take on* (just as momentarily) *his suffering and afflictions?*[8]

Ferenczi's answer to this question is an unambiguous "no," which he supports by making an inventory of the multifarious forms of rejection, laziness, and *no-entry signals* we all surrender to when it comes to receiving the internal "parental imagos" projected onto us by patients, and in particular (Ferenczi's most precious acquisition) the negative response given when it comes to *holding within our own bodies and minds the "dissociated and fragmented child"* who has lost his own voice because of the trauma he has undergone and the consequent, inevitable unconscious identification with the inattentive and unreliable adult. Ferenczi underscores that this is a child who, in spite of everything, is always *waiting to be recalled into existence* by a rescuer who brings him back to life by recognizing and slowly putting into words the infantile language he had exiled when finding himself under conditions of "great pain" (Ferenczi 1932b, p. 30). However, at the same time, his recognition and rebirth can only occur as long as the analyst *humbly* hosts (in his psychic space) and embodies on behalf of the patient both the feelings the latter has hitherto been unable to experience and the natural potentialities he has never expressed or even been aware of, but which he could have embraced as a child or teenager, had his life taken a different course. I would like to stress that Ferenczi's way of thinking in this respect is strikingly similar to that adopted by Winnicott in "Fear of Breakdown" (1963–1974) and that, as I have suggested (Borgogno, 2007), it also effectively illustrates the deep meaning of Ferenczi's notion of "new beginning," further developed theoretically by Michael Balint (1952).

Clearly, at this stage in his thinking Ferenczi is no longer referring to the kind of oedipal patients typically described by Freud, but to the categories of patients that most frequently enter our consulting rooms today (i.e., borderline, schizoid, etc.), whose main problem is a deficit in the functioning of the ego and in the ability to symbolize. With reference to these categories, the long analytic treatment of R.N. (*alias* Elizabeth Severn) thoroughly described by Ferenczi in *The Clinical Diary* constitutes a groundbreaking and paradigmatic antecedent. This is due to the fact that, in the diary, through a relentless scrutiny of his own transference and countertransference, Ferenczi ends up frankly exposing the reservations and difficulties that the analyst encounters in tolerating the transferences of the patient and the roles that the latter forces him to embody, particularly when the channel of the transference is nonverbal and the analyst is therefore supposed to *personify on behalf of the patient*—or "interpret", in the sense of "taking on the roles the patient asks us to play"—*the "lost" child* who "is gone" and has come to be "beside himself" (Ferenczi 1932b, p. 32; Borgogno and Vigna-Taglianti, 2008, 2013).

While, from Ferenczi's perspective, such difficulties and reservations also emerge in the context of positive countertransference[9] as well as (of course to a greater extent) in ordinary negative transference, permeated as it is by intense feelings of anger and hatred, they become definitely overwhelming and hard to deal with in the situation I have just outlined—that is, when in the "long wave" of the analysis and *through a process of role-reversal the analyst has to accept being transformed into the child* whom the patient had partially to give up or exile in the past; or even when, before getting to that point, the analyst is transformed into the "bad object" that has determined this specific negative transference—an object, it is worth stating again, that in all likelihood does not (and did not in the first place) originate from the hostile primary feelings of the patient, but rather from idiosyncratic deficits and faults of the parents and the analyst who have been unable to identify with the patient's infantile suffering.

To summarize, becoming the "bad object" because of their own deficits or faults, and going through the (often) resulting process of role-reversal,[10] are situations that analysts basically *do not want to know anything about* (Borgogno, 2007).

And yet, Ferenczi stressed, they are also precisely the situations that (above all, when dealing with trauma and its consequences) should by no means be avoided or neglected, as the recovery of unsymbolized and unrepresented parts of a patient's experience can only occur by "objectifying" them through the—ostensive!—passage of making them "something that happened to another person" (Ferenczi 1932b, p. 180)—someone who, in the framework of the treatment, must of course be the analyst. In Ferenczi's own words, this is a person who, "*in contrast*" to what the patient has experienced in the past, is ready to carry responsibly the burden of becoming the "murderer of the patient" (Ferenczi 1932b, p. 52; Schreber, 1903)[11] while, at the same time, granting to him (within himself, as well as externally) a different psychological environment where the hurt, seduced, unacknowledged, and betrayed childhood can finally step again into life and be completed, reconstructed, remembered and, eventually, integrated. This fundamental therapeutic function of offering a different psychological environment that can "make *contrast*" with the one the patient experienced in his/her infancy or adolescence is specifically described by Ferenczi in "The Principle of Relaxation and Neocatharsis" (1930) and "Confusion of Tongues between Adults and the Child" (1932a).

Conclusion

To conclude, what else would I wish to add? First, I shall point out explicitly that, throughout this overview, I have presented Ferenczi's psychoanalytic itinerary from a rather ideal perspective. Indeed, far from completely theorizing and developing the insights he had throughout his career, Ferenczi mostly glimpsed or fleetingly addressed them, thus entrusting us today with his brave attempt to improve and potentiate the impact of psychoanalytic intervention, especially when this is carried out in an environment overwhelmed by mental suffering and the massive hatred that usually accompanies it. Such situations of extreme pain are those in which the analyst is most likely to succumb to his fear of feelings and pain, and resort defensively to veritable forms of "terrorism of suffering" (Ferenczi 1932a; 1932b). While it is true to say that it is precisely in situations centered on being hated, hating, and (simultaneously) in his indiscriminately empathizing with the other's suffering, that Ferenczi revealed his limitations, often ending up by finding himself in entangled relationships with his patients, it is equally important to stress that in *The Clinical Diary* he also provided us with an unparalleled and very honest description of how, in order to achieve a worked-through understanding and mutual transformation, it is necessary for the *intra*psychic (which was produced by the *extra*psychic in the very early stages of life) once again to become *inter*psychic within the "here and now" of the analytic relationship. In this respect, Ferenczi also points out how the analyst needs to abide for a long time in this complex dynamic, if he is eventually to disentangle and set himself free from the various objects and aspects of the self of the patient. Incidentally, the latter consideration leads us to yet another fundamental aspect of Ferenczi's legacy, one that only gradually have we become able to appreciate and that has helped us to rediscover that in our work an element of "interpersonal action" is inevitable (and sometimes indispensable in order to identify and represent the events of the internal world that the analytic process brings to the surface); and consequently that it is frequently impossible to gain quick access to interpretations independent from an intense unconscious involvement on our part. This kind of clinical phenomena has been productively investigated by a number of American authors who, carefully differentiating them from "acting without thinking," have understood them in terms of "enactment" or "interpretive action" (see, for instance, Levenson, 1983; Jacobs, 1991; Ogden, 1994). As for the French authors (prominently, Botella and Botella, 2001), they have explored these phenomena by making reference to the notion of the analyst's "work of figurability," which they aptly connect to the analyst's need, in such circumstances, to allow his own thinking to regress formally during the session, so as to become able to reach patients who are themselves extremely regressed.

Second, I would like to take my leave with a succinct overview of a question I have not entirely addressed at the beginning of my chapter. In "*Ouverture: A 'Calling Card'*," talking about interpretation as a kind of *penetrative act*, I mentioned in passing (quoting Paula Heimann, Roger Money-Kyrle, Irma Brenman Pick, Heinrich Racker, and also Horacio Etchegoyen) that all "interpretative acts" are in fact always projective acts following the introjection of the patient's projections. In focusing on this complex point, it is important to underline that, as a projective act, the interpretation of the analyst should not only involve his passive reception of the aspects communicated projectively by the patient; in effect, in setting out to contain those aspects, the analyst should also be prepared to initiate their transformation, first and foremost through a *decontamination* of the severe catastrophic anxieties that characterize them.

However, unfortunately, not always is the analyst able to carry out this task within an adequate amount of time: partly because he may not manage to grasp entirely all the different aspects involved in the communications of the patient; partly because, even if he does grasp them, he cannot immediately separate his personal reaction to them from the actual content of the projections he has introjected. To an extent, the latter is a situation the analyst inevitably has to go through, particularly when the patient, positioning himself in a mental state that precedes individuation, requires that the analyst be willing to reside for a limited time in a state of chaos and confusion—both feeling to be nonexistent for the patient (just as the patient felt he was during his childhood) and, more simply and yet no less painfully, feeling not-yet-existent as an external object for the patient. These mental states should never be eluded when they emerge, if, following Bion, we really aim to "dream" the events ongoing in the session by reaching an authentic reverie on them.[12]

Notes

1 A version of this chapter was presented as the invited keynote lecture at the International Sándor Ferenczi Conference, "Introjection, Transference, and the Analyst in the Contemporary World," Buenos Aires, October 21–24, 2009, and was first published in the *Rivista di Psicoanalisi* (Vol. 56, N. 3, pp. 561–576, 2010) and then in English in *American Imago* (Vol. 68, N. 2, pp. 155–172, 2011). I wish to take this opportunity to thank the *Rivista di Psicoanalisi* and *American Imago* for granting the permission to republish it in the present book.

2 Ferenczi will equate this fanaticism for interpretation with a cruel, sadistic act of narcissistic subjugation, full of a "cerebral and masturbatory" stance that does not allow for the authentic recognition of the partner and his uniqueness (Ferenczi with Rank, 1924b; Ferenczi, 1928). As early as 1912, he refers to this kind of attitude as "performing onanism *per vaginam*" (1912a, p. 187), and later on, in an entry to his *Notes and Fragments* dated November 26, 1932, he will add that in many circumstances "ejaculation = cerebral haemorrhage" (1920–1932, p. 255).

3 On the relational meta-communications behind and beyond the transmission of contents Heimann (1970, 1975) and Rycroft (1956, 1957) followed Ferenczi's direction without knowing it.

4 On "unconscious hypnotic orders" and their grip on individuals, see also the 1913 essays "Taming of a Wild Horse" (1913a) and "Belief, Disbelief and Conviction" (1913b), as well as "Psychogenic Anomalies of Voice Production" (1915b) and "The Analysis of Comparisons" (1915a), both from 1915.

5 In *The Clinical Diary* (1932b), Ferenczi goes as far as to claim that first the analyst induces the transference and then denies having done so, and that—similarly—it is often the analyst who provokes the trauma or its repetition but then is not willing to acknowledge it.

6 As for "archaic strategies for survival" (including, for instance, "pretending to be dead" and other kinds of "animal mimicry," "clinging reflexes," "phenomena of hysterical materialization," "mutilating autotomy," "catatonia and catalepsy," "negativism," "petrification," "glaciation," "psychical suicide," etc.), see Ferenczi 1919b; 1919c; 1919d; 1921a; 1921b; 1924b; 1932b; and also 1920–1932. As far as "primary identification" is concerned, several references can be found in *The Clinical Diary*.

7 In the context of Ferenczi's late works, *revitalizing dead points* will become the equivalent of *reanimating the dead or agonizing parts* not only of the patient but also of the analyst himself.

8 In this respect, see the interesting case of the English-speaking, epileptic patient who asks Ferenczi to impersonate Julius Caesar—a request that, since in English the word "Caesar" sounds very much like "seizure," Ferenczi understands as meaning "Have an epileptic seizure, you too, so that you'll attain a deep understanding about what I feel in my condition" (Ferenczi 1932b, pp. 71–72). Is this fruitful process of reverie and transformation comparable to Bion's famous example of "ice cream / I scream" (1970, p. 13)? Quite possibly. Certainly, Ferenczi's thinking in this sketch prefigures Bion's insight in *Cogitations* (1992, p. 291) that the patient does not simply want to receive an interpretation from the analyst. Rather, he wants to find out whether the analyst is willing to get to know the situation he is in and see how he deals with it and what sort of compromises and antidotes he resorts to in doing so.

9 In Ferenczi's view, the difficulties connected with positive transference emerge both when this is too intense and informed by a dependence dating back to early life, and when the analyst mystifies the transference by concealing from the patient (and himself, to the extent that out of wishful thinking he relies on it) the considerable degree of idealization with which, due to the inevitable state of regression entailed by the analysis, the patient looks at the person who takes care of him.

10 Of course, I do not refer here to the rather frequent kind of "role-reversal" typical of children's games, which fundamentally reflects a reversal dynamic of a passive position into an active one. Such a dynamic, clearly observable in child analysis, is also present, if only more indirectly, in the analysis of adults when they—both children and adults— make the analyst experience what they feel or have felt in their more or less painful vicissitudes (see Borgogno, 2011; Borgogno and Vigna-Taglianti, 2013). A remarkable example of this kind of role reversal is offered by two patients described by Ferenczi in "On Transitory Symptom-Constructions during the Analysis" (1912b) who, feeling that he was treating them as if they were stupid, actually became stupid during the session, thus making in turn Ferenczi feel stupid and "idiotic." Ferenczi acutely interpreted their behavior as a communicative mode aimed at "mocking" what I once defined (Borgogno, 2005) as an "interpretative tic" of the analyst. Furthermore, and significantly, in presenting these two cases Ferenczi reports in a footnote a brief exchange he had with a child, highlighting how often children actually "mock" adults when the latter tell them "nonsense" (1912b, pp. 202–204).

11 See, in this regard, "The Analyst's Murder of the Patient," Chapter 7 of Rudnytsky's *Reading Psychoanalysis: Freud, Rank, Ferenczi, Groddeck* (2002), as well as *Soul Murder: The Effects of Childhood Abuse and Deprivation* by Shengold (1989), but also *Soul Murder: Persecution in the Family* by M. Schatzman (1973), a book which was very famous in the 1970s.

12 There is no space to discuss here in more detail Ferenczi's actual achievements in this respect, alongside the situations in which things went out of his control causing him to make what today we would regard as "gross mistakes," if not veritable forms of "acting in." On the one hand, it is certainly true that, due to the absence in the coeval psychoanalytic community of someone who could provide him with the assistance and consultation he needed, Ferenczi did occasionally "use" his patients (i.e., "mutual analysis") in order to overcome his own difficulties with himself and with them. On the other hand, however, as Elizabeth Severn's treatment clearly illustrates, in spite of his obvious shortcomings Ferenczi was also able (through the *working-through* of his transferences and his emotional responses to the projective identifications of that patient) to start working out an intrapsychic explanation of her internal world, connecting it with the "long wave" of his analytic relationship with her as well as with the past personal history of both. In this way, Ferenczi actually provided us with an example (which is anything but unsophisticated or superficial) of the type of work we have to carry out when dealing with these kinds of situations in analysis, we have to disentangle and set ourselves free from the restraints the patient has entrapped us with. For a more extensive analysis of this subject, see the last chapter of my book *Psychoanalysis as a Journey* (1999), entitled "On the *Clinical Diary*: Fear of Suffering and the Terrorism of Suffering."

References

Abraham, K. (1919). A particular form of neurotic resistance against the psychoanalytic method. In: *Selected Papers on Psychoanalysis* (pp. 303–311). Trans. D. Bryan and A. Strachey. London: Hogarth, 1942.

Balint, M. (1952). *Primary Love and Psychoanalytic Technique.* London: Hogarth and The Institute of Psychoanalysis.

Bion, W. R. (1970). *Attention and Interpretation: A Scientific Approach to Insight in Psycho-Analysis and Groups.* London: Tavistock.

Bion, W. R. (1992). *Cogitations.* Ed. by F. Bion. London: Karnac.

Borgogno, F. (1999). *Psicoanalisi come percorso.* Turin: Bollati Boringhieri. (English translation *Psychoanalysis as a Journey.* Trans. Ian Harvey. London: Open Gate Press, 2007).

Borgogno, F. (2005). Who is the author speaking to? The impact of the intended audience on theoretical framing of clinical material. *Psychoanalytic Dialogues*, 15(6):917–928.

Borgogno, F. (2007). *The Vancouver Interview. Frammenti di vita e opere d'una vocazione psicoanalitica.* Rome: Borla. [Partially translated in English as: Notes and fragments of a psychoanalytic vocation. *The American Journal of Psychoanalysis*, 68(1):69–99, 2008].

Borgogno, F. (2011). *La signorina che faceva hara-kiri e altri saggi.* Bollati Boringhieri, Torino 2011 (English translation: *The Girl Who Committed Hara-Kiri and Other Clinical and Historical Essays.* Trans. Alice Spencer. London: Karnac Books, 2013).

Borgogno, F. (2013). "Coming from afar" and "temporarily becoming the patient without knowing it": Two necessary conditions for analysis according to Ferenczi's later thought. Presented at the conference *Sincerity and Freedom in Psychoanalysis*, Freud Museum/Anna Freud Centre, London, 18–20 October 2013 and published in *The American Journal of Psychoanalysis*, 74(4):302–312, 2014.

Borgogno, F. and Vigna-Taglianti, M. (2008). Il rovesciamento dei ruoli: un "riflesso" dell'eredità del passato piuttosto trascurato. *Rivista di Psicoanalisi*, 54(3): 591–603 [English translation: Role-reversal: a somewhat neglected mirror of heritages of the past. *Ital. Psychoanal. Annual*, 3: 93–102, 2009].

Borgogno, F. and Vigna-Taglianti, M. (2013), Role-reversal and the dissociation of the self. Actions signaling memories to be recovered: an exploration of a somewhat neglected transference-countertransference process. In R. Oelsner (ed) (2013), *Transference and Countertransference Today*. Routledge/IPA-Psychoanalytic Ideas and Applications Series, London.

Botella, C. and Botella, S. (2001). *La figurabilité psychique*. Lausanne/Paris: Delachaux et Niestlé. (English translation: *The Work of Psychic Figurability: Mental States without Representation*. Trans. A. Weller with M. Zerbib. London: Routledge, 2004).

Brenman Pick, I. (1985). Working-through in the countertransference. In E. Bott Spillius (ed), *Melanie Klein Today: Developments in Theory and Practice. Vol. 2: Mainly Practice.* London: Routledge, 1988 pp. 34–47.

Etchegoyen, R. H. (1991). *The Fundamentals of Psychoanalytic Technique.* Trans. P. Pitchon. London: Karnac, 1999.

Ferenczi, S. (1908a). *The Effect on Women of Premature Ejaculation in Men.* In S. Ferenczi (1955), pp. 291–294.

Ferenczi, S. (1908b). *Psychoanalysis and Education.* In S. Ferenczi (1955), pp. 280–290.

Ferenczi, S. (1908c). *Actual- and Psycho-Neuroses in the Light of Freud's Investigations and Psychoanalysis.* In S. Ferenczi (1950), pp. 30–55.

Ferenczi, S. (1909a). *Introjection and Transference.* In Ferenczi (1952), pp. 35–93.

Ferenczi, S. (1909b). *The Psychological Analysis of Dreams.* In S. Ferenczi (1952), pp. 94–131.

Ferenczi, S. (1911a). Anatole France als Psychoanalytiker [Anatole France as psychoanalyst]. *Zentralblatt für Psychoanalyse*, 1:461–467.

Ferenczi, S. (1911b). *On the Organization of the Psychoanalytic Movement.* In S. Ferenczi (1955), pp. 299–307.

Ferenczi, S. (1912a). *On Onanism.* In S. Ferenczi (1952), pp. 185–192.

Ferenczi, S. (1912b). *Transitory Symptom-Constructions during the Analysis.* In S. Ferenczi (1952), pp. 193–212.

Ferenczi, S. (1913a). *Taming of a Wild Horse.* In S. Ferenczi (1955), pp. 336–340.

Ferenczi, S. (1913b). *Belief, Disbelief and Conviction.* In S. Ferenczi (1950), pp. 437–450.

Ferenczi, S. (1913c). *A Little Chanticleer.* In S. Ferenczi (1952), pp. 204–252.

Ferenczi, S. (1915a). *The Analysis of Comparisons.* In S. Ferenczi (1950), pp. 397–407.

Ferenczi, S. (1915b). *Psychogenic Anomalies of Voice Production.* In S. Ferenczi (1950), pp. 105–109.

Ferenczi, S. (1917). *Dreams of the Unsuspecting*. In S. Ferenczi (1950), pp. 346–348.

Ferenczi, S. (1919a). *Technical Difficulties in the Analysis of a Case of Hysteria*. In S. Ferenczi (1950), pp. 189–197.

Ferenczi, S. (1919b). *The Phenomena of Hysterical Materialization*. In S. Ferenczi (1950), pp. 89–104.

Ferenczi, S. (1919c). *On the Technique of Psychoanalysis*. In S. Ferenczi (1950), pp. 177–189.

Ferenczi, S. (1919d). *Psycho-Analysis of the War-Neuroses*. In E. Jones (ed), *Psycho-Analysis and the War Neuroses* (London/Vienna/New York: Int. Psa. Press, 1921, pp. 5–21).

Ferenczi, S. (1920–1932). *Notes and Fragments*. In S. Ferenczi (1955), pp. 219–279.

Ferenczi, S. (1921a). *On Epileptic Fits: Observations and Reflections*. In S. Ferenczi (1955), pp. 197–204.

Ferenczi, S. (1921b). *Psychoanalytical Observations on Tic*. In S. Ferenczi (1950), pp. 142–174.

Ferenczi, S. (1924a). *Thalassa: A Theory of Genitality*. Trans. H. A. Bunker. New York: The Psychoanalytic Quarterly, 1938.

Ferenczi, S. (1924b). *The Development of Psychoanalysis*. Trans. Caroline Newton. New York: Nervous and Mental Disease Publishing Company, 1925 (written with O. Rank).

Ferenczi, S. (1927). *The Adaptation of the Family to the Child*. In: S Ferenczi (1955), pp. 61–76.

Ferenczi, S. (1928). *The Elasticity of Psychoanalytic Technique*. In S. Ferenczi (1955), pp. 87–101.

Ferenczi, S. (1929). *The Unwelcome Child and His Death Instinct*. In S. Ferenczi (1955), pp. 102–107.

Ferenczi, S. (1930). *The Principle of Relaxation and Neocatharsis*. In S. Ferenczi (1955), pp. 108–125.

Ferenczi, S. (1931). *Child Analysis in the Analysis of Adults*. In S. Ferenczi (1955), pp. 126–142.

Ferenczi, S. (1932a). *Confusion of Tongues between Adults and the Child*. In S. Ferenczi (1955), pp. 156–167.

Ferenczi, S. (1932b). *The Clinical Diary of Sándor Ferenczi*. Ed. by J. Dupont, Trans. M. Balint and N. Z. Jackson. Cambridge, MA: Harvard University Press, 1988.

Ferenczi, S. (1933). *Freud's Influence on Medicine*. In S. Ferenczi (1955), pp. 143–155.

Heimann, P. (1949). On counter-transference. In P. Heimann (1989), *About Children and Children-No-Longer. Collected Papers 1942–1980*. Ed. by M. Tonnesmann. London: Routledge, pp. 73–79.

Heimann, P. (1970). The nature and function of interpretation. In P. Heimann (1989), *About Children and Children-No-Longer. Collected Papers 1942–1980*. Ed. by M. Tonnesmann. London: Routledge, pp. 267–275.

Heimann, P. (1975). Further observations on the analyst's cognitive process. In P. Heimann (1989), *About Children and Children-No-Longer. Collected Papers 1942–1980*. Ed. by M. Tonnesmann. London: Routledge, pp. 295–310.

Jacobs, T. (1991). *The Use of the Self*. Madison: International University Press.

Laplanche, J. and Pontalis, J. B. (1967). *Vocabulaire de la Psychanalyse*. Paris: Press Universitaires de France. (English translation: *The Language of Psychoanalysis*. Trans. Donald Nicholson-Smith. London: Hogarth, 1973).

Levenson, E. (1983). *The Ambiguity of Change. An Inquiry into the Nature of Psychoanalytic Reality*. New York: Basic Books.

Money-Kyrle, R. E. (1956). Normal countertransference and some of its deviations. *International Journal of Psychoanalysis*, 37:360–366.

Ogden, T. H. (1994). The concept of interpretive action. *The Psychoanalytic Quarterly*, 63:219–245.

Racker, H. (1949–1958). *Transference and Counter-Transference*. New York: International Universities Press, 1968.

Rudnytsky, P. L. (2002). *Reading Psychoanalysis: Freud, Rank, Ferenczi, Groddeck*. Ithaca: Cornell University Press.

Rycroft, C. (1956). The nature and function of the analyst's communication to the patient. *International Journal of Psychoanalysis*, 37:469–472.

Rycroft, C. (1957). An enquiry into the function of words in the psycho-analytical situation. *International Journal of Psychoanalysis*, 39:408–441, 1958.

Schatzman, M. (1973). *Soul Murder: Persecution in the Family*. London: Allen Lane.

Schreber, D. P. (1903). *Memoirs of My Nervous Illness*. Trans. I. Macalpine and R. A. Hunter. London: Dawson, 1955.

Shengold, L. (1989). *Soul Murder: The Effects of Childhood Abuse and Deprivation*. New Haven: Yale University Press.

Winnicott, D. W. (1963–1974). Fear of breakdown. In C. Winnicott, R. Shepherd, and M. Davis (eds), *Psychoanalytic Explorations*. London: Karnac, 1989, pp. 87–95.

11

CONFUSION OF TONGUES

Trauma and Playfulness[1]

Galit Atlas

"Let us then go down and there confuse their language, so that one will not understand what another says."

(Genesis 11:1–9)[2]

Entrances

On that evening Tomaz entered my office, smiled broadly, and apologized. "I've got to finish something here," he said, beginning to click a text message on his cell phone. "It seems to me that the treatment is over," he added humorously immediately after finishing. "I've achieved my goals, so it's time, isn't it? It's taken me ten years." I still did not understand what he was talking about, but I was well acquainted with his playful way. "I'll explain, I'll explain," he said, returning to his phone and reading: "'I can't meet you today, I'm not feeling well.' She wrote this to me this morning, and I felt like crying. You know how much I've been waiting for this meeting with her," he said, adding, "but then I thought of you, and I thought of myself immediately taking the back seat of the bus. As we've been saying, I understood that I'm afraid to sit up front, to demand, to initiate, instead of only being nice all the time. And then, a minute before I rang your bell, I wrote her: 'I can come bring you soup.' I don't know where I got the guts from to simply make it clear that I want to see her and that no sickness is going to get in my way."

I just smiled and nodded, well aware that underneath the humor and the playful language we were always touching on a trauma concerning the abuse of power and aggression, along with Tomaz's daily struggle related to money and women. It was difficult for him to connect with the parts of himself that wished to take something for himself; for years he said he had been terrified of approaching women for fear they would "smack him." I understood that fear as also representing the anxiety lest the woman would discover his "sexual-aggressive motives," to which she would respond aggressively and attack him. During the first years of treatment, Tomaz did not manage to get a job, and the sense of power associated with making money was a source of emotional engulfment and anxiety. Tomaz had struggled with depression and tried to commit suicide in his youth on a number of occasions. In those first years of treatment, he used to tell me that he would die by the age of 27, like Jimi Hendrix, Jim Morrison, Kurt Cobain. He all but mentioned his own name at the bottom of the list of dead rock stars, asking that I either let him die already or save his life. I was not worried that he might consciously take his own life, but I was very much alarmed by the mysterious accidents he would occasionally be involved in. I shared this fear with him, suggesting that he tended to get himself in harm's way "by mistake." Tomaz became aware of this tendency, and termed his 27th birthday as "the beginning of life after death." It was a special birthday that we celebrated together, though not before he made sure that it was important for me that he live.

While our work together over the years addressed many layers, in this chapter I would like to focus on the unique language that evolved between Tomaz and me, the language of tenderness. This was a way of relating that helped us form a safe environment, but it was only after we managed to process its significance that it enabled a transformation in Tomaz's ability to function in the world. The language I am referring to is soft, creative, and playful, replete with much humor. Together we co-created our language, co-constructed the collusion (Beebe and Lachmann, 1988, 2002), created tender contact, and avoided contact with the trauma, which I later understood consists of the abusive use of power and aggression.

Beginnings

In this chapter, I will explore the confusion of tongues that arises in the chasm and dialectic between the language of tenderness and the language of aggression as it appears in the therapeutic relationship. I will emphasize the way in which patient and therapist use playfulness to collude in avoiding aggression as a means of protecting the tenderness that evolves in the co-constructed third of the treatment and preventing the retraumatization of both parties. In referring to Ferenczi's (1933) notion of the confusion of tongues, my focus is on the mutual interactional processes between analyst and adult patient, taking into account the clear asymmetry between them vis-à-vis the significant differences in their roles, function, and responsibility (Aron, 1992b), yet acknowledging the fact that they both speak the two languages and act unconsciously to satisfy needs on two corresponding parallel axes.

Ferenczi (1933) draws an important distinction between children's needs and adults' needs on the sexuality–relatedness axis, attributing exclusive responsibility for sexual exploitation to the adult, while claiming that sexual behavior in children is a symptom that attests to a rupture between the child and his surroundings. He points to the child's fantasy of playing within the domain of tenderness, while the adult, on the other hand, harbors sexual fantasies related to power, domination, and aggression, and the abuser tends to project his unconscious desire, shame, and guilt onto the child, thereby ignoring the child's actual need for love and protection. Ferenczi (1933) analyzes the power component of therapist–patient relations and stresses the destructive, forceful element that can surface. He claims that the same structural dependence that exists between child and parent arises between patient and therapist too. This dependence enables the abuse of the therapist's power in the same way that the parent can abusively exert his power to harm his child. And like the abused child, the patient often reacts with anxiety-ridden identification and introjections of the menacing person or aggressor, since it is unbearable for her to be left alone, deprived of maternal care and tenderness (p. 228). Ferenczi adds that the abused child plays innocently and feels "blissfully guiltless" up to that point (1933, p. 228).

Viewing children in this manner is especially important in that it paved the way toward emphasizing the actual, reality-based trauma, as well as caregivers' structural power and complete responsibility for abuse. Furthermore, it helped to develop the concept of identification with the aggressor. Just as significant to note, however, is that this way of thinking disregarded the child's internal reality, his own impulses and unconscious fantasies (Blum, 2004), as well as vulnerabilities and susceptibilities (Atlas-Koch, 2007). Applied to the therapeutic relationship, this perspective posits patients as potential innocent victims—perhaps in tandem with the way that Ferenczi experienced himself in the analytic community of the early 1930s, where he felt attacked and could not find the care, tenderness, and support that he needed (Blum, 2004).

We are dealing, then, with the clear distinction made by Ferenczi between the child and the adult as well as between the therapist and the patient, as he discusses the differences in structural power, the exploitation of authority, and the repetition of torture in the therapeutic relationship: In this case, the adult, as the powerful party, is potentially exploitative, while the child is potentially exploited. Ferenczi conveys the implicit yet clear message that asymmetry, even the simple indication that someone has more power than we do, can be traumatic (Frankel, 1998, 2002). It is therefore not surprising that Ferenczi opted for symmetry in his clinical interactions, since the asymmetry of the therapeutic encounter provided a reminder of an early trauma associated with the abuse of power between adult and child. In his "mutual analysis," Ferenczi not only refrained from emphasizing asymmetry as a necessary and important aspect of the analytic encounter but also viewed it as a threat and renounced his own analytic authority (Frankel, 2002; Blum, 2004; Aron, 1992a).

Many of Ferenczi's concepts and ideas are used by contemporary psychoanalysts, including his emphasis on the importance of trauma and childhood sexual abuse, the significance of the affective experience in analysis, the conception of countertransference as a potential source of analytic insight rather than merely resistance, the value of the therapist's empathy, and the recognition of the real relationship

between patient and analyst and between parent and child, including the importance of honesty and sincerity on the part of the analyst (Aron, 1992a; Blum, 2004;
Rachman, 1993; Hazan, 1999). Ferenczi is viewed as a pioneer in that he allowed
for two participants and two interpreters in the analytic investigation; he shed
light on the importance of acknowledging two psychologies in the room. In his
"mutual analysis," Ferenczi and his patients would hold back-to-back sessions in
which they took turns free-associating—an hour as a patient and an hour as the
"patient's patient"—in a symmetrical analysis (Aron, 1992b). Today the relational–
perspectivist approach to a "two-person psychology" emphasizes the distinction
between symmetry and mutuality and the analytic situation as mutual but asymmetrical. It views the analyst as a co-participant with the patient in a mutually and
reciprocally constructed transference–countertransference integration, stressing the
interpersonal nature of transference and of the continual dialectic between transference and countertransference—not as isolated or artificially split off from each
other ("taking turns"), but as mutual interactional processes (Aron, 1992b).

Confusion and Collusion

Using this framework, I will discuss the therapeutic situation in which an unconscious collusion is co-constructed by the therapist and the patient, while recognizing that both victim and aggressor exist simultaneously in both participants; a child
who speaks the language of tenderness, as well as an adult who speaks the language
of passion, are present in both. The two participants collude to protect the one part
from the anxiety-provoking other. Davies and Frawley (1992) refer to the adult self
state and the child self state that exist simultaneously in adult survivors of abuse and
might introduce confusion into the analytic process. I adopt their perspective and
focus here on the dialectical way in which *both* therapist and patient speak *both* languages, i.e., the child's tender language (including the need for care, love, holding,
containment, recognition, etc.) as well as the adult's sexual and aggressive language
(including passion, rage, competition, envy, etc.). The confusion appears when the
coexistence of the two languages threatens to disrupt psychic regulation. When this
happens, aggression gets disguised as tenderness in an effort to avoid destroying the
benevolent, tender parts that evolve in the co-constructed third of the treatment.
This language shift becomes activated in response to an unconscious reminder of
our patient's—or our own—trauma. I will demonstrate the theory in the context
of two cases and raise questions about the analytic couple's ability to work through
these collusions.

Tomaz

When I met Tomaz, he was twenty-three years old, an artist, and the youngest son
of a Brazilian mafioso. He moved to New York a year after his brother, with whom

he had been very close and who had died under mysterious circumstances, and tried to set out on his professional journey as an artist. When Tomaz was a year and a half old, his father kidnapped him from his mother and, as he explained to me, "No one messes with my father. She knew he'd kill her if she did anything." And so she did nothing. The father took young Tomaz to live with his ex-wife and their joint children. The ex-wife became Tomaz's mother, and their children became his very close siblings. The stepmother was described as warm and loving, and Tomaz had only good things to say about her: "After all, she is the woman who saved my life." She never discriminated between him and her own children, she was attentive to him, and to this day she is the one who sends him warm sweaters that always fit him to keep him snug during the New York winters.

The stepmother used to arrange for Tomaz and his biological mother to meet behind his father's back. He barely remembers his mother from these visits; his recollection of her apartment is an empty room, the only noise coming from a rotating fan. Throughout the years, Tomaz's biological mother had been the one that "he doesn't care about," and in ten years of therapy, twice a week, we gradually established contact with his grief over the sudden separation from her, mainly by working through the grief over our separations.

The language of tenderness was the exclusive mode of communication between Tomaz and me for a long time; I represented a loving mother to him, and he represented a soft and loving mother to me. The bad, dangerous, and abandoning mother was erased. The father was not granted entry into the room, but he made a forceful entry nonetheless, and as expected of him aggressively penetrated Tomaz's mind as reflected by the associations that emerged. "One day my motorcycle was stolen. I was 16. I went home frightened. I was scared that my dad would be mad at me for maybe not tying up my bike properly. But he wasn't mad, he only quietly said to me, 'Nonsense, don't worry.' Twenty minutes later there was a knock at the door. Dad told me to open it, and a guy with a helmet stood in the entrance and said, 'I've come to apologize. Your bike's parked outside.' That's how my bike was returned, without any explanations. And I never spoke about it with Dad, because I understood that it was better not to talk."

On another occasion, Tomaz is late for a session because he could not find parking, and he describes to me how his father never had such problems in Brazil. "Whenever we arrived anywhere he would phone and say where he wanted to park, and the car that had been parked there before just disappeared. I guess they would simply lift the car and clear the parking space for my father." Tomaz experiences the associations as aggressively penetrating the therapeutic space. He is unwilling to invite his father into the room and tries to fend off the associations that come to the surface, but quickly gives in and "takes the rear seat of the bus." This metaphor of his symbolizes his place on the "life ride." "I'm not one to *fight* over a place," said Tomaz, "I'm willing to give in and watch the scenery. What do I care? I sit in the back, listening to music through my headphones."

While he suffered no physical violence from his father, Tomaz deeply felt the power and aggression his father symbolized. He knew that the women in his father's life—including both his biological mother and his rearing mother—suffered physical violence, as did his elder brothers. Frankel (2002) notes that we must emphasize not only the emotional defensive aim of behaviors such as identification with the aggressor, but also their survival function; that is, the manner in which a certain behavior actually repeats itself in therapy because it has saved the child in the past not only from emotional fragmentation but from real aggression that had been directed toward him. Tomaz certainly interpreted his playful behavior as a child as protecting him from his father's physical aggression, and with me there is an implicit agreement barring aggression from entering the room. Frankel (2002) explains that in certain ways the patient and the analyst perceived each other as inherently threatening and that both partly see and identify with the other as an aggressor. "The result is unconscious collusions: tenuous agreements to avoid areas of anxiety for both of them" (p. 102). In this sense, just as the traumatized children described by Ferenczi (1933) are hungry for tenderness in the form of love, attention, and protection, defending themselves from any experience or appearance of aggression (see, for example, children's playing out of the Little Red Riding Hood fairy tale, Atlas-Koch, 2007), I believe that our patients' traumatized self states may collude with our own in order to protect the tender parts of the self, the other, and the treatment from damage by the aggressive parts. This is an attempt at defending against the terror of being traumatized through attack, penetration, humiliation, and destruction. Jessica Benjamin posits that at the core of male anxiety, the aggressive penis is seen as hurtful or destructive to the mother's body—and, by extension, to the treatment's maternal–tender parts (personal communication, 2009). The fear is of being both destructive and destroyed, and denial of aggression serves to exclude any threatening contents that might destroy the "good" and tender parts of the treatment, as well as the therapist and the self.

The threat is sensed as very real and thus Tomaz remained constantly vigilant. Anything can prove dangerous, anything and anyone a threat. We acknowledge that this vigilance sometimes serves as a life-saver; when a closet falls on the son of a friend, Tomaz leaps toward him, "as though I knew the closet was about to fall and was waiting for it to happen," and he succeeds in getting hold of it a moment before it falls on the child's head. I sense this vigilance in the room. We are both vigilant, but communicate in an entirely different language, the protected language, the language of tenderness, which manifests itself primarily through what I take to be playful behavior. The father's entrance is strictly forbidden, aggression is strictly forbidden. There is no entry for phallic interventions or any negative emotion. And if there is an intervention that gives him the sense that I see him, that I have understood something profound about him, he smiles immediately and jokingly mimics Robert De Niro, the mafioso who goes to therapy in the film *Analyze This*: "You … you …" He points at me and winks. For a moment he is the mafioso in therapy, the therapeutic language is alien and threatening to him, but also one that he begins to discover and to be moved by. And at these moments I am a mafioso as well, who threatens him with an obtrusive intervention, who sees him and aims to hurt him. We cope through our play and humor, and I do not interpret or analyze his behavior, but rather genuinely and unconsciously cooperate with him.

Here I would like to briefly discuss the playfulness that was part of the language of tenderness between Tomaz and me, as it was in Ron's case, presented below. I do not mean to claim that playfulness always denies aggression or erotic transference, and neither will I discuss the developmental aspect of play (Winnicott, 1971). My focus here is on cases in which play operates as a form of tender language, the aim of which is to evade contact with other contents that might revive an early trauma.

We know that playfulness cannot be only a seductive way to express erotic and aggressive contents (Torras De Beà, 1987), but that it can also serve to obstruct erotic transference and countertransference. In the cases presented here, I understand the absence of erotic transference and countertransference as part of a broader avoidance I am addressing related to passion and aggression. Welles and Wrye (1991) explore women therapists' unconscious feelings of threat of the maternal erotic countertransference (MEC) and their tendency to avoid or block it. Welles and Wrye note Lester's (1985) analysis of the way she unconsciously avoided presenting herself as an erotic woman by adopting the role of the nurturing mother and point out how, among other things, female therapists perpetuate the mother–infant merger with male patients in order to deny threatening adult male sexuality (Welles and Wrye, 1991). For the purpose of our discussion, in the cases presented, I take the perception of male patients' sexuality as infantile to be one of the "contracts" between the female therapist and the male patient that is aimed at avoiding the language of passion, including sexual aggressive contents. As mentioned, I believe this to be a manner of blocking contact with the "unthought known" trauma (Bollas, 1987), which in split-off form, as part of the joint dissociative mechanism that protects the entire internal object world of the abused child (Davies and Frawley, 1992), cannot yet be fully processed in the treatment.

With female patients, I find that similar dynamics of collusion occur in different ways. I believe that an encounter between two women usually activates defenses of identity rather than of difference; two women who experience each other as a potential threat will usually tend more toward merging and denial of separateness to safeguard the tender, maternal parts. While the effect of these kinds of enactments is to reinforce the conviction that there are things too dangerous to feel or to know, Frankel (2002) suggests that the process of analysis can be understood as the working-through of these inevitable collusions in the therapeutic dyad. Davies and Frawley (1992) note that it is the analyst's ability to both participate in and interpret the unfolding historical drama that encourages the progression of insight, integration, and change. Through the presentation of my clinical work, I will try to touch upon the manners in which working through these collusions was enabled and space and growth were made possible, as well as question cases in which such working-through was not possible, as the danger remained perpetually tangible and even intensified, moment by moment.

Following years of therapy in which I did not perceive Tomaz as a man but merely as a child and he did not react to me as a woman but as a mother, one night I had a sexual dream about him. I woke up shaken, truthfully quite shocked and embarrassed. He appeared different in my dream from the way that I perceived him consciously. As stated, our collusion lasted for a number of years during which we worked through significant issues, especially concerning his mother and mourning his separation from her. While a stable and constant therapeutic relationship was established between us, the various levels of depressive symptoms with which Tomaz came for treatment, as well as the ways in which he deprived himself of women and money, remained virtually unchanged. He continued struggling financially and could not yet "hit on a girl." In light of the anxiety that the dream evoked in me, I realized that contrary to the way I viewed other male patients, I did not allow myself to perceive Tomaz as a sexual man. This was the beginning of an inner shift in me concerning our use of the language of tenderness, as I grasped that my dream arrived in unconscious response to a change that *had already* begun to occur in the room, and probably threatened me because it acknowledged that the contract between us was beginning to transform. In the wake of the dream, I began to examine the language we used in the room, my trauma surrounding aggression, and the scary mafioso in my inner realm. I observed our collusion, the way I entered the dissociative experience, and the manner in which this dissociation was designed to protect the treatment and parts of both of our selves.

In retrospect, I believe that Tomaz and I had built enough trust in each other and in knowing that the good maternal parts would survive what ensued. We began working through the aggressive parts that had heretofore remained outside the room. We started a new mourning process as we recognized the finality and irreversibility of the traumatic loss and the end of the split-off fantasy of embryonic heaven. I remember a certain moment when Tomaz said to me, annoyed: "You know, what you just said is unlike you." I was startled for a moment, and then thought, "It's also unlike you to be angry with me." I responded with something like, "That's true, it's unlike the way you and I are used to communicating." This was the point in our work together when we began making contact with the frightening and painful trauma initiated when a boy of a year and a half was forcefully torn away from his mother. We were finding the boy who cries and misses her, the boy who is scared. The trauma has to do with the exploitative use of power, as well as the aggressive potential in me as a threatening object, an aggressor, and the fear of his own aggressive and destructive parts ("After all, I'm my father's son"). This process gave rise in Tomaz to feelings of anger toward his father as well as identification with him, and yet it also catalyzed the development of Tomaz's ability to *use* his power rather than being afraid of *abusing* it. I believe that every use of aggression on his part served as a traumatic reminder, tainted by the fear of abuse. Therefore, integrating different self states and allowing the language of passion and aggression into the room could only become possible when the maternal parts were experienced as secure enough, not only in the sense that they would survive but that they could actually protect the child from the other, threatening parts.

We are dealing here with the representations of three major players, the victim, the abuser, and the protector. In the abused child's inner drama, the "aggressor" betrays the child, while the "protector" cannot protect him (Thomas, 2003). A child cannot survive without an affective witness–protector and will not be able to protect herself without an internalized effective witness–protector (Atlas-Koch, 2007). In this sense, I believe in the significance of Tomaz's perception of an object who survives, is not beaten, and cannot be murdered. I was forced to face my greatest fears, to process them through the work with Tomaz, and to acknowledge the parts of the frightened girl but also the parts of the aggressor, and the woman who looks fear in the eye. And when Tomaz sends the text message offering to bring soup to the woman he is dating, he knows that I understand the risk he is taking in expressing his desire to see her, feeling what he wants to have. He has begun to be able to "take for himself," to earn money, to enjoy the experience of being a desirable man. In the middle of the session, he gets a text: "Come, I want soup," and he smiles at me. "She didn't smack me." As mentioned before, when patients and therapists perceive themselves and each other as potential aggressors, it leads naturally to anxiety-driven, unconscious collusions. While each person feels threatened by the aggression, both agree to ignore the seemingly unresolvable and dangerous conflict that lurks between them and instead they create tenderness, a relationship that feels safe, but could ultimately stifle growth (Frankel, 1993, 2002). The question, then, is what prevents the working-through of these collusions? When are they experienced as too dangerous? Is the confusion of tongues in the dialectical interaction between therapist and patient and the ability to work through this confusion only linked to the extent of both sides' ancient traumas?

Ron

I would now like to present Ron, a handsome, witty, and creative thirty-two-year-old man who came for therapy with symptoms of obsessive thoughts and compulsive behaviors, accompanied by a vague sense of depression. Ron had never worked. For years he was supported financially by his mother, but he maintained no contact with her beyond the economic ties. He characterized his mother as depressive, and in the first session described a cold relationship with her, consisting mainly of secrets and unspoken matters. He conveyed her as having no past. She had never spoken of her childhood or who she used to be before her children were born. She had never shared any emotion with them and was a "nonselfish" mother, needless. Ron perceived her as someone "functional," someone who, as mentioned, was now transferring money to his bank account while during childhood she had cleaned, cooked, and washed. But he cannot remember her ever looking at him. Ron stresses the mother's lack of subjectivity; to him she was an empty object, a dead mother (Green, 1983), seemingly preoccupied with a loss that became inscribed in Ron's mind as an inaccessible, yet present, phantom.

Ron's father had died following a severe but short illness when Ron was 12. Ron asserts drily that this event is not one that bears much importance in his life. Years later he begins to speak about a feeling of happiness. "It's horrible, isn't it?" he says. "I was just happy he died. I'm shocked when I think of it, but I never miss him." Ron describes the mourning in his home as "a one-minute mourning," since a minute later everyone pretended nothing had happened. From that moment on, Father no longer left a trace in his memory.

We slowly gather details. We try to get to know his mother, himself as a child, acquaint ourselves with his childhood scenery, construct a puzzle with many missing pieces. He is afraid to expose the child that he used to be and keeps on protecting him, especially through humor. Ron is a very funny guy, and when I laugh, he breathes with relief and looks me in the eye for a moment. The rest of the time he does not look at me. It seems as though I pose a great threat to him, and the fact that he is seated in the patient's seat, with the asymmetry between us, renders him powerless and vulnerable in such ways that he needs constantly to protect himself. So he invites me to play with him, invites me to the zone where he feels safe. He knows he is funny and is well aware of the rules of this game, controls it, displays his ideas wittily and charmingly, makes sure we both talk continually in a language of playfulness.

The treatment with Ron lasted five years. I will try and focus the discussion on our collusion to protect the tender parts of the treatment and of ourselves. Throughout the years, Ron had often said to me, "You're soft ... You're fragile ... You're afraid." He presented me with an empty and terrifying world, and for a long while I thought that that was where our fears emanated from, a world from which he protected me through humor. Only years later did I begin to realize that Ron was also providing us protection from other contents that had been eradicated from his memory and that always remained outside the room, even while both of our psyches sensed them and colluded to protect us from the "unthought terror."

For the first years of therapy, we dealt mainly with his relationship with his mother and processed his father's loss. During this period, Ron could not tell me anything about his father. As mentioned earlier, he has no memories of him, only memories of Berlin, where he was born; a "ghost town," he says, full of ghosts and phantoms, all darkness, fear. "I had a nanny who used to threaten me that if I didn't behave, people would come and take me away." He describes a lonely child in a cold, threatening, rainy place, a city that sounds at times as though it were set in a horror film. He portrays his old German nanny as "keeping an eye on the graves." I know he is Jewish, and try to inquire whether these associations stem from the fact that he was born as a Jew in Germany, but he says he does not know. In fact, he knows nothing of his family's history, "whether we survived the Holocaust or not, maybe we came from another country altogether, maybe we pretended to be Holocaust survivors so that we'd be pitied, so that we'd be given money." The way he describes these matters is charged with terror and mystery, but also with cynicism and humor meant to soften such images and fantasies. The experience of nothingness is very powerful. Absence is the most tangible presence in the room, and the phantoms meet us everywhere. Nothing is certain, and questions of cultural, familial, and sexual identities arise.

Ron grew up in a house devoid of physical or emotional contact. He describes an experience of no presence in the world aside from his subjective experience, no presence that can provide a container and represent continuity (Gerson, 2009). Gerson writes: "… and this not-there-ness constitutes both the 'gap,' or absence, as well as what fills the absence. Perhaps this would be more simply imagined as the haunting presence of ghosts who, because they can never be banished, become primary objects of identification and so form the most enduring aspect of the self" (p. 13). Ron's world is full of "emptiness." He does not know where he came from, and therefore does not know where he is going to. His mother offers him no answers, but Ron has stopped asking questions long ago, and Father—he died a long time ago, and no memory of him has survived. The phantoms chase him into the room, and we work through the absence's strong presence as we attempt to welcome and live out his absence in the treatment.

Ron is constantly anxious and tells me of a sense that accompanies him "that I'm a bad person." A great deal of guilt is apparent in every step he takes. He tries to be a "good man"—he donates to charities, gives money to people on the street, helps old men get on the bus, and if he sees an old man without helping him, he feels like a "terrible person." He fears that the bad entities will attack the good ones, and this is manifest in the very first session when we discuss the fee. He tells me that I am "taking advantage of his decency," and after he leaves, I note that there are "good people" and "bad people," the exploiters and the exploited, who are always split.

For the first years, playfulness and humor are the only moments in our interaction when Ron actually looks at me. As mentioned, the rest of the time he shifts his head to peer out the window. Over time I gradually feel my presence emerging, changing from someone who is not looked in the eye and not seen to someone who exists. Ron begins inspecting the room, cynically remarks about the books on the shelf, and renders his opinion about the desk that I have replaced. He begins wondering aloud if he is really important to me and to what extent he is just "my work." Then he starts asking me about myself, in a very gentle, noninvasive way. I consciously choose to answer his concrete questions directly, and when after almost three years of therapy he asks me where I am from originally (my accent makes it obvious that I am not American, but he never asked and I never said), I choose not to investigate the underpinnings of his question but rather to reply first. I later inquire how he feels after learning something about me, when I turn into a person with a history.

We both knew this to be a new experience for him, and not a simple one. "Don't be frightened, it's not like I'm going to phone you at home now," he said jokingly, beginning to communicate his fear of needing me. And when I am leaving for vacation, he stands at the door and says to me, "I won't die while you're away, don't worry," and pretends to faint or die in the doorway. "I know you won't die, but I'm reminding you that you can contact me at any moment, not only if you're about to die," I say, always leaving him the option of calling me, even when I am on vacation; to which he replies once again, "You don't give up, huh? No chance." And he never calls. Then one day he asks me what would happen if I suddenly wanted to give up my job. "It happens, people want to make career changes. Poor thing, it'll probably be really difficult for you." While he does not mention himself, only me, I hear fear that I might leave "poor him." Only in hindsight do I understand that this utterance also contained the fear that I might give up the profession *because* of him, that he would frighten me so much that I would not be able to take it.

Throughout the years, I felt something was missing. I usually associated it with the issues we discussed, the emptiness and death that were so strongly present. But small, humorous utterances of his, and the very playful language that evolved between us, made me feel that something else was missing, something that I was not able to define. There is something "slippery" about Ron, something difficult to get a grip on, and every time it seemed to me that I was holding on to it, it slipped away again. Just as he was unable to access his lost memories, I, too, could not comprehend completely what was missing. And as we gathered evidence of his childhood together, so, too, did I seek to collect the evidence that would help me solve this puzzling feeling. When Ron spoke, I often felt fear, which I interpreted as a response to his scary and dark childhood stories. But as time passed, I began thinking he was trying to evoke fear in me not only so that I would acknowledge the affect that arose from these memories, but because there was another threat that did not register in either of our consciousnesses.

One day a mouse enters the room during a session. I get scared for a moment, but regain my composure rather quickly. Ron cannot calm down. Embarrassed, he tells me that it is one of his greatest fears, that he is disgusted by mice, that this is terrible for him. I become a "guard" in this session, and he laughs in great embarrassment that "a girl protects a boy." It is supposed to be the other way around, he tells me. "There, now you see I'm not a man," he says to me. The following session Ron brings me a gift—a mousetrap. We talk about the mouse that we are trying to catch together. "But don't murder it, if you can," he says. In that moment I am a potential murderer and the mouse is experienced as an invasive aggressor that keeps on escaping. "He probably won't eat the cheese," he says, "he's a clever mouse." I realize we are dealing with a mouse that represents at that moment bits of both of us: the aggressor, the victim, the piece that we are searching for. The mouse might expose the fear in the room, as well as the embarrassment about the wish that I protect him, along with his doubt about whether

I would be able to do so. "Don't pretend, you're afraid of mice yourself," he says repeatedly.

In another session, Ron tells me that when he was seven years old he had a couple of hamsters that he loved. One day the female gave birth to six offspring, but then the mother suddenly "went crazy." She attacked the father and killed him, and afterwards ate one of the newborns every night. Each morning his mother forced him to clean up the "disgusting mess." He remembers the cage as looking like "someone had been murdered in it." We talk about the threat of a mother who eats her children, kills her spouse, while he needs to clean up the mess every morning. Questions arise that are to crop up again and again over the years, questions about who the murderer was and who killed whom. Did we die in the Holocaust or not? Who is the aggressor and who is the victim? Where exactly did the danger stem from? Am I a dangerous killer? Is he? "Have you killed and also taken possession?" (Book of Kings 1, Chapter 21) he asks in another session, speaking of his father's death and the money that he and his mother use to this day, its origin unknown to him.

As always there were more question than answers, but as I write now, I realize that the form of my writing demonstrates how I deferred my conscious under-standing and joined Ron's dissociated experience. I write one line after the other, beating around the bush, and precisely like in our therapeutic encounter, I cannot comprehend what I already know—and probably knew about Ron long before I could admit it to myself—that he was a victim of abuse, which was "the unthought known." The knowledge that there is a relation between the emptiness and the bru-tality encompassed therein but cannot be reached now permeates. I entered Ron's dissociated world, felt the fragmentation and terror, but could not "hold" anything other than the affect.

One day Ron brought in a diary he found. It was his sister's journal from the period before his father died. She described in minute detail the father's aggression and brutality toward the family members and her wish that he would die. Ron does not share many details with me. He says laconically, "Yes, there were beatings. Harsh words. Rage." In an indifferent tone, he recalls, "We were very scared of him throughout the years," unable to connect with that child, unable to feel the boy's pain, to love or understand him. Ron has no recollection of physical or emotional pain, only death and nothingness. The child's self state is totally dissociative, while the adult's self state perceives him as a demanding, screaming, mushy little boy, one whom he needs to get rid of. The adult does not allow the child to present himself, and there is a constant battle between the two self states, each holding different needs. I join Ron's dissociated state and for a while deny the traumatic childhood terror as a way to protect the adult from the child's experience, as well as the little boy from being exposed. In retrospect, I was providing Ron with the protection the little girl I used to be had so wished for. Davies and Frawley (1992) believe that only within the dissociative state can the analyst come to understand the internal object world of the abused child. Only by allowing herself to enter, rather than interpret, the dissociative experience will the therapist come to occupy the same relational matrix as the patient.

As I related to my own experiences of old terror and helplessness, I was not sure for some moments what was real and what wasn't. Ron smiles. "Nonsense," he says, his sister has always been a girl who exaggerates. And so nothing is reliable. Language does not succeed in being reliable, either. Words have no meaning, they only provide a form that illustrates an emotional experience that lacks words, lacks a body, just like a ghost. And so we never spoke of the diary again. Ron refused to expose the child he is, and at these moments I feel like being the only helpless child in the room. His adult self was terrified of the child's experiences and trying to keep him silent (Davies and Frawley, 1992). And the wordplay, the playfulness, is the only way to connect, to relate, to experience something safe and solid. I understand the playful form to be illustrating a very early form of relatedness, a reminder of "the state of happiness that existed prior to the trauma—a trauma which it endeavors to annul" (Ferenczi 1933, p. 164). This was Ron the playing baby, the baby who could make eye contact and smile, and receive the smile, the gaze, the excitement back from the caregiver. It is the co-construction that Beebe (2005) exemplifies in the "video micro-analysis" of infant research, and the manner in which both participants take part in a moment-to-moment interactive and self-regulatory process. While playing, something else happens between Ron and me; nonverbal interactions are created that for moments contain a relationship—a smile, contact—and then are once more annulled.

Over time, as the connection between Ron and me intensified, he became more fearful for our life as an analytic couple as well as for our individual lives and worried that the tenderness we'd managed to create in therapy might be destroyed. Once his father entered the therapeutic space, the sense of danger became more real. The danger that had always been in the room became more intense, and it was unclear who was going to be hurt. Is it a risk to his life if he recalls what he has forgotten? Is my life in danger if he gets in touch with the brutal parts in himself? Or maybe if his and/or my aggression surfaces, I will be the one to attack him?

Ron, the child, had survived. His father was the one who had died. He identifies himself as the aggressor, "the bad man," the one who "killed and also possessed," and defends against being a vulnerable victim. Davies and Frawley (1992) have noted that the abuser within the child persona is, after all, the part of the patient who was determined to survive and who borrowed from his abusive parent ways of protecting the vulnerable parts of himself. Ron had turned a passive trauma into an active one and thus reconfirmed an unconscious belief that he was responsible for his own abuse and for his father's death. There is always a split, then. He is the evil survivor, and his father is the destroyed victim. Ron is not in touch with the victim that he is and the potential aggressor I am, and I believe our "protector" appears only in the form of the collusion surrounding our tender language.

Ron does not believe that the treatment can survive the aggression as it emerges. He tries to forcefully preserve our language of tenderness, but this becomes increasingly difficult, for me as well as for him. Trying to disguise the traumatic contents that rise to the surface, his playfulness becomes tinted with a hostile hue. Ron begins talking about terminating the treatment. We speak very directly about his fear of the contents that have been emerging; he fears something is going to be ruined soon and prefers ending therapy before that happens. "If we weren't close, I could talk to you," he says. "I think the moment has come and I have to end the treatment." I hear his great fear that the aggressive parts will annihilate the "good," and I remind him that he left the only girl he loved so dearly because he was afraid that he was about to destroy everything, preferring to end the relationship before that happened. Then, too, he had been afraid of his destructiveness, and now he is again afraid of the rage and the hatred, trying to preserve what he calls "the love" by ending the treatment, wanting to store the good parts in a closed and protected place.

Ron was afraid that what was tender could not survive—whether it was me, whom he described over the years as "too tender," or him, whom he described in the exact same words, only derogatorily. We were both tender children in hiding, who could be hurt, and the tender language we created and used together was meant to protect us. I understood that the only trustworthy protector was the one we had created in our collusion, which had for a time prevented the destructive contents from entering. Any other protection was experienced as ineffectual. He could not trust his mother to stand guard over him. He could not rest assured that I would remember and protect the good parts of myself, himself, and of the treatment, that I would survive the attack of the other parts, and that we will be able to protect him and the therapy from disintegration. His mother had not succeeded in witnessing what her child had gone through, and he did not believe that I would be able to be such a witness without becoming empty; Ron said he feared the moment I would empty out and become absent, that I would wish to make a career change. The silent witness that Gerson (2009) describes is not only the one who is absent but also the one who permits the violence to go on. Gerson writes that "we have learned that the presence of an other who can bear living with that which cannot be represented in words, is what gives meaning both to life and to death" (Gerson 2009, p. 23).

Exits

The collusion that Ron and I co-created to fend off the anxiety borne by the aggression bred zones full of goodness that had to be protected from emptying. There is a sense of contamination (Gerson, 2009), and the "healthy" parts have to be protected in solitary confinement. The unconscious collusion is therefore a mutual agreement between the two (each containing both a victim and an aggressor simultaneously) that the aggression poses a threat for each other and for the treatment. Together they summon the "guard" who obstructs the language of passion and aggression, only granting entry to the language of tenderness as a means of preventing retraumatization and protecting the tender parts of each of the participants and of the treatment. Ron and I separated, each of us containing the good, but also the empty parts of the treatment.

Discussion

"[The patient's mind] lacks the ability to maintain itself with stability in face of unpleasure—in the same way as the immature find it unbearable to be left alone, without maternal care and without a considerable amount of tenderness" (Ferenczi 1933, p. 228).

I have attempted to use the parallel drawn by Ferenczi between the patient and the child who speaks the language of tenderness and to shift the perspective to the confusion of tongues within the dialectical encounter between therapist and patient, who both harbor a child and an adult, a victim and an aggressor, simultaneously. I believe that the working-through of the original trauma is linked to the manner in which the two paradigms exist in the transference and the countertransference and are represented in both the therapist's and the patient's inner worlds, as they exchange representations and roles, and experience themselves as seductive and being seduced, exploitative and being exploited, together creating a third role, the effective witness-protector. That protector is not only an inner representation in each of the participants but one that is co-created in the analytic third between therapist and patient, enabling both to securely play the risky game of working through the trauma.

In both cases presented, the collusion embodied an attempt to protect the tender and benevolent parts of the treatment, even as this protection was associated with the dissociation and denial that was co-experienced by therapist and patient. I believe that when a split between the representations of the abuser and the abused, the adult and the child, takes place—and when each side permanently holds on to one experience only—there is no possibility for movement and development in the "analytic third." It is this move away from a collusive, defensive protector that splits tenderness and aggression, to an effective, more developed protector, that enables all parts to exist simultaneously, without the threat of any part attacking the other.

Notes

1 An earlier version of this chapter appeared in *Psychoanalytic Perspectives,* Volume 7.1, and appears here with permission of the publisher.
2 Ferenczi's reference to the Tower of Babel.

References

Aron, L. (1990). One-person and two-person psychologies and the method of psychoanalysis. *Psychoanalytic Psychology,* 7:475–485.

Aron, L. (1992a). From Ferenczi to Searles and contemporary relational approaches: Commentary on Mark Blechner's "Working in the countertransference." *Psychoanalytic Dialogues,* 2:181–190.

Aron, L. (1992b). Interpretation as an expression of the analyst's subjectivity. *Psychoanalytic Dialogues,* 2:475–507.

Atlas-Koch, G. (2007). *Toward an Assessment of Susceptibility to Sexual Abuse: An Expressive Psychoanalytic Perspective.* Ohio: Union Institute & University.

Beebe, B. (2005). Mother-infant research informs mother-infant treatment. *Psychoanalytic Study of the Child, 60,* 6-46.

Beebe, B. and Lachmann, F. (1988). Mother–infant mutual influence and precursors of psychic structure. In A. Goldberg (ed), *Frontiers in Self Psychology: Progress in Self Psychology, Vol. 3.* Hillsdale, NJ: The Analytic Press, pp. 3–25.

Beebe, B. and Lachmann, F. (2002). *Infant Research and Adult Treatment: Co-constructing Interactions.* Hillsdale, NJ: The Analytic Press.

Blum, H. (2004). The wise baby and the wild analyst. In M. Bergman (ed), *Understanding Dissidence and Controversy in the History of Psychoanalysis.* New York: Other Press.

Bollas, C. (1987). *The shadow of the object.* London: Free Association Books.

Davies, J. M. and Frawley, M. G. (1992). Dissociative processes and transference-countertransference paradigms in the psychoanalytically oriented treatment of adult survivors of childhood sexual abuse. *Psychoanalytic Dialogues,* 2:5–36.

Ferenczi, S. (1933). The confusion of tongues between adults and children: The language of tenderness and passion. In M. Balint (ed), *Final Contributions to the Problems and Methods of Psycho-Analysis, Vol. 3.* New York: Brunner/Mazel, 1980, pp. 156–167.

Frankel, J. (1993). Collusion and intimacy in the analytic relationship. In L. Aron and A. Harris (eds), *The Legacy of Sándor Ferenczi.* Hillsdale, NJ: The Analytic Press, pp. 227–247.

Frankel, J. (1998). Ferenczi's trauma theory. *The American Journal of Psychoanalysis,* 58:41–61.

Frankel, J. (2002). Exploring Ferenczi's concept of identification with the aggressor: Its role in trauma, everyday life, and the therapeutic relationship. *Psychoanalytic Dialogues,* 12:101–139.

Gerson, S. (2009). When the third is dead: Memory, mourning, and witnessing in the aftermath of the holocaust. *International Journal of Psychoanalysis.*

Green, A. (1983). The dead mother. In A. Green, *On Private Madness.* London: Hogarth Press, 1986, pp. 142–173.

Hazan, Y. (1999). From Ferenczi to Kohut: From confusion of tongues to self object transference. *Sihot-Dialogue,* March, No. 2.

Lester, E. P. (1985). The female analyst and the erotized transference. *International Journal of Psychoanalysis,* 66:283–293.

Rachman, A. W. (1993). Ferenczi and sexuality. In L. Aron and A. Harris (eds), *Sándor Ferenczi's Clinical and Theoretical Contributions.* Hillsdale, NJ: The Analytic Press, pp. 81–100.

Thomas, P. M. (2003). Protection, dissociation, and internal roles: Modeling and treating the effects of child abuse. *Review of General Psychology,* 7:364–380.

Torras De Beà, E. (1987). A contribution to papers on transference. *International Journal of Psychoanalysis,* 68:63–68.

Welles, J. K. and Wrye, H. K. (1991). The maternal erotic countertransference. *International Journal of Psychoanalysis,* 72:93–106.

Winnicott, W. D. (1971). *Playing and Reality.* London: Tavistock Publications.

12

THE PERSISTENT SENSE OF BEING BAD

The Moral Dimension of Identification with the Aggressor

Jay Frankel

Ferenczi's signal theoretical contribution, I believe, was identification with the aggressor[1] (Ferenczi, 1933; Frankel, 2002a, 2012)—a concept at the core of both his understanding of the response to trauma and his move toward a more open technique. And he saw its most destructive element—"The most important change, produced in the mind of the child by the anxiety-fear-ridden identification with the adult partner"—as "*the introjection of the guilt feelings of the adult*" (p. 162, italics in original; and see Bonomi, 2002; Frankel, 2002b).

Ferenczi was talking about the abused child's feeling of being bad. He believed the abused child takes on the abusive parent's feeling of guilt. My own observations suggest that the feeling of badness also includes a sense of shameful defect. Shame was not overlooked by Ferenczi, but was not emphasized. In what follows, I will not restrict myself to Ferenczi's definition of what the parents feel or what the child's feeling of badness consists of.

I will, however—following Ferenczi, and my own clinical observations—keep my focus on actual environmental dangers and deficiencies. While intrapsychic conflict indisputably plays a role in shaping the *fantasy elaboration* of traumatic events, and in *defensively ensconcing* feelings of badness, my own experience points to parental failure as the origin of these feelings.[2]

The child's readiness to take on a sense of badness can be thought of as the *moral dimension of identification with the aggressor*—a name that echoes Fairbairn's (1943) term *moral defense*, designating his similar concept, to be discussed below. The advantage of my own term is that it illuminates this phenomenon within its larger context; indeed, the moral dimension of identification with the aggressor works in synchrony with its *behavioral* and *mental* dimensions, as I will elaborate at the end of this chapter.

Identification with the Aggressor

In his landmark paper "Confusion of Tongues" (1933), Ferenczi defined identification with the aggressor: Child victims of an assault are compelled by their anxiety *"to subordinate themselves like automata to the will of the aggressor, to divine each one of his desires and to gratify these; completely oblivious of themselves, they identify themselves with the aggressor"* (1933, p. 162, italics in original).

Here, Ferenczi described both behavioral compliance and the mental accommodations necessary to support it: hyperattunement to the aggressor's feelings and intentions; creating emotions and thoughts the child senses the aggressor needs the child to have, which will help her stay safe in the frightening situation; *not* perceiving things that might be threatening to notice, or having independent thoughts, especially those that could stir unease and undermine compliance; dissociating feelings that could undermine playing the role that the child senses is essential to survival (see Frankel, 2012). Also sacrificed, as these aspects of personal experience are lost, are feelings of agency and authenticity, and a sense of self.

As I have become more alert to the moral dimension of identification with the aggressor, I have observed it in many of my patients, to varying degrees—and in line with the great prevalence of the other dimensions of identification with the aggressor (see Frankel, 2002a, for an extensive discussion of this point), not only in people who were grossly abused as children, in whom Ferenczi first discovered it. This observation forces us, following Ferenczi (1929, 1930, 1931, 1932, 1933), to broaden our understanding of what situations constitute trauma (see Frankel, 2002a)—an idea I will elaborate.

Ferenczi's Ideas about the Sense of Badness

Ferenczi's discovery of identification with the aggressor came late in his life—a culmination of much of his life's work. Consequently, he wrote relatively little about it, and less about its "most important," moral, aspect—a few paragraphs in his short Congress paper, "Confusion of Tongues" (1933), written during the summer of 1932, as the pernicious anemia to which he would succumb the following spring was developing, and working formulations in his *Clinical Diary* (1932), written that same year.

"The most important change, produced in the mind of the child by the anxiety-fear-ridden identification with the adult partner," Ferenczi wrote, "is *the introjection of the guilt feelings of the adult* which makes hitherto harmless play appear as a punishable offense" (1933, p.162). He continued: "When the child recovers from such an attack [i.e., a traumatic assault], he feels enormously confused, in fact, split—innocent and culpable at the same time—and his confidence in the testimony of his own senses is broken. Moreover, the harsh behaviour of the adult partner tormented and made angry by his remorse renders the child still more conscious of his own guilt and still more ashamed. ... Not infrequently after such events, the seducer becomes over-moralistic or religious and endeavors to save the soul of the child by severity" (1933, pp. 162–163).

The child's immaturity is an important factor in her response. Ferenczi wrote that "The children feel physically and morally helpless, their personalities are not sufficiently consolidated in order to be able to protest, even if only in thought, for the overpowering force and authority of the adult makes them dumb and can rob them of their senses" (1933, p. 162). He called children "semifluid" (1932, p. 176) beings with a natural tendency, in this "purely mimetic period" of life (1932, p. 148), to take in without resistance, to identify (1932, pp. 147–149), and to imitate fear, hatred, and love (1932, p. 175).[3] Only when children receive "support on all sides" (1932, p. 176) from their environment will they be able to overcome and outgrow this tendency (1932, pp. 210–211). Otherwise, "Freud's death instinct" will prevail (1932, p. 176)—the child will lack the will to live (1929), will disintegrate and become "inclined to 'explosion'" (1932, p. 176). The immature child, subjected to assault, now has "a mind which consists only of id and super-ego, and which therefore lacks the ability to maintain itself with stability in the face of unpleasure" (1933, p. 163). Does this mean that the child who has introjected the adult's guilt feelings is unable to modulate her superego harshness through reality testing and perspective—ego functions—and feels she deserves only punishment? This lack of self-esteem persists into adult life. As adult patients, these people "refused so obstinately to follow my advice to react to unjust or unkind treatment with pain or with hatred and defense" (1933, p. 163).

Ferenczi also suggested that the child may *make* himself "bad": "The misused child changes into a mechanical, obedient automaton or becomes defiant, but is unable to account for the reasons of his defiance" (1933, p. 163).

We can speculate that such apparently senseless defiance may represent compliance—an effort to actualize the parents' projections—or a compromise: the child refuses to submit meekly to injustice, but refuses to blame the oppressor. Additionally, in line with his belief that children need most of all to be wanted and loved and to receive empathic accompaniment from their parents (1929, and see notes 5 and 7 in this chapter), Ferenczi thought that successfully provoking parents through misbehavior establishes for the child that she is not alone in her badness (1932, p. 167).

With similar logic, an abused child who engages her parent *sexually* may feel not only that doing so is required for her own safety, but that it is the only way she can elicit what feels like the love and tenderness she desperately needs (1932, p. 191). But her pleasure may feel like complicity, suggesting to her that she wanted the abuse and is therefore responsible for it (1932, p. 191)—an attribution that can be reinforced if the adult blames the child.

Ferenczi also wrote about an "autochthonous sense of guilt" based on "impoverishment of the libido, artificial pumping out of libido without internal pressure" (1932, pp. 188–191), whether done alone or provoked by someone else—that is, from sex or love that is obligatory rather than desired.

I will hold in reserve what Ferenczi wrote about parents' traumatizing behavior, as a frame for my own observations.

Fairbairn and Others[4] on the Child's Sense of Badness

Of all subsequent psychoanalytic writers, W. R. D. Fairbairn, a decade after Ferenczi, most directly addressed the phenomenon of the child's attachment to being "bad," with his concept of the "moral defense" (1943, p. 65)—a concept better known than Ferenczi's. Fairbairn was writing about delinquent children, but his ideas also seem to apply to children who may *feel* they are bad even though they *act* especially "good."

Fairbairn wrote that "the [mistreated] child would rather be bad himself than have bad objects. ... In becoming bad he is really taking upon himself the burden of badness which appears to reside in his objects. By this means he seeks to purge them of their badness; and, in proportion as he succeeds in doing so, he is rewarded by that sense of security which an environment of good objects so characteristically confers" (1943, p. 65). By the child's logic "it is better to be a sinner in a world ruled by God"—a "conditional," more tolerable form of badness—"than to live in a world ruled by the Devil. A sinner in a world ruled by God may be bad; but there is always a certain sense of security to be derived from the fact that the world around is good" (1943, pp. 66–67). Fairbairn's explanation, unlike Ferenczi's, does not assume feelings of guilt in the parents.

Earlier, in a similar vein, Ferenczi had written that a child, faced with the possibility of opposing or disbelieving what her abusive parents tell her, is confronted with the question: "Is it the whole world that is bad, or am I wrong?—and chooses the latter" (1932, p. 80). The child would rather be bad than alone. Ferenczi also suggested that the child takes on the parent's badness (1932, p. 64) or craziness (1932, p. 161) in order to protect her idealized image of her parent.

Also like Ferenczi, Fairbairn (1941) understood identification to be the most basic form of relatedness, meaning that a child's sense of goodness may derive more from her identification with a parent experienced as good than from her own behavior. That is, the child needs to feel she is bad for reasons of both attachment security and, paradoxically, self-esteem.

Kohut's (1972) seminal contributions in this area focused on shame, which he understood essentially as a reaction to the narcissistic injury of an unexpected lack of a mirroring response, whether from external objects or the idealized superego, when exhibitionistic wishes are aroused. Rather than receiving the expected admiration and confirmation of a sense of omnipotence and wholeness, the person feels that a defect has been exposed. Kohut understood mirroring as a basic developmental need. While he had developed his understanding of shame within his particular elaboration of narcissistic development, his conclusions are roughly consistent with Ferenczi's and Fairbairn's ideas that children's primary (not their only) needs involve receiving love and empathic understanding. For all three, the sense of badness—whether guilt, or shame and defect—involved a sense, at least, of emotional abandonment, broadly understood.

Other writers, whether focusing on children who have been grossly abused or damaged in more subtle ways, have also addressed the child's tenacious sense of badness, generally along similar lines. Rothstein (1977) explained the child's sense of being defective as an "attitude of self that derives from internalizing mother's narcissistically-deflated and/or depressed, disinterested or inappropriately angry facial representation into the germinal 'self-as-agent'. ... as if the subject felt, '... it must be my fault. ... if I can be perfect, then mother would love me. If mother doesn't love me, it must be because I am defective'" (pp. 414–415). Grotstein (1992) suggested that the abused child feels guilty and ashamed, first, as a result of introjecting and identifying with her abusers—the child feels she is what she feels she contains inside her. Grotstein also pointed to the child feeling she is bad because, through her identification with her abusive objects, she exposes them publicly, in order to shame, blame, and punish them.

Bemporad (1994) observed how, as adults, these people "so desperately need to hold on to the delusion that, in spite of mounting evidence to the contrary, the parents were good (or justified in their maltreatment) ..." (pp. 405–406). In one patient, "extremely brutal treatment was passed off as caring behavior. ..." (p. 408). Children accept this perception because "the powerful parents present a world view that denies the existence of any ... support beyond themselves. Living in virtual psychological isolation, the child's only means of psychological survival is to believe in the goodness that is espoused by the parents while reconciling the pain caused by them as deserved on the basis of personal badness" (p. 408). Bemporad criticized Fairbairn's moral defense as overemphasizing the intrapsychic element and neglecting the parents' active role in promoting the child's sense of badness.

In my own earlier discussion of the topic (Frankel, 2002b), I questioned both Ferenczi's assumption, implicit in his term "*introjection of the guilt feelings of the adult*" (1933, p. 162, italics in original), that parents always feels guilty about abusing their child—this cannot always be so, and Fairbairn's explanation, in contrast to Ferenczi's, did not require it—and whether the feeling of badness is only, or even mainly, guilt. Jones (1995), for instance, understood emotional abandonment, which Ferenczi saw as the core of the trauma,[5] as closely tied to shame: "the ultimate threat [of shame is] banishment. Thus guilt threatens punishment—perhaps even death—but not exclusion from the community; shame threatens an end to the relationship" (Jones 1995, p. 138).

I seconded Fairbairn's emphases on the child taking on the parent's badness in order to exonerate the parent, the child's preeminent need to have a good parent in order for the child to feel secure and good, and the child deriving her sense of goodness more from her identification with a parent seen as good than with her evaluation of her own behavior.

And I raised the possibility that "a victim identifies with the aggressor's actions while maintaining her own values. In this case, she feels ashamed of what the other has done as if she had done those things herself" (2002b, p. 166). I also suggested that the abused child may identify with the *feeling* of the relationship—good or bad—and asked "whether a feeling of shame is inherent in victimization and even in suffering. Perhaps helplessness naturally tends to feel like a fault and power like a virtue" (2002b, pp. 164–165).

I proposed that "a more parsimonious Ferenczian hypothesis than Ferenczi's own questionable idea about introjecting the aggressor's guilt feelings … [is that] perpetrators may treat the child/victim as if she is guilty, and the child may simply identify and comply with this attribution owing to her fear of the aggressor" (2002b, p. 165).

And further: "not simply acting but feeling guilty makes [the child's] display of guilt more convincing. In this way, feeling guilty or ashamed are part of an act of identification and submission motivated by fear" (2002b, pp. 165–166). Additionally, "a display of guilt may signal the other not to hurt oneself … a preemptive strike against oneself in order to neutralize the other as a threat," and I cited Jones's idea of "shame as an 'appeasement ritual' (Jones 1995, p. 147), a sign of submission in order to avoid attack by a more powerful figure" (p. 166).

"Feeling guilt," I continued, may be "preferable to feeling fear since guilt, unlike fear, represents only an internal, illusory danger that is somewhat under one's control. In this way, guilt confers a feeling of power when one is powerless. This is precisely what Fairbairn (1944) meant by internalizing bad objects" (Frankel 2002b, p. 166) and—I add now—what Ferenczi was getting at when he said that "Through the identification, or let us say, introjection of the aggressor, he disappears as part of the external reality, and becomes intra- instead of extra-psychic … a dream-like state … The attack as a rigid external reality ceases to exist and in the traumatic trance the child succeeds in maintaining the previous situation of tenderness" (1933, p. 162).

Clinical Observations

I turn now to my own clinical observations of people's dogged attachment to their sense of being bad—a phenomenon present, to different degrees, in many if not most of my patients (also true, I assume, of most other analysts' practices), though I have been more alert to it as I have given the concept more focus. And as with identification with the aggressor more broadly (Frankel, 2002a), its moral manifestations are not restricted to survivors of severe childhood abuse, but are much more widespread, suggesting that many virtually ubiquitous childhood experiences are often traumatic and leave their mark—foremost, the many, often subtle, iterations of emotional abandonment.

Nature of the Observations and How I Will Refer to People

In what follows, I abstract the elements of the moral dimension of identification with the aggressor that I have observed repeatedly in many adult patients over a span of years and have recorded more systematically during various extended periods.

My descriptions are based on my patients' memories of their childhoods and accounts of their adult lives that appear in many ways to mirror intrapsychic and interpersonal patterns established in childhood. Such accounts have been explored in detail, have often been confirmed in transference–countertransference interactions, and have repeatedly appeared in similar form in different patients. While the following descriptions will inevitably reflect my particular attunements, the detail and consistency of my patients' stories, and the depth of feeling and conviction with which they have been presented, make them convincing to me.

While I will often refer to the "child," similar responses are likely to persist and to apply equally well to the adults these children become. I will mostly talk generically about the "parent" and the "child" and use female pronouns, but the phenomena I will describe are well represented in both my men and women patients, and the parents I will describe have been both their fathers and their mothers.

Description of the Phenomenon

The feelings of badness may be powerful or mild, pervasive or present only at moments of heightened interpersonal conflict and anxiety. There are two main aspects of the feeling of badness, which find their own proportions in each person: feelings of responsibility and guilt, and a shameful sense of being defective.

A person may feel *responsible* even for events she sees she had no control over—often accompanied by feelings of *guilt*. She insists on taking the blame any time things go wrong—despite the facts—or even when they don't. "Bad" perceptions of others may be quickly split off and discounted, if they threaten the child's ownership of being the bad one in a situation. When something bad happens *to* her, she wonders what she has done wrong and may apologize. She feels her anger can hurt other people and may apologize when angry.

She may also feel that her success in life is not only undeserved, and that someone else should be rewarded rather than she, but that it is an abandonment or otherwise hurtful to someone. And she may fear that it will draw others' anger and revenge.

Guilt feelings undermine her sense of being entitled to do what she wants and make ordinary self-assertion feel like being too demanding.

She feels *shamefully defective*. Specifics differ according to age, gender, culture, and other factors, but generally involve feeling different from, and inferior to, other people: physically or morally grotesque, repulsive, too big or too small, not feminine or masculine enough, not pretty enough, not strong or athletic enough, not smart enough, incomplete, incapable, inadequate, unimportant, lacking substance, empty, with nothing or only badness inside her. She may feel she has nothing of true value to offer. Her self-doubts may cover the gamut: physical, cognitive, emotional, and moral. And she is unlikely to be dissuaded by contradictory evidence. She may see her imagined mental and moral defects as disqualifying her from judging, criticizing, or even disagreeing with others.

She feels she will always ultimately be disappointing to others, and may feel unlovable, or lovable only as someone's stand-in for the real thing. She may try to hide major parts of herself. When others are pleased with her, she seeks explanations that reflect badly on her or feels they don't see the real her. Indeed, her "bad" experiences of herself are often directly opposite to others' perceptions of her.

But she may have a *split perception of herself*, her sense of badness and defectiveness existing alongside knowledge of her own value, capabilities, and positive contributions, and her awareness that she is loved and respected—often by people she herself loves and respects.

She may also feel she *doesn't deserve what she longs for and needs*—not respect, or affirmation of her value as an autonomous person with rights and feelings; not attention, especially when her parents (often the case, as I will describe shortly) are suffering and needy; not comfort—although she desperately wants these things.[6] She may feel that there is no place for her—for the real her, at any rate—in her family or in the world, and even that all she deserves is to be alone (suggesting a compulsive repetition of her traumatic emotional abandonment, as I will describe). Her pathological sense of *un*entitlement may be rooted in her belief that she is a defective person.

Unsurprisingly, the sense of badness is sometimes, not always, accompanied by a depressed mood. Or someone may be anxious—that their badness will be discovered or punished. Other people—far from all—fight back against their sense of badness and *un*entitlement, at least at moments, with angry, compensatory narcissistic assertions of entitlement.

Family Dynamic: Parents' Coercive Emotional Abandonment and the Child's Identification

In this and the following section, I will start with Ferenczi's observations and then add my own. According to Ferenczi, a typical traumatic sequence involves parents who "mistake the play of children for the desires of a sexually mature person" (1933, p. 161), and may sexually abuse and also humiliate and punish the child. A parent, for instance, the father, denies his own impulses and guilt feelings—often implicitly, through a silence that Ferenczi called "hypocritical" (1932, p. 53; also p. 191)—and projects these feelings into the child. The mother may collude with the father's disavowal, blinding herself to the father's responsibility and blaming her daughter, completing the child's emotional abandonment—the most damaging element of trauma, in Ferenczi's view.[7] The mother may even see her child as a rival and punish her (1932, p. 118).

The adult's denial can create what Ferenczi called "traumatic confusion" (1932, p. 178) in the child, and press the child to accept and internalize the adult's "implantation" (1932, pp. 58, 76, 79) of sexuality and guilt into the child (1932, p. 178; also see pp. 47–48, 50, 57–59, 64, 76, 81, 82, 139, 175).

Ferenczi hinted at other psychological factors in the child that may press her to identify with the abusive adult and take on the badness of the situation. For instance, he noted that causing someone else pain can soothe an enraged person—implanting the poison, one rids oneself of it (1932, p. 76). Perhaps—at least in some cases—identifying with, and taking care of, the aggressor (see the discussion of the child's caregiving response, below) requires the child to experience pain, including the "moral" pain of feeling guilty and ashamed.

Ferenczi also noted that punishment creates guilt and fixation, impeding separation from the parent (1932, p. 208). Identification further blocks the child's separation: "Because I identify myself (to understand everything = to forgive everything), I cannot hate." *(Ferenczi 1932, p. 170)*

My own observations, which, unlike Ferenczi's, include a majority of patients who have *not* suffered gross familial child abuse, point to a typical set of family dynamics in patients struggling with feelings of badness. Most basically, a narcissistically compromised parent, grappling with depression, anxiety, or self-esteem problems, uses her child in an instrumental, oppressive way—often outside the parent's full awareness. The parent's urgent need to feel better makes her intolerant of her child's needs—the need to have her personal boundaries and separateness respected, to be loved unconditionally, to be recognized in the many aspects of her own developing individuality for their own sake and not because her interests, talents, or sensitivities gratify the parent.

Haydée Faimberg (2005)—whose observations, like mine, focus mainly on adult children of narcissistically compromised but not overtly abusive parents—has described parents' narcissistic use of their children as consisting of *intruding* parts of the parents' mind into their children, and *appropriating* aspects of their children's mind for themselves. Alice Miller (1997) has observed that these kinds of needy parents invert the parent–child relationship to meet their own needs rather than those of their children and has described the consequences for these children: fragile self-esteem and a readiness to blame themselves when others fail to understand them.

While physical or sexual abuse may be present—perhaps disguised and disavowed—the core of the trauma often seems to be the parent's emotional abandonment and exploitation. A common variant consists of a parent centering her life on her child. She broadcasts a need for constant, intense emotional engagement from a child she places in some kind of idealized role—admiring, for example, the child's great achievements, extraordinary intelligence, unusual beauty, or selfless devotion (to the parent); the parent may require close, constant emotional accompaniment from the child, or make the child, in essence, a romantic partner.

A child, seduced by her parent's admiration, may accept this job, but may feel that nothing short of perfection will be acceptable to the parent (and herself), and end up feeling inadequate to the task, shamefully disappointing, and a fraud. If a parent identifies with her idealized child as a way to protect herself against feeling envious and inferior to other people, the child's self-image may align with the parent's self-contempt, or with the parent's *unconscious* hatred of her envied, idealized child. If the parent needs the child to play a sexualized role, the child may then make sexuality, perhaps in attenuated form, the currency of interpersonal relationships more generally. An idealized child is often made into a caregiver—a very damaging role, as I will elaborate at length, below.

The adult partner to such a parent may tacitly collude in his spouse's possession of the child, reinforcing his "gift" by making himself, in important ways, unavailable to his child. This compounds the trauma of abandonment and reinforces the needy parent's definition of reality, including the relative lack of importance of the child's needs.

When a parent centers her whole life on her child, the parent's exploitation may be clear but she hardly seems emotionally abandoning. Yet her overinvolvement hides the fact that she is mainly looking after her own needs, leaving the child alone with needs unrecognized and unmet.

In an apparently opposite configuration, emotional abandonment may be obvious while exploitation is hard to see. For instance, a parent may scapegoat or otherwise exclude her child from a sense of belonging in the family, or devalue the child as a person or as precious to the parent—forms of emotional abandonment that can feel just as punishing as gross abuse. Elements in the parent's emotional life certainly drive this kind of treatment—depression, preference for the child's sibling, identification of the child with a problematic figure in the parent's own life, or the child having been an unwelcome "accident" that locks the parent into an unhappy marriage. Such a child may come to feel her very existence is destructive, disturbing to someone she loves.

While these parents may appear withdrawn or rejecting, they are colonizing and exploiting their children no less than the overinvolved parent—just projecting a bad object into their children rather than a good one. Both apparent overinvolvement and apparent withdrawal involve emotional abandonment and exploitation. The parents in some families may both play the same role; in others, the roles are split. Or one parent may alternate between both roles.

Whether the parent appears withdrawn or overinvolved, the child is likely to feel that her needs and her failures are responsible, and to identify with the implicit message that she has no place in the family *as the person she really is,* and has no right to have her own needs met. The child may conclude that something is wrong with her—a conclusion supported by a parent's rage at the child, rationalized as discipline or correction the child needs. The effectiveness of these modes of enforcing the child's identification and compliance suggests the umbrella term *coercive emotional abandonment.*

Implied in many of these observations, and as Ferenczi (1931, p. 138; 1932, pp. 2, 178, 182; 1933, pp. 162–163) and Balint (1969, pp. 432–433) both emphasized (see notes 5 and 7 in this chapter), there is one other element that completes the parent's desertion of the child. The parent who is the main source of coercive emotional abandonment, perhaps unable to face her own (perhaps unconscious) guilt, and sometimes with the support of the other parent, may disavow her responsibility for the hurtful things she has done to the child—disavow it to herself as well as to her child and others, or diminish the importance and impact of her actions. A parent who behaves in a disappointing, hurtful, disturbing, or provocative way toward her child, for example, may characterize her own behavior as reasonable, the child's reaction as an overreaction, and the child as oversensitive. Such disavowal constitutes yet one more layer of coercive emotional abandonment.

The child, following the parent's explicit or implicit disavowals—backed up by the various forms of emotional blackmail I have been describing—may buy into this story, suppress her anger, and feel something is wrong with her feelings and needs, that she is not a good child, that she is ungrateful. But she remains aware, perhaps marginally, that something feels wrong and that her own needs are not being met. Her suppressed anger and offended sense of justice may find an outlet in passive or open defiance—as Ferenczi also noted (1933, p. 163)—which the child, in compliance with the story the parents are pushing, may see as irrational and for which she may punish herself with guilt feelings.[8]

The Terrorism of Suffering and the Never-Ending Separation-Guilt Cycle

In addition to sexual abuse and violence—"passionate love and passionate punishment"[9] (Ferenczi 1933, p. 165)—Ferenczi proposed a third primary traumatic event: "the *terrorism of suffering*" (1933, p. 166, italics in original).

In Ferenczi's (1933) words, from "Confusion of Tongues": "Children have the compulsion to put to rights all disorder in the family, to burden, so to speak, their own tender shoulders with the load of all the others … A mother complaining of her constant miseries can create a nurse for life out of her child, i.e. a real mother substitute, neglecting the true interests of the child" (p. 166).[10] And from the *Clinical Diary* (Ferenczi, 1932), a little more bluntly: "[T]he child becomes a *psychiatrist, who treats the madman with understanding* and tells him he is right. (This way he will be less dangerous.)" (1932, p. 172, emphasis in original). The child may "understand" the aggressor in order to calm him, perhaps in hopes of receiving understanding in return (cf. 1932, p. 158).

My own observations flesh out how the terrorism of suffering acts as a particularly destructive threat of coercive emotional abandonment—brutally effective at controlling a child and preventing her from separating by evoking in her an unbearable traumatic compassion. The child feels that her devotion to caring for her parent, sacrificing her own needs and will, is all that allows the vulnerable parent to bear up and not collapse.[11]

A parent's fragility may be confirmed by her inability to be present *as a parent*, that is, her inability to face or empathize with her child's emotional pain—at least pain that does not flatter or bolster the parent, for instance when the child's suffering can be blamed on the child's other parent, with whom the parent is at war, and in contrast to whom the parent can feel like the good one. Or a parent may hijack the child's pain by flooding the child with her *own* pain and anxiety *about the child's suffering*. The parent may even get angry and blame her suffering child for upsetting her—a burden of guilt the child may be all too eager to accept if it will soothe her parent.

Taking blame can be a tactic to manage an out-of-control parent. Ferenczi wrote: "[T]he child even *commits* mistakes *on purpose* in order to justify and satisfy the adults' need for aggression" (1932, p. 172, italics in original). Taking blame also blinds the child to the parent's frightening difficulties and allows the child to continue to see the parent as good and to feel she herself has not been abandoned. On an internal-conflict level, the child may blame herself in order to preemptively absolve the parent of the child's disavowed accusations. The child may sense, in her own marginally perceived angry feelings, confirmation that—as the parent may have charged—the child "started it" due to her own badness.

But when the caregiver child's natural urge to separate nevertheless asserts itself, the parent, afraid to lose her needed child, is likely to counter with an aggressive display of suffering. The outmatched child has two options, both bad: submission and shame, on one hand, or self-assertion weighed down by guilt, on the other.

1. *Relinquishment of self, failure, falseness, and shame.* The child shields herself from the parent's assault-by-suffering by reverting to a caregiver mode: complying, flattering, understanding, soothing, validating, and empathizing. But such stabilizing of the parent's mood and self-esteem is more than a full-time job for a child—it is a terrible loss. A child focused so exclusively on someone else's needs can lose virtually all sense of what she herself feels, what she thinks, and who she really is.[12]

Further, the parent's continued suffering—clearly, such parents are unlikely ever to feel better more than transiently; certainly not in response to the child's caregiving—makes the child feel like a helpless failure in her very purpose for existing and may infuse her with a broader sense of failure and futility. She may conclude that she is not able to cheer up, enliven, or calm her parent down because of some deep-seated inadequacy or *defect* in herself—a "fact" that feels deeply *shameful* and undermines the child's confidence that she is qualified to hold her own as an independent person in the larger world. Shame *prevents separation* from the parent.

The child also senses, perhaps dimly, that the feeling of specialness she gets from being her parent's caregiver is built on collusive omnipotent fantasies that she has bought into. This compounds her feeling of being a fraud and feeds her doubts about being able to function independently in the real world. She also doubts that she is capable of genuine empathy or real love—since these feelings have been scripted by the unreal fantasy scenario she has signed on to, which also requires that her many contrary, more authentic, wishes be suppressed—or that she can truly be loved.

2. *Thwarted self-assertion, resentment, and guilt.* The deprived child naturally longs for the care she has never adequately received and for the opportunity to grow and develop as a person. But she feels that her own needs, *ipso facto*, are burdensome and hurtful to her fragile, suffering parent and must be choked off—though, of course, killing off one's own needs is an impossible task. Nevertheless, she must appear only submissive, compliant, caring, selfless, and "good," in order to protect her parent and protect herself from terrible guilt.

Most of all, she must thwart any sign of a wish to separate, or of interest in people or things that could pull her out of her fusion and her caregiving role—interest likely to be stimulated when someone in the child's wider world recognizes her capacities. Any hint of separation is likely to trigger anxiety in the parent, who may then isolate the child, devalue people to whom the child may become attached, and ramp up the terrorism of suffering.

The child may also unconsciously hate her parent for forcing her to throttle self-expression, contort her inner life, give up self-determination, and let herself be exploited, forfeit living in a real and honest way—that is, for colluding in her own "partial death" (Bonomi, 2002). All hatred and urge to defy must be hidden, perhaps behind a mask of sadness, anxiety, rumination, or cheerfulness. But at times the child's unhappiness is also felt by the parent as a burden, as disloyalty, and as an accusation of failure—which, unconsciously, it may be—and this, too, must be hidden.

But no child is able to fully stifle her own needs and feelings. The child may feel unbearably guilty for this "failure," and flee from her guilt through renewed submission, compliance, and fusion with her suffering parent, along with a sense of failure, defect, and shame that undermines her impulse to separate. But the urge to separate will not be silenced and will push her out toward the world again. An unstable emotional oscillation—a cycling between concealed urges to separate and guilty withdrawal—is set into perpetual motion.

Another source of a caregiver-child's guilt feelings is a parent's use of her child as a weapon, requiring the child to be her ally against someone—the child's other parent, a sibling, or someone outside the immediate family—or using her idealization of the child to demean someone else by comparison. The child feels pressed to acquiesce, lest the parent feel betrayed and abandoned and make the child her target. But the child feels complicit. She feels she should have resisted and may punish herself with guilt feelings out of a sense of justice.

Feeling and Acting "Bad" in Order to Preserve a Sense of Realness and Separateness

For some children, embracing an inner sense of badness—painful as it is—feels like the only way to hold onto some sense of authenticity and of being one's own person, separate from a parent's oppressive, and unreal, idealizations. Children who feel their badness is the only real piece of themselves not appropriated by a parent may even need to *show* it to others, partly to create a barrier that protects their sense of being real and separate from those who might trespass. An impervious display of guilt or shame will often ultimately push others away, as will hurtful, disobedient, or otherwise "bad" behavior (which may also constitute a protest, a refusal to collude silently in an injustice against oneself, however disguised the complaint). Demonstrating one's incompetence or defectiveness can be similarly isolating and also supply a cover story for *resisting* parental demands—it's not that the child doesn't want to take care of or please her parent, it's that she's not able to do so.

These observations complement Ferenczi's and Fairbairn's emphases on guilt as a *tie to the parent* and a *loss of self* by illuminating how a child can use feeling and acting bad as ways to *separate* and to *protect a sense of one's real self.*

A Note on the Synergy of the Moral Dimension with the Other Dimensions of Identification with the Aggressor

Identification with the aggressor is a way to manage an aggressor's threat from a position of weakness, by accommodating (Frankel, 2002a). Within the family, what frightens a child most is that her parent will abandon her in some way, including emotionally. The different dimensions of identification with the aggressor work synergistically to prevent the parent's abandonment.

The child's sense of defect, shame, and guilt—*moral* accommodations—which feel to the child like the basis for her connection to the parent, depend on certain *mental* accommodations. Critical perceptions and thoughts and angry feelings toward the parent must be *excluded*, along with attention to the child's own values, needs, and good qualities. And a heightened sensitivity and empathy toward the parent's feelings must be *created*. These moves keep the child's focus *off* her own needs and the parent's failure to meet them, preserving the child's image of the parent as the good one and the child as the problem. Conversely, moral accommodations make it easier to disregard forbidden perceptions, thoughts, and feelings, disqualifying them as products of a faulty mind or moral deficiency. And behavioral compliance with an aggressor, to be convincing, must be backed up by fully committed inner compliance in both the mental and moral realms.

Treatment Issues

I offer a few brief, general comments about particular dynamics that a persistent sense of badness can inject into a treatment. A patient's attention to the freer associations that naturally emerge in the analytic setting threatens to liberate perceptions, thoughts, and feelings from dissociation—experiences that could challenge her irrational feeling of badness. Anxiety and guilt may follow, as a patient fears that her sense of badness is all that anchors her most important interpersonal relationships and sense of self, and that greater self-confidence might irreparably damage someone she loves. A patient may find temporary refuge in an idealizing transference to the therapist—a backup source of security for a patient afraid to see her own strength. But the patient may feel torn, her devotion to two idealized figures—therapist and parent—pulling her in opposite directions, in terms of her freedom to psychologically separate and express herself openly.

A sense of badness can also be activated in the therapist. A patient's self-torment may evoke a compassion in the therapist that is hard to bear, based on the therapist having been traumatized in his own childhood by a parent's terrorism of suffering—which my own impressions suggest is a not-uncommon element in therapists' personal histories. In such a situation, a therapist may react with her own forms of compulsive submission and caregiving (cf. Racker, 1968, Chapter 7) in lieu of a more thoughtful and genuinely compassionate response to the patient—for instance, by providing excessive reassurance, overaccommodating, or passively accepting too much aggression. Such responses mirror the patient's parent's pattern of responding to her own anxieties rather than to the patient's needs. When this happens, the therapist's acknowledgment of her empathic lapse may differentiate her from the parent and help reestablish trust (Ferenczi, 1933), though the therapist's anxieties can take charge here too, turning acknowledgments into confessions (cf. Balint 1968, p. 116).

Notes

1 Ferenczi's concept is different from, though related to, Anna Freud's (1936) later use of the term to denote coping with aggression against oneself by becoming an aggressor toward someone else.

2 As such, Freud's and others' ideas about guilt stemming from universal Oedipal conflicts and a harsh superego understood largely as a reflection of innate fantasy, will be omitted. Ferenczi (1933) believed that the Oedipal situation is only pathogenic if a disturbed parent responds to the child's playful overtures as attempts at actual seduction or otherwise reacts to the child in a passionate or pathological way, and that a harsh superego is mainly an "implantation" by a troubled parent rather than the result of intrapsychic conflict (1932, pp. 58, 76, 79)—essentially, that the sexual, rivalrous, and aggressive feelings and the fears of retaliation that comprise the Oedipal fantasy situation are essentially benign, absent a pathogenic response from a parent. Klein's intrapsychic conception of the depressive position as a source of guilt will be addressed (see note 10 in this chapter) as it contrasts with Ferenczi's ideas. I will not discuss survivor's guilt directly, which is by definition a traumatic response and clearly connects with the "terrorism of suffering" and its consequences, which I will elaborate at length.

3 Ferenczi related the tendency to take in and imitate to what he saw as the primal principle of self-sacrifice and altruism, in contrast to the selfish principle (1930–1932, pp. 252–253).

4 While Bonomi (2002) elaborated compellingly on Ferenczi's idea of introjecting the aggressor's feelings of guilt, his focus was on an *actual* process of destruction—what Ferenczi called "partial death"— that results from "the malignant inclusion of the other as a parasitic foreign body" (p. 156), not on the topic of this chapter: the child's feeling of being bad.

5 "Ferenczi (1932, pp. 18, 182, 193; 1933, p. 163) believed that the most damaging aspect of the traumatic situation is the second parent's turning her back on her child, discounting the terrible reality of what he experienced; the child is then left feeling profoundly, unbearably alone. To the extent that trauma causes someone to feel outcast from human community, the response may be a more basic feeling of badness: shame rather than guilt" (Frankel 2002b, p. 165). Also, see note 7 in this chapter.

6 See Modell (1965) "on having the right to a life."

7 See Ferenczi's (1929, 1930, 1931, 1932, 1933) expanded ideas about what is traumatic, starting with his discussion of not being wanted or loved by parents, which he saw as literally essential to life (1929)—a hypothesis later confirmed by Spitz's (1945) systematic study of the effects on infants of being raised in an institution with good physical care but without maternal care and love.

Ferenczi referred explicitly to the aggressor's "threat of withdrawal of love" (1932, p. 190), and, in my reading, saw the threat of emotional abandonment as the most frightening aspect of the aggression, the potent factor behind all the aggressor's manipulations, and the aspect of trauma that does the greatest damage to the child's moral, mental, and behavioral functioning by enforcing compulsory identifications and dissociations. In regard to an assault, Ferenczi believed that the most destructive element of familial child abuse is the emotional abandonment of the child through parental denial *after* the assault. "Probably the worst way of dealing with such situations is to deny their existence, to assert that nothing has happened and that nothing is hurting the child ... These are the kinds of treatment which make the trauma pathogenic. One gets the impression that children get over even severe shocks without amnesia or neurotic consequences, if the mother is at hand with understanding and tenderness and (what is most rare) with complete sincerity" (1931, p. 138; 1932, pp. 18, 182, 193;1933, pp. 162–163).

8 To speculate: the default to self-blame may reflect an innate tendency to complementary thinking, in which there often must be a doer and one who is done to (cf. Benjamin, 1990); if the parent is suffering, then it must be the child who caused it.

9 Ferenczi also included their more subtle, disavowable variations (Ferenczi, 1930, 1931, 1933).

10 Cf. Melanie Klein's (1935) ideas about the depressive position, in which the child's fear that her own (essentially innate) sadism will damage the loved object and cause her to lose it—or to have already done so—lead to the child's concern about, and attempts to repair, the object. Klein's strongly intrapsychic emphasis in her discussion of guilt feelings and reparation is very different from Ferenczi's focus on guilt and caregiving as responses to traumatic factors such as parental terrorism of suffering.

11 There is empirical support relating factors very close to the causal elements of feeling one is bad that I have been discussing—coercive emotional abandonment and the terrorism of suffering—to compulsive caregiving.

Bowlby (1980), in the third and final volume of his landmark study on attachment, examined the then-existing literature on compulsive caregiving—which at that time consisted of clinical accounts and the study of individual cases, "no systematic study" then being available—and concluded that there were two factors that led children to become compulsive caregivers. The first was related to emotional abandonment; Bowlby wrote of "intermittent and inadequate mothering during early childhood" (p. 222). "[S]ome individuals respond to loss or threat of loss by concerning themselves intensely and to an excessive degree with the welfare of others" (p. 206), he wrote.

More recent attachment research supports these ideas, finding that compulsive caregiving is linked both to insecure attachment and to a preoccupation with relatedness (Bartholomew and Horowitz, 1991; Blatt and Levy, 2003; Holmes, 2000; Kunce and Shaver, 1994; Levy and Blatt, 1999)—that is, to anxieties about the other's emotional connection.

And in terms strongly overlapping with the terrorism of suffering, Bowlby's second factor occurred "when pressure is put on a child to care for a sick, anxious or hypochondriacal parent. In some such cases, the child is made to feel that he himself is responsible for his parent's being ill and therefore has an obligation to act as caregiver. In others, whilst not held responsible for the illness, he is none the less made to feel he has a responsibility to care for his parent" (p. 222).

Bowlby also found that "Should this [compulsive caregiving] pattern become established during childhood or adolescence, as we know it can be …, that person is prone, throughout life, to establish affectional relationships in this mould. Thus he is inclined, first, to select someone who is handicapped or in some other sort of trouble and thenceforward to cast himself solely in the role of that person's caregiver. Should such a person become a parent there is danger of his or her becoming excessively possessive and protective, especially as a child grows older, and also of inverting the relationship" (p. 206)—a reversal of roles resulting in a kind of intergenerational transmission of compulsive caregiving. He noted that a pattern of compulsive caregiving can make someone prone to chronic mourning.

12 In my observations, this self-sacrificing sense of responsibility occasionally exists without the conscious self-punishing guilt that often accompanies it.

References

Balint, M. (1968). *The Basic Fault: Therapeutic Aspects of Regression*. London/New York: Tavistock.

Balint, M. (1969). Trauma and object relationship. *International Journal of Psychoanalysis*, 50:429–435.

Bartholomew, K. and Horowitz, L.M. (1991). Attachment styles among young adults: A test of a four-category model. *Journal of Personality and Social Psychology*, 61:226–244.

Bemporad, J. R. (1994). The negative therapeutic reaction in severe characterological depression. *Journal of the American Academy of Psychoanalysis*, 22:399–414.

Benjamin, J. (1990). An outline of intersubjectivity. *Psychoanalytic Psychology*, 7S:33–46.

Blatt, S. J. and Levy, K. N. (2003). Attachment theory, psychoanalysis, personality development, and psychopathology. *Psychoanalytic Inquiry*, 23:102–150.

Bonomi, C. (2002). Identification with the aggressor—An interactive tactic or an intrapsychic tomb?. *Psychoanalytic Dialogues*, 12:153–158.

Bowlby, J. (1980). *Attachment and Loss, Volume III: Loss, Sadness, and Depression*. New York: Basic Books.

Faimberg, H. (2005). *The Telescoping of Generations*. New York: Routledge.

Fairbairn, W. R. D. (1941). A revised psychopathology of the psychoses and psychoneuroses. In *Psychoanalytic Studies of the Personality*. New York: Tavistock/Routledge, 1952, pp. 28–58.

Fairbairn, W. R. D. (1943). The repression and the return of bad objects (with special reference to the "war neuroses"). In *Psychoanalytic Studies of the Personality*. New York: Tavistock/Routledge, 1952, pp. 59–81.

Fairbairn, W. R. D. (1944). Endopsychic structure considered in terms of object-relationships. In *Psychoanalytic Studies of the Personality*. New York: Tavistock/Routledge, 1952, pp. 82–136.

Ferenczi, S. (1929). The unwelcome child and his death instinct. In M. Balint (ed) and E. Mosbacher et al (Trans.), *Final Contributions to the Problems and Methods of Psycho-Analysis*. London: Hogarth, 1955, pp. 102–107.

Ferenczi, S. (1930). The principle of relaxation and neocatharsis, M. Balint (ed) and E. Mosbacher et al (Trans.), *Final Contributions to the Problems and Methods of Psycho-Analysis*. London: Hogarth, 1955, pp. 108–125.

Ferenczi, S. (1930–1932). Notes and fragments. In M. Balint (ed) and E. Mosbacher et al (Trans.), *Final Contributions to the Problems and Methods of Psycho-Analysis*. London: Hogarth, 1955, pp. 219–279.

Ferenczi, S. (1931). Child-analysis in the analysis of adults. In Ferenczi, S. (1955), *Final Contributions to the Problems and Methods of Psycho-Analysis*, M. Balint (ed) and E. Mosbacher et al (Trans.). London: Hogarth, pp. 126–142.

Ferenczi, S. (1932). *The Clinical Diary of Sándor Ferenczi*, J. Dupont (ed) and M. Balint and N. Z. Jackson (Trans.). Cambridge, MA: Harvard University Press, 1988.

Ferenczi, S. (1933). Confusion of tongues between adults and the child, in Ferenczi, S. (1955), *Final Contributions to the Problems and Methods of Psycho-Analysis*, M. Balint (ed) and E. Mosbacher et al (Trans.). London: Hogarth, pp. 156–167.

Frankel, J. (1993). Collusion and intimacy in the analytic relationship: Ferenczi's legacy. In L. Aron and A. Harris (eds), *The Legacy of Sándor Ferenczi*. Hillsdale, NJ: The Analytic Press.

Frankel, J. (2002a). Exploring Ferenczi's concept of identification with the aggressor: Its role in trauma, everyday life, and the therapeutic relationship. *Psychoanalytic Dialogues*, 12:101–139.

Frankel, J. (2002b). Identification and "traumatic aloneness": Commentary on discussions by Berman and Bonomi. *Psychoanalytic Dialogues*, 12:159–170.

Frankel, J. (2012). Psychological enslavement understood through Ferenczi's concept of identification with the aggressor: Clinical and sociopolitical aspects. Plenary presentation at "Faces of Trauma" conference, Budapest, Hungary, June 1.

Freud, A. (1936). *The Ego and the Mechanisms of Defense*. New York: International Universities Press.

Grotstein, J. S. (1992). Commentary on "Dissociative processes and transference-countertransference paradigms …" by Jody Messler Davies and Mary Gail Frawley. *Psychoanalytic Dialogues*, 2:61–76.

Holmes, J. (2000). Attachment theory and psychoanalysis: A rapprochement. *British Journal of Psychotherapy*, 17:157–172.

Jones, J. M. (1995), *Affects as Process: An Inquiry into the Centrality of Affect in Psychological Life*. Hillsdale, NJ: The Analytic Press.

Klein, M. (1935). A contribution to the psychogenesis of manic-depressive states. *International Journal of Psychoanalysis*, 16:145–174.

Kohut, H. (1972). Thoughts on narcissism and narcissistic rage. *Psychoanalytic Study of the Child*, 27:360–400.

Kunce, L. J. and Shaver, P. R. (1994). An attachment-theoretical approach to caregiving in romantic relationships. In K. Bartholomew and D. Perlman (eds), *Advances in Personal Relationships, Vol. 5: Attachment Processes in Adulthood*. London: Jessica Kingsley, pp. 205–237.

Levy, K. N. and Blatt, S. J. (1999). Attachment theory and psychoanalysis. *Psychoanalytic Inquiry*, 19:541–575.

Miller, A. (1997). *The Drama of the Gifted Child*. New York: Basic Books.

Modell, A. H. (1965). On having the right to a life: An aspect of the superego's development. *International Journal of Psychoanalysis*, 46:323–331.

Racker, H. (1968). *Transference and Counter-Transference*. New York: International Universities Press.

Rothstein, A. (1977). The ego attitude of entitlement. *International Journal of Psychoanalysis*, 4:409–417.

Spitz, R. A. (1945). Hospitalism—An inquiry into the genesis of psychiatric conditions in early childhood. *Psychoanalytic Study of the Child*, 1:53–74.

Weiss, J., Sampson, H., and the Mount Zion Psychotherapy Research Group. (1986). *The Psychoanalytic Process*. New York: Guilford.

13

ON THE THERAPEUTIC ACTION OF LOVE AND DESIRE[1]

Steven Kuchuck

Love Sweet Love

Shortly after my uncle died, his widow came to visit us. Only in her 50s at the time, I remember that she seemed old to my five-year-old self, sad perhaps but also vibrant and very much alive. As she took me for a walk through the courtyards of the large garden apartment complex we lived in, my aunt sang a song that has stayed with me ever since: "What the World Needs Now, Is Love, Sweet Love." Sadness and longing permeated and etched the sounds and rhythm into my soul—they have never left. Looking back, I'm certain that I learned something on that walk not only about my aunt's experience of pining and loss; now I, too, had a piece of music that articulated and held a probably already familiar part of my experience.

Though perhaps it should not, it sometimes troubles me to consider the possibility that many of us may be drawn to this field in quest of love. If we subscribe to the notion put forth by Alice Miller (1981) and others that what draws us to our work is in large part an attempt to rescue and heal our parents, then I do not see it as being much of a leap to suggest that part of what motivates us in this endeavor is the hope that we will be able to instill or restore a capacity for nurturing and loving, which often springs from or leads to our own loving feelings. Of course, if we are speaking of love between parents and children, we must also speak of oedipal dynamics and Freud's (1900) mention of the parents' sexual partiality for their sons and daughters, Ferenczi's (1925) efforts to explore the full range of analyst-patient love, and much more recently, whether as parent or child, as Stephen Mitchell (2003), Jodie Davies (2003), and others point out, falling in love. Whether or not a quest for love is part of what drives some to become analysts, we would probably all agree that our work is often intimate and at its core relational, dyadic, and, though not always or exclusively, loving. Not surprisingly—all in a day's work, I might add, we sometimes fall in love.

This chapter is an exploration of that love (and accompanying component, sexual desire) and its curative nature, especially within the gay male analyst-heterosexual male patient dyad. I present theory and a case from my practice to illustrate this line of thinking. Though I offer a new paradigm for exploring the therapeutic use of love and attraction, the roots can be traced to Ferenczi's ideas about love and therapeutic action (1925, 1932; Rachman, 1993, and this volume, among others), as well as his emphasis on use of the countertransference, especially as further developed by Mitchell and his followers. I recognize that there can sometimes be a fine line between Ferenczi's or any analyst's therapeutic *use* of love and what Wolstein (1993, p. 181) refers to as Clara Thompson's "questions about Ferenczi's irrational dependency on *being* loved" (italics added).

In the Beginning

Almost from the beginning of psychoanalytic time, much has been written about the (usually) female patient's tendency to fall in love with her (usually) male analyst (Freud, 1958/1915). This early writing and a somewhat later literature addresses the analyst's erotic countertransference as well, though until recently, mainly as a cautionary tale (Blum, 1973; Jacobs, 1986; Kernberg, 1994; Gabbard, 1989). Freud, at least in writing, was clear about the dangers inherent in acting on erotic feelings that arise as part of treatment (Crews, 1998). Though writing primarily about non-treatment situations, Ferenczi also warns us to avoid enacting confusion of the language of (sexual) passion with that of tenderness and to avoid retraumatizing patients in other ways as well—although we know that he himself transgressed (Ferenczi, 1932, 1933; Rachman, 1993). An important part of our work has always been to emphasize the difference between thought and deed; as mentioned, Ferenczi was adamant that analysts must allow themselves to acknowledge all countertransference feelings (1932), an important component of this differentiation. Still, because the dangers and repercussions for sexual acting out as a result of love or lust were so severe, this freedom to explore sexual and romantic stirrings was mostly denied us, save for a brave and revolutionary paper by Harold Searles in 1959. Today, we have interpersonal and relational writing that explores the full range of the analyst's affective and fantasy life, including the erotic, and a literature that examines this still relatively new frontier of the analyst's psyche for diagnostic and intersubjective data.

To quote Freud, analysis is "a healing through love" (F/JU, 6.12.1906). Though Freud was referring to transference love, it seems likely that Ferenczi, the first to really explore the nature of the analyst's love, understood (or at least applied) Freud's words to mean the analyst's loving feelings and attitudes towards the patient. "Only sympathy heals," declares Ferenczi, but: "can one love everyone?" (1932/1995, p. 200). In an earlier paper, he writes, "The child, with its desire for love ... lives on literally in every human being" (1916, pp. 53–54). It is well known that Ferenczi wanted more direct expression of caring from Freud, and as his patient and friend, longed to offer the same to him as well. He was deeply disappointed and likely angry that Freud abandoned his earlier mission to offer patients warmth and ministering in favor of scientific detachment, observation, and interpretation. In his clinical diaries and elsewhere, he states it is not abstinence—which he believes can actually be retraumatizing—that the patient needs, but rather the analyst's open, loving attitude and behavior (the language of tenderness) that is of primary importance in the presence of the patient's internalized child (1932). Ferenczi was also the first to recognize the necessity of acknowledging and making use of the analyst's whole personality (not only the aforementioned countertransference responses) in conducting a treatment. As perhaps each contributor to this volume has pointed out, every analyst who values and incorporates these ways of thinking and practice is an heir to the work of Ferenczi.

Stephen Mitchell was one such heir, though certainly not only an heir. His ideas about relational psychoanalysis evolved through an integration of British object relations theory and interpersonal psychoanalysis (1988). Because Michael Balint and Clara Thompson, both major contributors to each of these earlier traditions, were patients, students, close colleagues, and enthusiastic supporters of Sándor Ferenczi, it is not surprising that the seeds for much of Mitchell's groundbreaking work can be found in the writing of Ferenczi (see Bass, Chapter 14 of this volume). As Mitchell and others have noted, theory develops in the context of the current intellectual and cultural milieu, and Mitchell, a postmodern thinker, challenges notions of hierarchy, categorization, and positivism in ways that Ferenczi was only beginning to imagine and outline in his lifetime (1932). Still, one certainly does hear clear echoes of Ferenczi in Mitchell's discussions of mutuality, self-disclosure, two-person psychology, focus on the transference-countertransference, and recognition of the analyst's "real" (non-transferential) impact on the patient and treatment. When Mitchell states that technique cannot be related to the analyst's specific behaviors but is instead something that can only be understood as contextual and coconstructed (1988), we might be reminded of Ferenczi's plea to move away from a one-size-fits-all approach to treatment that declares some patients unanalyzable (Ferenczi, 1932). Both men wrote about love, each believing that the topic was poorly or under-addressed: for Ferenczi, regarding analytic love, and for Mitchell, on romantic love (2003). The two believed that it was the individual analyst's flexible and creative approach to the work rather than a unitary, static set of theories that would determine the outcome of a treatment, and each of these men viewed the therapeutic relationship as being the primary vehicle for change.

Early Stirrings

Jody Davies (2003), building on the legacy of Sándor Ferenczi, Stephen Mitchell, and others, credits Searles' (1959) pioneering work when she discusses the rarely articulated mutual erotics of the oedipal phase and compares the analyst who experiences an erotic countertransference to the oedipal parent in the throes of passion and fantasy, the analyst in most cases needing to withhold disclosing these feelings, though not in one controversial case that she shares. Davies is one of the first to elaborate on the therapeutic benefits of recognizing an erotic countertransference position, though Ferenczi, Mitchell, and others certainly set the stage for this work. Like Irwin Hirsch (2010) and Andrea Celenza (2010), Davies mentions the curative aspect of oedipal/now clinical erotic love for the patient who may never have had the chance to be adored and be the object of the parent's idealized romantic interest. As it can be for the parent in love with her child, the analyst who may be feeling not only love but deep attraction for a patient can utilize this subjective state in a way that leads to experiences of hopefulness, agency, and contentment for patients, even or perhaps especially if these feelings are contained by the analyst rather than articulated. Hirsch, actually, is more open to disclosing these feelings than I am, as was Ferenczi at various points in his work, here writing about the benefits of mutual analysis: "Any kind of secrecy … makes the patient distrustful; he detects from little gestures … the presence of affects, but cannot gauge their quantity or importance; candid disclosure regarding them enables him to counteract them or to instigate countermeasures with greater certainty" (1932, p. 11). To be fair, he also mentions "the limits of mutual analysis" (p. 10), which in later years led him to abandon this experiment. He goes on in the same diary entry to make clear that the patient's capacity to tolerate and make good use of the analyst's disclosures is of ongoing concern to Ferenczi (pp. 11–12), but at least during the periods of time before he renounces mutual analysis, he seems to favor disclosure over withholding. I believe that among other problems, flooding and disregualtion—a confusion of tongues, in Ferenczi's own language (1933)—can easily result from an overt disclosure of the erotic.

All these writers also note the importance of the associative value of our fantasies and reverie and the data that would be missed were we to close ourselves to the erotic in our patients or ourselves. Indeed, we need to consider the clinical dangers inherent in rejecting any patient or analyst self-states as Mitchell and his followers discuss, or what Ferenczi referred to as the need to more fully know oneself via ongoing self-inquiry, training analysis (he was the first to emphasize the need for specialized, qualified training analysts), and openness to the "real countertransference" (Haynal, 1993 and this volume) and "the dialogue of unconsciouses" (Ferenczi 1932, p. 84).

Gender and the Erotic

There is very little mention of male (or even female) homoerotic countertransference in the literature. In the next section, I show how this differs slightly, although not significantly, in work with homosexual patients and/or analysts. This absence in the literature might very well be related to the fact that erotic transference-countertransference material of any type often gets dissociated, especially by men according to some studies (Person, 1985; Thomas, 2003), and therefore often remains unrecognized by patients or analysts. Hirsch (1994), a heterosexual analyst, does disclose an awareness of his own erotic countertransference with male patients that he believes falls just short of sexual arousal only because of his own anxiety and inhibition. Hirsch and others believe that the male analyst who cannot be open to this aspect of the countertransference deprives the male patient of an opportunity to experience what Jessica Benjamin calls the developmentally necessary "homoerotic love affair with the father" (1995, p. 60). The analyst's fear and lack of recognition of these feelings might mirror or induce the same responses in the patient, a sure sign that unacceptable desire is being blocked from the treatment.

Sexual Orientation and the Erotic

Just as we can't separate gender from our conversation about the erotic countertransference, neither can we overlook sexual orientation. Until this point, my focus has been primarily on the heterosexual analyst. But what of the gay male analyst? If we bypass outdated reports of assumed pathology, we find almost nothing in the literature about gay male analysts prior to the 1980s or 1990s and then, minimal reporting or exploration of erotic countertransference. Mitchell may have been the first analyst to outright depathologize homosexuality—I am fairly certain he was the first heterosexual analyst to do so, and at a time when the Diagnostic and Statistical Manual (DSM) and psychoanalytic texts and institutes asserted it was a manifestation of arrested development and mental illness (Mitchell, 1978, 1981). Ferenczi, working more than half a century earlier in an era when homosexuality was seen in an even more absolute pathological light—as a degenerative disease—attempted to free himself of this bias and without judgment, to empathically understand his "female homosexual transvestite" patient Rosa K (Rachman 1993, p. 82). Haynal (2002), in referring to this same patient and to Ferenczi's sensitivity and activism regarding what we would now call the LGBTQ community, mentions "his activity in favour of homosexuals" (p. 10) and the important role that Ferenczi thought psychiatrists should play in this fight against social repression.

The gay male analyst's clinical work with heterosexual male patients specifically is even more rarely mentioned prior to the last decade, and there is almost no writing dealing with the gay male analyst's erotic countertransference to his heterosexual male patients, save for a contribution by Eric Sherman (2005). Sherman discusses his sexual arousal with one particular straight male patient as an antidote to an otherwise deadened clinical experience. He believes that his fear and shame around these sexual feelings prevented the erotic countertransference from being as accessible and useful as it might have been had the patient been gay and Sherman less terrified of being discovered and vulnerable to embarrassment and rejection.

Indeed, shame, fear of discovery and rejection, vulnerability, and a host of other painful remnants of childhood, adolescence, and earlier stages of adulthood are familiar feelings for gay male analysts. Hiding, from oneself and from others, is often the norm. Until recently, non-disclosure of orientation was necessary at most psychoanalytic training programs, though due to the work of Mitchell and other relational writers and activists, this is no longer the case. These fears, then, are likely contributing factors to the dearth of published material about erotic countertransference feelings among gay male analysts. Shame and concern about vulnerability of exposure and accusations of pathology have made it difficult for straight female, male, and lesbian analysts to publish in this area as well, although to a lesser extent.

Though it can be understood as an attempt to answer theoretical and clinical questions, as is the case with most writing, this chapter springs from a deeper well. It is also, of course, an effort to sublimate and compensate for earlier experiences of shame, identity, coming out, training-related traumas, and needs to hide—for historical/developmental reasons, for training and referral reasons, and under the burden of a first training that was classical and taught all candidates and members to hide evidence of our subjectivity (Kuchuck, 2008).

Therapeutic Action of the Gay Analyst's Erotic Experience

Though I work with a significant number of female and gay male patients, a large and sometimes majority portion of my practice is made up of heterosexual men. Consequently, a large if not majority portion of my countertransference contains an erotic element that I believe enhances the therapeutic work with many of these men. It is this phenomenon—the therapeutic action of the gay male analyst's erotic countertransference to his heterosexual male patients—that will be the focus of the remainder of this chapter. Much of what follows can also be applied to all the various gender and sexual orientation dyadic configurations. However, because others have written about those configurations—even if minimally—and because there are dynamics that are specific to this particular analyst-patient population, the above-mentioned dyad is the focus of my current work.

Some writers differentiate between erotic, quasi-erotic, loving, and romantic (Hirsch, 2010; Lichtenberg, personal communication, October 13, 2011) when discussing the parents' oedipal feelings, and/or in later life with regard to what I call the analyst's erotic countertransference responses. Although I believe that to a limited extent these distinctions can be made in some cases, I also assume that there is usually an erotic component on both sides of an oedipal love affair and in most intensely loving or romantic adult relationships. Therefore, I use the terms "erotic transference/countertransference" or "erotic experience" to mean the erotic, quasi-erotic, romantic, and deeply passionate, loving feelings that the analyst and/or patient feels emotionally, physically, and/or sexually. In a rare and important consideration of this topic, psychoanalyst and Ferenczi scholar Judith Vida writes, "André Haynal (1993) wrote that an analysis begins with a 'moment of mutual seduction' (p. 19). Those who trained me called it, in private conversation, 'falling in love.' It is not possible for me even to enter my office in the morning of a clinical day without the hope and the possibility of love" (Vida 2002, p. 437).

When I reflect on additional aspects of personal history and personality that are stirred by and potentially enhancing of the work with these men, a number of factors come to mind, including Herzog's notion of father hunger, and how in various manifestations and degrees of intensity this has gnawed at me and propelled me forward, always seeking, longing for, male contact, for feeding that might sate. In my work, I am often aware of a need and aptitude for making contact with and feeding the hungry boys—they and me—who inhabit the bodies of the men who sit before me. As Celenza (2010) says, we are in love with our little boy and little girl selves. It is not difficult to love or even to fall in love with these men. Ferenczi, who lost his beloved father when he was only a boy of 15, would likely have experienced some degree of this dynamic emergent in relation to Freud (1/17/30 letter, in *The Clinical Diary*, 1932/1995, p. xiii; Aron and Harris, 1993), Groddeck (see Fortune, Chapter 5 of this volume), and other male figures. Perhaps this hunger, as well as a corresponding desire to heal through rescuing traumatized patients with whom he identified due to his own loss, harsh treatment at the hands of a stern, unavailable and likely grieving mother, and earlier sexual molestation (Ferenczi 1932, p. 61; Aron and Harris, 1993) fueled Ferenczi's work in similar ways to those I am outlining in this essay.

If we can return to my aunt for just a moment and what "the world"—or at least she and I "need now,"—I do believe that on some level, it may be in part this need to love and be loved, that has enabled me to be particularly attuned to a similar need in patients and in particular, patients whose gender and core issues of paternal absence and abuse resonate with my early history. Heterosexual identifications that live alongside what for many gay men are easily accessed strong female, nurturing internalized objects further the projection of, recognition of, and compelling desire to care for and heal these wounded child states; an important part of the healing power of the erotic.

Clinical Example

Mark first came to see me close to fifteen years ago when he was in his mid-30s and burdened by issues of depression, intimacy, and social anxiety. A struggling painter, Mark's father left his mother and older siblings when he was 3, disappearing for years and reappearing for only sporadic contact—usually amounting to no more than a birthday call every year until he reached his early 20s when minimal, inconsistent, and disappointing contact became established. Mark's mother pined for her ex-husband and fluctuated between neglect and overreliance, leaving him to feel exposed, vulnerable, and responsible for her physical and emotional well-being. In separate fits of rage less than a year apart, his mother threw his beloved brothers out of the house, sending them to live with the father that Mark barely knew. There were additional childhood traumas, including instances of inappropriate sexual overstimulation and play with a teenage boy in the neighborhood and anal penetration by a man his mother barely knew but had asked to babysit one evening shortly after his father had left the home. In sessions, he is terrified that I will seduce and penetrate him—physically, sexually, and otherwise.

In the early days, I keep my interpretations to a minimum and mostly to myself, aware of his fragility and feeling the need to prove my benign caring even while feeling not only erotically and romantically stimulated at times but uncharacteristically predatory as well, not an unusual feeling when working with a survivor of sexual abuse. Fears of being penetrated yielded to simultaneous or alternative wishes to sexually and otherwise turn me on and be penetrated by me. I understood this wish as not only residue of the sexual abuse but also an inevitable remnant of intense father hunger, albeit more consciously sexualized than for many though to some extent a normative desire of the pre- and oedipal child. The wish is that I, unlike his real father, will want to claim him as my own just as he longs to be my son and romantic partner, a buffer against and an alternative to his erotically charged relationship with his mother and abusers. This terrifies Mark in our first years while he questions his sexual identity, preferences, and safety around and hunger for a man; it is exciting and more pleasurable in recent years as he becomes more comfortable acknowledging his heterosexuality and exhibitionistic creative, erotic, and other urges—coming out of the closet, as he calls it with some irony.

Though I do not articulate my erotic and romantic fantasies, I do believe that on a pre- or unconscious level, much as the oedipal child knows he is passionately loved—or not—in similar probably quasi-sexual ways, Mark was able to make use of my attraction and fleeting romantic fantasies in ways that over time allowed him to believe in his capacity to love and be loved romantically and begin to rework previously defeating and defeated internalizations. I also believe that as is almost always the case with an erotic countertransference, my never sleepy or deadened state meant I could be with him more consistently and completely than we are sometimes able to be with patients and probably contributed to my heightened state of attunement. Mirror neurons are likely at work at times like these, awareness of my body in relation to his leading to awareness of his body in the presence of mine, making space in the treatment for us to explore previously dissociated or repressed feelings of shame around his body and physical self.

Transference-Countertransference Implications

Most typically, reports of the analyst's erotic countertransference are offered as a response to the patient's romantic feelings and sexual attraction. Relational thinking about transference-countertransference, however, suggests that we cannot always know where the feelings initiate. Though my hunch is that whether consciously or not, it is often the analyst who first experiences these feelings, this is not always the case. Regardless of where the feelings begin, the most important thing to note is that the analyst's erotic state becomes part of the therapeutic action through the means discussed above, and that this awareness often mirrors or creates space for a similar state in the patient.

Even with a patient who has not been sexually and otherwise exploited in the ways that Mark has been, it can be difficult for the analyst to tolerate erotic feelings without feeling a preponderance of anxiety, guilt, and shame, especially if the patient does not share the analyst's minority sexual orientation. However, to the extent that I have been able to contain and even enjoy these feelings when they come up—Mitchell's "feel irresponsibly but behave responsibly" comes to mind—it is my sense that I have been able to help Mark learn to contain and enjoy his own initially frightening erotic feelings, including a wish to sexually excite and allow himself to be sexually excited by women, without feeling that his sexual appetite will be out of control and destructive.

When abuse is not part of one's history, power still often gets sexualized. Because of the inherent power differential in therapy, the erotic may become a central dynamic for analyst and patient alike. Stoller (1979) believes that hostility is a component of most sexual excitement, coexisting with affection at one end of the continuum, serving as "an attempt to undo childhood traumas ... that threatened the development of one's masculinity or femininity" (p. 6). While Ferenczi calls for mutuality and a loving attitude in the treatment as an antidote to the asymmetry and hypocrisy of an abusive childhood home (Hidas, 2012; Szekacs-Weisz and Keve, 2012), these elements of the therapeutic environment may revive or lead to sexual and/or romantic feelings. Additionally, Mitchell believes that idealization, so much a part of my work with Mark and many treatments, also fuels romantic feelings. My patient and I have, in fact, been surviving enactments of romance, power, sexuality, and hostility, including identification with the aggressor that has been stirred for each of us in various ways (Ferenczi, 1933; Rachman, 1989, 1997). Sexual desire—including his wish for me to desire him—love, and aggression emerge in fantasies of ownership (Atlas and Kuchuck, 2012); purchasing me as he would a prostitute. With regard to having to share me with other patients, he wonders, "how can you have so many lovers? How can I ever feel ok with this open relationship?"

When not feeling aggressed upon, I am flattered and sometimes aroused by this attention, the beaming father-lover he has longed for.

Discussion

In this and other cases I have written about (Kuchuck, 2012, 2013), male patients who most crave (and flourish as a result of) the male analyst's unarticulated sexualized response have often experienced some form of paternal neglect, rejection, or physical abuse and may be traumatized in some of the ways Ferenczi describes (1932), although this is not necessary for the erotic countertransference to be of therapeutic value.

It is the absence of physical appreciation, attraction, holding, and/or the presence of violent physical contact at the hands of father or other men that most creates the need for and, in some cases, induces the presence of this mirroring attunement and set of bodily and adoring responses in the treatment. As discussed, there is often a corresponding set of erotic feelings in the patient that might induce, parallel, or emerge in response to the analyst's erotics, sexual excitement fueled for each, according to Mitchell, by the unknowable; the "otherness" that colors the relationship.

With Mark, there were moments in the countertransference during which I was acutely aware of becoming the sexually attracted, gentle rather than abusive physical father I never had, and the sometimes erotically attached brother that I have enjoyed being and relating to throughout my life; holding and loving as I wished to be held and loved, and attuned to what I perceived to be a corresponding need for these elements in Mark. I also experienced an attraction to early, idealized heterosexual self-other states as embodied by and projected into my patient.

Conclusion

Although heterosexual male analysts (and female analysts, though there are different dynamics and therapeutic benefits) can also experience these erotic responses to male patients, it is because of the nature of the primary erotic attraction that the gay male analyst is more likely to experience, without dissociation, an erotic response. Therefore, if he is not too frightened by or ashamed of these feelings, the gay male analyst is likely to be in a position to consciously feel and make therapeutic use of them. Certainly, at times, gay male analysts do have similar erotic experiences with heterosexual or lesbian female patients and, of course, with gay male patients, but those configurations and resulting dynamics have not been the focus of this chapter. Although I contend that analysts who do not experience an erotic, affective, and/or bodily response can still provide the needed mirroring, empathic attunement, and appreciation that Ferenczi (1928), Mitchell, and others note these patients need, in some cases it might not be enough to address and sate the kinds of deficits discussed.

For the analyst who finds himself in the midst of an erotic countertransference, as with our patients' erotic transferences, we must also wonder about the possibility that patient or analyst deadness, aggression, or hate is being defended against by way of a sexualized or romantic experience. We must therefore consider the possibility that, in some cases, these responses might serve as a defense against knowing or relating to our patients in more emotionally intimate, less sexualized ways, and might inadvertently blind the analyst to the patient's or analyst's non-erotically desired self and body states that also need to gain entrance into the room. Likewise, we need to investigate the opposite possibility, when the erotic seems nowhere to be found.

Note

1 Some portions of this chapter appeared earlier in "Please (Don't) Want Me: The Therapeutic Action of Male Sexual Desire in the Treatment of Heterosexual Men" (2012), *Contemporary Psychoanalysis*, and appears here with permission of the publisher.

References

Aron, L. and Harris, A. (1993). Discovery and Rediscovery. In L. Aron and A. Harris (eds), *The Legacy of Sándor Ferenczi*. London: The Analytic Press, pp. 1–36.

Atlas, G. and Kuchuck, S. (2012). To have and to hold: Psychoanalytic dialogues on the desire to own. *Psychoanalytic Dialogues*, 22:93–105.

Benjamin, J. (1995). *Like Subjects, Love Objects: Essays on Recognition and Sexual Difference*. New Haven, CT: Yale University Press.

Blum, H. P. (1973). The concept of eroticized transference. *Journal of the American Psychoanalytic Association*, 21:61–76.

Celenza, A. (2010). The guilty pleasure of erotic countertransference: Searching for radial true. *Studies in Gender & Sexuality*, 11:175–183.

Crews, F. (ed) (1998). *Unauthorized Freud: Doubters Confront a Legend*. New York: Viking.

Davies, J. M. (2003). Falling in love with love: Oedipal and post-Oedipal manifestations of idealization, mourning and erotic masochism. *Psychoanalytic Dialogues*, 13:1–27.

Ferenczi, S. (1916). *Contributions to Psycho-Analysis*. Boston, MA: R. G. Badger.

Ferenczi, S. (1925). Psycho-analysis of sexual habits. *International Journal of Psychoanalysis*, 6:372–404.

Ferenczi, S. (1928). The Elasticity of Psycho-Analytic Technique. In S. Ferenczi (ed), *Final Contributions to the Problems and Methods of Psycho-Analysis*. London: Karnac Books, Maresfield Reprints, 1980, pp. 87–101.

Ferenczi, S. (1932). *The Clinical Diary*. (J. Dupont, ed). Cambridge, MA: Harvard University Press, 1988, 1995.

Ferenczi, S. (1933). The confusion of tongues between adults and children: The language of tenderness and passion. In M. Balint (ed), *Final Contributions to the Problems and Methods of Psycho-Analysis*, Vol. 3. New York: Brunner/Mazel, 1980, pp. 156–167.

Freud, S. (1900). Interpretation of Dreams. *SE*, 4/5.

Freud, S. (1906). Letter from Sigmund Freud to C. G. Jung, December 6, 1906. *The Freud/Jung Letters: The Correspondence Between Sigmund Freud and C. J. Jung*, pp. 11–13.

Freud, S. (1958). Observations on transference love. *In The standard edition of the complete psychological works of Sigmund Freud*, Vol. 12: The dynamics of transference 1911–1913. London: Hogarth Press, pp. 159–171. (Originally published 1915).

Gabbard, G. O. (ed) (1989). *Sexual Exploitation in Professional Relationships*. Washington, DC: American Psychiatric Press.

Haynal, A. (1993). *Psychoanalysis and the Sciences*. London: Karnac.

Haynal, A. (2002). *Disappearing and Reviving. Sándor Ferenczi in the History of Psychoanalysis*. London: Karnac.

Hidas, G. (2012). Ferenczi and trauma: a perilous journey to the labyrinth. In J. Szekacs-Weisz and T. Keve (eds), *Ferenczi and His World: Rekindling the Spirit of the Budapest School*. London: Karnac, pp. 111–128.

Hirsch, I. (1994). Countertransference love and theoretical model. *Psychoanalytic Dialogues*, 4:171–192.

Hirsch, I. (2010). On some advantages of mutual sexual fantasy in the analytic situation: Commentary on paper by Christopher Bonovitz. *Psychoanalytic Dialogues*, 20:654–662.

Jacobs, T. J. (1986). On countertransference enactments. *Journal of the American Psychoanalytic Association*, 34:289–307.

Kernberg, O. F. (1994). Love in the analytic setting. *Journal of the American Psychoanalytic Association*, 42(4):1137–1157.

Kuchuck, S. (2008). In the shadow of the towers: The role of retraumatization and political action in the evolution of a psychoanalyst. *Psychoanalytic Review*, 95:417–436.

Kuchuck, S. (2012). Please (don't) want me: The therapeutic action of male sexual desire in the treatment of heterosexual men. *Contemporary Psychoanalysis*, 48:544–562.

Kuchuck, S. (2013). Reflections on the therapeutic action of desire. *Studies in Gender and Sexuality*, 14:133–139.

Miller, A. (1981). *The Drama of the Gifted Child: The Search for the True Self.* (rev. ed.). New York: Basic Books.

Mitchell, S. (2003). *Can Love Last?: The Fate of Romance over Time.* New York: Norton.

Mitchell, S. A. (1978). Psychodynamics, homosexuality, and the question of pathology. *Journal for the Study of Interpersonal Processes*, 41(3):254–263.

Mitchell, S. A. (1981). The psychoanalytic treatment of homosexuality: Some technical considerations. *International Journal of Psychoanalysis*, 8:63–80.

Mitchell, S. A. (1988). The intrapsychic and the interpersonal: Different theories, different domains, or historical artifacts? *Psychoanalytic Inquiry*, 8:472–496.

Person, E. S. (1985). The erotic transference in women and in men: Differences and consequences. *Journal of the American Academy of Psychoanalysis & Dynamic Psychiatry*, 13:159–180.

Rachman, A. W. (1989). Ferenczi's contribution to the evolution of self psychology framework in psychoanalysis. In D. W. Detrick and S. P. Detrick (eds), *Self Psychology: Comparisons and Contrasts*. Hillsdale, NJ: Analytic Press, pp. 89–110.

Rachman, A. W. (1993). Ferenczi and sexuality. In L. Aron and A. Harris (eds), *The Legacy of Sándor Ferenczi*. Hillsdale, NJ: Analytic Press, pp. 81–100.

Rachman, A. W. (1997). *Sándor Ferenczi: The psychotherapist of tenderness and passion*. Northvale, NJ: Jason Aronson.

Searles, H. F. (1959). Oedipal love in the countertransference. *International Journal of Psychoanalysis*, 40:180–190.

Sherman, E. (2005). *Notes from the Margins: The Gay Analyst's Subjectivity in the Treatment Setting*. Hillsdale, NJ: Analytic Press.

Stoller, R. J. (1979). *Sexual Excitement: The Dynamics of Erotic Life*. New York: Simon & Schuster.

Szekacs-Weisz, J. and Keve, T. (eds) (2012). *Ferenczi and His World: Rekindling the Spirit of the Budapest School*. London: Karnac.

Thomas, S. (2003). Talking man to man: Transference-countertransference difficulties in the male same-gender analytic dyad. *British Journal of Psychotherapy*, 19(3):335–347.

Vida, J. E. (2002). The role of love in the therapeutic action of psychoanalysis. *American Imago*, 59:435–445.

Wolstein, B. (1993). The problem of truth in applied psychoanalysis. *Psychanalytic Review*, 80:661–664.

14

THE DIALOGUE OF UNCONSCIOUSES, MUTUAL ANALYSIS, AND THE USES OF THE SELF IN CONTEMPORARY RELATIONAL PSYCHOANALYSIS[1]

Anthony Bass

"If it doesn't belong in my analysis, what is it doing in my analysis?"
(Benjamin Wolstein to Clara Thompson in his analysis,
personal communication to Anthony Bass in his analysis)

"We analysts must admit to ourselves that we are much indebted to our patients for their sharply critical view of us, especially when we promote its development" (p. 26)

"One could almost say that the more weaknesses an analyst has, which lead to greater or lesser mistakes and errors, but which are then uncovered and treated in the course of mutual analysis, the more likely the analysis is to rest on profound and realistic foundations" (p. 15)

(*The Clinical Diary* of Sándor Ferenczi)

Ferenczi's Clinical Legacy and the Relational Turn in Psychoanalysis

My intention in this chapter is to explore the links between Ferenczi's understanding of psychoanalysis as a radically mutual endeavor in which unconscious communication between patient and analyst sustains currents that flow in both directions, his experiments in mutual analysis, and the subsequent development of contemporary relational theory and technique. Since the (1988) posthumous publication in English of his (1932) clinical diary, there has been a growing appreciation of the ways in which Ferenczi's clinical investigations have had a profound impact on contemporary psychoanalytic thought (Aron and Harris, 1993). Developments in a relational theory of technique, in particular, bear the imprint of Ferenczi's grasp of the nature of psychoanalytic relations, shaped by his understanding of the depth of mutuality at the core of the process, as well as the self-corrections and caveats that emerged from his experimental efforts to test the limits of the therapeutic possibilities and applications of mutuality at the level of technique.

His late work, as reflected in his (1933/1949) paper, *Confusion of Tongues between Adults and the Child*, and *The Clinical Diary* (1932/1988) offer a profound counterpoint to approaches to psychoanalytic technique associated with the classical tradition. His work has served as a point of departure for approaches to clinical psychoanalysis that have expanded the frame of how analysts may effectively use themselves with reference to their countertransference. Contemporary relational approaches rooted in Ferenczi's clinical investigations emphasize intersubjectivity and recognize mutuality and reciprocity as central to therapeutic relations, with broad and diverse implications for technique. While such innovations have been noted to reflect contemporary American democratic, feminist, and post-modern values (Mitchell and Harris, 2004), Benjamin Wolstein noted (1993) that the discovery of Ferenczi's work more than a half century after his death embedded our contemporary understanding of analytic therapy and the therapeutic relationship deep in the history of psychoanalysis itself.

Ferenczi's radical experiments in analytic technique expanded the possibilities for joint, direct transference/countertransference exploration, illuminating the complex permutations of expressive and transparent ways therapist and patient can utilize the full range of feelings and thoughts that emerge in the field of therapy. He reformulated transference as something other than how it was traditionally conceived: an endogenous unfolding of inner psychic contents projected onto a blank screen analyst trained to interpret its unconscious meanings to the patient. A multiply determined, highly selected but not inevitably distorted patient response to the person and psychic activity of the analyst, and to the analyst's technique, called for new forms of psychoanalytic participation on the analyst's part, taking as their point of departure the recognition that the patient's views of the analyst are likely to include accurate, as well as distorted, perceptions. Such perceptions frequently touch on areas that are beyond the awareness of the therapist and that may evoke strong defenses against their recognition. How does a therapist deal constructively and therapeutically with a patient's views of him when such perceptions touch on areas of his inner life that are unconscious or subject to dissociation?

Much of the development of contemporary relational technique over the past thirty years has been stimulated by challenges similar to those Ferenczi grappled with in the 1920s and early 1930s, which led him to realize that each analytic journey is actually two journeys, requiring a conjoint working through of complementary personal obstacles, with the potential for deepening self-awareness and working through new realms of psychic experience for both participants. While psychoanalytic work is defined in part by the intention of the therapist to help the patient to grow and to change, it is also at its best a process of mutual transformation.

Ferenczi's experiments in direct, expressive, countertransference utilization opened doors to new realms of psychoanalytic exploration, expanding the possibilities for deepening and enlivening analytic work. Beyond careful, disciplined attention to the analyst's personal reflections and affect states in the presence of the patient, made possible by the depth of commitment to his or her personal analysis (and ongoing self-analysis), Ferenczi came to recognize that such foundational commitments must be complemented by careful, receptive attention to patients' views of us as well. He recognized that our patients' perceptions serve not simply as windows into the unconscious transferences awaiting interpretations meant to illuminate their own unconscious life, but also as signals that can orient us through our countertransference to our own unconscious life as well.

In this chapter, I will focus on two themes that were central to Ferenczi's thinking about the analytic relationship and the nature of therapeutic change: the dialogue of unconsciouses and mutual analysis. They represent linked focal points in Ferenczi's *The Clinical Diary*, illuminating a path for therapeutic exploration and the transformation of clinical technique first forged by Ferenczi, and further pursued today as relational psychoanalysis continues to evolve.

Ferenczi, Freud, and the Dialogue of Unconsciouses between Analyst and Patient

Ferenczi's dedicated efforts to explore in depth the implications of understanding the relationship between patient and analyst as "a dialogue of unconsciouses" followed from his discovery, described as early as 1910, of an unconscious dialogue central to human relations, development, communication, and symptom formation. He would come to understand over time that unconscious dialogues have special relevance in the psychoanalytic situation itself, where attention to, clarification, and elaboration of unconscious realms of experience are important components of the engine that drives therapeutic action.

In a 1915 paper describing a case he conducted in 1910, Ferenczi described symptom formation in a young man he was treating for impotence, megalomania, and a "peculiar voice symptom" (he had two different voices: a high soprano voice and a fairly normal baritone voice). Ferenczi came to understand through the course of this analysis that these symptoms constituted the outcome of a series of communications between the young man and his mother, of which neither had the slightest awareness. Ferenczi's stunning insight was that the source of his patient's symptoms could be found in the unconscious of his mother! "In my opinion," Ferenczi noted, "we have to do here with one of those numerous cases that I am in the habit of calling Dialogues of the Unconscious, where namely, the unconscious of two people completely understand themselves and each other, without the remotest conception of this on the part of the consciousness of either" (p. 109).

As the years passed, and Ferenczi continued to track the secret responsiveness of one unconscious to another, his grasp of how psychological and psychogenic symptoms are co-created came to have an increasingly prominent place in Ferenczi's understanding of the therapeutic relationship and of therapeutic action. Ferenczi's understanding of the bi-directional, reciprocal nature of communication between therapist and patient at an unconscious level that shaped their experience of the therapy would forge a deep divide in the way Ferenczi and Freud viewed the therapeutic process, psychoanalytic technique, and the nature of the relationship between analyst and analysand. And so two roads diverged in the psychoanalytic woods.

While for both pioneers, the analyst's attention to and ability to grasp the unconscious experience of the patient was fundamental to their method, a fateful difference emerged in their understanding of the nature of relations between the patient's unconscious and that of the analyst. From its inception in Freud's thought, the unconscious mind of therapist and patient had been at the center of the discipline of psychoanalysis, involving two minds engaged with each other, at both conscious and unconscious levels of experience. The revelation of unconscious dimensions of human minds that shaped experience was Freud's groundbreaking discovery, essential to the process of psychoanalytic work, a key to its method and its therapeutic action. "It is a very remarkable thing," wrote Freud (1915, the same year that Ferenczi first formulated his understanding of dialogues of the unconsciouses), speaking of what was quintessentially psychoanalytic about the kind of conversation that psychoanalytic work entailed, "that the unconscious of one human being can react upon that of the other, without passing through the conscious mind" (p. 140).

Freud (1912) recognized that the analyst's state of mind in free floating attention was the requisite counterpoint to the patient's commitment to the fundamental rule of free association and the sine qua non of analytic listening. He taught that the analyst's unconscious must be the prime instrument of the endeavor. "The analyst must bend his own unconscious like a receptive organ toward the transmitting unconscious of the patient. He must adjust himself to the patient as a telephone receiver is adjusted to the transmitting microphone. Just as the receiver transmutes the electrical oscillations induced by the sound waves back again into sound waves, so is the physician's unconscious able to reconstruct the patient's unconscious, which has determined his free associations" (p. 115–116).

For Freud, the analyst's role was to decipher the unconscious of his patient with his own, while the patient remained naïve to what lay beneath, the workings of his therapist's mind. The analyst's disciplined efforts to remain hidden, an anonymous blank screen, were conceived as fundamental to his technique and were meant to sustain a pristine field in which the patient's mental productions could emerge endogenously, uncontaminated by the actual person of the therapist. Analytic relations were not perceived in dialogic terms when it came to the workings of the unconscious. Rather, the process was conceived as a monologue of the patient's free associations to be deciphered by the analyst, functioning as an observer rather than as a participant, an interpreter rather than a co-creator. The analyst showed the patient what he came to understand about his or her unconscious through the interpretations that he (the analyst) alone provided. Freud believed that he could view the unconscious of his patient from a kind of blind viewing post, his own unconscious safely out of view. He had anticipated the telephonic mute button in his telephonic metaphor by almost a century!

Ferenczi's revelation that communication between patient and analyst, on an unconscious level, took place on a two-way line would ultimately set the two (and psychoanalysis itself) on divergent paths of psychoanalytic understanding. Ferenczi realized that neither participant is privileged when it comes to hearing the sounds of his own unconscious, while both had the advantage when it came to apprehending the unconscious of the other. This insight upended the fundamental bulwark of the analyst's anonymity and neutrality and introduced a new set of problems and opportunities that flowed from the recognition of a far more permeable and translucent boundary between patient and analyst than had been previously conceived.

As Ferenczi wrote in the diary (Dupont 1988, p. 84), "when two people meet for the first time, an exchange takes place, not only of conscious, but of unconscious stirrings. Only analysis could determine for both why inexplicitly to either of them, sympathy or antipathy has developed in either of them. Ultimately I meant by this that when two people converse, not only a conscious dialogue takes place, but an unconscious one, from both sides. In other words, next to the attention cathected conversation, or parallel to it, a relaxed dialogue is also pursued." Ferenczi realized that Freud's effort to keep his own unconscious contribution to the therapeutic situation to himself could only go so far and that a "relaxed" dialogue, unconscious to unconscious, would inevitably take place, unfettered by conscious intentions, whether the analyst liked it or knew it or not.

In exploring the intricate, delicate choreographies of "dialogues of unconsciouses" as their movement shaped the psychoanalytic field of experience, Ferenczi noted that a patient's perspicacity regarding the sensitivities and vulnerabilities of the analyst is often obscured, as the patient is moved to protect the therapist from insights that he has reason to think the therapist would be loath to hear.

Ferenczi observed that a confusing maze of collusive mutual avoidances often left the therapist and patient running around in circles, with mystifications exacerbated by the very elements of psychoanalytic technique meant to clarify them: Ferenczi concluded that "natural and sincere behavior constitutes the most appropriate and favorable atmosphere in the analytic situation: desperately clinging to a theoretical approach is quickly recognized by patients as such, and instead of telling us (or even admitting it to themselves) they use the characteristic features of our own technique, or one-sidedness, in order to lead us ad absurdum" (p. 1).

The reciprocal nature of the ways in which we come to read one another is an aspect of what a "dialogue of unconsciouses" describes. Ferenczi's efforts to create a sufficiently elastic technique and psychoanalytic frame to accommodate this finding and to help patient and therapist alike through the thickets of their unconscious contributions to shaping the therapeutic (or antitherapeutic) process is what fueled his experiments in mutual analysis.

Mutual Analysis and the Dialogue of Unconsciouses

The ways in which a sense of mutuality at the heart of the therapeutic process came to be seen as the *sine qua non* of deeply transformative work and a fundamental principle that guided Ferenczi's experiments with psychoanalytic technique grew out of his understanding of the "dialogue of unconsciouses." Ferenczi's recognition of his own resistance to the awareness of aspects of his own countertransference which his patients had grasped and about which they had steadfastly been trying to inform him led to his pursuit of mutual analysis. His efforts to encourage his patients to offer their most brutally honest assessments of him took many different forms. In one case, with his patient RN, mutual analysis meant a literal switching off of the roles of patient and analyst, from session to session. With other patients, the mutual analytic process was more seamlessly integrated into the back and forth of therapeutic sessions in a way that is better reflected in the kind of quotidian mutual explorations of transference and countertransference as an integral part of therapeutic relations, in which role asymmetries between analyst and patient are steadfastly maintained.

Ferenczi's efforts flowed from his recognition that the inevitable limits of his self-awareness meant that he needed to listen to his patients in new ways: "It is in fact what led to the story of the origins of the most recent modification. The motive for reversing the process (the analyst being analyzed) was an awareness of an emotional resistance, or more accurately, of the obtuseness of the analyst" (Dupont 1988, p. 85). The possibility should not be rejected out of hand that the analyst's habit of identifying any obstacle encountered as resistance on the part of the patient can be misused in an equally paranoid, that is delusional way, for the projection or disavowal of his own complexes (p. 26), a phenomenon that his patients were the first to identify.

Ferenczi came to recognize that some of what had been understood as the patient's transference represented an iatrogenic response to the process itself, to an analytic technique that in representing the analyst as neutral observer rather than a participant bearing his own subjectivity and unconscious contribution to the proceedings, could subject the patient to a kind of gas lighting effect. "A part of what we call the transference situation is actually not a spontaneous manifestation of feelings in the patient, but is created by the analytically produced situation, that is created by analytic technique. At the very least, the interpretation of every detail as expressing a personal affect toward the analyst, which Rank and I perhaps exaggerated, is likely to produce a kind of paranoid atmosphere, which an objective observer could describe as a narcissistic, specifically erotomaniacal delusion of the analyst. It is possible that one is all too inclined to assume too quickly that the patient is either in love with us or hates us" (Dupont 1988, p. 95).

Ferenczi's explorations in mutual analysis constituted his effort to explore the implications for psychoanalytic technique of his discovery that in the psychoanalytic situation, no less than in other forms of intimate human relations, unconscious communication takes place on a two-way street. This insight made possible the understanding that our patients take note of and develop hypotheses regarding our own ways of being and relating, including those that elude our consciousness in much the same way that we dedicate ourselves to attending to aspects of our patient's inner lives of which they are unaware. It was his dawning recognition of his patient's sensitivity to aspects of his own psychic life to which he had little or no access that led him to explore the possibilities that a mutual form of analysis might help him to help them.

When his patient, RN, first shared her insights into his own inner psychic life, he denied their relevance, interpreting them as transference in the usual way. But as she persisted in her interpretation of her analyst's blind spots, Ferenczi began to listen and found that his "counter analysis confirmed, almost word for word the assertions of the analysand" (Dupont 1988, p. 85). As Ferenczi delved deeper into his own psychic life, with her insistent "help," he began to recognize that what she had seen, what he had up until now understood as a reflection of her transference and projections actually represented an accurate picture of aspects of himself that he had failed to see. Whatever his patients' reflections about him had to tell him about their minds, they provided quite accurate portrayals of his as well.

The recognition of such forms of mutuality in the psychoanalytic dyad includes the appreciation of the limits of self-awareness that each person's unconscious imposes, as well as its potential for generating insights into the mind of the other. In a vivid passage in the diary, in one of the earliest demonstrations of how the analysis of the patient and analyst may converge, Ferenczi shows how his analysis of RN, involved not one, but two analyses taking place simultaneously. Neither analysis could have taken place without the other. "The patient feels that this dream fragment is a combination of the unconscious contents of the psyches of the analysand and the analyst. The analyst is for the first time, to link emotions with the above primal event (his own memory) and thus endow that event with the feeling of a real experience. Simultaneously, the patient succeeds in gaining insight, far more penetrating than before, into the reality of these events that have been repeated so often on an intellectual level. ... It is as though two halves had combined to form a whole soul. The emotions of the analyst combine with the ideas of the analysand, and the ideas of the analyst (representational images) with the emotions of the analysand: in this way the otherwise lifeless images become events, and the empty emotional tumult acquires an intellectual content" (Dupont 1988, p. 14).

The analysis made possible a fuller integration of thoughts and feelings for both patient and analyst, enlivening the work as it did so, a phenomenon to which

Ferenczi referred in his final diary entry. Writing shortly before his death in 1933 under the heading, "Mutuality—Sine Qua Non," Ferenczi raised the following question: "must every case be mutual, and to what extent?" His answer: "An attempt to continue analyzing unilaterally. Emotionality disappeared; analysis insipid. Relationship—distant. Once mutuality has been attempted, one-sided analysis is no longer possible, not productive" (Dupont, 1988, p. 213). Now the question: must every case be mutual—and to what extent?

These last words ("once mutuality has been attempted, one-sided analysis is no longer possible") summed up the findings of his final year of clinical, constituting a kind of last will and testament to his psychoanalytic progeny.

It is a remarkable fact of psychoanalytic history that Ferenczi's last words of psychoanalytic speculation, the echoing question that he left us with (in 1932), was finally sprung from his psychoanalytic grave with the publication of his diary in 1988, the same year that Stephen Mitchell's *Relational Concepts in Psychoanalysis* (the first explicitly relational text) was published, and the New York University Relational Track came into being, establishing the relational perspective as an active, vital psychoanalytic orientation at a major psychoanalytic training program in the United States. With the publication of the diary, the first generation of relational psychoanalysts discovered an ancestor whose work conducted some sixty years earlier offered inspiration, affirmation and a treasure trove of clinical accounts that illuminated the journey that they were now themselves undertaking.

From our current vantage point, Ferenczi's question (and response) read as a trail marker pointing the way forward into the future of psychoanalysis as he envisioned it—a future that we now inhabit. The findings of his lifelong psychoanalytic investigations, pushed to the limits in his final year, dedicated to taking his mutual analytic investigations as far as time would allow, revealed that there could be no turning back.

Unconscious Dialogue and Mutual Analysis Today

Ferenczi's discoveries of the ways in which psychoanalysis is most vital and transformative when practiced as a radically collaborative, mutual process, has come to be a core operating principle for many analysts working today. A lone voice in 1932 when he proposed his revisionist reconstruction of the way psychoanalysis should be practiced, Ferenczi would be pleased to find a psychoanalytic culture today in which his vision has been substantially realized. The recognition of the ways in which increased personal self-awareness and growth of patient and analyst as integrally linked is widely taken for granted among relationally informed therapists today, having incorporated the very insight that Ferenczi chased down the rabbit hole in a solitary leap of faith when he became convinced that his patient was in a privileged position to give him the analysis he needed in order to be able to analyze her. He found that to reach a patient in the deepest possible way, complementary areas of his own psychic life inevitably became engaged, resonating like a tuning fork connecting one unconscious to another. He could no longer sustain the illusion of the neutral, dispassionate, objective observer. He came to see instead that important aspects of himself were exposed to his patients whether he meant such exposure or not, and that far from countertransference detritus, such communications played an important role in the analytic process itself.

Benjamin Wolstein (1993), who recorded his discovery of Ferenczi through the diary and his realization of his personal psychoanalytic ancestry to him by way of his own analyst (Clara Thompson, DM in the diary), recounted a vignette from his analysis to me in my analysis with him. In referring to something that Thompson had said or done in a session, he inquired of her about what she took to be its countertransference basis. She responded that she would consider his question in her own self-analysis: it didn't belong in his, she averred. He responded in a way that captured the spirit of Ferenczi and his own, recognition of the ways that transference and countertransference interpenetrate. Since countertransference is an evoked response to the patient, its presence offers the potential through its joint exploration to shed light on both participants, in much the way that the exploration of transference does. Wolstein reported that he replied, "Well, if it doesn't belong in my analysis, what is it doing in here?" Wolstein shared that personal vignette with me to encourage me to take my analysis of his countertransference as far as we both were capable of taking it, expressing an analytic value which constituted an important dimension of his own clinical and theoretical work (1975, 1977, 1983, 1992, 1997), and which has undoubtedly played an important role in informing my own approach.

Mutuality is inherent in many forms of human relatedness that are growth producing and healing. For many analysts working relationally today, the absence of mutuality and reciprocity in a psychoanalytic relationship is not so much a matter of preferred technique as a symptom of analytic sclerosis. Its relative absence in a psychoanalytic couple may be a warning sign; a symptom of what ails patient or therapist, or something gone awry in the unique mix of these two personalities, warranting curiosity, and the joint exploration of its parameters. Such joint exploration of personal obstacles within the therapeutic dyad is often a key to opening the process to new possibilities and experiences and crucial to understanding communications that are taking place in enacted dimensions of experience, and to identifying dissociative and restrictive processes at work in patient or therapist (Bass, 2003).

Both Sides Now: Forms of Mutual Analysis in Contemporary Relational Work

To employ a Joni Mitchell lyric originally referring to life and to love, analytic therapists are in a position to look at therapy from both sides now: that is, with reference to their experience as patients as well as therapists. This allows us to take note of a paradox at the center of traditional understandings of the analytic process:

when it comes to the limits of awareness of ourselves imposed by our own uncon-scious, and our capacity to apprehend something that is unconscious in another, we come to see that both our limits and capacities are not distributed according to our assigned roles in any given therapeutic encounter. So we come to ask: during the hours of the week that we spend as patients, do the powers of observation that we rely on during our working hours forsake us? Does a patient's capacity to perceive the unconscious psychic experience of others, including his psychoanalyst, shut down by virtue of taking the socially defined role of patient?

Ferenczi's disruptive discovery that this was indeed not the case resonates power-fully for many relational therapists today: transference notwithstanding, the patient sometimes may have the greatest insight into what is troubling the analyst, who may be encountering aspects of himself, and trouble spots, for the first time, as they are evoked and identified by the patient. Such was Ferenczi's experience with RN, who saw aspects of Ferenczi with which he had been unfamiliar. His own analysis with Freud had in fact failed to draw his attention to facets of himself that emerged only as they became implicated in his work with patients. Ferenczi attributed their joint failing to the limits of the brief training analyses characteristic of the time. He pointed out that it was not unusual for patients with whom he worked to have had far more analysis than he, and this form of asymmetry placed severe limits on many analyses. He urged more intensive training analysis, carried to "rock bottom" as a necessary corrective. Yet, we find today that notwithstanding the extensive, and often multiple analyses of which contemporary analysts avail themselves, that we nevertheless frequently encounter unfamiliar and anxiety-fraught aspects of our-selves in our work with our patients. I do not believe that such observations suggest that the analyst's analysis has been found wanting, though such encounters with oneself do often properly lead to a therapist's decision to pursue further therapy or supervision: rather, we recognize that no analysis can ever be "complete," and that new challenges to our psychic equilibrium and new opportunities for deepening self-awareness inevitably arise in the cauldron of deep analytic work.

We take note, whether from behind the couch, sitting or lying upon it, that when analytic work is stalling, or at impasse, the analyst's anxieties, inhibitions, and personal restrictions are frequently as prominent in the mix of troubles as the patients'. We work in our own analysis, and in supervision when it is good enough and safe enough, and with our patients themselves when we are both capable of it and interested, on what it is that is restricting the range of our thought and responsiveness. Our most challenging "difficult" patients are usually those in whom we encounter parts of ourselves with which we are unfamiliar and uncomfortable, which we cannot bear to recognize. Further personal work is required to keep pace with these patients and allow us to accompany them into realms of experience as yet untraveled, and much of this work takes place in the analysis itself.

A patient with whom I work recently noted, upon the completion of his final analytic clinical paper requirement for training, that if I read his paper, I would be likely to think he was writing about himself, so identified was he with the kinds of issues with which his patient was struggling. I have found that analysts in their training years and beyond are often struck by the ways in which issues that they recently confronted in their own analysis begin to appear regularly in their work with patients, and vice versa. It is not unusual for an analyst in analysis to say something like: my patient is like me. I, too, have an eating disorder (or a sexual problem, or a marital problem, or a money problem), not so different from that of my patient. A patient of mine recently said: "My patient just asked me to reduce her fee, because she doesn't want to take money from her husband for her therapy. But, even so, she has more money than I do. She actually earns more than I do, and her husband is wealthy. I find myself handling this in an awkward way, and submitting to her request against my will, because I find that I am too anxious to face this squarely with her. It is hard for me to know how to explore her worry about money, because my worry about money is getting in the way."

Another patient, speaking about a patient of hers that is thinking about ending therapy, noted the strong anxieties that are activated by such thoughts. "I find that I get quite anxious when she brings up the question of ending. My referrals have been down lately, and I am worried about my finances. But I am not sure that that is the main thing. I think when a patient is talks about ending therapy, it brings up for me a question about how good an analyst I am. This makes it difficult to explore her thoughts about stopping, what it means to her in a genuinely curious way, rather than something that I have a personal stake in. So I tend to either respond to it as though I am trying to talk her out of it, or I get very neutral about it because I don't want her to feel that I need her to stay." In each of these cases and many more, the work of the patient and the therapist is interpenetrating, as they worked out complementary areas of conflict, anxiety, and shame conjointly. We might say that they were working things out together. Analytic work can profitably be seen as a process of mutual working through of issues that touch therapist and analyst alike.

This does not mean that patient and therapist work together as Ferenczi did with his patient RN, switching roles from session to session. How could he have risked such boundary blurring and role negating self-exposure? With hindsight, the benefit of what we have learned from Ferenczi and others, and the development of relational technique over the past three decades, we see that Ferenczi was struggling to find a way to work with and through his countertransference together with his patients. His experiments in mutual analysis, harrowing as they were at times, constituted his initial (and as it turned out, final) creative efforts to make therapeutic use of his encounters at the edge of his patients' and his own deepest vulnerabilities. But Ferenczi's motivation to risk exposing such vulnerability to patients whom he had little reason to trust came from his startling insight into the potential of the psychoanalytic situation. He realized that his patient needed to give him the psychoanalysis he needed to give her the psychoanalysis that she needed.

Her psychoanalysis and his were woven into a single process and became indistinguishable. She drew his attention to aspects of his own unconscious life, as it was making its appearance in hers.

One understanding that has emerged in contemporary relational work is that the image of the anonymous, neutral analyst is a fiction (Singer, 1977). Ferenczi may have been the first to observe that while the analyst may sit behind the patient who reclines on the couch, the analyst's perch is no place to hide. "Subtle, barely discernable differences in handshake, the absence of color or interest in the voice, the quality of our alertness or inertia in following and responding to what his patient brings up. All these, and a hundred other signs, allow the patient to guess a great deal about our moods and feelings" (Dupont 1988, p. 35). The analyst's efforts to avoid personal transparency and to eschew self-disclosure, essential elements of a classical theory of technique, does not go unnoticed by the patient, suggesting to the patient an air of secrecy that is not without consequences to the way analytic work unfolds, and to the quality of the therapeutic relationship. "Any kind of secrecy, whether positive or negative in character, makes the patient distrustful; he detects from little gestures—form of greeting, handshake, tone of voice, degree of animation, etc.—the presence of affects, but cannot gauge their quantity or importance; candid disclosure regarding them enables him to counteract them, or to instigate countermeasures with greater certainty"(Dupont 1988, p. 11).

Ferenczi explored such "countermeasures" against retraumatization and other iatrogenic exacerbations of patients' difficulties in the various experiments to mutual analysis that he attempted. Although there is wide variation among contemporary relational therapists when it comes to matters of technique, many therapists today apply some version of mutual analysis as a matter of course, in attending to intersubjective dimensions of the dyad, in negotiating enactments and, more generally in working to expand mutual awareness within the transference–countertransference field. Interest in and curiosity about what the patient detects about the analyst's contribution to the process is central to the way that many therapists work. The recognition that therapeutic conversation constitutes a two-way dialogue at both conscious and unconscious levels informs therapeutic choices in fundamental ways that have been incorporated into our quotidian approach to technique.

An Example of Ordinary Mutual Analysis

A patient of mine recently noticed me yawning during a session and inquired whether I had not gotten enough sleep, whether I was affected by the overheated atmosphere of the room, or whether he was "making me" sleepy. The question was a genuine inquiry, not rhetorical in form or tone. He was interested in the impact he had on others and believed that he could be boring at times, and we were accustomed to using our experiences in therapy as a point of departure for exploration of his inner life and its interpersonal representations. I had yawned without paying much attention to the origins of the psychic state the act might have represented. Rather than starting with a query about his "fantasy" about what my yawn might signify, I thought about his question and told him that the combination of not having gotten a great night's sleep and the heat of the room as he suggested were probably behind the yawn, at least as far as I knew at the time.

At the same time, I acknowledged that what I "knew" was unlikely to be the entire story, and I would be interested in coming to know more about it if we could. I wondered if he might have entertained other hypotheses about my condition. Had he noticed a feeling, a thought, a physical sensation, or anything that might turn out to be relevant to his observation of my physical/mental state as represented by the yawn? Did he notice something in himself or in me that might shed some light on what the sleepy symptom might represent for me, for him, or between us? My interest was not as a transference fishing expedition. In noticing and thinking about my yawn, perhaps he had touched upon an area of my lack of awareness, something that I was missing, in my own experience or his. I didn't think that the occasional yawn in a session was unusual for me, as I know that I frequently have too little sleep, so I wondered if there might have been something in particular that drew his attention to the phenomenon this time. Had he picked up something in the session that may have raised a question about my responsiveness to him, and perhaps put it together with the yawn, to come up with his query about what it might suggest? Whatever caught his attention may well have escaped my awareness altogether, having been enacted in the autonomic form of a yawn.

His question stimulated my own curiosity about whether something in my physical/affective state was relevant to something transpiring in the session. I noticed that with my own curiosity primed, my head had cleared and I felt suddenly as if I had had a much better night's sleep. I also knew that any further insight into the matter was as likely to come from his associations and introspections as my own. After a minute of quiet reflection on both our parts, he said it occurred to him that he had had some thoughts about me, before my yawn, that he hadn't bothered to mention. It seemed possible to him that I registered some holding back on his part, which I might have experienced in some subliminal way as soporific. Now that we were thinking about it together, he was able to hone in on the thought that had eluded us, and we were able to delve further into considering what might have made the missing thoughts go missing. The conversation came to include his further ideas about how it was that he lost track of what he was thinking before he could tell me (it didn't feel like a conscious choice), as well as his astute sense of why his losing track of the thought might have had the effect of "making me foggy." His insight into the nature of my response and how it related to what he sensed about me felt accurate. His construction of the moment included observations and speculations about the way I unconsciously respond to information withheld, leading me to new insights about its origins in my own history. This didn't seem necessary to either of us to pursue. As Ferenczi came to recognize, the patient's analysis of the analyst proceeds "only to the extent that the patient's needs require it" (Dupont 1988, p. 34). Our discussion of the yawn, its likely origins in both of us, and newly emergent links to other moments in our therapy that we now could consider retrospectively was helpful to both of us and led each of us to greater awareness about ourselves, each other, and our relationship.

Conclusion

The centrality of psychoanalytic mutuality is, for me, at the heart of what makes psychoanalysis relational and distinguishes its unique approach to listening and engaging. We see the evidence of a dialogue of unconsciouses shaping therapeutic work in a variety of ways, some of which are taken up directly between patient and therapist, while others operate at a more implicit level. An analysand of mine, a therapist herself, found that as she was beginning to think new kinds of thoughts in her own therapy, her patient began to move into new, parallel areas of his own. The opposite of an "attack on linking," as Bion (1959) has described, the freeing of space within the therapist's mind seems to make new connections possible for the patient too, in a kind of mutual linking process. My patient realized that her patient had not been able to risk thinking about certain aspects of her own experience until she (her therapist) could inhabit a place in her own mind where she could receive these thoughts and think about them along with her. She believed that her patient sensed her greater comfort in areas that they had both struggled with, which made it possible for her own patient to begin to do new work. It seemed to my patient that her patient had waited until she was ready to take the next step. In the exploration that followed, her patient was able to say that she had sensed a shift in her therapist that had preceded a shift of her own.

The recognition of the bi-personal, bi-directional, and mutually transformative quality of analysis is central to a relational perspective. A special kind of analytic expertise is born from the experience we gain pursuing the pathways of our inner lives, as well as that of our patients, as they intersect and interpenetrate in the work. Therapeutic work is a process of joint self-discovery, in which each dyad finds unique ways to expand the possibilities for deep and transformative experience, encountering limits, and finding ways of transcending them, as far as it is capable.

In discussions of psychoanalytic mutuality, the asymmetrical aspect of the psychoanalytic situation is often emphasized. Concerns about the roles and boundaries that protect therapeutic work are meant to minimize abuses of power and outright abuses. Analytic discipline requires different things of us as analysts and patients. We cannot function optimally as either patient or analyst without taking our different roles and responsibilities to heart. These distributions of responsibilities involve largely conscious identifications, commitments, and intentions represented by the structuring of the analytic frame, however flexible and elastic it may be. When it comes to our own unconscious processes, these asymmetries recede into the background. Benjamin Wolstein used to say (personal communication) that we get the patients we need. I have found that the transference–countertransference field of analysis is a realm particularly well suited to a mutually constructed working-through process. That is, the analyst and patient must engage in a way that challenges, stimulates, and expands the psychic models that they each have relied on up to that point. In that sense, psychoanalysis involves a kind of symmetry at a level of psychic experiencing and processing that facilitates change and transcends more conscious professional asymmetries that define the workaday assignment of daily responsibilities in the work.

If the analyst's discipline requires holding the asymmetrical elements of therapeutic work in mind, the analyst's art includes a softer focus, to create a comfortable atmosphere for the emergence, identification, and elaboration of unconscious experience from both sides.

As Loewald (1975) put it, patient and analyst, each in his own way, become both artist and medium. "For the analyst as artist, his medium is the patient in his psychic life; for the patient as artist, the analyst becomes his media. But as living human media they have their own creative capabilities so that they are both creators themselves" (p. 369).

The dawning recognition that we are all swimming in the same psychic waters is the linchpin of relational psychoanalysis and leads to new ways of understanding the skills that make up psychoanalytic technique. Each therapist finds his or her own way to sustain the elasticity that allows for a rigorous, flexible enough frame (to support the asymmetrical necessities of the work) and a listening stance that is disciplined in its intent yet softly focused, allowing us to remain receptive to what we come to know about ourselves as we come to know our patients. What we find in our patients' analysis points us toward the patient and toward ourselves too. This is what ultimately makes every analysis a mutual analysis. Analyst or patient, we discover aspects of ourselves that we have not encountered before. Born out of our mutual exploration, we are challenged to gain access to new realms of experience, for our patients and for ourselves, in the relationship that we call psychoanalysis.

Note

1 An earlier version of this chapter appeared in *Psychoanalytic Dialogues*, 2015, Vol. 25. No 1. This current adaptation appears courtesy of the publisher.

References

Aron, L., & Harris, A. (Eds.) (1993). *The Legacy of Sándor Ferenczi*. London: The Analytic Press, pp. 1–36.

Bass, A. (2003). "E" Enactments in psychoanalysis: Another medium, another message. *Psychoanalytic Dialogues*, 13:657–675.

Bion, W. R. (1959). Attacks on linking. *International Journal of Psychoanalysis*, 40:308–315.

Dupont, J. (1988). *The Clinical Diary of Sándor Ferenczi*. Cambridge, MA: Harvard University Press. (Originally published 1932).

Ferenczi, S. (1915). Psychogenic anomalies of voice production. In S. Ferenczi, *Further Contributions to the Theory and Technique of Psychoanalysis*. New York: Brunner/Mazel, 1980, pp. 105–109.

Ferenczi, S. (1949). The confusion of tongues between adults and children: The language of tenderness and of passion (M. Balint, Ed.). *International Journal of Psycho-Analysis 30*(4), 225–230. (Originally published 1933).

Freud, S. (1912). Recommendations to physicians practicing psychoanalysis. *SE*, 12:109–120. London: Hogarth Press, 1958.

Freud, S. (1915). The unconscious. *SE*, 14:166–215. London: Hogarth Press, 1957.

Loewald, H. (1975). Psychoanalysis as an art and the fantasy character of the psychoanalytic situation. *J Am Psychoanal Assoc, 23*, 277–299.

Mitchell, S.A. *Relational Concepts in Psychoanalysis*. Cambridge, MA: Harvard University Press.

Mitchell, S. A. and Harris, A. (2004). What's American About American Psychoanalysis?. *Psychoanalytic Dialogues*, 14:165–191.

Singer, E. (1977). The fiction of analytic anonymity. In K. Frank (ed), *The Human Dimension in Psychoanalytic Practice*. New York: Grune & Stratton, pp. 181–192.

Wolstein, B. (1975). The psychoanalyst's shared experience and inquiry with his patient. *Journal of the American Academy of Psychoanalysis*, 3:77–89.

Wolstein, B. (1977). Countertransference, counterresistance, counteranxiety: The anxiety of influence and the uniqueness of curiosity. *Contemporary Psychoanalysis*, 13:16–29.

Wolstein, B. (1992). Resistance Interlocked with Countertransference—R.N., Ferenczi and American Interpersonal Relations. *Contemporary Psychoanalysis, 28*:172-189.

Wolstein, B. (1993). Sándor Ferenczi and American interpersonal relations: Historical and personal reflections. In L. Arons and A. Harris (Eds.), *The Legacy of Sándor Ferenczi*. Hillsdale, NJ: The Analytic Press.

Wolstein, B. (1997). The first direct analysis of transference and countertransference. *Psychoanalytic Inquiry*, 17:505–521.

15

FERENCZI WITH LACAN

A Missed Encounter[1]

Lewis Kirshner

Lacan was familiar with the work of Sándor Ferenczi, but of course came too late on the scene to have had personal contact with him. He did mention Ferenczi several times in his seminars and writings, and several features of his work clearly made an impact, both positive and negative. Ferenczi's independence from doctrinaire approaches and his freedom to experiment with analytic techniques could have made him a symbolic ancestor of Lacan. Nonetheless, this possible filiation of a pioneer innovator with a later dissident did not materialize and, in the end, as previous authors have remarked, the tone taken was dismissive. In this chapter, I summarize the major references to Ferenczi in Lacan's work and some of the parallels that readers have found between them. I use the case of G. from Ferenczi's *The Clinical Diary* (1988) as material to illustrate these affinities and differences, which can be viewed as representing complementary or mutually corrective positions.[2]

The relationship between Lacan and Ferenczi seems best described overall as a missed intellectual encounter. Ferenczi's thinking was perhaps strongest in grappling with the inherent problems of the analytic relationship and the application of Freudian technique to traumatized patients. His sensitivity to suffering led him to stress an active engagement and openness that was inimical to Lacan. Ferenczi's critique of the classic position of abstinence and reserve contrasts markedly with Lacan's endorsement of the impersonal stance characteristic of perhaps most French psychoanalysts of his day. Likewise, his attention to the impact of the analyst's inevitable countertransference speaks to the limitations of Lacan's highly abstract conception of the place of the Other in the transference. In this regard, Ferenczi's awareness of the power imbalance of the analytic situation and its potential to repeat trauma might have at least raised questions for Lacan about the difficulty of escaping the position of master in the analytic relationship.

Conversely, Lacan's notions of the imaginary, his reflection on the status of the subject, his notions of the real of trauma, and his attention to the spoken language of his patients, among other features of his work, offer a critique of many post-Ferenczian ideas about the effects of the "real relationship" between analyst and patient and the nature of their intersubjective engagement. That is, Lacan was strongest in delineating the various components of the analytic relationship that are often neglected in a two-person model. A focus on the dyad, Lacan taught, promotes mirroring and reciprocal identifications—what he called imaginary transference—and tends toward repetition, rather than opening the determining unconscious structure of the relationship for change. Likewise, although Ferenczi was certainly interested in language, he was prone to construct explanatory scenarios to explain what he heard, rather than use the ambiguity of language to access unconscious meanings. Perhaps in part for these reasons, it has taken many years for the current growing interest among Lacanian analysts in reconsidering the legacy of Ferenczi[3] to emerge.

Lacan (1953) did refer favorably to Ferenczi in his important "Rome Discourse" lecture, in which he set out his views on the centrality of speech in psychoanalysis, just at a time when the split of the Paris Society in which he played a major part had aroused concerns in the International Psychoanalytic Association about his bona fides as a psychoanalyst. Here he commented on "the confusion of tongues by which Ferenczi designated the law of the child/adult relationship" (1953, p. 37)—a sally directed at the "officiating mothers of psychoanalysis" who in his mind were replacing symbolization as the key process of the mother–child relation with object relations psychology (Melanie Klein, of course, being the central figure). Object relations theory was a *bête noire* for Lacan, a one-sided expansion of the imaginary register that was taking psychoanalysis in the wrong direction. Apart from this one comment, he did not take note of Ferenczi's interest in language either in this paper or in other places. In the same year, however, Lacan wrote a letter to Michael Balint in which he expressed admiration for Ferenczi (Lugrin, 2013).[4] Ferenczi's famous "Confusion of Tongues" paper (1932) was not published in French until some years later, and Ferenczi was known in France, as elsewhere, primarily as a troubled, if brilliant dissenter. Lacan's contemporary rival Granoff did read Ferenczi and made use of his work (Granoff, 2001), which may have served to further Lacan's distancing.

In his inaugural seminar of 1953–1954, Lacan recognized Balint as a disseminator of Ferenczian ideas, centered on "an emphasis on the relation between the analysand and the analyst, conceived as an interhuman situation and … implying a certain reciprocity" (Lacan 1953–1954, p. 209). Lacan consistently regarded contemporary work in this vein as a serious misunderstanding of psychoanalysis. He opposed Balint's position with what he termed "a radical intersubjectivity" (p. 217), a refraction of the complex field of interaction between two persons that he elsewhere theorized. The mirroring aspect of human relations and the exchanges of signifiers in Lacanian terms create an inevitable blurring of positions that must be taken into account, even though Lacan seems to have believed in the efficacy of the analyst's own analysis to solve or at least minimize this countertransference problem. The same session of the 1953–1954 seminar closes with praise for Ferenczi's recognition "in a magisterial fashion" (p. 219) of the importance for analysis of the manifestations of the child within the adult.[5]

Later, in his Royaumont lecture on "The Direction of the Treatment," Lacan (1958, p. 239) cites Ferenczi for posing "the question of the analyst's being ... almost fifty years earlier in the history of analysis." The question of *being*, perhaps inspired by his reading of Heidegger, is recurrent in Lacan's seminars. However, he does not take up this question in terms of the impact of the analyst's countertransference nor of his authority itself, as Ferenczi did. Speaking of Ferenczi's essay entitled "Introjection and Transference" (1909), he refers to him as the analyst "most tormented by the problem of analytic action." According to Lacan, the essay "anticipated by a long way all the themes later developed about this topic" (1958, p. 239). These bits suggest Lacan's awareness of Ferenczi's role in questioning received analytic wisdom and being open to experimentation—both of which figured prominently in Lacan's practice. He did comment that Ferenczi reevaluated his own modifications of technique, a desirable step prominently lacking in Lacan's writings.

In short, Ferenczi's ideas on "elasticity" of technique and on the analyst's "activity" might have made him a worthy predecessor for Lacan's experiments with variable length sessions and with taking actions in his treatments; yet this spiritual kinship was not acknowledged. Meanwhile, citation of Ferenczi gradually disappears from the seminars. However, in her biography of Lacan, Roudinesco mentions in passing that in 1973 he travelled to Budapest to speak with Imre Hermann about Ferenczi (Roudinesco 1997, p. 356). One would like to know what transpired during that conversation!

Returning to Lacan's important first seminar, which reviewed and challenged many post-Freudian conceptions of analytic technique and therapeutic action, we find a strangely harsh condemnation of Ferenczi's 1913 paper on the sense of reality. Lacan attributed to this paper a decisive and negative influence through its promotion of the idea of developmental stages (Lacan 1953–1954, p. 127), a notion he labelled "truly stupid," an inanity, and a kind of "poison." Although elsewhere Lacan inveighed against the fatuity of a developmental approach, which he set up in straw man fashion to imply a belief in the natural harmony of psychic growth, his choice of Ferenczi as an example seems misplaced. Ferenczi was far from holding any such simplified view of human development. Yet, if a tendentious reading of Ferenczi was far from unique in psychoanalytic circles, as famously illustrated by Jones' treatment in Volume 3 of his biography of Freud (1957), Lacan seems to have gone well out of his way to distance himself from any possible filiation. No doubt his attacks should be assessed in the context of Lacan's equivocal position within the International Psychoanalytic Association and the Paris Society, with its many hidden agendas, but we may also wonder about the threat to his originality that Ferenczi represented.

The remarkable absence of Ferenczi from Lacan's attention to trauma in his later writings may reflect a similar avoidance of a significant predecessor. Lacan's approach to trauma as the presence of an unsymbolized set of real physical experiences seems on its face a version of Ferenczi's notion of the unprocessed foreign body in the psyche (Garon, 2012). Moreover, Lacan's criticism of Melanie Klein in his Seminar VII that opposes the reality of trauma to her emphasis on fantasy almost demands a discussion of Ferenczi. Fantasies about traumatic experiences or the guilt evoked retrospectively by the memories of childhood fantasies do not negate the importance of the primal events, the real of traumatic experience, which may remain unrepresented in mental life and conscious memory. In Freudian terms, these events have left a trace of some kind but cannot be thought or communicated in signs. While obviously their attention to the reality of trauma belongs to different kinds of theory, Lacan's and Ferenczi's approaches redirected analysts to the impact of actual events and thereby departed from conventional analytic approaches of their time that emphasized fantasy over actuality.

One obvious difference between them is that Lacan's interest in trauma and the impact of "the real" was part of a metapsychological model and not an attempt to solve a pressing clinical problem, as was Ferenczi's effort in *The Clinical Diary*. Nonetheless, his concept of an inassimilable "real" that cannot be contained in the symbolic (of speech) suggests an implantation of otherness in the psyche that produces effects, like Ferenczi's notion of the foreign body. This is an old idea in trauma theory, coming from the original work of Freud and Breuer (1893).[6] The "Confusion of Tongues" paper more specifically addresses the incapacity of the child to translate the sexual messages coming to it from the adult, much as Freud first proposed with his concept of Nachträglichkeit and as Jean Laplanche, perhaps influenced by Lacan, emphasized in his innovative theory of "the fundamental anthropological situation" of human infancy. Although again differing in important respects, these authors all dealt with something in the child's experience of the adult that cannot gain direct mental representation in language but that insists psychically in some way and thereby produces effects. In the Case of G. in *The Clinical Diary*, Ferenczi (1988) speaks of his patient as an example of the cases "certainly not rare—in which ... incestuous fixation does not appear as a natural product of development but rather is implanted in the psyche from the outside" (p. 175).

The Case of G.

G. was a patient of Ferenczi treated in Budapest. She is described as having suffered the shock of witnessing the primal scene, which Ferenczi considered traumatic. Her parents appear to have endured a bad relationship (mother habitually unfaithful), and father turned to his daughter for affection. The mother is described as cold and unavailable, leaving her father when G. was ten years old, at which point she was placed in a new symbolic role as woman of the house. G. seems to have regarded the "passionate genitalization of the relationship with her father" (p. 177) inflicted on her by this promotion as the source of her distress, although there was no overt sexual contact described. The Oedipal situation was thereby "forced upon her." Ferenczi writes that it was only because of an adult seduction that what would otherwise have been a playful aspect of childhood development became pathogenic (he cites Freud for support, p. 178). The actual history seems vague here, perhaps because Ferenczi retained the Freudian idea of wishful fantasy being a predisposing factor for later traumatic impact.

What was Ms. G.'s real problem, and how does it relate to the analytic treatment of trauma? For Ferenczi, the process of analysis could not cleanly separate her difficulties in her family from her analyst's own subjective reality and its influence on the treatment. This realization led to his numerous efforts to modify the actualized transference by various maneuvers designed to create a more equal or less oppressive relationship and, by implication, a reparative experience. These clinical experiments do suggest at times a simplification of psychoanalysis as an "inter-human relationship" between two partners, as Lacan wrote. On the other hand, Ferenczi was extremely aware of how his own unconscious might impact on the patient and become part of a repetition of trauma, as indicated by the constant self-analysis in his diary. Many of his experiments in technique were aimed to avert this outcome, which has become a concern of contemporary analysts as well. Still, statements like "The presence of someone with whom one can share and communicate joy and sorrow (love and understanding) can HEAL the trauma. ... (like 'glue')" (p. 201) display a grandiose passion for cure (also the self-cure of "mutual forgiveness," p. 202) for which he was criticized. Ferenczi may have been excessive in his belief in the curative possibilities of a purified countertransference love and its implicit corollary of a whole subject to receive it (Kirshner, 1993). Of course, analysts continue to debate the nature of the intersubjective relationship and how it influences treatment.

The central issue in contrasting arguments about intersubjectivity, radical or otherwise, is how to conceive of the individual subject in the interaction of two separate persons. Lacan's writings are extremely relevant to this debate, as they constantly explore and reformulate traditional philosophical and psychoanalytic ideas about the nature of subjectivity. As noted, Ferenczi's contributions suggest points of discord with Lacanian principles about intersubjectivity. Perhaps most notably, he privileged the lived experience of transference–countertransference interaction in the here and now over dynamic causes and unconscious desires that may have determined it. To put it another way, he may have regarded the analytic relationship as a real encounter between complete subjects who can speak directly to each other. By contrast, Lacan saw the subject as constantly fading in relation to the linguistic content of speech, its tenuous sense of identity undermined by words and images expressed outside of conscious control. Moreover, the analyst's words are heard only in the immediate context of transference and cannot lead to any genuine authenticity of encounter.

In Ferenczi's brief report of his treatment of G., his presentation of the analytic experience, rather than resembling an objective case study, is constructed within a relationship, out of which grows a new entity that many contemporary analysts call "the analytic third." The "third" can represent a shared framework built up over time. In Ferenczi's rendering of this mutual construction with G., we discover a mythic story of a mother who has deserted her family, leaving behind a husband terrified of losing his remaining love relationship with his daughter and a daughter who has no sense of her own desires but identifies with the desire of others. At the base of this self-abandonment by G. lies her earlier experience of the primal scene, which, in Ferenczi's formulation, acted as a severe trauma, splitting off her affective, desiring self from a detached and intellectualized observing self. Her survival henceforth would depend upon her unconscious identification with the desire of her mother. G. describes the primal scene experience as one of betrayal and loss of confidence in her important relationships, which left her alone to deal with the traumatic situation by drastic means. Perhaps the being alone was itself the traumatic situation.

What Ferenczi is thinking about G.'s desire takes the form of what appears in retrospect to be a rather poor interpretation, which carries many implicit ways of defining the Oedipal situation and the unconscious sexual wishes of his patient. He declares that the domestic situation she has described as consisting of an abandoned, possessive father and a devoted daughter represented "a happy marriage." G. hears this depiction as a metaphor for her imputed wishes to take the mother's place as her father's partner, which results in a devastated reaction of betrayal and anger toward him. It seems that repetition of trauma, a confusion of fantasy and reality, has entered the analysis. She subsequently dreams of Ferenczi lying with her on the couch and then of the analyst A. Brill kissing her and arousing the beginning of an orgasm! Ferenczi immediately recognizes this as her unconscious reading of his own desires, as transmitted through the signifier "a happy marriage." He emphasizes her inability to reach orgasm, which he connects somewhat obscurely with a defensive or wishful identification with her mother in the primal scene. Perhaps he alludes to her alienation from her own desire. Clearly, this is a mistaken or, at best, partial interpretation of G.'s unconscious wishes. The text rather suggests the destructive effects of her father's possessiveness on her development and the overshadowing history of an absent mother. The sexual dream–fantasy can be understood in many ways but here suggests the power of the analyst's words to produce effects in the transference (as Ferenczi himself taught us).

Ferenczi's response to his mistake or countertransference enactment is to recant in a kind of cleansing of conscience, confessing that he has imputed adult sexual wishes to the child (but perhaps he was more accurately imputing childish sexual wishes to the adult patient)—an example of a confusion of tongues. His confession seems somewhat hypocritical, however, as shown by a subsequent note in *The Clinical Diary* on 8/24. He (1949, p. 209) then writes that "the child's fantasies were suddenly realized in the departure of the mother," suggesting his persistent formulation of G.'s classical Oedipal position. He also sees father's warning to G. not to be like her mother as forcing her to regard the incest fantasy as real—an ingenious but at best highly inexact interpretation. On the most obvious, superficial level, father's statement could be telling G. not to become a sexual woman like mother who would leave him for another man, but, instead, to remain his devoted daughter. Of course, we would want to listen to the patient's associations before leaping to such formulations, to which Ferenczi may have been prone. Lacan reminded analysts of the dangers of false certitude and supposed knowledge based on their ideas of the psychology of the patient. "When it comes to our patients, please give more attention to the text than to the psychology of the author—the entire orientation of my teaching is that" (Seminar II, p.153) was Lacan's aphorism.

A contemporary understanding of this situation with a focus on the intersubjective relationship might be instead that G.'s unconscious has become figured or organized symbolically in the field of the Other—that is, within a dialogue filled with messages about her position from the powerful analyst. Ferenczi's model in the "Confusion of Tongues" paper implicated the Other from the start in the creation of a traumatic experience, which was much more, he saw, than a matter of excessive stimulation. "Psychoanalysis," he wrote to Freud, "deals far too one-sidedly with obsessive neurosis and character analysis—that is, ego psychology ... overestimating the role of fantasy and underestimating that of traumatic reality." At its heart, traumatic reality, for him, consisted in a betrayal by the other. Given that the case of G. involves a young subject attempting to find her way in a family structure in which she is facing two vastly more powerful parents, it makes sense in her case to refer to Lacan's more generalized "big Other" than the specific persons ("others" like her parents).

Ferenczi and Lacan: A Complementary Reading

Many contemporary analysts in the relational and intersubjective schools who have been influenced by Ferenczi's clinical experience might concur with Lacan's pithy formulation that the unconscious is the voice of the Other. This means that the personal unconscious is an effect of exposure to language and the cultural symbolic order (the Other). The origins of the subject lie in its initial exchanges with the parental Other, and the diverse maternal/paternal responses to the child will provide its basic structures of subjective experience. As Ferenczi wrote, the infant does not have a self. It lacks "a protective skin, so that infants communicate with the environment over a much broader surface" (*The Clinical Diary*, June 30, p. 148). This statement speaks to the infant's enormous vulnerability to being shaped by the Other.

To further develop this theme of the influence of the parental Other, Lacan's conception of the importance of mirroring as foundational for the ego of the child is also relevant to Ferenczi's clinical thinking. At the mirror phase of Lacan, the child sees itself as a cohesive object in the image of the mother, founding the organization of the ego as imaginary (a product of images). Winnicott's different reading of this stage emphasized that the infant sees itself in the mother's affective responses to it (a kind of mirror, to be sure). His more interactive version of the mirror stage seems more compatible with subsequent infant research, yet it also describes the state of capture by an image of the mother (with its enigmatic affective messages). This form of influence by mirroring is not limited to early life. Narcissistic phenomena, for example, can be understood in part as attempts to identify with idealized images as a mirror to represent the self. Mirroring identifications are an attempt to reduce the flux of self to a concrete, durable entity. Ferenczi emphasized the exquisite sensitivity of his traumatized patients to be mirrored in his private feelings and judgments as though they could be defined by them. Hence, he made efforts at mutual analysis, to level the playing field between himself and his vulnerable patients.

Lacan repeatedly highlighted the danger of remaking the patient in the analyst's image (for example, by encouraging identification with the analyst, which he saw as the clinical goal of ego psychology). His concern with sidestepping the patient's imaginary fantasies and the risk of becoming a mirror for them supported his endorsement of the classical abstinent posture for the analyst. In addition, he conceived of the act of speech as conveying a demand for something—love in the first place. The more the analyst speaks, he taught, the more she reveals her lack and the desire that flows from it, which amounts to a seduction of the patient. Since the goal of analysis is the freeing of the patient to follow her own desire, it is important that the analyst as a person not want anything from her. Ferenczi might have reminded Lacan that silence does not protect the patient from the analyst and may even be more likely to repeat a traumatic situation of power imbalance (not to speak of other channels of affective communication).

Infant research, again opposing Lacan, confirms the importance of an active interplay of the infant's gestures and cries with the words and affects of the mother, perhaps especially because only the mother has command of language. In that sense, it is from the first a question of the infant's communications with the mother, not an unfolding internal process of id modulated by ego or an impersonal assimilation of a given structure, even if the mother in her all-importance for the infant transmits or represents the Other. Subjectivity (at least of the reflective or secondary type) involves a mediated emergence into the symbolic order, as a universal developmental sequence, with its hazards of going awry if the primary relationship is not "good enough." This fundamental point about development was implicit in Ferenczi's attention to the actual circumstances and events of early childhood (including what was left unspoken or denied). In this sense, he did take the developmental approach for which Lacan, emphasizing the constant reprocessing of psychic life in the *après-coup*, with its ongoing revision of prior meanings, accused him.

At the same time, Ferenczi's writings are consistent with Lacanian ideas about trauma and the divided role of the analyst in treatment, where the analyst represents both the specific other of transference (the person of the analyst) and the symbolic place of the generalized Other. As Other, the analyst generates a movement of the unconscious in the patient's speech, a revival of the process of his becoming a subject in the first place. The analytic process thereby furnishes further opportunity for symbolization of experience that has been excluded from thinking (the foreign bodies of which Breuer and Freud first spoke, 1893). A common ground for Ferenczi and Lacan might be here, in the definition of trauma as a failure of symbolization—a failure to capture or signify embodied and emotionally charged experiences. Verhaeghe, a contemporary Lacanian, has argued that the process of finding representations of experience depends on a link to the Other (Verhaeghe, 2004), which offers a bridge between Lacan and an object relational approach.

Taking this perspective, the essence of trauma can be redefined as the failure of the Other to provide an integrated affective–verbal representation of a joint (intersubjective) experience. It might be a product of pure neglect by a caretaker who has abandoned a distressed child—as in "fear of breakdown"—or the direct effect of an active abuse that remains unacknowledged or denied. Under optimal circumstances, exposure to the Other's signifying responses in early childhood enables the child to elaborate its experiences along associative semiotic pathways. Failure of the symbolic role of the Other, however, can lead to the splitting off of a fragment of life experience—a somatic memory lodged like a foreign body in the psyche that is inaccessible to the child's subjective consciousness. This unrepresented foreign element can return later in the form of symptoms or, as Lacan wrote, "in the real."

In the case of Ms. G., her traumatic memory became active as present experience within the unfolding transference–countertransference constellation, to which Ferenczi contributed a large and obvious part, repeating a past overstimulation or seduction (as he realized). Lacan would later describe this as the danger of an object relations (two-person) approach, creating a dyadic hothouse of shared fantasy. Ferenczi's behavior in the case of G. seems to be an example of this pitfall in which boundaries are blurred or lost because they lack a frame or code that provides symbolic meanings. The analytic relationship, Lacan insisted, cannot undo or literally replay an original experience. What is reproduced in analysis inevitably departs from the real of traumatic experience, which lacks an original symbolic inscription. What remains are the traces that can achieve new figuration through an expanding dialogic field. Perhaps Ferenczi, with his zeal to heal the original injury, was unclear about this limitation of analytic work. For Lacan, the important feature of analysis of trauma is not reliving, but the creative potential of language to build new chains of signifiers to represent the real. Around this issue, an approach holding in mind the contrasting Lacanian and Ferenczian positions may be most useful.

If the analyst does not naively seek to replace the lost primary objects in the manner of a rescue operation, derided by Lacan, she can still assume a symbolic caretaking function for the patient. Here, a rapprochement between Ferenczian and Lacanian positions may be possible. That is, the analyst can provide symbolic functions lacking in many early relationships—functions like recognition of the child as a separate person with "rights" in the world to be respected by a responsible parent. By maintaining an analytic attitude of respect for the otherness of the patient, acknowledging participation in the unfolding of the transference (much as a parent will monitor her own behavior), and remaining attentive to the patient's responses for indications of what may have been communicated unconsciously, the analyst supports a form of intersubjectivity analogous to the inaugural dialogues of the child with its mother. Although Lacan did not speak explicitly about the analyst taking this kind of active symbolic role, the general notion seems consistent with his views on the infant's process of subjectivation through its reciprocal exchanges with the mother.

On the other hand, just as Lacan's advocacy of abstinence can have an effect opposite to what was intended, an analyst's zeal to reverse early traumatic injuries can produce a paradoxical result. Attempting to become a "real object" to repair past wounds can revive a dyadic relationship of unequal power, intrusive influence, and lack of boundaries. In this way, too much investment in being the good Other can end up recreating in a new form an old abusive interaction. For this reason, Ferenczi's desire to use his personal sincerity and openness as a way to directly counteract the traumatic failure of the parents could be usefully modified by introducing a third position, a triangulation, in which the healing wishes of the analyst can be contextualized within the field of the Other. That is, the analyst has her own personal wishes and countertransference feelings towards the patient—loving or otherwise—but she also accepts a role as symbolic Other in the analytic setup. In that position, she is subjected to the condition of being a divided human being who is not the master of her own discourse nor of the messages she transmits, and who can only support, but not intentionally restore or repair, the subjectivity of her patient.

As noted, it may be in the area of technique that Ferenczi and Lacan seem most incompatible. Although Lacan talked about the unconscious being transpersonal (and thereby shared to some extent by both subjects in his radical intersubjective model), and also commented about the inevitability of a strong countertransference in any real analysis, he did not see the analyst as a true interactive partner. No doubt he would have seen this approach carried too far by current relational and intersubjective analysts. For him, the patient's transference (mostly unconscious) dictated the form of the relationship, which was not a relationship at all in the ordinary sense of the term. Lacan did not place the small other (o), the person of the analyst, at the heart of the analytic experience. Instead, he saw the patient's discourse as propelled by a transference to the big Other, who represents a potential source of knowledge about the unconscious, the whys and wherefores of her subjectivity. Again, this view of the analytic situation may be a useful corrective to an exaggeration of the relational component (versus the patient's own subjectivity as the focus of treatment). Of course, therapeutic interventions always come from a particular analyst and her countertransference, a point acknowledged by Lacan when he spoke of the analyst's interventions coming both from the registers of O and o (Lacan 1955, p. 132); yet given the asymmetrical form of the analytic relationship, the distinction between other and Other may be a question of emphasis more than substance. Lacan referred to the analyst as o in terms of his need to overcome his own resistances, while as O he was to remain mainly silent like the dummy in bridge (*le mort* in French, Lacan 1955, pp. 132–133). This doctrine can carry analysis to an extreme of unrelatedness, which, as Ferenczi saw, could also reproduce a form of trauma.

Lacan seems correct in insisting that the analyst represents something for the patient beyond the actual person sitting behind the couch, even if the direction of the dialogue is influenced by countertransference and the analyst's sentiments and interests. The inseparable combination of the personal and the role of Other endows the analyst with power and authority that can be misused, wittingly or unwittingly. Lacanians sometimes speak of an "oscillation" of the analyst's position to refer to the constant back and forth of listening and responding to the patient, in which every response sends a message communicating a kind of interpretation of what has been said. In this regard, Ferenczi gave us a powerful conception of the analyst as an attentive, if often wrong, participant listener who is being read constantly by the patient. By implication, the flow of the clinical dialogue grows from the intrication of the two subjectivities, but this may have more to do with shaping the expression of the transference than a shared co-creation like the "third."

Certainly, Ferenczi's clinical work presaged the contemporary shift towards a relational view of psychoanalysis as a mutually constructed, reparative process that revises a traumatic history. But the details of this model are still contested and may benefit from the Lacanian focus on the unconscious and the specific language (signifiers) expressed by the patient to a largely symbolic Other. These divergent conceptions of the analyst's role can be maintained dialectically in practice. That is, the analyst is not simply relating person to person, but is trying to aid the patient to recover something unidentified or unexpressed in conscious awareness.

Ferenczi may have been excessive in his belief in the curative possibilities of a purified countertransference love and its implicit corollary of a whole subject to receive it (Kirshner, 1993). In this respect, in reading *The Clinical Diary*, it seems to me that his dramatic confessions to analysands have a strained and not wholly convincing ring to them. Nonetheless, for all its flaws, the therapeutic model presented in *The Clinical Diary* has the considerable virtue of validating the analyst's participation in a way that could correct the Lacanian position. Combining their perspectives, I conclude that the essence of our work with traumatized patients lies in actively reestablishing the missing or lost link to the Other, which may be the ultimate ground of trauma (Kirshner, 1994; Verhaeghe, 2004).

Notes

1 An earlier version of this chapter appeared in the *Canadian Journal of Psychoanalysis/ Revue Canadienne de Psychanalyse*,Volume 23: 1 (Spring), 2015 and appears here with permission of the publisher.
2 A panel on this theme for which the case of G. was utilized was presented at the IPA biannual Congress in Rio de Janeiro in 2004.
3 See for example Barzilai, 1997; Gorog et al, 2010; Lugrin, 2013; and Solers 1985.
4 "I know, however, from psycho-analysis of neuroses that suppressed or repressed psychical material becomes in fact through the blocking of association a 'foreign body' in the mental life, which is capable of no organic growth and of no development, and that the contents of these 'complexes' do not participate in the development and constitution of the rest of the individual" (Ferenczi 1952, p. 144).
5 The text is not entirely clear—the phrase may have been Lacan's irony.
6 Without entering into Lacanian theory in detail, it suffices to say that the "big Other" is a structural concept incorporating the field of culture and language that organizes human subjectivity. Specific individuals are designated with a small o, as other.

References

Barzilai, S. (1997)."History is not the past": Lacan's critique of Ferenczi. *Psychoanalytic Review*, 84(4):553–572.
Breuer, J. and Freud, S. (1893). *On the Psychical Mechanism of Hysterical Phenomena: Preliminary Communication from Studies on Hysteria, Standard Edition of the Complete Psychological Works of Sigmund Freud, Vol. II, 1893–1895, Studies on Hysteria*, 1–17.
Ferenczi, S. (1932). The confusion of tongues between the adults and the child: The language of tenderness and passion, *International Journal of Psychoanalysis*, 30: 225–230, 1949.
Ferenczi, S. (1952). *First Contributions to Psycho-Analysis*. The International Psycho-Analytical Library, 45:1–331 (London: The Hogarth Press and the Institute of Psycho-Analysis).
Ferenczi, S. (1988). *The Clinical Diary of Sándor Ferenczi*, J. Dupont (ed) and M. Balint and N. Z. Jackson (trans.). Cambridge, MA: Harvard University Press.
Garon, J. (2012). Un écart qui estrange. *Revue Française de Psychosomatique* 2(42): 89–99.
Gorog, J. J., et al (2010). *Ferenczi après Lacan*. Paris: Hermann.
Granoff, W. (2001). *Lacan, Ferenczi et Freud*. Paris: Gallimard.
Jones, E. (1957). *Sigmund Freud: Life and Work, Vol. 3: The Last Phase, 1919–1939*. London: Hogarth Press.
Kirshner, L. (1993) Concepts of reality and psychic reality in psychoanalysis as illustrated by the disagreement between Freud and Ferenczi. *International Journal of Psychoanalysis*, 74:219–230.
Kirshner, L. (1994) Trauma, the good object, and the symbolic. *International Journal of Psychoanalysis*, 75:235–242.
Kirshner, L. (2007). Figurations of the real, representation of trauma in a dream. *The American Journal of Psychoanalysis*, 67:303–311.
Lacan, J. (1953). The field and function of speech in psychoanalysis. In B. Fink (trans.) *Écrits: A Selection*. New York: Norton, 2002, pp. 31–106.
Lacan, J. (1953–1954). *The Seminar of Jacques Lacan, Book I: Freud's Papers on Technique*, J. A. Miller (ed) and J. Forrester (trans.). Cambridge: Cambridge University Press, 1988.

Lacan, J. (1954–1955). *The Seminar of Jacques Lacan, Book II: The Ego in Freud's Theory and in the Technique of Psychoanalysis*, J. A. Miller (ed), S. Tomaselly (trans.), 1988.

Lacan, J. (1955). The Freudian thing. In B. Fink (trans.) *Ecrits: A Selection.* New York: Norton, 2002, pp. 107–137.

Lacan, J. (1958). The direction of the treatment and the principles of its power. In B. Fink (trans.), *Ecrits: A Selection.* New York: Norton, 2002, pp. 215–270.

Lacan, J. (1964). *The Four Fundamental Concepts of Psychoanalysis,* J. A. Miller (ed) and A. Sheridan (trans.). New York: Norton, 1977.

Lugrin, Y. (2013). *Lacan and Ferenczi: A Paradoxical Kinship?* Paper presented in London at Sincerity and Freedom in Psychoanalysis: A Studio Conference Inspired by Ferenczi's *The Clinical Diary*, London.

Roudinesco, E. (1997). *Jacques Lacan,* B. Bray (trans.). New York: Columbia University Press.

Solers, C. (1985). L'acte manqué de Ferenczi, Ornicar? N. 35. Paris: Navarin, 1985, pp. 81–90.

Verhaeghe, P. (2004). *On Being Normal and Other Disorders*, S. Jottkandt (trans.). New York: Other Press.

16

A SECOND CONFUSION OF TONGUES

Ferenczi, Laplanche, and Social Life

Eyal Rozmarin

My friend Marlowe is four years old. We play a lot together. Sometimes we play as two boys will: we chase each other around the house and wrestle. Marlowe loves to overpower me. I have to fight back, or he would not feel like he is winning. But in the end he has to win, or he will get upset. One Sunday afternoon, in the midst of such play, we are taking a breather. I am on his bed, lying on my back, panting. He is standing next to me with a big smile on his face. All of a sudden he slips and begins to roll off the bed. Things move in slow motion. I jump up and reach towards him. First, I'm alarmed, but then it seems that his fall is controlled, and it will be OK. But then his little back hits the dresser that stands next to his bed. I know that this hurts. "Are you okay, Marbs?" I ask, as I continue to reach over. The expression on his face is strange. He looks more frightened than hurt.

Before I know it, he is running away from me to the next room and crouching in the furthest corner. I follow him. He is crying and yelling, "You hit me! You hit me!" I hear myself saying "sweetie, I didn't hit you, you fell!" Now I feel strange. Of all the things to say or do now, is this the most urgent, that I explain what "really" happened? It is my instinct, I think in retrospect, to assure him that I did not mean to hurt him, so that he will let me get closer and see how badly he's hurt. But I am also aware that his parents are in the next room and might be already aware of the drama, and I know that I am saying it not only to him but also to them.

I am shocked that he really does look frightened, as if he really believes that I did it, on purpose. I can reason about it in retrospect, that his perception of the moment where he was standing next to me was different, that in his mind, it was not separate from the moment before and most likely after. Maybe for him, the game did not stop. Maybe he was planning his next move when he slipped, and it felt to him as if I intercepted. But in this moment, where he is crouching and crying in the corner, there is no reason. I want to hold and soothe him, but I am facing a frightened accusation. And this situation is unsettling me as well.

And then it gets worse. He shoots out of the corner as if running away from a terrible monster, out to the next room and on to his mother's lap. "Lovey hit me, lovey hit me," he cries bitterly. (He calls me lovey because this is my nickname in his household.) I follow him into the next room and again, all I have to say is "I didn't hit you Marlowe, you fell." Then Marlowe's mother speaks: "Lovey didn't hit you Marlowe, lovey would never hit you, lovey loves you. It's not nice, what you're saying." She also finds it necessary to establish the truth of the event. No doubt, like me, she wants to expel the thought that I intentionally hurt him, and so make him feel better, but all the same—a child is in pain, crying, frightened, and the adults respond by trying to establish the facts and social etiquette. It's as if making him see the error of his beliefs—both the immediate, that I hurt him, and the general, that I might want to hurt him—is the solution to his crisis in the spirit of "there are no monsters under the bed."

Yet the obvious is this: not only is he hurting and spooked, but he is forced, first by me, then by his mother, to attend to a confusing and invalidating argument: what you believe is wrong, and how you feel about it is wrong as well. I can see on his little face a pained bewilderment. Whatever it is that he is asking for at this moment, he is not getting. What he is getting is making him feel worse.

A long moment later, he seems almost pacified. It might be that he is beginning to be convinced. The dissonance of being attacked by someone he trusts is lifting, the element of fear is losing its edge. It might be that he is tuning out the words, being soothed despite our narrative. All along this fretful communication, his mother has been caressing his back, where it hurts. It takes a bit longer for him to warm up to me again. He agrees to resume playing, another game. But he still looks at me with suspicion. I can see that he is making a big effort to process the dissonant message, to travel across the gap between his experience, and what has been said.

I began with the story of that moment I experienced with Marlowe and his family, in order to open for consideration the many such moments that occur in a child's life, and what transpires in them. I would like to suggest that such moments, which are both routine and formative, are difficult, sometimes traumatic, and that the difficulty or trauma that mark them, mark our lives as adults, in profound ways.

If we apply a Freudian (1933) framework, we might say that these are the moments where the superego is instated, the superego and its inevitable discontents. The child's impulse, be it desire, aggression, or fear, is met by an ambiguous mix of social normativity and reason. "You should not feel what you are feeling" is the essence of the message. "You are wrong" in both the factual and ethical sense. "This is how one should feel and think in this situation." Bit by bit such messages are internalized to form a socially consonant, morally hued part of the self. Fantasies are dispelled, affect is channeled, right and wrong, guilty and shameful, are formed into a common, that is, normative sense. Experience is structured along permissions and prohibitions that may be compromising, but they also establish the safety of civilized knowing; knowing what can be thought, what can be done, and what can be said. The later Freud indeed emphasizes the internalization of messages, rather than identification with the parent (father), as the root of the superego's formation. "Thus a child's super-ego is in fact constructed on the model not of its parents, but of its parents' superego; the contents which fill it are the same and it becomes the vehicle of tradition and of all the time-resisting judgments of value which have propagated themselves in this manner from generation to generation" (Freud 1933, p. 67).

But if the notion of the superego helps in formulating this process of internalization in terms of its eventual hypothesized psychological structure, if indeed it affords us a way of locating and understanding the effects of social normativity in the subject, it is less successful in accounting for the experience and trouble that this gradual, by necessity, intimate process involves. What actually happens in such formative moments? How do they register? What are the meanings, unconscious and conscious, that join the narrative of the budding self? It seems to me that if we want to better understand the struggle and disorientation that such moments entail for children, and the ways in which such moments continue to structure our adult experience, we need to look elsewhere in psychoanalysis. I would like to suggest for this purpose two additional, different, yet related notions: Ferenczi's (1949) seminal "confusion of tongues," and Laplanche's (1995) enigmatic message.

In what follows, I will pull these two notions together and place them on a spectrum. I will suggest that, as they are both concerned with the enigmatic and potentially traumatic differences between adults and children, they are better suited to account for such moments where children learn from adults. I will further suggest that if Ferenczi speaks explicitly of one confusion of tongues, his body of work implies two confusions, the second more general and perhaps more profound. I will find evidence to support this suggestion in Ferenczi's critique of the superego, and in another of his great contributions, the idea of identification with the aggressor. I will also have something to say in this context about the so-called death instinct. I will argue that, far from any ingrained destructiveness, it is the traumatic loss of meaning that makes people want to die.

A brief reminder is in order here. The confusion of tongues Ferenczi (1949) speaks of is a confusion between "the language of tenderness and the language of passion." It is about how adults can mistake a child's need for gestures of affection, for sexual advances, and respond in the language of adult sexuality. In the extreme, the confusion of tongues is about the sexual abuse or rape of children—adults seducing or forcing children to have sex. The sexual abuse is usually followed by another kind of abuse: punitive denial. "Almost always the perpetrator behaves as if nothing had happened, [...] Not infrequently after such events, the seducer becomes over-moralistic, or religious and endeavors to save the soul of the child by severity" (p. 227).

As a result of this double abuse, the child suffers severe trauma. "The fear of the uninhibited, almost mad adult changes the child ..." (p. 229). It leads to the fragmentation and atomization of the personality, to a mind that "consists only of the Id and superego, and which therefore lacks the ability to maintain itself with stability ..." (p. 228). Love, hate, and terror form a perpetual emotional storm that the child can weather, only through pervasive dissociation and splitting. It is as if he is destined to live in an eternally present, unsymbolizeble, primal scene. In short, the confusion of tongues Ferenczi speaks of is a catastrophe.

Laplanche (1995) explores the more ambiguous and nuanced domains of the relations between adults and children. The concept that he develops to account for the effect of adult sexuality on children is "the enigmatic message." The enigmatic message refers to the inherently overwhelming excess and enigma presented to the child by the mere presence of the sexuality of his parents. In the context that Laplanche explores, this sexuality is implicit, not forced, yet it is ubiquitous and powerful. And it is registered by the child as a mysterious language that is both frightening and exciting. It is a language of excess, since it exceeds the child's ability to process its complex conscious and unconscious messages. But unlike in Ferenczi, it is evocative rather than destructive. This is because in the Laplanchian scenario, the child is not attacked and subjected to an actual primal scene. The adult's language hovers. The child is allowed to process it in his own time, privately, and for the most part unconsciously. Moreover, as it is hinted as much as evident, the exchange harbors equal measures of fantasy and reality. And so the child is able to translate it into his own, evolving world of meanings, able to engage his curiosity and creativity.

Laplanche considers the excess of adult sexuality the driving force in the formation of the unconscious, and its basic quality of otherness. We become the layered beings that we are as we struggle to take in more than we're capable of. We develop an enigmatic and othered experience of our own selves, as we become in relation to the other's mysterious desire.

We may say that Laplanche also speaks of a confusion of tongues, a confusion related, like in Ferenczi, to the excess and otherness of adult sexuality, as it impacts children. But the confusion explored by Laplanche is inherent to human development. It does not involve the extremes of violence and denial. It is therefore enigmatic rather than shocking, difficult, but not destructive.

What Ferenczi and Laplanche share, which is why we can pull them together in this context, is a view of child development contrary to the post-seduction theory of Freud. They see the child not as the author of disturbing urges, that are then put in order by adult intervention, but as the subject of alien desires that he must struggle to accommodate. For both Ferenczi and Laplanche, the child is the object of the adult's power and desire intermingled. It is not the child's but the adult's desire that emerges on the horizon; moreover, it is imposed within the imbalance of power that exists between children and adults. It is how children negotiate their own and others' desires within this unfair field of power that marks their development. The adults bring on disorder as much as order.

But the confusions explored by Laplanche and Ferenczi are also very different. It may be useful therefore to see them as anchoring two points on a spectrum. Laplanche captures a confusion where the language of the adult is excessive but for the most part benevolent and implicit enough to be evocative. Ferenczi exposes a confusion where the language of the adult is blatantly raw, often malevolent, and for this reason catastrophic.

Let me now try to read the moment I described earlier through this framework. Marlowe is having a complex bad experience. It involves shock, pain, a scary perception of the events, a crisis of trust, and most of all helplessness. He goes through it both as an enigmatic internal event and in relation to the adults around him. He recoils in fear and suspicion from me; he reaches to his mother for comfort and safety. Both of us wish to address his trouble. His mother holds him. I would have, if he'd let me. But at the same time, we argue with his perceptions and challenge his feelings. "I didn't hit you," I say. "He didn't hit you, he would never hit you," his mother consoles him. It is our instinct that he would feel better if he believed what we say. This is reasonable. Accidents are less scary than bad intentions and planned violence; they do not involve the frightening prospect of malevolence.

But what I would like to suggest is that, in another register, what the adults are doing, perhaps inevitably and hopefully with good intentions, is forcing on him a foreign language. This language not only fails to meet his needs at the moment, but it also does them injustice. It demands of him to accommodate to how we need to make sense of things, so that we are not overwhelmed and put to shame by his trouble. It requires of him to subject and translate his experience according to the premises we present to him. It puts the shame on him. Moreover, it requires of him to accept a degree of denial that we all need, in order to feel good in these troubling circumstances.

Yes, I did not hit him that moment, and I never quite hit him. He is allowed to jump on me, punch and pull almost as much as he wishes. My reaction is limited to evading and containing. But it is also true that throughout the game Marlowe was subject to my superior physical and mental power. There was much fun and excitement. But was there also a moment where play was exceeded, and we crossed into an ominous realm of real fear and pain? We are supposed to pretend to be really fighting, pretending being my charge to maintain. But did I get carried away at some moment? Was I too rough, was I really scary? Was there a moment where the boundaries faded, where he no longer felt safe, and where he was overwhelmed?

Neither I nor his mother could consider the prospect that the game might have gone too far and that I failed my responsibility. Neither of us wanted to think that I might have put him in real danger. And so we asked him to forget that this might have happened, that he might have been exposed to too much aggression. We asked him to deny the possibility of transgression. We forced on him a dilemma—adopt our logic or remain isolated. For a while he protested, but eventually he had to accept.

Moments like this entail a serious gap of meaning and of recognition—a gap that opens when any given experience that is too difficult for the adults to handle is met with general narratives that aim to alleviate it by negating its premises. What you think is happening is not really happening. What is happening is something else altogether, and you will see it if you listen. The language of singularity, the need of the child to be recognized in his present moment, is met by the language of what presents itself, what needs to believe itself, as reason and objectivity. It is, from another angle, the language of social norm and prescribed modes of meaning making. It is from yet another angle, the language of omnipotence and narcissism. I will tell you what's right, I will tell you what's normal, and I will make you believe what I need you to believe in order to feel good about myself. The singular need expressed by the child is indigestible. It exceeds the adult's common sense, defies his sense of knowing, and challenges his need for control of the circumstances. It requires of him to acknowledge thoughts and behaviors that make him feel ashamed and guilty. And so he asserts the power he shares with all the adults, to determine the truth, to accept or reject meaning and feeling, and to deny the destructive potential of his power and the grave consequences of his lapses of responsibility.

Such moments also involve a dilemma of identifications. It might be difficult for the adult to identify with an injured, helpless child; it is easier to identify with internalized narratives that dilute injury and helplessness by putting them in context, while absolving the adult of responsibility. And so a minor instance of indoctrination, or as Althusser (1970) might call it, interpellation, follows. The child is called to align with the adult and the narratives that inform his sense of self and identity. If he wants to be taken care of, he must conform to these narratives. The alternative is remaining isolated, without words or sense. For most of us, such isolation is impossible. And so the child takes in this foreign language and makes it his own. He learns to identify and be identified by the same narratives. He puts away the domains of experience that these narratives refuse to acknowledge. The gap between the singular and the objective-normative is internalized and formalized and becomes a basic structure of his subjectivity.

This process is a common aspect of what we call socialization, yet already since Freud, and even more so Lacan, we have come to see that it involves profound compromises. It instills in us a register where self-consciousness means self-alienation. It brings about the fundamental conflicts of civilized living, where the self never feels quite at home in the world. It seems to me, however, that if we add to the equation the sensibility formulated by Ferenczi, we may be able to look further into the nature of this process and its troubled consequences. One of these consequences is the emergence in our experience of what Freud could not explain until he looked beyond the pleasure principle and proposed a death instinct—that aspect of our existence that is about withdrawal from, or destruction of, meaning and life (Freud, 1920). From another angle, it is what Ferenczi left unformulated between two ideas that he did not integrate. First, what he called "identification with the aggressor," and second, what he must have meant when he wrote in his *Contributions to Psychoanalysis* (1939)[1] that "a real character analysis must do away, temporarily, at least, with every idea of the super-ego, including the analyst's own" (p. 394).[2]

Ferenczi (1949) speaks of identification with the aggressor in the immediate context of the confusion of tongues. Identification with the aggressor is how the child resolves the anxiety aroused by the confusion and its aftermath: "… children feel physically and morally helpless, their personalities are not sufficiently consolidated in order to be able to protest, even if only in thought, the overpowering force, and the authority of the adult makes them dumb and can rob them of their senses." The same anxiety, "… if it reaches a certain maximum, compels them to subordinate themselves … to the will of the aggressor, … to identify with the aggressor" (p. 228).

Ferenczi is portraying here his own scenario of superego development. It is a superego that emerges more dyadically than in a triangle, a superego formed in the merger, rather than the opposition of desire and retribution. It is a superego whose founding premise is denial rather than prohibition. Its basic structure is dissociation rather than repression. The adult says: it didn't happen, it couldn't have happened, and if it happened, it's not what you think it is. The child is incapable of resisting and accepts the message. He identifies with the adult's aggression and his denial. In other words, he internalizes an evident paradox. This paradox becomes his own agent of authority and knowledge, a fragmented, internally preoccupied, and haunted superego. This is a superego dramatically different than Freud's. Ferenczi's superego does not enforce what Lacan (1966) called "the law of the father," a set of meanings and directives predicated on a coherent, if also alienating, symbolic order. Rather, it enforces a law based on the delinking of meanings and the negation of experience, a disorder of splitting and foreclosure. The excessiveness and otherness inherent in this superego is annihilating.

When Ferenczi (1939) writes that in analysis we need to rid the individual of every idea of the superego, it must be this scenario that he has in mind. The superego of identification with the aggressor is not a fantasy policing agency. It is not a psychological structure whose harsher effects need to be recognized and put in relief. It is a superego founded not on the narrowing of experience along the lines of (gendered) prohibition, but on identification with raw violence and blatant lies. This is why Ferenczi speaks of the need to suspend it in analysis. If we want to heal the evisceration of experience necessitated by such identification, we must protest the lies, untangle the paradoxes, and expose the perpetual attacks on linking that are required to keep it functional. A superego formed in the denial of actual suffering and the destruction of awareness should be rejected completely for the individual to thrive. As Adorno (1966) shows in his critique of Ferenczi, Ferenczi does not fully hold to his rejection of the superego. Perhaps his identification with his own psychoanalytic aggressor, Freud, made such full rejection impossible. But we may note that there is a deep ambivalence.

In fact, if you followed me to this point, you might have registered a certain gap or confusion in Ferenczi's own conceptual framework. After all, not all of us suffered the kind of sexual abuse upon which Ferenczi based his idea of the confusion of tongues. Not all of us identified with the aggressor such that our superegos are paradoxical, self-negating, and deeply destructive. Yet Ferenczi seems to suggest that psychoanalysis should always involve a suspension of the superego, in both patient and analyst. Why this extension of the principle from the severely traumatized to all of us?

I would like to suggest that this is because Ferenczi already deliberates the two kinds of confusion I have been talking about. But for his own reasons he names only one. When he speaks of the denial that usually follows the imposing on the child of the language of adult passion, he gives the denial a role secondary to this confusion. But elsewhere in his writing, Ferenczi (1931) speaks of far more pervasive and routine kinds of trouble in the relations between children and adults. He writes of "the insincerity and hypocrisy" of parents, and of the child's ensuing sense of abandonment, and of "not being loved." He writes, for example, that children's "naughtiness, fits of passion and uncontrollable perversions are generally a later result of tactless treatment of those around them" (p. 473). He reports on his own "feeling of outraged authority" (p. 471) in the countertransference with patients who protest his interventions, a feeling that he considers a reenactment of earlier interactions with parents who responded to the child's protest with frustration and anger. In other words, Ferenczi recognizes a far more general kind of mismatch, or confusion, between the tender language of a child's emotional needs and a mis-attuned, aggressive, and authoritative language used in response by the adults. And he writes that "when a child feels himself abandoned, he loses, as it were, all desire for life or, as we should have to say with Freud, he turns his aggressive impulses against himself" (p. 479). He adds that as patients re-encounter such experiences in analysis, "Sometimes this process goes so far that the patient begins to have the sensations of sinking and dying" (p. 478).

It seems from such passages that Ferenczi sees this second confusion (to repeat, a confusion between the language of the child's emotional need and the indifferent, authoritative adult discourse) as devastating on its own account. It results in the experience of abandonment and of not being loved. It makes children and the adults they become self-hating. It leads to the loss of the desire for life. Ferenczi recognizes the protest against this aggressively mis-attuned discourse emerging in the transference. And he refuses to consider such instances of protest as mere resistance to the knowledge and authority of analysts. He considers the resistance justified. The child in analysis is protesting the variety of misrecognitions: the insincerity, hypocrisy, and tactlessness present in adult authority in general. It appears that Ferenczi considers this second kind of confusion no less consequential in the formation of a superego based on identification with adult aggression, or indifference, which in either case involves destructive gaps of meaning and denial. This may explain why he suspects the superego in general.

This is where the death instinct becomes relevant. Freud's shift to a theory of development, based on conflicts in fantasy rather than the denial of reality, made it impossible for him to understand why some people become so deeply demoralized. If all we seek is pleasure, why are some people capable only of suffering? Why do some people become so identified with aggression that they want to destroy themselves and others? (This is the so-called masochism problem.) Freud's (1920) answer was to posit an independent instinct whose essence is destructive. But Ferenczi, when he observes that some children and adults feel like dying, sees no instinctual propensity for self-destruction. He sees aggressive invalidation internalized. People feel like dying when inhabiting the parts of their subjectivities, or in another language, self-states, where too much of their experience, their need and capacity for love, has been unrecognized.

All this may seem quite far from the story I began with. The misrecognition Marlowe faced was of the kind most of us must have faced repeatedly in our childhoods. Marlowe, I would like to assure you, is a robustly alive child who feels loved more than enough and loves back with great passion. It seems to me that, as he does regarding the confusion between tenderness and sexuality, the confusion Ferenczi captures in this context is also of the extreme kind. Perhaps what most of us faced, and what Marlowe faced in the story I told you, is closer to what Laplanche conceives of in the realm of the enigmatic message.

I did not hit Marlowe on purpose. But we played an aggressive game where boundaries might have become unstable and where his sense of safety was clearly compromised. He experienced my adult power. More than that, he was actually hurt. There was enough cause for him to be frightened. Yet, following his injury, I was overwhelmed by the potential lapse that made it possible, and so there was a quick, defensive denial. "I did not hit you Marlowe, you fell." In what must have been to him a disorienting harmony, his mother repeated the same message.

But if the adults consorted to argue with his experience, there was also soothing and our good intentions must have been palpable. Our denial was invalidating and confusing, but it was not overtly aggressive or punishing. Marlowe was presented with a wide range of responses to his trouble. We pressed upon him a logic that he was not able to process fully. He must have sensed the complex emotions and relations that transpired in those moments in and between us. But he was also given the time and space to digest the mis-attunement, the excess, and the otherness of our spontaneously consonant responses. The acoustic bath that surrounded him, as Adrienne Harris (1998) would call it, was not as deep or stormy as to drown him. It was as if he had been exposed to a strangely consistent yet incomprehensible adult language that clashed with his own, but it clashed rather softly. If there were hypocrisy and tactlessness, there were also benevolence and sincere love. The gap of meaning and recognition was not negating to the point of trauma. It was probably internalized as a troubling enigma.

If we follow the framework offered by Laplanche further, we may theorize that this was one moment in many, in which another kind of unconscious has been forming in him. An unconscious mirroring the excess of the adults' own experience, their anxieties and conflicts vis-à-vis social normativity and the responsibilities it demands of them. An unconscious holding the enigmas of adult logic and conventions, the confusion between guilt and responsibility, and between shame and self-awareness—the confusion that we all suffer from, precisely because we are all formed by such moments. An unconscious, hopefully, where these enigmas can be sustained in relative safety and elaborated to inform Marlowe's own creative compromises.

Notes

1 All the quotations to follow from Ferenczi's *Contributions to Psychoanalysis* are taken from "Baunsteine zur Psychoanalyse," the original translation to German from Ferenczi's original Hungarian, as translated to English by E. B. Ashton, the translator of Theodore Adorno's *Negative Dialectics to English*.

2 The full quotation is: "a real character analysis must do away, temporarily, at least, with every idea of the super-ego, including the analyst's own. After all, the patient has to be freed from all emotional ties that go beyond reason and his own libidinous tendencies. Nothing but this sort of dismantling of the super-ego can bring about a radical cure. Successes that consist only in the substitution of one super-ego for another still have to be classified as successes of transference; they certainly fail to satisfy the ultimate purpose of therapy, which is to do away with the transference." You will notice that Ferenczi speaks here of "reason" as something antithetical to the superego, but this is before we have come to see the notion of reason through the lens developed by Foucault.

References

Adorno, T. (1966). *Negative Dialectics*. [Trans. E. Ashton]. New York: Continuum, 1973.

Althusser, L. (1970). Ideology and ideological state apparatuses. [Trans. B. Brewster]. In *Lenin and Philosophy and Other Essays*. New York: Monthly Review Press, 1971.

Ferenczi, S. (1929). The unwelcome child and his death-instinct. *International Journal of Psychoanalysis*, 10:125–129.

Ferenczi, S. (1931). Child analysis in the analysis of adults. *International Journal of Psychoanalysis*, 12:468–482.

Ferenczi, S. (1939). *Bausteine zur Psychoanalyse*, Vol. III and IV. Bern: Hans Huber Verlag.

Ferenczi, S. (1949). Confusion of tongues between the adults and the child: The language of tenderness and of passion. *International Journal of Psychoanalysis*, 30:225–230.

Freud, S. (1920). Beyond the pleasure principle. *SE*, 13:1–64.

Freud, S. (1933). New introductory lectures on psycho-analysis. *SE*, 12.

Harris, A. (1998). Psychic envelopes and sonorous baths. In *Relational Perspectives on the Body*, L. Aron and F. Anderson (eds). New York: Routledge, pp. 58–70.

Lacan, J. (1966). *Écrits*. [Trans. B. Fink]. New York: Norton, 2006.

Laplanche, J. (1995). *Essays on Otherness*. London: Routledge, 1999.

17

SOME PREVENTIVE CONSIDERATIONS ABOUT FERENCZI'S IDEAS REGARDING TRAUMA AND ANALYTIC EXPERIENCE

Haydée Christinne Kahtuni

Sándor Ferenczi surprises me every time I reread him. For over twenty years, I have been studying and researching his writings, and I can testify that the entirety of his work has been an ongoing help in my own clinical practice. In addition to an admirable ability to have reconciled in a singular way theory with practice—the result of constantly enhancing his therapeutic skills over the years (since for him there are no unanalyzable patients[1]), the incredible modernity and relevance of his writings, ideas, and conceptualizations always catches my attention.

Ferenczi, along with Sigmund Freud, belongs to the first generation of psychoanalysis. Paradoxically, despite all of the constant shifts and changes of clinician behavior and values presented in these past centuries and especially in the twenty-first century, his work is revolutionary. His therapeutic methods and the new tools he developed have opened and continue to open doors for a wide range of psychotherapeutic possibilities, especially those referring to the understanding, treatment, and even discovery of certain psychopathologies (difficult patients, traumatized patients, psychosomatic, psychotic, "as if personalities," etc.), which are so prevalent now. I refer, for example, to the pioneering study of the early relationship between mother and baby and the significant role this relationship plays in personality development. Also, the emphasis that he originally assigned to the role of external objects as the main factor in the etiology of various psychiatric diseases, particularly when related to trauma, was then controversial in its challenge to Freud, but today speaks to contemporary psychoanalysts.

Many subsequent generations of psychoanalysts found a teacher and guide in Ferenczi. Melanie Klein, Donald W. Winnicott, Michael Bálint, Margaret Mahler, Heinz Kohut, Renee Spitz, Masud Khan, and so many others benefited from his writings and used them as a springboard to develop important work that not only

expanded the possibilities of psychoanalytic treatment but also led to new therapeutic modalities such as the analysis of children, infant observation, institutional
psychotherapy, etc.

For these above-stated reasons, I decided to write in co-authorship with
Gisela Paraná Sanches, the first published dictionary[2] of Sándor Ferenczi's work
in order to share the knowledge we have accumulated over many years of studying this author. Without any pretense of exhausting all the work of Ferenczi,
our goal was to provide the reader with a more integrated view of his writings.
At the same time, we wanted to facilitate the study of Ferenczi's work, for both
beginners and more experienced psychoanalysts, mental health professionals, and
scholars by including entries (which include his main concepts, original ideas,
newly developed but related theory, some relevant biographies, etc.) that complement each other and act as guides for learning from Ferenczi's legacy. In this
present paper, based on more extensive entries from the dictionary, I would like
to discuss the following:

1.   Specific topics related to the trauma theory of Sándor Ferenczi, pointing out
     some technical innovations he presented in *Child Analysis in the Analysis of
     Adults* and *Confusion of Tongues between Adults and the Child*.
2.   The risks of retraumatization in current psychoanalytic practice.

Trauma

Trauma occupies a major role in the development of Sándor Ferenczi's psychotherapeutic theory. Referring to the first Freudian notion of trauma based on the
theory of seduction,[3] Ferenczi pointed out the fundamental role that external
objects played in the configuration of trauma. For Ferenczi, the trauma *is really
caused* by specific events, which are *external to the subject and relatively independent
of psychical reality*. Ferenczi treated many patients traumatized by war and others
called "difficult" by his colleagues, who would end up referring these patients to
him. He noticed that trauma has very specific characteristics. For instance, it derives
from a set of events that happened in the subject's life. Trauma is a psychic wound,
provoked by one or more exogenous factors that cause harmful and lasting psychological consequences. In trauma, whether caused by war, disasters, or abuse,
some features are repeated with individual variations: the symptoms may vary in
their intensity; they usually prevent the individual from functioning appropriately
without being harmed in their mental or physical health, and these symptoms can
cause other mental disorders and pathogenic, lasting effects on the subject's psychic
organization.

All traumas have in common an inevitable consequence, a *typical drastic effect*
upon the personality that always implies a break in the individual's psychic structure, damaging important functions of the ego such as judgment, memory, and

temporal and spacial orientation, among others. This drastic effect leads to the splitting of the personality, a subject we will discuss later. Patients who suffered traumas may also present many other symptoms characteristic of ego divisions that indicate the occurrence of psychic shocks, such as diffuse anxiety, depression, distorted self-image, feelings of emptiness, helplessness, tedium, symptoms of eating disorder, deficits of critical judgment, psychosomatic symptoms, acting out, etc.

The Traumatic Violation of the Adult over the Child

In one of his most striking contributions, *Confusion of Tongues between Adults and the Child* (1933), Ferenczi describes three types of trauma: enforced love, the unbearable punitive measures, and terrorism of suffering. It is through enforced love that he explained the dynamics of the formation of trauma in general. Let us see how it works: Initially, there is a child in a dependent relationship with an adult who is supposedly their protector and someone that the child trusts. The adult attacks the child. The child submits themselves to the adult's commands and is initially excited. However, the adult, *not forbidden by the laws against incest*, makes a *confusion of languages* and runs over the child in their pre-genital tenderness with the language of passion. The child, though excited, gets scared, as they are also afraid. *Nevertheless, they have no alternative but to give in to the adult domain* since the younger they are, the more defenseless they will be. The child is then seduced/abused. To defend themselves, they *identify with the aggressor* and not only learn their *modus operandi* but also *introject their guilt,* absorbing it psychically. Later, the perpetrator behaves *as if nothing happened.* This *double bind* will cause the child to be unable to think, perceive, or feel.

The child can ask for help from other significant adults, but again, these adults also often deny the occurrence of violence and in fact sometimes respond with additional violence, since the child may be accused of being responsible for the original abuser's behavior and be wildly punished for it. The child then reacts in an autoplastic way and suffers a split in their ego. We note that according to Ferenczi trauma is established *after* the first assault, when *the adult denies the child's perceptions of the brutal event,* which will consequently lead to the split of personality.

Denial and Splitting of the Ego

Denial involves two or more people in a nefarious network of suffering. After having attacked the child, the abuser denies their perception of reality and replaces it with a false and contrary version of reality opposite to the truth. Consequently, the child develops a deficient pattern of reality testing that makes them doubt their own perceptions and ambivalent painful feelings. Denial plays a definitive role in the formation of trauma because to an even further extent than sexual, psychological, or physical abuse, denial assures that psychic inscription of events is recorded in only one of the cleaved parts of the ego. This makes it impossible for the child to believe in facts and events that actually occurred and prevents validation of feelings and perceptions.

Let us consider some of Ferenczi's thoughts about denial:

> The worst is really the denial, the claim that nothing happened, that there was no suffering or even be beaten and scolded when traumatic paralysis of thought or movements is manifested; this is, above all, what makes the pathogenic trauma.
>
> *(Ferenczi 1931, p. 79)*

In *The Clinical Diary*, he considered:

> What is traumatic: an attack or its consequences? The adaptive potential "response" of even very young children to sexual or other passionate attacks is much greater than one would imagine. Traumatic confusion arises mainly because the attack and the response to it are denied by the guilt-ridden adults, indeed, are treated as deserving punishment.
>
> *(Ferenczi 1932, pp. 223–224)*

About "double denial", he also wrote in *The Clinical Diary*:

> The trauma involved (and mostly involves) the child at a stage of already-established sphincter-morality; the girl feels soiled, indecently treated, would like to complain to her mother, but she is prevented by the man (intimidation, denial). The child is helpless and confused, should she struggle to prevail over will of adult authority, the disbelief of her mother, etc. Naturally, she cannot do that, she is faced with the choice—It is the whole world that is bad, or am I wrong?—and chooses the latter.
>
> *(Ferenczi 1932, p. 116)*

Specificities of Splitting

It is important to notice that Ferenczi refers to splitting as a *primary process of repression*. This is because splitting, unlike repression, is a very archaic defense mechanism. Developmentally, it occurs before repression, which, to be activated, requires a stronger and more cohesive ego, a more developed and sophisticated psychic apparatus. This means that in terms of libidinal development, splitting is a mechanism that precedes the repression itself, being present in the early stages of psychosexual development or in people whose ego development is stunted or underdeveloped due to internal or external circumstances. More often, what happens is a combination of these factors. Although Ferenczi occasionally refers to what we know to be the defensive mechanism of splitting as a primary process of repression (and sometimes uses the term *narcissistic splitting* instead), it is important to clarify that there are fundamental structural, topical, and phenomenological differences between repression and the splitting mechanism.

Splitting *does not occur between* the different psychic structures (id, ego, and superego). In the case of neurosis, for example, the mechanism of repression involves all psychic structures. In splitting however, division occurs in the ego and superego and stays limited to those structures.

As we can see, what happens in the process of splitting is different than what leads to the emergence of neurotic or psychotic symptoms as seen in phobias, obsessive and hysterical conversion, or even hallucinations and delusions. Those symptoms are the result of a compromise-formation between the psychic agencies, which though strained, remain in contact and are not split. In splitting, on the other hand, *two or more parts of the personality coexist simultaneously and independently without any conflict between them.* Understanding these differences and their consequences is fundamental to the establishment of a differential diagnosis and therefore to the proper psychological treatment of the split patient.

The importance of this distinction is also due to the necessity of adapting psychotherapy to the needs of each patient based on psychic organization.

The Elasticity of Technique

Beginning in 1928, Ferenczi adopted a noticeable modification in his clinical approach. Similar to the "maternal" proposals, which Donald Winnicott would adopt years later for the care of pediatric and regressed patients, Ferenczi's technical innovations are part of a set of therapeutic proposals developed in an effort to heal trauma.

His paper *The Elasticity of Psychoanalytic Technique,* written in 1928, is very emblematic of this shift in his approach to trauma and can be considered a turning point, a milestone regarding his changes in clinical attitude, the intellectual independence (from Freud and his other disciples) he now displayed, and the quality of relationships he started to establish with his patients. Listening to his patient's complaints about the coldness of the analyst and realizing the trauma caused by active technique, Ferenczi completely changed his perspective on intervention and, in contrast to Freud, began to worry about the technical use of countertransference in the analytical process.

Recognizing that countertransference is an instrument that enables the analyst to develop fundamental psychic qualities[4] for healing traumatized patients, Ferenczi realized that the analyst needs to investigate their own feelings, modes of object relations, levels of narcissism, defensive mechanisms, and so on. Moreover, when his patients complained about the coldness of the analyst, he comprehended the hypersensitivity of traumatized patients, not only in relation to countertransference movements, but also toward the characteristics of the personality of the analyst. At this point, Ferenczi's break with the positivist paradigm of science really stands out:

> ... a recent analysis of the Ferenczi epistemological work makes us realize the magnitude of its content: much more than a psychoanalytical technique innovator, more than the creator of a new conception of the analyst-analysand relationship, Ferenczi broke with the positivist paradigm of science in which he was formed.
>
> Without having lived long enough to realize the epistemological leap that he had made, Ferenczi ditched the consecrated idea of his era of the possibility of objective separation between researcher and object of research. His clinical work was slowly undoing the limits that discriminate the individual psyche of each member of the analytic pair to realize the absolute necessity that certain regressed and symbiotic patients have to temporarily use psychic resources of their analyst. Ferenczi led us to the concept of intersubjectivity, in which the assumption of neutrality is abandoned and replaced by the assumption that the researcher (the psychoanalyst) is always and inescapably implicated in the phenomenon that they note (analyzing). It is therefore imperative that the analyst be aware not only of their countertransferential psychic movements reactive to the patient, but also to aspects of their own personality and to the technical or ethical mistakes that they can commit, and be responsible for their anti-therapeutic gestures.
>
> *(Kahtuni and Sanches, 2009)*

Ferenczi noted that traumatized patients usually perceive very subtle desires, trends, moods, sympathies, and antipathies of the analyst, even when the analyst himself is completely unaware of them. However, because these patients suffered during their childhood a violent attack on their perceptions, they automatically doubt them. Moreover, as they are generally identified with their abusers, they do not have the ego strength to defend themselves and to protest. Instead, patients may suffer melancolization and turn against themselves the aggressiveness that was originally addressed to the analyst. Ferenczi then considered:

> So he [the patient] "retrojects," we might say, the censorship directed against us. Indeed, recrimination is thus laid down: You do not believe me! Do not take seriously what I am communicating! I cannot admit that you are sitting there, insensitive and indifferent while attempting to imagine something tragic from my childhood! The reaction to this accusation (never expressed spontaneously by the patient and having to be guessed by the analyst) cannot be considered other than in a critical way, their own behavior and their own emotional attitude, the spirit of what was emphasized, and admit the

possibility, even the reality, of something as fatigue, monotony, or even bore-dom. ... The naturalness and honesty of behavior ... are the most appropriate and favorable climate to the analytic situation.

(Ferenczi 1932, pp. 31–32)

Taking Care of Potential Retraumatization in Psychotherapy

Aware of these phenomena, Ferenczi began to advocate the need for an attitude of honesty from the analyst in opposition to what he called "professional hypoc-risy." Additionally, according to Ferenczi, the analyst's honesty is a powerful tool for accessing stunted traumatic situations that caused splitting. Honesty is also a healing instrument in itself as far as it allows the patient to experience in the transference new patterns of emotional reactions and more integrated and mature behavior.

Admitting a mistake, validating a patient's perceptions, and legitimating their feelings are therapeutic attitudes that help the patient to trust the analyst and believe in their own perceptions. Keeping in mind that what leads to trauma is denial, the validation by the analyst of the patient's perceptions is the key to achieving integra-tion of the separated parts of personality. Insensitivity, disbelief, coldness, and profes-sional hypocrisy are considered iatrogenic and in the case of traumatized patients can be retraumatizing.

It may therefore be recommended that a careful and judicious use of the princi-ples of abstinence and neutrality be utilized in the treatment of traumatized patients:

> For contemporary psychoanalysis (which prioritizes the quality of the ana-lyst-patient relationship rather than the technique per se), abstinence is pri-marily limited to the analyst not satisfying, under any circumstances, sexual (genital) desires of the patient at the same time that they do tend to satisfy certain incipient and primarily unmet needs (pre-genital) whose satisfaction is necessary for the healthy development of the self.
>
> *(Kahtuni and Sanches, 2009)*

In certain situations, especially with difficult patients, it is essential that the ana-lyst deliberately abandon the principle of neutrality and take sides on behalf of the patient in order to demonstrate that he really does supports the patient. With regard to professional hypocrisy, it is very illustrative to read some of Ferenczi's considerations:

> A lot of repressed criticism concerns on what might be called professional hypocrisy. We politely welcome the patient when he comes, ask them to participate in their associations, and promise to listen to them carefully and to devote all our interests to their well-being and to the work of elucidation.

In reality, it is quite possible that certain traits, external or internal to the patient are difficult to bear. Or, we can feel that the analysis session generates an unpleasant disturbance in a most significant professional concern, or in a personal and intimate concern. Also in this case, I see no other way but to become aware of our own discomfort and talk about it with the patient, admit it, not only as a possibility, but as fact.

Let us remark that to resign the "professional hypocrisy," considered until now as inevitable, rather than injure the patient, gave them the contrary, an extraordinary relief. ... the analyst admits his own mistake gave him the gain of patient trust.

(Ferenczi 1933, pp. 98–99)

In *The Clinical Diary*, he wrote:

The analyst must be an authority that for the first time realizes his error, but above all, hypocrisy. The child can deal much better with rough but honest treatment than with so-called pedagogical objectivity and detachment that, however, conceals impatience and hatred. This is one of the causes of masochism; one prefers being beaten to feeling simulated calm and objectivity. Another fault, which must be recognized, admitted, and changed, is moodiness.

(Ferenczi 1932, p. 160)

Reflecting on the very likely harmful consequences of these occurrences between analyst and patient, I believe it is important to point out that it is the analyst's responsibility and not the patient's to address these dynamics. This is where Ferenczi warns us about the urgent need for a well-done analysis of the analyst in order that he or she may face themselves and their own narcissistic injuries, denial, and unpleasant character traits; when this does not occur, the analyst will inevitably be unduly influenced by the darker aspects of their personality that patients perceive. For Ferenczi, much repressed or dissociated patient criticism relates to what the analyst continues to deny.

Child-Analysis in the Analysis of Adults

It is possible that by now the reader is finding great similarity between the analysis of children and the analysis of adults in treatment with Ferenczi.

So, let us discuss some important ideas on this topic addressed by him in 1931 when he wrote *Child Analysis in the Analysis of Adults*. Despite not having been a child analyst himself, Ferenczi pointed out that many factors led him to decrease considerably the contrast between child analysis and adult analysis. As the free association of ideas was not enough to facilitate the emergence of deeper emotions,

Ferenczi used the relaxation technique to obtain rich material for analysis. The more relaxed the patient was, the more he started to communicate through bodily expressions and temporary symptoms. Ferenczi noticed that these bodily manifestations were representative of physical memories of childhood trauma. With relaxation, previously cleaved memories could emerge and then be subjected to analysis. Commenting on the relaxation measures he had adopted and that were opposed to his old active technique, Ferenczi said:

> When discussing with Anna Freud some of my technical measures, she made the following relevant comment: "You treat your patients like I treat the children in my child analyzes"… reminding me that in my last publication, a short article about the psychology of "unwelcome" children [*The Unwelcome Child and His Death Instinct*] that would later seek psychoanalytic treatment, I pursued a kind of warm reception in preparation for the actual examination of the resistances. The relaxation measures that I have just proposed declined even further, for sure, the difference, excessively marked today between child analysis and the analysis of adults.
>
> *(Ferenczi 1931, p. 65)*

As mentioned previously, Ferenczi had great faith in the curative possibility of psychoanalysis. For him, unlike most analysts of his time, the resistance and narcissism of the patient were not necessarily factors that made analysis impossible. His observations of traumatized patients, considerations of the analysis, and management of the transference—countertransference and the fact that resistance and narcissism are psychic phenomena which are not restricted solely to the patient— led him to conclude that the problem of non-analyzability was due to technical inadequacy of classical procedures used for traumatized patients. It then became necessary to modify the techniques so that they fit a new demand. Thus, in the face of the encountered obstacles such as the absence of associations, negative transference, treatment interruption, etc., Ferenczi began to use some techniques that were already commonly used in psychoanalysis of children. He also developed some others which were particularly effective in the treatment of the so-called "difficult cases" (traumatized patients) and borderline and regressed patients.

Game of Questions and Answers

Since the callous attitude of the analyst added to a lack of candor, and the analyst's failure to recognize his errors were factors that reaffirmed childhood trauma, Ferenczi suspended interpretation and other protocolary questions of analysis and started to interact with patients using another technical innovation, the game of questions and answers. This technique was effective because it entailed communication adapted to the special capacity of the patient's split memory, that is, the analyst using this technique makes direct contact with the dissociated, infantile parts of the personality. This way of working also enabled expression of the patient's psychic pains stored in the split part of the personality that may manifest as true staging (acting in) during the therapeutic process.

Similar to the mode of communication between analyst and child patient, this game as well as other techniques allowed him to communicate with some adult patients by favoring the emergence of memories whose contents were dissociated on the basis of early traumatic experiences and therefore sometimes unsymbolized and inaccessible through free association. Another important discovery reported by Ferenczi was that very often he noticed that healing happens in analysis with the replacement of remembering with acting. This reversal of Freud's order of events—remembering, repeating, and working through (which works with neurotic patients for whom recollection and elaboration precede resolution)—proved to be necessary in cases when traumatic memory was affected by splits and division, as is the case for traumatized patients for whom traumatic events could not simply be allocated in the unconscious, but still manifest themselves through the patient's body. In terms of the similarity between analysis of children and analysis of adults, Ferenczi considers that adult patients should also have the right to behave in the analysis as if they are a difficult child. In his own words:

> In this regard, I would issue the hypothesis that the emotionally expressive movements of the child, especially libidinal, dated back mainly to the tender mother-child relationship, and that the elements of malice, of passionate rapture and perversion are present, most often, as consequences of treatment devoid of touch, by the environment. It is an advantage for the analysis when the analyst can, thanks to patience, an understanding, benevolence and a nearly limitless kindness, go as far as possible to meet the patient. ... The patient impressed with our behavior, contrasting with the events experienced in his own family, and, as we know, now protected from repetition, will dare the plunge in playing the unsavory past. What happens then reminds us vividly what the analysts of children tell us. It happens, for instance, that the patient confesses a fault, takes our hand and suddenly begs us not to hit him. Often patients seek to provoke our supposed hidden perversity, using evil, sarcasm, cynicism, severe unkindness and even grimacing.
>
> (Ferenczi 1931, pp. 74–75)

Ferenczi goes on to ask himself what the analyst's limit of tolerance should be for an adult "acting in" the analysis. Again, he considered the use of sincerity rather than professional hypocrisy:

> There is no advantage to play in these conditions the role of man who is always nice and forgiving; it is more advisable to honestly confess that the

patient's behavior displeases us but we must control ourselves, knowing that if he strives so much to be evil, there must be some reason.

(Ferenczi 1931, p. 75)

Conclusion

I wrote this chapter to offer the English language reader a small sample of what the Ferenczi dictionary addresses. By translating some of the dictionary's content under the entry "Trauma" into English and presenting it here, I explore Ferenczi's understanding of trauma and more specifically shine light on the potential for the patient's retraumatization to occur in the context of psychoanalytic treatment.

Ferenczi's work has helped me try to avoid that potential danger by *adapting therapy to the patient*. This adaptation—via some of the techniques described in this chapter—is especially crucial when working with traumatized and regressed patients for whom the environment not only failed to meet their needs for care, love, protection, and development of confidence, but also proved to be violently abusive and dramatically pathogenic.

Notes

1 Ferenczi had solid faith in the possibilities of the so-called depth psychologies to cure. He used to say that there is no such thing as an unanalyzable patient; because they ask for help or continue to come for therapy, it is the therapist's job to find the proper way to help them. His faith was one of the qualities that drove him to develop, among other things, his set of new techniques, including the controversial mutual analysis.
2 Kahtuni, H. C. and Sanches, G. P. (2009). *Dictionary on the Thought of Sándor Ferenczi—A Contribution to the Psychoanalytic Contemporary Clinic*, Elsevier Editora: Rio de Janeiro e FAPESP: São Paulo. The dictionary was originally written in Portuguese and has not been translated yet.
3 I refer to the seduction theory, which Freud abandoned in order to increasingly prioritize psychic over external reality and assign to the unconscious conflicts originated in childhood and related to sexuality as the source of psychological distress.
4 I refer for example to empathy, sympathy, self-observation, the capacity of judgment, the ability to reality test, etc.

References

Aron, L. and Harris, A.(1993). Sándor Ferenczi: Discovery and Rediscovery. In *The Legacy of Sándor Ferenczi*. Hillsdale, NJ, & Londres: The Analytic Press.

Bálint, M. (1949). *Changing Therapeutic Aims and Techniques in Psychoanalysis. Primary Love and Psychoanalytic Technique*. London: Tavistock Publications, 1959.

Bálint, M. (1966). *Experiências técnicas de Sándor Ferenczi*. Benjamim Wolman (org.) As técnicas psicanalíticas. Rio de Janeiro: Imago, V. 2, 1976.

Dupont, J. (1985). *Prefácio. Sándor Ferenczi. Diário Clínico*. São Paulo: Martins Fontes, 1990.

Ferenczi, S. (1927). *O problema do fim da análise. O.C.* São Paulo: Martins Fontes, V. 4, 1992.

Ferenczi, S. (1928). *A adaptação da família à criança*. *O.C.* São Paulo: Martins Fontes, V. 4, 1992.

Ferenczi, S. (1928). *A elasticidade da técnica psicanalítica*. *Obras Completas*. São Paulo: Martins Fontes, V. 4, 1992.

Ferenczi, S. (1929). *A criança mal acolhida e sua pulsão de morte*. *O.C.* São Paulo: Martins Fontes, V. 4, 1992.

Ferenczi, S. (1930). *Princípio de relaxamento e neo-catarse*. *O.C.* São Paulo: Martins Fontes, V. 4, 1992.

Ferenczi, S. (1931). *Análises de crianças com adultos*. *O.C.* São Paulo: Martins Fontes, V. 4, 1992.

Ferenczi, S. (1932). *Reflexões sobre o trauma*. *O.C.* São Paulo: Martins Fontes, V. 4, 1992.

Ferenczi, S. (1932). *The Clinical Diary of Sándor Ferenczi*, (ed.) J. Dupont [Trans. M. Balint and N. Z. Jackson]. Cambridge, MA: Harvard University Press, 1988.

Ferenczi, S. (1933). *Confusão de língua entre os adultos e a criança*. *O.C.* São Paulo: Martins Fontes, V. 4, 1992.

Figueira, S. A. (1994). *Freud e a difusão da psicanálise*. Porto Alegre: Artes Médicas.

Haynal, A. (1995). *A técnica em questão: controvérsias em psicanálise de Freud e Ferenczi a Michael Balint*. São Paulo: Casa do Psicólogo.

Hoffer, A. (1991). The Freud-Ferenczi controversy: A living legacy. *International Journal of Psycho-Analysis*, 18:465–472.

Kahtuni, H. C. and Sanches, G. P. (2009). *Dicionário do Pensamento de Sándor Ferenczi—Uma Contribuição à Clínica Psicanalítica Contemporânea*. Rio de Janeiro: Elsevier; São Paulo: FAPESP.

Sabourin, P. (1988). *Ferenczi, paladino e grão-vizir secreto*. São Paulo: Martins Fontes.

INDEX

Ferenczi's letter to, recalling incident in Palermo 153–4, 162–3; Freud and 96, 97, 99–100, 103, 104, 108; Groddeck's letters 99–100; importance and influence on Ferenczi 100; inspiration and influence on Ferenczi's writings 102–6, 108; overview of Ferenczi-Groddeck correspondence (1921–1933) 96, 97–9; sanatorium at Baden-Baden 56, 96, 98, 120, 162; significance of mother, recognition of 101–2

Grotstein, J. S. 130, 208

guilt: of caregiver-child, terrorism of suffering and 216; child's introjection of guilt feelings of adult 204, 205–6, 208, 276; as internal, illusory danger somewhat under one's control 209; sense of badness and 210, 214; separation-guilt cycle 214–16

Gyógyászat [Therapy] 27–8

Hann-Kende, Fanny 21

Harris, Adrienne xi, 2–5, 8, 9, 127–33, 272

Haynal, André E. and Véronique D. xi, 3, 229; on discovering Ferenczi as missing link 29; on Ferenczi's attitude 7, 52–74; on Ferenczi's sensitivity regarding homosexuality 227; on Freud's relationship to Ferenczi 44

Heilprin, Michael 151–2

Heimann, Paula 68, 172, 181

Hermann, Imre 69, 253

Herzog, James M. 229

Heywood, Mrs. *see* Severn, Elizabeth (RN)

Hidas, György 3

Hirsch, I. 226, 227

Hirschfeld, Magnus 153

Hitler, Adolf 164

Hoche, Alfred 140

Hoffer, Axel 21

homoerotic countertransference 226–31

homoerotic longings: of Ferenczi for Freud 154, 155; of Freud for Fliess 157, 158, 161

homophobia 153, 154, 157, 159; Freud's internalized 161

homosexuality: Ferenczi's sensitivity and activism regarding 153, 227; Freud's view of 161; Kraft-Ebbing's theory of 161; paranoia and 155–8; pathologizing of 157

honesty from the analyst, need for 155–7, 280, 281, 283–4

hospitalization syndrome 23

humanist perspective 29

Hungarian Psychoanalytical Society 27, 117

Hungarian Republic of Councils 163

Hungary, Jews in 150, 151

Huszadik Század ("Twentieth Century," monthly) 53

hypocrisy: parents' emotional abandonment and 211, 271; professional 280–1, 283

hysteria: complementary paranoiac/hysteric roles of Freud and Ferenczi 158–9, 160; conversion, Ferenczi's conception of war trauma as 128, 131; as quintessentially female, return to 161–2

identifications, confusion of tongues and dilemma of 269

identification with the aggressor 10, 25, 69, 89, 162, 176, 192, 269–70; in context of confusion of tongues 270; defined 205; development of concept of 189; enforced love and 276; family dynamic in 211–14, 219n7; passive trauma of abused child turned into active trauma 200; superego of 270–1; *see also* moral dimension of identification with the aggressor

identificatory play 178–9

imaginary transference 252

Imago (journal) 103

indoctrination/interpellation, confusion of tongues as instance of 269

"Inner Child," New Age notion of 105

insensitivity of analyst 33–4, 43

internal attitude 52

International Ferenczi Center 5

International Forum of Psychoanalysis 19

International Humanitarian Committee for the Defense of Homosexuals 153

International Journal of Psychoanalysis 4, 27, 135

International Psychoanalytical Association (IPA) 4, 19; establishment of 19, 27–8; Lacan's equivocal position within 252, 253

International Psychoanalytic Congress: in Berlin (1922) 61, 72n5; in Budapest (1918) 58; Sixth (Hague, 1920) 97; Symposium on War (Budapest, 1919) 127, 132

International Sándor Ferenczi Foundation 5

interpersonal psychoanalysis 1, 8, 77, 124, 181

interpretation: analyst's fanaticism or over-keenness for 172–3, 182n2; as penetrative act 172, 181

intersubjectivity 255, 279

"Interview with Dr. Elizabeth Severn" (Eissler) 112

introjection 9, 162; Abraham on 175; development of notion of 175–7; Ferenczi as "introjective analyst" 171–86; of guilt feelings of adult 204, 205–6, 208, 276 (*see also* moral dimension of identification with the aggressor); pathogenic forms of 176–7; transference and 57, 62, 175–6, 177

"Introjection and Transference" (Ferenczi) 57–8, 175–6, 177; Lacan on 253

IPA. *see* International Psychoanalytical Association (IPA)

Jackson, Edith 84, 91
Jelliffe, Smith Ely 138
Jews: anti-Semitism and 151, 158–64; of Austria-Hungary 150; divided Jewish Enlightenment identity shared by Freud and Ferenczi 150–67; Eternal, Wandering, "unmanned" Jew 158–9, 161; Freud's and Ferenczi's polarized poles of reaction to anti-Semitism and homophobia 158–9; tradition of migration, acculturation, and assimilation 150

Jones, Ernest 64, 92n18, 158; criticism of Ferenczi 61–2, 69, 71, 79, 107, 253; on emotional abandonment and shame 208, 209; on Freud's view of Severn 111; Fromm's rebuttal of 136

journals, special issues devoted to Ferenczi's legacy 5

Jung, Carl 54, 60, 68; Freud and 37, 38, 157, 158; Sprielrein case 124

Kahtuni, Haydée Christinne xi, 11, 274–85
Katasztrofak (Catastrophe) [Ferenczi] 40
Kirshner, Lewis A. xi, 10, 251–63
kissing incident with Thompson 78, 83, 84–5, 136–7
Klar, Vilma 164
Klein, Melanie 66, 68, 218n2, 219n10, 252, 254
Kohut, Heinz 124, 139, 207
Kovacs, Vilma 66
Kris, Ernst 35
Kuchuck, Steven xi–xii, 10, 223–34
Kurzweil, Edith 4

Lacan, J. 251–63: approach to trauma 254, 259; complementary reading of Ferenczi and 257–61; endorsement of classical abstinent posture for analyst 251, 258, 260–1; on imaginary transference 252;

inaugural seminar of 1953–1954 252–3; on "law of the father" 270; references to Ferenczi 10, 252–3; relationship between Ferenczi and 251–2, 253

Lampl-de Groot, Jeanne 66
Language of Psychoanalysis, The (Laplanche and Pontalis) 175
language of tenderness and passion. *see* confusion of tongues
Laplanche, Jean 175, 254; enigmatic message of 11, 266, 267–73
Legacy of Sándor Ferenczi, The (Aron and Harris) 3–4, 52; new, updated introduction to 5
Lester, E. P. 193
Lévy, Lajos 22, 23
liberalism 20–3
literary theorists, on impact of World War I 129
literature, contributions to Ferenczi 4–5, 8
"Little Chanticleer, A" (Ferenczi) 176
Loewald, Hans 12, 79, 249
love: enforced 276; Ferenczi's preoccupation with 90–1; Severn's capacity to, after analysis with Ferenczi 122–3
love, therapeutic action of 223–34: analysis as "a healing through love" 10, 91, 224; analyst's erotic countertransference 224, 226–33; Davies on 226; Ferenczi's understanding of analyst's loving approach 224–5; gender and the erotic 226–7; sexual orientation and the erotic 227–8; therapeutic action of gay analyst's erotic experience 228–31; transference-countertransference implications 231–2
Lowell, Alice 89–90, 93n28
Lueger, Karl 151

Mack-Brunswick, Ruth 66
Magistretti, P. 70
Magyar nation 150, 151
Mahler, Margaret 22, 69
marginalized voices, inclusion of 1–2
masculine protest, Adler's concept of 158
masochism problem. 272
Masson, J. M. 112
maternal erotic countertransference (MEC) 193
Meaning of Illness, The (Groddeck) 97
medicine, Jews and 150
Meigs, Katy 134
Memoirs of My Nervous Illness (Schreber) 157